THE ORIGIN OF APHRODITE

.

THE ORIGIN OF APHRODITE

Stephanie Lynn Budin

CDL Press
Bethesda, Maryland

Library of Congress Cataloging-in-Publication Data

Budin, Stephanie
    The origin of Aphrodite / Stephanie Budin
        p. cm.
    Includes bibliographical references and index.
    ISBN 1-883053-70-6
    1. Aphrodite (Greek deity) I. Title.

  BL820.V5 B83 2002
  292.2'114–dc21   2002034972

Cover design by Duy-Khuong Van.

TABLE OF CONTENTS

ACKNOWLEDGMENTS

There are many people and institutions who deserve a world of thanks for helping me at various points in the completion of this study. At the University of Pennsylvania, I thank Sheila Murnaghan, Keith DeVries, Jeremy MacInerney, and Earl Leichty for help on matters feminist, geometric, and Assyriological. Special thanks go to Philip Betancourt at Temple University for guidance in Bronze Age matters, especially concerning contacts between Crete and Cyprus; and to Neal Walls of Emory University, for help in the study of Levantine goddesses. My gratitude also goes to former Dean Licht for the Pennfield Fellowship that enabled me to spend my first year in Athens at the American School of Classical Studies, and the Samuel H. Kress Foundation for the Samuel H. Kress Joint Athens-Jerusalem Fellowship, which let me continue my studies at the American School in Athens as well as work at the Albright Institute in Jerusalem.

At the American School of Classical Studies in Athens, thanks go to the late William Coulson, Connie and Ronald Stroud, Charles K. Williams II, Molly Richardson (for help with epigraphy), Sandra Blakely, Barbara Olsen, and Albert Morales. At the Albright Institute of Archaeological Research in Jerusalem, I thank Sy Gitin, Edna Sachar, Gerald Bilkes, and F.W. "Chip" Dobbs-Allsopp.

I am eternally indebted to the people who helped me in areas of Cypriot research. First and foremost is Jenny Webb of LaTrobe University. Gratitude and extreme fondness go to Nancy Serwint, former acting director of CAARI, and to Diane Bolger, for organizing the excellent conference "Engendering Aphrodite," which contributed much data for Chapter Six and for their willingness to discuss their work with me. Such thanks also go to Edgar Peltenberg of the University of Edinburgh, who discussed with me his work at Lemba and allowed me to use some of his materials in this book.

To the east, I thank Garth Gilmour for reviewing the section on Levantine archaeology and offering extremely helpful bibliography on east-west connections. I am also grateful to Steve Wiggins and M. Dijkstra for allowing me to quote their works here, and for showing general enthusiasm in this topic.

On a more personal level, I thank my friends Kellee Barnard, Eric Robinson, Jenny Wilson, and John Crimmins for help, good cheer, and empathy. I thank the Summer Session Office at Rutgers University, Camden, for office and technical support. Regards to Janice, Tina, and especially Tom Venables. I thank my parents for all sorts of support.

Finally, most of all, I thank my husband Paul Butler. He drew most of the illustrations in this book. He also provided technical and moral support, transportation, trips to the zoo, and remarkable patience and good humor.

All these people contributed to the completion of this book. I again express my deepest gratitude to each.

When quoting from translations prepared by other scholars, I have maintained the spelling of proper nouns in that translation, e.g., Aštart, Astarte, or Attart. Transcriptions or transliterations of texts translated have been gathered in Appendix B. However, I have not included the Ugaritic transliterations, since they are easily accessible in M. Dietrich, O. Loretz, and J. Sanmartín, *The Cuneiform Alphabetic Texts from Ugarit, Ras Ibn Hani and Other Places* (2nd ed.; Münster: Ugarit-Verlag, 1995) and H. Donner and W. Röllig, *Kanaanäische und Aramäische Inschriften* (Wiesbaden: Otto Harrassowitz, 1962).

S. L. B.

ABBREVIATIONS[1]

AAA	Αρχαιολογικα αναλεκτα εξ Αθηνων/*Athens Annals of Archaeology.*
ABD	*Anchor Bible Dictionary.*
ADelt	Αρχαιλογικον Δελτιον/*Archaiologikon Deltion.*
AION	*Annali. Istituto Universitario Orientali (Napoli).*
AJA	*American Journal of Archaeology.*
AJBA	*Australian Journal of Biblical Archaeology.*
Alasia I	*Mission Archeologique d'Alasia.* Cl. F.-A. Schaeffer (ed.) E.J. Brill. Paris. 1971.
Ant Cl	*L'Antiquité Classique.*
ArchAnz	*Archäologische Anzeiger.*
ARSIA	*Annuario. Regia Scuola Archeologia Italiana Atene.*
ASAA	*Annuario. Reale Scuola Archeologica di Atene.*
ASCSA	American School of Classical Studies at Athens.
ASOR	American Schools of Oriental Research.
Ath Mitt	*Mitteilungen. Deutsches Archäologische Institut. Abteilung Athens.*
BA	*Biblical Archaeologist.*
BASOR	*Bulletin. American Schools of Oriental Research.*
BCH	*Bulletin de Correspondance Hellénique.*
BSA	*British School at Athens. Annual.*
BSRAA	*Bulletin. Société Royale d'Archéologie d'Alexandrie.*
CA	*Current Anthropology.*
CAA	*Cyprus and the Aegean in Antiquity: From the Prehistoric period to the 7th century A.D.: Nicosia 8–10 December 1995.* Department of Antiquities, Cyprus. Nicosia. 1997.
CAH	*Cambridge Ancient History.*
CAJ	*Cambridge Archaeological Journal.*
CANE	*Civilizations of the Ancient Near East.* J.M. Sasson (ed.). Scribner. New York. 1995.

---

1. Based on Alkire 1998: *passim.*

ix

CBOO	*Acts of the International Archaeological Symposium "Cyprus Between the Orient and the Occident."* Nicosia 8–14 September 1985. V. Karageorghis (ed.). Dept. of Antiquities, Cyprus. Nicosia. 1986.
CPh	*Classical Philology.*
CRAI	*Comptes Rendus: l'Académie des Inscriptions et Belles. Lettres.*
CW	*Classical World.*
HSPh	*Harvard Studies in Classical Philology.*
ICr	*Inscriptiones Creticae.* M. Guarducci (ed.).
IEJ	*Israel Exploration Journal.*
IG	*Inscriptiones Graecae.*
JAOS	*Journal. American Oriental Society.*
JAR	*Journal of Anthropological Research.*
JARCE	*Journal. American Research Center in Egypt.*
JEA	*Journal of Egyptian Archaeology.*
JFA	*Journal of Field Archaeology.*
JHS	*Journal of Hellenic Studies.*
JNES	*Journal of Near Eastern Studies.*
JRAS	*Journal. Royal Asiatic Society of Great Britain and Ireland.*
KAI	*Kanaanaische und Aramaische Inschriften.* Donner, H. and W. Rölling (eds.). Otto Harrassowitz. Wiesbaden. 1968.
Kret Chron	Κρητικα Χρονικα/*Kretika Chronika.*
KTU	*Keilalphabetischen Texte aus Ugarit.* Dietrich et al. (eds.).
LIMC	*Lexicon Iconographicum Mythologicae Graecae.* Boardman, J. et al. (eds.). Artemis Verlag. Zurich. 1981–1994.
Marb W Pr	*Marburger Winkelmann-Programm.*
M.A.R.I.	*Mari: Annales de Recherches Interdisciplinaires.* Éditions Recherches sur les civilizations. Paris. Volumes 3–8. 1984–1997.
MEM	*Acts of the International Archaeological Symposium "The Mycenaeans in the Eastern Mediterranean."* Nicosia 27th March – 2nd April 1972. Dept. of Antiquities, Cyprus. Nicosia. 1973.
MIO	*Mitteilungen des Instituts für Orientforschung.*
MUSJ	*Mélanges. Université Saint Joseph.*
OA	*Opuscula Archaeologia.*
Op Ath	*Opuscula Atheniensia.*
PAAH	Πρακτικα της εν Αθηναις Αρχαιολογικης Εταιρειας/*Praktika tes en Athenais Archaiologikes Hetaireias.*
PBA	*Proceedings. British Academy.*

PEQ	*Palestine Exploration Quarterly.*
Praktika 1985	Πρακτικα Του Δευτερου Διεθνουσ Κυπριολογικου Συνεδριου: Αρχαιον Τμημα. Λευκωσια. 1985.
Praktika 1972	Πρακτικα του Πρωτου Διεθνουσ Κυπρολογικοψ Συνεδριου: Αρχαιον Τμημα. Λευκωσια. 1972.
PRU	*Palais Royal d'Ugarit.* C. F.-A. Schaeffer (ed.).
PW	*Pauley-Wissova Realencyclopädie der Classischen Alterwissenchaft.*
RAA	*Revue d'Assyriologie et d'Archéologie Oriental.*
RBCC	*Acts of the International Archaeological Symposium "The Relations Between Cyprus and Crete, ca 2000–500 B.C."* Nicosia 16th April – 22nd April 1978. Dept. of Antiquities, Cyprus. Nicosia. 1979.
RDAC	*Report. Department of Antiquities of Cyprus.*
Rend Linc	*Rendiconti. Reale Accademia dei Lincei.*
Rend Pont	*Rendiconti. Pontificia Accademia Romana di Archologia.*
RlA	*Reallexikon der Assyriologie.* Walter de Gruyter. Berlin and New York.
SCE I	*The Swedish Cyprus Expedition: Finds and Results of the Excavations in Cyprus: 1927–1931.* E. Gjerstad, J. Lindros, E. Sjöqvist and A. Westhold (eds.). Swedish Cyprus Expedition. Stockholm. 1934.
SEG	*Supplementum Epigraphicum Graecum.* Alphen aa den Rija. Sijtheff and Noordhoff.
SEL	*Studi Epigrafici e Liguistici.*
SHA	*Sitzungsberichts. Heidelberg Akademia der Wissenschaft.*
SIMA	Studies in Mediterranean Archaeology.
Stud Or	*Studia Orientalia [Helsinki].*
TAPA	*Transactions and Proceedings. American Philological Association.*
UF	*Ugarit-Forschungen*: Internationales Jahrbuch für die Altertumskunde Syrien-Palästinas. Verlag Butzor & Bercher Kevelaer. Neukirchener Verlag Neukirchen-Vluyn.
WO	*Welt des Orients.*
ZDPV	*Zeitschrift. Deutscher Palästinaverein.*

I.
INTRODUCTION

This book is an examination into the origins of the Greek goddess Aphrodite, whose main areas of concern and power were erotic love and sexuality. She was revered in the Greek-speaking world by the names Aphrodite, Aphrodita, and Aphordita, as well as by the epithets *Kythereia*, *Paphia*, and *Kypris*. This study addresses how this goddess came into being.

It is clear that Aphrodite existed in the Greek pantheon as a Greek goddess by the end of the eighth century BCE (as per the dating of the inscription on the so-called Nestor cup from Pithekoussai) and that she was well entrenched in Greek mythology and folklore by the early seventh century BCE (as per her presence and prominence in the works of Homer and Hesiod).[1] The question remains, however, as to whether and when she evolved in Greece, or whether she was imported into Greece and under what influences.

Three hypotheses exist concerning the possible origins of Aphrodite: (1) Aphrodite was an indigenous Greek goddess; (2) Aphrodite was not an indigenous Greek goddess, but was imported from outside the Greek-speaking world before c. 750 BCE; (3) there were elements of Aphrodite in a deity or deities of the pre-Iron Age Aegean that combined with external elements to create the Hellenic goddess. All hypotheses will be considered in the following pages, and I shall attempt to determine which of them, or combination of them, is best supported by the available evidence.

Over the centuries various historians and scholars have adopted one or more versions of these hypotheses to explain the origins of Aphrodite. What follows is a brief survey of the various schools of thought that have emerged since the days of Homer regarding either the origins of the goddess or her introduction into the Greek pantheon.

The Ancient Opinions

There is a general consensus among the ancient authors that Aphrodite came from the east, with the extent of her eastern origins extending outward throughout the passing centuries. Both Homer and Hesiod see the goddess as being at home on Cyprus, notably at her sanctuary at Paphos. In the *Theogony*, ll. 188–202, the goddess first alights on land at Paphos,[2] while in the Song

---

1. More on these in Chapters Two and Three.

2. The goddess passes by Kythera before landing on Cyprus. This first landing makes Cyprus especially important in this context. The interjection of Kythera is an attempt

1

of Demodokos (*Odyssey*, VIII, 360–64) she retires there after her tryst with Ares.

> When the two were free of the bonds (which seemed even stronger than they
>   were to them),
> immediately Ares went off to Thrace,
> while smile-loving Aphrodite went to Cyprus,
> to Paphos, where are her temple and altar of sacrifice.[3]

Herodotos is the first to assert that Aphrodite (specifically Aphrodite Ourania) is Phoenician in origin. He claims that the Paphian sanctuary of the goddess was actually preceded by the cult of the goddess in Ashkalon in the southern Levant, and that it was the Phoenicians who brought this cult to Cyprus:

> This is the sanctuary, as I discovered through inquiry, the oldest of all the
> sanctuaries of this goddess; for the sanctuary of Cyprus originated from there
> (Ashkalon), as the Cypriots themselves say, and as for the one among the
> Kytherians, the Phoenicians are its founders, who are from Syria too. (*Histo-
> ries* I.105, 2–3).[4]

Aphrodite's origins are placed even farther to the east by Pausanias, who claims that the cult of Aphrodite Ourania was originally practiced by the Assyrians, who taught her rites to the Phoenicians, who then passed the cult on to the Cypriots, before she was finally brought to Greece:

> Nearby is a sanctuary of Aphrodite Ourania. It is held that the first people
> to revere Ourania were the Assyrians, and after the Assyrians the Paphians
> of Cyprus and those of the Phoenicians who dwell in Ashkalon in Palestine;
> Kytherians worship her having so learned from the Phoenicians (Pausanias
> 1, XIV, 7).[5]

In these claims, aspects of her cult (if not the cult entirely) were said to have been originated by Easterners and passed on to the Greeks by way of the Phoenicians.

The "Orientalist" School of Thought

This school of thought has endured since the Archaic Age, but emerged especially as a topic of debate among Classicists in the nineteenth century. Both Röscher in his *Lexikon* and L.R. Farnell in his *Cults of the Greek States* understood Aphrodite to be a more-or-less Hellenized Aštart-Ištar figure. Farnell,

---

on the part of Hesiod to explain the epithet "Kythereia" and the belief, held by later authors, that this was the site of Aphrodite's earliest sanctuary in Greece. These hypotheses will be taken up in Chapter Four in the section on Kythera.

3. All translations, unless otherwise noted, are my own. See Appendix B 1.1.

4. See Appendix B 1.2.

5. See Appendix B 1.3.

having noted the correlations between Aphrodite and Ištar, claimed that, in spite of wide prevalence in the Greek world, there is no reason to believe that Aphrodite belonged to the "aboriginal" religion of ancient Greece. He believed, rather, that the texts and artifacts confirmed that she was an "oriental" deity and that even after her adoption into Greece she retained her eastern flavor. Furthermore, this adoption into the Greek pantheon from abroad rendered hazy her familial connections to the other Greek deities.[6]

Almost a half-century after Farnell, H.J. Rose emphasized the connections between Ištar and Aphrodite, stating that her true origins were heavily, if not totally, indebted to "oriental" influences. Her associations with Cyprus and Phoenician Thebes, as well as her questionable Greek name, made it quite unthinkable that she was an indigenous Greek goddess. It stood to reason, then, that she was an adaptation of some manner of Ištar goddess, such as those whom Rose believed to have been worshipped throughout the greater part of Asia.[7]

Perhaps the most significant scholar to deal extensively (and recently) with Greek religion and eastern influences is W. Burkert, who, in *Greek Religion*, examines the various parallels between the cultic, artistic, and literary portrayals of the eastern "love goddesses" and those of Aphrodite. Burkert argues that the Semitic, specifically Phoenician, origins of Aphrodite as expressed as early as Herodotos are supported by the correspondences in cult and iconography that go beyond just the sexual characteristics of Greek Aphrodite and eastern Aštart/Ištar. He notes the androgynous quality of Aphrodite/Aphrotitos and the bearded Ištar and the male/female pair Aštar/Aštart; the militaristic qualities shared between Ištar and armed Aphrodite; heavenly designations; and similar uses of doves and incense in cult ritual.[8] Burkert insists that there is no trace of Aphrodite in the Mycenaean world, so that the cult of the goddess must have been imported no earlier than the Dark Ages by way of Cyprus.

The "orientalist" school sees Aphrodite as a Greek cognate of Phoenician Aštart, and often of Mesopotamian Ištar as well. This female deity of sexuality moved east to west by way of Cyprus, where, most probably, the Greeks first encountered her.

The Cypriot School of Thought

In the twentieth century, alternate theories emerged concerning the origins of Aphrodite, with many scholars now looking to the west of the Levant for the goddess's origins. These scholars claim that the island of Cyprus was just

---

6. Farnell 1896: 618 and 622.

7. Rose 1964: 122.

8. Burkert 1985: 152–53. For more on Aphrodite Armed, see Chapter Two, the section on iconography, and Chapter Four, notably the sections on Kythera, Sparta, and Corinth.

as influential in the development of the eventual Hellenic goddess of love as was the Levantine coast and its northern and eastern neighbors. For example, G. Hill in *The History of Cyprus* states his belief that Aphrodite is the final, anthropomorphic manifestation of an indigenous mother-goddess venerated in Cyprus at least since the Early Bronze Age.[9] Hill sees no oriental influence in the early development of this deity, certainly none before the Iron Age, but finds in Cyprus, the Aegean, and Anatolia all the elements of the eventual Greek goddess.[10]

Taking a somewhat different view of Cypriot origin, H. Herter in his article "Die Ursprünge des Aphroditekultes" argues that, although Aphrodite must owe much of her character to the Near Eastern sex goddesses,[11] nevertheless, it was ultimately a Cypriot goddess, the goddess of Paphos, who made her way into the Greek mainland by way of the island of Kythera. Thus, he claimed that Cyprus was not an intermediary station in the evolution of Aphrodite, but its starting point, with a true cult of Aphrodite appearing specifically in Mycenaean Cyprus.[12] Although Herter maintains that the Greeks revered this early, Cypriot form of Aphrodite in the Bronze Age, before the colonization of that island by the Phoenicians, he sees considerable Eastern influence within the Greek Aphrodite, which surely must have come through Phoenician contact.[13] Unfortunately, due to the chronological difficulty of the question, Herter declines to address the issue of *why* the oriental/Greek similarities exist, and merely lists the similarities.

J. Karageorghis in *La grande déesse de Chypre et son culte* also places considerable emphasis on native Cypriot origins, noting that Cyprus played a very important role in the transmission of religious ideas at the end of the Bronze Age. From this basis she offers the hypothesis that Aphrodite existed originally as a "humble Cypriot goddess of fertility" who became the glorious Aphrodite of Greek mythology beginning at the interface between the Bronze and Iron Ages. Like Herter, Karageorghis sees Near Eastern influence in the development of the goddess, at least in terms of iconography, as early as the Early and Middle Bronze Ages, when Anatolian and Levantine styles manifested themselves in the Cypriot iconography. Thus, as she believes, although the

---

9. Hill 1940: 80.

10. *Ibid.*, 71.

11. The term "sex goddess" refers to a goddess who has sexuality as one of her powers or spheres of influence. This is to be distinguished from a "sexual goddess" who is erotic in character, but who does not have sex as one of her powers or spheres of influence. Hera may be "sexual," but she is not a "sex goddess."

12. Herter 1975: 29–30.

13. *Ibid.*, 32.

goddess who would become Aphrodite is clearly indigenous to Cyprus, Kara-georghis admits to considerable, long-term oriental influence.[14]

Maier and V. Karageorghis in *Paphos: History and Archaeology* maintain the views of Herter and J. Karageorghis and state their belief that Aphrodite arose as a combination of an indigenous Cypriot fertility goddess with some elements of a Near Eastern "Great Goddess" such as Ištar.[15] However, they, like J. Karageorghis, emphasize the idea that although the Near East may have influenced the development of this goddess, the goddess and her cult were indigenous to Cyprus. In support of their hypothesis, Maier and Karageorghis refer to the Chalcolithic female figurines from the area of Paphos, arguing for an age-old continuous fertility cult in that region that evolved into the cult of Aphrodite.[16]

According to this school of thought (with the exception of Hill), Middle and Late Bronze Age contacts between the Near East and Cyprus permitted the Cypriot adoption of some aspects of Near Eastern religion, including aspects of the Near Eastern "Great Goddess," which the Cypriots combined with their native religion to create the "Great Goddess" honored especially at Paphos. The Greeks who migrated to Cyprus at the dawn of the "Time of Trou-bles" would have then encountered the cult of this Paphian goddess, whom they would eventually reconstruct as their own Hellenic Aphrodite. J. Kara-georghis and V. Karageorghis, to greater and lesser extents, however, regard Aphrodite as ultimately an indigenous, Cypriot goddess, whose existence in Cyprus dates back into the Chalcolithic.

The "Indigenous" School of Thought

Contrary to the previous schools of thought that, to one extent or another, recognize Near Eastern influence in Greek Aphrodite, K. Tümpel in his article on that goddess in Pauly's *Realencyclopädie* claims that she is indigenous to Greece and that her proper homeland is in Thessaly.[17] This indigenous Aph-rodite was later "lost" behind layers of foreign, eroticising influence, thus causing even Herodotos to theorize a foreign origin for the goddess.[18]

The "Indo-European" School of Thought

A. Enmann initiated the Indo-European school of thought with his 1886 arti-cle "Cyprus und der Ursprung des Aphroditekultus." Enmann believed that

---

14. J. Karageorghis 1977: 117.

15. Maier and Karageorghis 1984: 365.

16. *Ibid.*, 101–2. This argument will be addressed fully in Chapter Five.

17. Tümpel in *PW*, 2769, 49–55.

18. *Ibid.*, 2771, 53–56.

Aphrodite emerged out of an Indo-European moon-goddess, along with almost all the other female deities of the Greek pantheon.[19] In this, Enmann appears to have been heavily influenced by the two dominant myth theories of his day: Indo-Europeanism as begun and advanced by the linguistic theories of the Grimm brothers; and celestialism, according to which all divinities ultimately emerged as numens of heavenly bodies. In addition to this, Enmann, while maintaining his belief in her Indo-European nature, argues that Aphrodite derived from the spirit of the (Greek) people, that it was "not through the Phoenicians, nor from Cyprus or Kythera, but from the dark womb of the people's spirit, from which sprang in time primordial the Greek religion."[20] Thus one might say that Aphrodite originated in the earliest formation of the Greek culture.

G. Nagy in his article "Phaethon, Sappho's Phaon, and the White Rock of Leukas: 'Reading' the Symbols of Greek Lyric," D. Boedeker in *Aphrodite's Entrance into Greek Epic*, and P. Friedrich in his *The Meaning of Aphrodite* also argue that Aphrodite is ultimately of Indo-European origin, but claim that she originally arose out of an Indo-European dawn-goddess.[21] According to Nagy, a dawn-goddess is one of the original and commonly shared members of the Proto-Indo-European divine family. As the Indo-Europeans spread across Europe, the proto-Greeks brought this goddess, Eos, with them. At some point in prehistory, this Eos bifurcated, rendering both Eos and Aphrodite. That they are, in fact, the same goddess (originally) is determined through comparison with their Indian cognate Ushas, the Vedic goddess of the dawn and daughter of the Vedic sky-father (*Dyáus Pitar*). Their key to this identification is that the title "Daughter of the Sky Father," which in the *Vedas* belongs to the dawn-goddess, is applied not to Eos but to Aphrodite in epic diction.[22]

Such is an overview of the various theories concerning the origins of Aphrodite. They range from the extreme indigenous/psychological to the result of trade and evolution among the various cultures of the ancient eastern Mediterranean. Some theories are mutually exclusive, whereas some might interact to form varying approximations of the answer. Ultimately, none of them is exhaustive, and none of them resolves the question adequately.

---

19. Enmann 1886: 75.

20. *Ibid.*, 84.

21. This theory was originally expounded in the nineteenth century by M. Müller, *Vorlesung über die Wissenschaft der Sprache (2) II*, and by L. Meyer, *Bemerkungen zur ält. Geschichte der griechische Mythologie.* I specifically consider Nagy's treatment of the issue in this section as the information and theories are more in line with modern thought, and the later authors, Boedeker and Friedrich, follow his thinking.

22. Nagy 1990: 248. This theory will be considered in greater detail in Chapter Three.

A NEW ATTEMPT

In the past twenty years there have been great strides in Cypriot archaeology, Levantine archaeological and literary studies. Any theories based on previous understandings of these regions must now be reconsidered. There also have been exceptional accomplishments in the field of feminist theory in the past three decades. Any study that considers the role of the feminine in a society, be it divine or secular, must also be considered through this lens.

Whenever possible, literature will be examined as a prelude to and a means of understanding the physical data. The literature to be considered will come from a variety of sources, notably Greek, Ugaritic, Akkadian, Sumerian, Phoenician, Biblical Hebrew, and Egyptian, with references as well to the Roman, Vedic, and Norse.

Throughout this work, when investigating various deities and cults in different regions, the literary evidence will be considered in two ways. First, it will be used to examine the personae of deities, beginning, naturally, with Aphrodite. What roles do the deities play in the literature, how are they portrayed, when are they prayed to and for what purpose(s)? Chapter Two presents the persona of Aphrodite as she appeared in the earliest Greek literature and art. This material will establish Aphrodite specifically as a goddess of sex, rather than as a generic fertility-goddess/earth-mother, as often has been assumed. Once we distinguish between ancient Greek notions of fertility, sexuality, and maternity, we will consider the early artistic evidence, noting Aphrodite's associations with sex, sea and sky, and doves. After the literary data have revealed the nature of Aphrodite's persona, this information is utilized to compare Aphrodite to other goddesses revered in the ancient world who may have contributed to her evolution or development.

Furthermore, information derived from the literary analysis of the persona of Aphrodite helps to establish the identification of an Aphrodite-type goddess in an iconography where no written evidence is available. By definition, an "Aphrodite-type goddess" is a female presented in the iconography, likely to be a goddess, who portrays one or more of Aphrodite's known characteristics as revealed through the literary analysis. Depending on place and chronology, an Aphrodite-type goddess may be interpreted as a possible forerunner of or contributor to the goddess named Aphrodite, should it prove that this goddess did emerge through an evolutionary process.

As this is a search for the *origins* of Aphrodite, it is most important to understand the goddess as she existed in her earliest extant literary and iconographic manifestations in the Greek world (eighth through sixth centuries BCE). Likewise, when considering the personae of Near Eastern deities, it is critical to understand them as they existed during periods relevant to the possible development and influence on Aphrodite. For example, it is important to understand Aštart as she was known and revered *before* being recast in the literature as the cognate of a Greek deity (thus, before Aštart was portrayed as the Near Eastern Aphrodite). As it is consistently necessary to deal with earlier, "untainted" literary sources, the lower limit placed on this set of data is 500 BCE (with exceptions for drama, to note either continuity or change, and biblical references that also show continuity with earlier attestations).

Beyond the question of persona, literature will be used to study the history of the cult of the deities. Where, when, and how was each goddess worshipped? How did the Greeks themselves understand the history and origins of this goddess? For the purposes of the history of the cult, authors and texts from periods after 500 BCE will be analyzed, notably Pausanias.

One caveat is extremely important in this analysis. The Greeks clearly believed that all their deities existed at least since the period of time known as the Age of Heroes, the Bronze Age. Even the "newcomer" Dionysos lived in the age of Kadmos, which preceded the Trojan War.[23] Thus, literary assertions of foundation dates and other cultic chronologies may prove to be far earlier than the actual archaeological evidence allows. Furthermore, the dating of certain cults may be pushed back in time to serve political functions.[24] Thus, literary historical evidence must be checked against archaeological and artistic evidence.

Archaeological evidence will be examined in areas throughout the ancient eastern Mediterranean, focusing on sanctuary sites in the Bronze Age Aegean, the Hellenic world, Cyprus, and the Levant. The data so derived will be used to determine where deities were worshipped, when, and how. The chronology of sanctuaries, temples, and other relevant areas will be based on stratigraphy and comparative artistic evidence from pottery and/or votives. When this is unavailable, epigraphy and literary sources will be used. The extent to which architecture is native or foreign to the area will be considered and, in the latter instance, used as evidence of foreign contact and/or influence. As with the literature, evidence before the year 500 BCE will be considered as relevant.

---

23. Dionysos is represented in the Linear B corpus and, therefore, is not exceptionally "new" in the Greek pantheon. However, in this instance it is important to note that the Greeks themselves seemed to think of Dionysos as the "newly arrived" deity in the age of Kadmos, when the other gods were, in most cases, already well entrenched (exceptions include Herakles). It must be noted that many of the tales surrounding this god revolve around the concept of the new deity who must establish his cult in the face of Greek traditionalism (the theme of the *Bakkhai*, for example). Thus the issue is not whether the god Dionysos is "new" in the Greek pantheon, but whether the ancient Greeks understood him as being "new."

24. For example, the myth that it was Theseus who instituted the cult of Aphrodite Pandemos in Athens during the period when Theseus was being used in Athenian propaganda during the sixth and fifth centuries BCE, *contra* its introduction by Solon as explained by Pseudo-Aristotle in the *Ath. Pol.*

Epigraphy will be used to determine when and where deities were worshipped, especially as it identifies cult places, memorializes offerings or sacrifices, and points to the local, personal, or official nature of the cult. Focus will be on evidence before the year 500 BCE, unless a later inscription offers evidence of a structure, cult, etc. before 500.[25] Sources of epigraphy will derive from records in Linear A, Linear B, first-millennium Greek, Phoenician, and Egyptian.

The art historical evidence will mainly (although not exclusively) be focused on religious iconography. It is of primary importance in this endeavor to determine what one must look for as indicative of either Aphrodite or an Aphrodite-type goddess as defined above. Chapter Two will offer a description of Aphrodite as per the earliest literary and artistic materials. Based on this understanding of the goddess and her attributes, certain iconographic motifs will be considered as indicators of an Aphrodite-type goddess in those contexts for which no literary data are available, most notably Bronze Age Crete and Cyprus. When written evidence is available in specific cultural contexts (Ugarit, for example), the method established for the Greek data will be followed, whereby the persona is first determined according to the extant literature and then correlated to the iconography present in the region under question so as to offer a fuller understanding of the goddess (or iconography itself) under question. Thus, iconography will either be used to complement written evidence or, in the absence of such, as a primary source of data. Furthermore, the iconographic and archaeological evidence will help determine possible foreign influence on cult practices, iconography, and religion. As with the literary data, art historical data will be taken from the Bronze Age Aegean, the first-millennium Greek world, Cyprus, the Levant, Egypt, and Mesopotamia.

As far as possible, this study will proceed from the known to the unknown, thus, going from west to east backward in time. It is established that Aphrodite was worshipped in the Greek-speaking world since at least the Late Geometric Age. Therefore, the search for Aphrodite's origins begins in the Aegean. After an analysis of the persona of Aphrodite based on the data of the eighth to fifth centuries BCE, the study turns to the question of whether a chronology and geography of this goddess's cult can be established. Chapter Three will use literary and linguistic analysis to consider—and reject—the Indo-European school of thought. Then follows an examination, using all data as listed above, of the Bronze Age Aegean. Chapter Four continues that examination in the Archaic Aegean and the Greek world of the early first millennium. This survey, moving geographically from southern Greece northward, will show that Aphrodite's cult is oldest in Crete, especially at the site of Kato

25. Note that a fourth-century inscription points to the joint cult of Aphrodite and Hermes at the Samian Heraion dating back into the Archaic Age.

Symi, which shows continuous cultic activity since the Middle Minoan period.

The cult then spreads northward, hitting other points in Crete before
reaching Kythera and Sparta, and then reaching farther north, to regions such
as Attica and Boiotia. It becomes clear that, with the exception of Kato Symi,
no evidence from the Greek world is as old as that found for Aphrodite's cult
in Cyprus. The sanctuary of Aphrodite at Paphos on Cyprus was constructed
at the latest by 1200 BCE, and the literary data from the earliest Greek sources
attest to Paphos as being a primary, if not the original, home/sanctuary of the
goddess. Therefore, from Greece and Crete the study will proceed to Cyprus
and will consider whether Aphrodite or aspects of Aphrodite may have originated there.

Although, according to my thesis, Aphrodite emerged in Cyprus in the Late
Bronze Age, Chapter Five considers the evidence from the Chalcolithic
through Middle Cypriot periods, since some scholars have sought Aphrodite's
origins in that timeframe. The chapter begins with an explanation of the
most recent understanding of Cypriot chronology and proceeds to consider
the archaeological and art historical evidence in a chronological fashion.

Chapter Six considers the later Cypriot material and Near Eastern contacts. Here, a clear Aphrodite-type goddess appears in the archaeological
record. From here, archaeological evidence for contacts between Cyprus
and Greece in the Dark Ages is considered. The data show that there were
close contacts between Cyprus and Crete during the period when it would
appear that Aphrodite is first introduced into the Greek pantheon, explaining
how and why the goddess's cult first appears in Crete.

As Eteo-Cypriot is not yet readable, the data from Chalcolithic through Late
Bronze Age Cyprus will be almost exclusively archaeological and art historical. Particular emphasis will be placed on goddess iconography as it changes
over time on the island, votive remains and what information they might yield
about the deity in question, and religious architecture for information about
the spread of the cult on the island. Foreign influence will be considered
when analyzing all sets of data. Literary data will be examined to see if they
support the information yielded by the archaeology, especially that which
concerns the history of the cult at Paphos itself. The data will show that a goddess who clearly conforms to the Aphrodite-type appears throughout the
island by the beginning of Late Cypriot II, and that this iconography is heavily
influenced by Levantine iconography. This Levantine influence is also per-
ceptible in the religious architecture.

Chapter Eight will consider what deity or deities in the Near East may have
been the progenitress(es) of Aphrodite. After examining the contacts between Cyprus and the Near East so as to determine the strongest points of
contact, we will establish what deities were revered in the areas of contact,
thus creating a possible repertoire of deities who may have contributed to

the earliest stirrings of Aphrodite. The literary evidence is then considered to establish the personae of the Near Eastern goddesses, and will help determine which of these have the closest parallels to Aphrodite. Contrary to much modern opinion, Aštart is not the most likely progenitress, being a goddess associated with hunting and war, rather than love or sex. By contrast, the goddesses Ištar and Išhara are offered as the most likely ancestors of the Greek goddess. This is borne out by the study of iconographic evidence, which revolves mainly around the image of the "nude goddess."

The evidence considered here shows that the closest parallels to the bird-faced figurines, which show the earliest evidence for an Aphrodite-type goddess in Cyprus, are to be found in the region of Alalakh, where the cults of both Ištar and Išhara were strong. These two are once again presented as the most likely progenitresses of Aphrodite.

Chapter Nine considers the long-held belief that Aphrodite was the Greek version of Phoenician Aštart. After showing that the rise and spread of Aphrodite's cult in Greece does not correlate with contacts with the Phoenicians during the Dark Ages, we shall consider how the persona of Aštart as presented in the Levantine Iron Age evidence does not correlate with the persona of Aphrodite as established in Chapter Two. We shall then examine how the contemporary cults of the "Paphian" and Aštart in Cyprus caused both goddesses to be viewed as the "Goddess of Cyprus." This, in addition to sexual iconography of the Phoenicians on Cyprus, led the ancient Greeks to believe that the Phoenician goddess of Cyprus was the same goddess as their own, thus leading to the conflation of the two deities in Classical literature.

The final chapter of this book provides a summary of the evidence and arguments presented throughout this work regarding the origins of Aphrodite. We shall consider briefly the various ways by which the ancient Greeks Hellenized the Cypro-Levantine goddess into Greek Aphrodite, including consideration of early martial qualities in the goddess and the apparent Greek fear of the power of Aphrodite.

II.
THE PERSONA OF APHRODITE

Literature

When investigating the origins of Aphrodite, we must examine the earliest literary sources, mainly, the works of Homer, the Homeridai, Hesiod, and the Archaic poets, such as Sappho. We shall consider also some of the writings of the fifth-century dramatists on the grounds that this later material may shed further light on the Archaic data, and with an eye toward what changes or remains constant in the persona of Aphrodite from the time of Homer to that of Euripides. The artistic representations of the goddess up to approximately 500 BCE will also be considered.[1]

SEX-GODDESS VERSUS FERTILITY/MOTHER-GODDESS

Aphrodite is, above all, a goddess of sexuality and love. According to Hesiod, "this honor she has from the beginning, having received this / portion among men and immortal deities:/ maidens' fond discourse and smiles and deceits/ and joy and sweet love and gentleness."[2] As the author of the *Homeric Hymn to Aphrodite* describes her in Hymn V, she is "golden-throned Aphrodite, of Cyprus, who in deities stirs up sweet desire and who subdues the race of mortal men" (ll. 1–3). This identification is apparent even in her name, where "*Aphrodisia, aphrodisiazein* as a verb, denotes quite simply the act of love, and in the *Odyssey*, the name of the goddess is already used in the same sense."[3]

Methodologically, this identification of the goddess has engendered several problems vis-à-vis a search for Aphrodite's origins. One such problem is the overwhelming tendency of scholars of the past century to identify sexuality with maternity and fertility. Taken at face value, this conception would suggest that Artemis, a virgin goddess who wields power over animal and

---

1. The pre-500 BCE corpus, both of literary and iconographic data, is quite limited, especially in contrast to the plethora of materials after 500 BCE. Although it can be argued that the basis of an analysis of early Aphrodite might be hindered by such a small quantity of available materials, it is perhaps better to think of such a study as a random sample analysis. What remains from the Archaic period is, in fact, a random sample of the complete Archaic corpus and, thus, statistically speaking, might be used as an access to, a microcosm of, the whole.

2. *Theogony*, ll. 203–6 (Appendix B 2.1).

3. Burkert 1985: 152 (*Odyssey* Bk. 22, l. 444).

human fertility, is not qualitatively distinct from Aphrodite, whose domain is sexuality with minimal associations with fertility, animal or otherwise. This conflation also affects the interpretation of iconography, so that any goddess portraying characteristics such as breasts becomes blanketly identified as a "fertility-goddess" or "earth-mother," as though these attributes could not be distinctively sexual rather than fertility oriented. With the various specific areas in which goddesses hold power being conflated, the goddesses of the ancient pantheons lose their distinctiveness in modern scholarship; they become identified as cognates of each other, and many ancient depictions of females come to be interpreted as one and the same archetype.

This tendency toward conflation has also hampered the study of Aphrodite especially in terms of iconography. In general, any nude female in the Aegean corpus[4] not specifically portrayed as mortal is identified as Aphrodite, regardless of chronology or geography. For example, in her chapter on Aphrodite in *Die Götter der Griechen*, E. Simon sees Aphrodite in the Early Bronze Age marble Cycladic figurines; the gold-foil nude females from the Mycenaean shaft graves; the "goddess" under a tree on the gold signet rings from Minoan Crete; and any nude female figure from Geometric times onward in Greek art.[5] This not only confuses the study of Aphrodite's origins by placing the goddess in all Aegean societies in all times, but it can blind one to the non-erotic portrayals of the goddess in the Greek repertoire.

In order to avoid such conflations, it is important at this juncture to establish a working distinction between the concepts of sexuality, maternity, and fertility, specifically as these distinctions would have been understood by the ancient Greeks. As mentioned above, sexuality, in the form of Aphrodite's honors, to re-quote Hesiod, is "whispers and smiles and deceptions, sweet pleasure and sexual love and tenderness." Thus, love and flirtation, physical eroticism, and the act of coitus constituted sexuality, and these acts were within the province of Aphrodite. Maternity encompasses not only the conception and bearing of a child, but also the manifestation of a continued mother-child relationship. For a goddess to be regarded specifically as a mother-goddess, she must derive power from procreation and her relationship(s) with her offspring. Fertility, in terms of the power of deities, encompasses the ability to provide abundant live offspring of all living creatures, with divisions of power being recognized for vegetal (grain and vine) and animal categories.

The interplay of sexuality and maternity is manifest in Hera, the goddess of marriage, who derives power from her role as mother, and who reproduces both sexually and asexually. She is, like Aphrodite, a sexual being, a quality

---

4. "Aegean" limits this identification to specific references to the Greek goddess Aphrodite. Such nude female representations as far afield as France and Germany, such as the "Willendorf Venus" in a less specific fashion, are identified similary.

5. Simon 1985: 229–54.

perhaps best brought forth in Book XIV of Homer's *Iliad*, where, with Aphrodite's aid, the queen of the gods plots a successful seduction of the king of the gods. As the spouse of Zeus, Hera conceives and brings forth children— Ares, Hebe, and Eileithyia with Zeus (*Theogony*, ll. 921–23), and Hephaistos (*Theogony*, l. 928) and Typhoios (*Homeric Hymn to Apollo*, ll. 306ff.) independently (*without* sexual union). One might argue that it is this power of Hera, the power to bring forth children, specifically sons, without the aid or "permission" of Zeus, that is her greatest asset; using this power, she is able to threaten Zeus with the potential of bearing a son stronger than his father, the bane of gods in the Succession Myth. Thus, Hera might be viewed as a mother-goddess, a goddess who derives power through her ability to give birth. Furthermore, she is a force of civilization, imparting the institution of marriage to humans and, thus, setting them apart from the rest of the animal kingdom.[6] Her institution of marriage places restraints upon human sexuality, trading pure/wanton eroticism for a stable familial structure, thus enhancing maternity and her own role as a mother-goddess. Hera, then, is a goddess whose persona is focussed on maternity, less so on sexuality. Likewise, her use of sexuality, as in the *Iliad*, and maternity, as in the *Theogony*, are distinct from one another, showing the separate categories into which these concepts are placed.

Fertility encompasses both animal (including human) and vegetal procreation and abundance. In many instances in ancient Greece, the relationship between sexuality and fertility is made explicit, most notably in the practice of sexual abstention during fertility rituals such as the Thesmophoria (whereby the innate fertile powers of women are redirected into the earth). However, fertility is also distinct from sexuality, insofar as fertility may, and often does occur in the absence of sexuality. This is especially evident in the character of Artemis. This is the goddess most overtly associated with animal and human fertility. It is she who regulates the birth, life, and, through her hunting, death cycles of the sylvan animals. She is the protectress of children, being revered as a *kourotrophos* specifically in Sparta,[7] the patroness of unwed girls, the goddess who oversees menstruation and defloration, the deity most commonly invoked for conception and successful pregnancy,[8] and as Artemis Eileithyia and Lokhia she aids women in childbirth. And yet, just as Artemis herself never "grows up" or participates in the blood rites of womanhood, so, too, she remains a perpetual virgin, a regulator of fertility completely divorced from sexuality and personal motherhood.

The goddess in whom all these elements come together in a somewhat balanced fashion is Demeter. She, like Artemis, is associated with earthly fertility,

---

6. Rehm 1994: 201, no. 48.

7. Vernant 1991: 195–261.

8. Demand 1994: *passim*.

although for her it is vegetal fertility (whereas Dionysos is patron of the more liquid bounty of earth). Demeter is a mother *par excellence*, with the tale of her bonds with her daughter Persephone being the dominant theme of her Homeric Hymn. Furthermore, she "mingled" with the mortal Iasion in a "thrice-ploughed field" and bore the son Ploutos ("Wealth"), yet another reference to her associations with fertility and fecundity.[9] This tale also expresses her sexual nature, a role also brought out both in the figure of Iambe/Baubo, who pleases the goddess either by speaking obscenities to her or by exposing her genitals, and in cult, in the use of ritual obscenities and sexual abstinence during the Thesmophoria and other women's rites associated with Demeter.[10]

One must observe, then, that the Greeks recognized separate categories of sexuality, fertility, and maternity, and that these categories might be grouped or excluded in a variety of ways. The main difference among the roles of various goddesses such as Hera, Demeter, and Aphrodite is the focus of the individual goddess' powers. For Hera, the focus is on her maternal aspect; for Aphrodite, it is her sexual aspect. For, although Aphrodite takes part in all three areas (sexuality, maternity, and fertility), always the greatest focus is on her role in sexuality, a power that she wields over god, human, and animal. In Homeric Hymn V she is seen on earth inspiring the wild animals, who fawn over her to "pair off" in her wake.[11]

> She came to well-springed Ida, mother of beasts,
> and walked straight through the mountain dwelling.
> The grey wolves and bright-eyed lions fawned over her,
> bears and nimble leopards insatiate for game
> approached her. And she seeing these was delighted in her mind
> and in their breasts cast desire; through her all of them
> in pairs lay together in the shadowy haunts. (ll. 68–74)

Likewise, at the beginning of her Hymn the poet extols her thus:[12]

> Muses, relate to me the works of golden-throned Aphrodite,
> of Cyprus, who in deities stirs up sweet desire and
> who subdues the race of mortal men
> and air-borne birds and all wild creatures,
> and as many creatures the mainland rears, and also the sea.
> To all these are the works of well-crowned Kythera a concern. (ll. 1–6)

---

9. *Theogony*, ll. 969ff.

10. For further information on these topics, see Foley (ed.) 1994: *passim*, and Parke 1977: 82ff. On Baubo iconography, see Olender 1990: *passim*. For the use of ritual obscenity, see A. Brumfield 1996: *passim*.

11. Although I would argue here that the emphasis is on the animals having sex rather than on their reproducing; see Appendix B 2.2.

12. See Appendix B 2.3.

In the late seventh century, the poet Mimnermos further accentuates the nature of the goddess, asking: [13]

What life, what joy without golden Aphrodite?
I should die, were these things not a care to me,
Secret love and sweet gifts and the bed.

The Lesbian poet Sappho prays to Aphrodite to be her "ally" when she, Sappho, wishes to possess the object of a her longing, a woman who does not return the poet's affections. Thus, invoking Aphrodite's power over mortals, she writes (Sappho I):[14]

And you, O blessed one,
Smiling on your immortal face,
Asked on what account I am suffering again, and
On what account was I summoning again,
And what did I want most in my raving heart to happen.
"Whom do I persuade on this account
To lead you back to her dearest love?
Who, O Sappho, wrongs you?
For if she flees, soon will she follow;
And if she does not receive gifts, then she will give.
And if she does not love, soon she will love even if she does not wish it."
Come to me now, release me from this grievous care!
What my heart desires to come to pass, make happen.
And you yourself be my ally.

The power of Aphrodite and sexual union is also made manifest in the words of Apollo, speaking in Aeschylus's *Eumenides*, where the god suggests that the union created by Aphrodite is stronger than that of blood ties:[15]

In your argument, Aphrodite is discounted utterly—
yet from her the very dearest things come to human kind;
for man and woman, the bed,
when justly kept, their fated bed,
is greater than any oath that can be sworn. (ll. 215-18)

Aphrodite's power over the gods, even Zeus, is a major feature of her role in the epics and hymns. Most notable is her role in Book XIV of the *Iliad*, where she helps Hera seduce and deceive Zeus. Once again, at the beginning of Homeric Hymn V, she "leads astray" the mind of Zeus:[16]

...of all others there is none who can escape Aphrodite,
neither of the blessed gods nor of mortal men.

---

13. Skiadas 1979: Μίμνερμος, frag. 1, ll. 1-3 (Appendix B 2.4).

14. Campbell 1982: 52-54, ll. 13-28 (Appendix B 2.5).

15. Translated by Grene and O'Flaherty 1989: 142 (Appendix B 2.6).

16. See Appendix B 2.7.

And she led the mind of thunder-loving Zeus astray,
who is greatest and holds the greatest share of honor.
Whenever she wishes, she easily turns his firm mind
to mingling with a mortal woman,
forgetting entirely Hera, his sister and wife. (ll. 34–40)

Aphrodite's power, her embodiment of love and sexuality, for better or worse, over all creation is, perhaps, best expressed in a fragment attributed to Sophokles, where an unknown character states:[17]

> Children, Kypris is not Kypris alone, but she is called by many names. She is Hades, she is immortal life, she is raving madness, she is unmixed desire, she is lamentation; in her is all activity, all tranquillity, all that leads to violence. For she sinks into the vitals of all that have life; who is not greedy for that goddess? She enters into the swimming race of fishes, she is within the four legged brood upon dry land, and her wing ranges among birds ...among beasts, among mortals, among the race of gods above. Which among the gods does she not wrestle and throw three times? If I may speak out—and I may speak out—to tell the truth, she rules over the heart of Zeus, without spear, without iron. All the plans of mortals and of gods are cut short by Kypris.

Like many goddesses in Greek tradition, Aphrodite is a mother. Hesiod calls her the mother of Harmonia, Phobos, and Deimos by Ares (*Theogony*, ll. 933–37), and Pindar relates that she bore Rhodos and Herophilos to Poseidon. Her main hymn, Homeric Hymn V, relates the story of how she seduced Ankhises and, as a result, bore the hero Aineas. Later tradition, both literary and artistic, presents Aphrodite as the mother of Eros, Himeros, and Peitho.[18] Nevertheless, these relationships are not entirely consistent, except for Aineas. The identification of Aphrodite as the mother of Eros (as well as Himeros) stands in contrast to the Hesiodic tradition, whereby Eros was one of the four primordial gods, older than Aphrodite or even Ouranos, and both of these gods, Eros and Himeros, welcomed Aphrodite when she rose from the sea on Cyprus. The role that younger versions of these gods play on vase paintings and artistic representations is also somewhat ambiguous. In some cases Aphrodite holds them in her arms, in a maternal gesture, other times they accompany the goddess as attendants.[19] This last-named role is supported by a passage from Maximus of Tyre's *Orations*, in which he speaks of Sappho saying,[20]

---

17. Lloyd-Jones 1996: fragment 941 adapted (Appendix B 2.8).

18. For Sappho, who calls Aphrodite the "mother of Peitho," see Barnestone 1988: fragment 160. For Pindar, who refers to Aphrodite Ourania as the mother of the Erotes, see Pirenne-Delforge 1994: 110–11 (Athenaios, XIII, 573e–74b =Pindar fragment 122). For the iconographic reference to Aphrodite as mother of Eros and Himeros, see below.

19. Delivorrias *et al.* 1984: 3.

20. Campbell 1982: fragment 159 (Appendix B 2.9).

Aphrodite says to Sappho in one of her songs:
"you and my servant (θεράπων) Eros."

In some cases, as on a Roman silver medallion (see fig. 2a), Eros is portrayed helping the goddess from the sea, also referring back to the Hesiodic
tradition.[21] The list of Aphrodite's offspring grows through time and she
becomes a more "maternal" goddess in later eras, culminating in the Roman
period when *Venus Genetrix* is virtually the national mother, a nice bit of
political propaganda on the part of those Roman emperors claiming descent
from her through Aineas.

In spite of her brood, maternity is not a prime focus of Aphrodite's persona
in her early representations in ancient Greece, especially when compared to
Demeter or Hera. Aphrodite is less than enthusiastic about her conception of
the hero Aineas, wailing to Ankhises:[22]

> But for me this will be a great disgrace among the
> immortal gods for all days everlasting because of you.
> Before they continually feared my words and wiles, by which
> ever I made all the gods mingle with mortal women;
> for all minds were tamed by me.
> But now indeed no longer will my mouth be able to boast
> of this among the immortals, since I greatly erred,

Fig. 2a
Silver Medallion. Roman Period.

---

21. Simon 1985: 232.

22. See Appendix B 2.10.

> Wretch, most unblameworthy, having gone out of my mind,
> and I put a child under my belt having lain with a mortal.
> As for him, as soon as he sees the light of the sun.
> Deep-bosomed mountain nymphs will rear him. (ll. 247-57)

Even when Aineas reaches maturity, Aphrodite proves less than helpful. For, although he is her dearest (φίλτατός, *Iliad* 5.378) among mortals, she is unable to save him in battle in Book V of the *Iliad*, being driven away from him by a piercing blow from Diomedes.[23] While this is certainly due to the apparent non-military character of the goddess, one cannot help but notice that she is far more helpful to Paris in Book III—even the dead hero Hektor in Book XXIII—than she is to her own son, however good her intentions. Although Aphrodite is a mother in the early Greek tradition, perhaps even quite a loving mother to the hero Aineas—this aspect of her persona is not a source of her power. We see quite the opposite, for the tales of Aineas show her power being used against her to her humiliation. As such, it would be imprudent to refer to Aphrodite as a mother-goddess, and maternity should not be viewed as one of her dominant characteristics.

Finally, there are Aphrodite's associations with fertility, associations that have been exaggerated in past studies. The clearest association between Aphrodite and fecundity in the epic tradition is seen at the end of Hesiod's *Theogony*, where the children born of goddesses through unions with mortal men are described as occurring "through golden Aphrodite" (διὰ χρυσέην Ἀφροδίτην), a reference to reproduction through sexual intercourse, as opposed to the parthenogenic reproduction prevalent in the earlier verses of this work. In the goddess' Homeric hymn (ll. 50-51), she causes mortal sons to be born to the "deathless gods" through their sexual unions with mortal women.

The next extant references to Aphrodite's role in earthly fertility are much later, occurring in the works of the fifth-century dramatists Aiskhylos and Euripides. Two of these fragments are preserved in a passage of Athenaios' *Deipnosophistai* (XIII, 600, b). Referring to Aiskhylos' "Danaids," Athenaios quotes Aphrodite as saying:[24]

---

23. Burkert 1992: 96-99 suggests that this interchange between Aphrodite and Diomedes refers back to the meeting between Ištar and Gilgameš in the Gilgameš Epic, wherein the hero insults and rejects the goddess after her attempts to seduce him. Although some similarities do exist (goddess vs. hero; the "goddess of love" flees back to heaven to her parents to complain; the sky-god rebukes the goddess), it is important not to read too much into this seeming parallel. Gilgameš and Enkidu slaying a demon is quite a different scenario from a war battle, and seduction remains distinct from an attempt to rescue one's child. Furthermore, Ištar takes revenge upon the pair of heroes, whereas Aphrodite remains humiliated.

24. Gulick 1967: XIII, 600, b (Appendix B 2.11).

The chaste heaven loves to violate the earth, and love lays hold on earth to join in wedlock. The rain from the streaming heaven falls down and impregnates the earth; and she brings forth for mortals the pasturage of sheep and Demeter's sustenance; and the ripe season for trees is perfected by the watery union. Of all this I am the cause.

A similar fragment appears also from Euripides, likewise quoted by Athenaios:[25]

The earth is in love with the rain, whenso'er the dry ground, fruitless in drought, hath need of moisture. And the august heaven, filled with rain, loves to cast itself upon the earth through Aphrodite's spell. And when the twin mingle as one, they cause all things to grow for us, and nurture them as well,—all things by which the race of mortals lives and flourishes.

Likewise, in Euripides' *Hippolytos*, the nurse tells Phaidra that:[26]

Kypris moves through the air, she dwells in the sea wave, and all things come from her. She it is that gives and implants love, the love of which all we of earth are begotten.

The ideas presented in the first two quotations are heavily laden with sexual imagery, whereby the sky irrigates the earth through sexual union, much as later gynecological texts claimed that the uterus had to be "watered" by frequent sexual intercourse. (There is actually a certain irony in this imagery, considering the Hesiodic birth of Aphrodite, in which she emerged from the severed genitals of Ouranos. The sky, by this story, should not be able to "violate" the earth or anything else.) Thus, the fertility aspects of Aphrodite are brought back to her role as a goddess of sexuality. The nurse's lines in *Hippolytos* have the same effect, crediting Aphrodite's role in fertility and generation to her role in love. Aphrodite's associations with fertility depend heavily on sexual imagery. Thus, I would argue that although Aphrodite does have a role to play in fertility, especially in later Greek and Roman tradition, in the earlier periods Aphrodite should not be identified as a fertility-goddess, for fertility is only a symbolic extension of her primary attributes of love, desire, and sexuality.

ASSOCIATIONS WITH THE SKY AND THE SEA

Associations with both sky and sea are evidently important among the Greeks in their conception of Aphrodite. This manifests itself in Aphrodite's parentage. According to Hesiod, Aphrodite emerged from the sea, generated from the severed genitals of Ouranos:[27]

---

25. *Ibid.*, XIII, 600, a (Appendix B 2.12).

26. Kovacs 1995: ll. 447–50 (Appendix B 2.13).

27. *Theogony*, ll. 188–95 (Appendix B 2.14).

> When he [Kronos] first cut off the genitals with adamant
> he tossed them from the land into the loudly surging sea
> where long they were borne upon the waters. White foam
> arose about the immortal flesh, and from therein a girl
> was engendered. First to the holy Kytherians
> she drew near, thence she went to sea-girt Cyprus,
> and the reverend fair goddess walked forth, and about
> her slender feet grass sprung forth.

By contrast, according to Homer, Aphrodite is the daughter of Zeus and Dione, a sea-goddess.[28] The difference is considerable; Aphrodite is either of the earlier, "primordial" generation of deities in Hesiod or of the final, "most civilized" generation in Homer; she is either the daughter of Zeus (θυγάτηρ Διός) or his potential love interest; she is either "naturally" born of male and female or is the "parthenogenic" offspring of a single male deity.[29] However, both origin tales associate the goddess with both sky and sea, either in being the transformation of the genitals of the primordial sky-god mixed with sea foam or the daughter of Zeus, the supreme sky-god, and Dione, the daughter of "Ocean."

The associations with sky and sea are also borne out by the goddess' epithets. Her celestial character is evident in her common epithet among the Greeks: Ourania. The fact that this title is common throughout the Greek world, being attested in Athens, Elis,[30] Argos,[31] Epidauros,[32] Sparta,[33] Kythera,[34] Aigira,[35] Megalopolis,[36] Thebes,[37] and Cyprus,[38] suggests that this, along with Kypris and Kytheria, was perhaps one of her most important attributes. Aphrodite's association with the sea is found in other epithets:

---

28. Although it is true that etymologically Dione is the feminine counterpart of Zeus, and thus linguistically a sky-goddess as in her cult at Dodona, she is, nevertheless, in the earliest literature (Hesiod, *Theogony*, l. 353) the daughter of Okeanos and Tethys, the primordial sea deities. As such, it is impossible to ignore Dione's aquatic associations, which, by familial ties, also affect Aphrodite.

29. An identification usually associated exclusively with Athena.

30. Pausanias, VI, 20, 6.

31. Pausanias, II, 23, 8.

32. *IG*, IV(2), 283.

33. *IG*, V(1), 559. Of Roman date, but of interest nevertheless.

34. Pausanias, I, 14, 7.

35. Pausanias, VII, 26, 7.

36. Pausanias, VIII, 32, 2.

37. Pausanias, IX, 16, 3–4.

38. Herodotos, I, 105, 2–3.

according to the *Anth. Pal.* 9, 143, she has the epithets *Euploia, Pontia*, and *Limenia* and, as such, receives homage from sailors and fishermen.[39] So, too, ancient commentators saw deliberate connections between the first element of the goddess' name, *aphros* "foam," and her maritime birth, thus, seeing in the goddess' name her associations with the sea. Finally, images of Aphrodite's birth from the sea or, often in later tradition, being borne upon a shell are common in Greek art as early as the Archaic period—and even through the Renaissance! Clearly these associations were of significance to the Greeks.

The early literature shows Aphrodite to have a well-developed persona. She is the goddess of sex and love, who exerts her power over all except Hestia, Athena, and Artemis. She is a mother, if not a very effective one, and her extant associations with fertility are minimal in comparison to her role in sexuality and are dependent upon it. She is seen as the heavenly one and her birth, as related by Hesiod and Homer, provides her an association with the sea.[40]

Early Iconography

Aphrodite's iconography—dating back to the seventh century—is not quite as old as her literary presence in Greece. It is, nonetheless, important for forming a fuller picture of the goddess' persona in early Greece.

The earliest portrayals of the goddess (as identifiable through inscription) are the Naxian vase,[41] the Protocorinthian Chigi vase,[42] the Attic Erskine dinos by Sophilos,[43] the Attic François vase,[44] the Lydos dinos from the Athenian Akropolis,[45] and a black-figure pinax from the Athenian Akropolis.[46]

The piece from Naxos (mid-seventh century) shows Aphrodite standing in a chariot; the name ΑΦΡΟΔΙΤΗ appears to the left of the goddess (see fig. 2b).[47] Aphrodite wears a long veil (descending to the hips) and a few curls of hair appear upon her forehead. She wears a long garment with linear patterns

---

39. Graf in van der Toorn *et al.* 1995: col. 121-22.

40. It is admittedly difficult to determine if Homer has in mind the same aquatic associations for Dione as does Hesiod. In the *Iliad*, Dione is mentioned only once, where she is shown to be on Olympos, which may suggest a heavenly, as opposed to maritime, persona. However, Poseidon resides also on Olympos according to the "Song of Demodokos" in the *Odyssey* and, thus, area of residence might not be taken exclusively as a sign of persona.

41. Delivorrias *et al.* 1984: #1285.

42. CVA: Italia, Museo Nationale de Villa Giulia in Roma. Tav. 4, #3.

43. Williams 1983: *passim*.

44. Boardman 1991: 22, #1.

45. Delivorrias *et al.* 1984: #1394.

46. Delivorrias *et al.* 1984: #1255.

47. Carpenter 1991: 42.

and her two arms are bent at the elbow toward the person standing before her in the chariot. The chariot itself obstructs the view of the goddess from her knees downward. Neither the face nor the name of the person in front of Aphrodite remains. However, it is clearly a male wearing a helmet and he can be identified as Ares through comparison with several similar and contemporary pieces.[48] This piece is quite similar to a seventh-century Melian sherd that depicts the upper portion of a veiled woman with tresses on her brow. Her left hand holds her veil back from her face. Before her is a man holding the reins of a chariot(?). Delivorrias suggests that this pair may also represent Aphrodite and Ares.[49] Beyond these two portrayals, Delivorrias records another fourteen representations of Aphrodite and Ares together in the Greek repertoire before the year 500 BCE.[50]

Fig. 2b
Naxian Vase Naxos Museum.

48. See Delivorrias *et al.* 1984: #1285–1317 for examples.

49. Delivorrias *et al.* 1984: #1286.

50. *Ibid.*, 123–25.

The Chigi vase (650–640 BCE), portraying the Judgment of Paris, shows Aphrodite, along with Hera and Athena, before the youth Paris, with Hermes partially preserved at the edge of the sherd. In what remains of the Chigi vase itself, to the left there is a standing youth with long hair facing right. He is dressed in a black robe and a himation, and is labeled "Al[exandr]os." To his immediate right is a large break. As restored, to the right of the break are the heads of three females. Only the top of the head of the first female is visible, whereas the other two women are visible from the shoulders up. The last in this line of females is labeled "Aphrodite."

This scene is frequently repeated in the early iconography, enabling us to reconstruct fully the scene in question. One well-preserved version is a sixth-century black-figure Tyrrhenian amphora (see fig. 2c),[51] on which all three

Fig. 2c
Tyrrhenian Amphora, Judgment of Paris. Schefold 1966: Plate 67 b.

---

51. Schefold 1966: Plate 67 b.

goddesses, Hermes, and Paris are fully preserved (although unidentified by inscription). Here, to the right, Paris attempts to flee from the deities. Hermes, in full herald's paraphernalia, chases the youth. Behind the god are the three goddesses. The first goddess behind Hermes appears to be Athena, as she wears a rudimentary helmet on her head. The second two goddesses, Aphrodite and Hera, are indistinguishable from one another, although it is probable that Aphrodite is the final goddess on the basis of comparison with the Chigi vase.

One of the most famous representations of Aphrodite and Ares is the Erskine dinos by Sophilos (c. 570 BCE), [52] which portrays a procession of deities on their way to the house of Peleus (labeled) for his marriage to Thetis. In procession, riding together in a chariot, behind Poseidon, Amphitrite, and the Charities are Ares and Aphrodite. Both are identified by inscription, although Aphrodite's head is missing. From what remains it is evident that Aphrodite wore a rather simple gown and himation, and that she held her right arm to her face. Otherwise she is devoid of all attributes other than being paired with Ares.

At the top of the François vase (570–560 BCE) is a procession leading Hephaistos into the company of the deities (see fig. 2d). [53] At the center of the

Fig. 2d
François Vase. Florence Museum, 4209.

---

52. Hurwit 1985: 223.

53. *Ibid.*, 225.

frieze, on the left side of the procession, Aphrodite faces Dionysos, who is entering from the right, leading Hephaistos, who is riding upon a mule. In his wake are silens. Behind Aphrodite, Zeus and Hera are seated on thrones, and behind these are Athena, Ares, Artemis, Poseidon, and Hermes. Aphrodite is fully clothed and devoid of any and all attributes except the inscription of her name. Her central position in the procession, however, is of importance. According to Hurwit, the repeated theme of the François vase is marriage (dominated by that between Peleus and Thetis but alluding to others, as that between Aphrodite and Hephaistos, and Zeus and Hera). In the return of Hephaistos, Aphrodite is to be given to Hephaistos in exchange for his freeing his mother Hera from her throne.[54] Thus, the (unhappy) marriage of Aphrodite and Hephaistos is expressed in early art.

MARTIAL IMAGERY

The Lydos dinos (560–540 BCE; see fig. 2e) portrays a gigantomakhy; on this specific fragment a female, identified by inscription as Aphrodite, appears on the left.[55] The outline of the face is preserved, as is a leafy stephanos upon her head. The left shoulder with elaborately decorated garment remains, holding a round shield visible from the interior. The right arm is beyond the break in the fragment, but the spear passing before the goddess'

Fig. 2e
Lydos dinos, Athens Acropolis 607.

---

54. *Ibid.*, 226ff.

55. Boardman 1974: 52.

forehead is clearly held by the goddess. To the right of the fragment is a giant, identified by inscription as Mimos. His face is preserved, including the cheek-piece of a helmet. He carries a round shield decorated with a bee in front of him and, like Aphrodite, he wields a spear.

This is an unexpected rendering of Aphrodite, who is usually portrayed, especially in the *Iliad,* as non-martial. Part of this incongruity might be attributed to the gigantomakhy theme of the work, in which the whole ensemble of the gods throws itself into the fight enthusiastically. However, further evidence of Aphrodite's early martial iconography is preserved in the writings of Pausanias:

> Kythera is about ten stades inland from Skandeia. The sanctuary of Ourania, the most holy and sacred, is the most ancient of all the sanctuaries of Aphrodite among the Greeks. The goddess herself is represented by an armed *xoanon.*
>
> Pausanias, 3, XXIII, 1.[56]
>
> Heading not much further on is a small hill, upon which is an ancient temple and a *xoanon* of Aphrodite Armed.
>
> Pausanias, 3, XV, 10.[57]
>
> Going up to Akrocorinth is a temple of Aphrodite; the statues are: Aphrodite Armed, and Helios and Eros with a bow.
>
> Pausanias 2, V, 1.[58]

In none of these instances does either the image itself or a Roman copy survive. A middle Protocorinthian *krateriskos* from the Heraion at Samos may offer a pictorial version of such an armed representation of Aphrodite.[59] However, in the absence of an identifying inscription, it would be unwise to attribute this image to the goddess. Nevertheless, there is iconographic and literary evidence for both a link between Aphrodite and Ares in the early sources and portrayals of Aphrodite herself armed.

MOTHER

The fragmentary black-figure pinax from the Athenian Akropolis (560–550 BCE) shows a female holding two small boys (see fig. 2f).[60] The one boy who is complete is identified by the name "Himeros," while the other boy only has the letter 'ε' remaining. It appears that these are the gods Himeros (desire)

---

56. See Appendix B 2.15.

57. See Appendix B 2.16.

58. See Appendix B 2.17.

59. Walter 1959: 57–60, Beilage 99: 2 and Beilage 114: 1. Walter identifies this image as Athena.

60. Delivorrias *et al.* 1984: #1255.

and Eros (love) in the arms of Aphrodite. The young gods are nude. Aphrodite wears a dress decorated with geometric designs, a belt, and a himation. Her hair is not veiled and she bears a cap on her head. Her arms hold the two gods under their legs and her hands meet together at her chest. This pinax shows Aphrodite as mother of Himeros and Eros, associating her with the realms of love and sexuality, as expressed in the literary sources.

Fig. 2f
Black figure pixis. National Museum, Athens, Acr. 2526.

DOVES

There are no named representations of Aphrodite with doves before 500 BCE.[61] However, two sources—one epigraphic and one iconographic—associate Aphrodite with doves before 500 BCE. A 284 BCE inscription from Athens refers to the cult of Aphrodite Pandemos:

As the astynomoi ever chosen by lot
have cared for the rites

---

61. The general tendency is to associate Aphrodite with doves, perhaps also with swans. Pirenne-Delforge remarks, however, that references to περισετερά and πέλεια might be used without the limiting word *leuke*, "white," and thus refer equally to a dove or pigeon. Furthermore, later artistic renderings of the goddess show her with geese. Thus, the limited number of birds usually attributed to Aphrodite should be increased. See Pirenne-Delforge 1994: 415–17.

of the sanctuary of Aphrodite Pandemos
according to the rule of the forefathers (κατὰ τὰ πάτρια).
For good fortune, it has appeared good to the boule;
that those who chance to hold the prohedria in
the coming council bring forth
the kin of the priestess and consult
with them, and the opinion of the boule
that they put forth to the demos
concerning that which seems good to the boule (is that):
the astynomoi who are ever chosen by lot,
when there is a procession for Aphrodite Pandemos,
will provide for the purification of the
sanctuary a dove (περιστερὰν) and
the anointing of the altar and they will
coat the gates and clean the temple.[62]

Although the inscription dates to the Hellenistic period, the expression κατὰ τὰ πάτρια suggests that this rite is considerably older than the inscription itself and, thus, may serve as evidence for much earlier use of the dove (περιστερὰν) in the cult of Aphrodite.[63]

Further evidence associating Aphrodite with doves is a red-figure vase from Tarquinia dating to c. 520 BCE,[64] which shows an assembly of the gods. One of these deities is clearly Ares, as he holds a spear and a war helmet in his hands. Seated directly before him is a goddess in an elaborate chiton, holding a dove with outstretched wings in her left hand. Although the goddess' name does not appear on the vase, the association with Ares (see above) makes it almost certain that the goddess in question is Aphrodite. Furthermore, as Ares is portrayed with his attributes (spear, helmet), one might understand that Aphrodite is portrayed also with her attribute, namely, the dove.

A Synthesis

The most difficult issue to address in the interpretation of the goddess in the ancient sources is her lack of attributes in the Archaic iconography. Aphrodite, in general, has no specific attributes and, thus, is indistinguishable in many instances from Hera (as in the Judgment of Paris scenes) or any other lesser goddess in the Greek repertoire.[65] Often it is only literary references, such as the tale of the Judgment of Paris or the Song of Demodokos that allow for the identification of Aphrodite in the iconography when her name is not present. Nevertheless, such images as the Judgment of Paris refer back to the

---

62. *IG*, II2, 659 (Appendix B 2.18).

63. Pirenne-Delforge 1994: 29-30.

64. Delivorrias *et al.* 1984: #1298.

65. Boardman 1974: 219.

goddess' beauty and power over love (especially considering the outcome of the beauty contest). Thus, the imagery in the iconography reinforce that aspect of the goddess' persona from the literary materials.

The area in which the literary and iconographic sources are in greatest, if confusing, accord is Aphrodite's maternal status. Both sources maintain a long-standing ambiguity concerning Aphrodite's exact relationship to Eros (and to a certain extent, Himeros). Hesiod's *Theogony*, the fragment of Maximus of Tyre, and the silver medallion indicate that Eros is older than Aphrodite and that he was one of the deities who greeted the goddess at her watery birth. By contrast, the pinax from the Akropolis suggests that Aphrodite is the mother of Eros and Himeros. In either event, Aphrodite is mother at least to Aineas, although, unlike Hera and Demeter, she does not derive her primary power from maternity. She is a mother, without being a mother-goddess.

The greatest contrasts between the literary and iconographic sources occur in the areas of Aphrodite's eroticism and militarism. Unlike the literary sources, in which Aphrodite is portrayed as blatantly erotic, there are no overtly sexual, erotic, or even nude portrayals of Aphrodite in the Archaic and early Classical materials. This lack must be seen in the context of Archaic art in general, where nude or eroticised images of goddesses are, in fact, quite rare.

A broad gulf separates the nude images of the Bronze Age and (Proto-) Geometric periods from the Archaic and Classical depictions. When considering the lack of nude females in early Archaic Greek art, A. Stewart surmises: "Any explanation must take into account that nakedness in post-Mycenaean art develops in two phases: the first, when both men and women are generally shown naked; and the second, when women cover up but men usually do not."[66] Stewart further argues that in the Geometric period both men and women were shown nude for the sake of gender distinction, but that as the late-Geometric period turned into the early Archaic, artists from Athens to Sparta came to cover up the females portrayed in art.[67] There were, of course, a few exceptions to this trend. The figures on the so-called "Aštart-plaques" of the seventh and sixth centuries were portrayed fully or almost fully nude.[68] Likewise, Athenian black-figure pottery occasionally depicted nude women, such as Kassandra when violated by Ajax.[69] But otherwise, "female nudity is rare in black-figure and confined to nymphs, maenads, and hetairai."[70] It is only after artists such as Oltos and Euphronios, at the end of the sixth century,

---

66. Stewart 1997: 38–39.

67. *Ibid.*, 37–40.

68. See Chapter Three, below.

69. Cohen 1992–93: *passim*; Jackson 1996/97: *passim*.

70. Jackson 1996/97: 57.

adopted the motif of the nude prostitute and made it common in Greek vase painting that the nude female made its way into the artistic repertoire.[71] Even then, the motif was limited to society's "liminal" females. In the fifth century, depictions of the nude Kassandra come to show her, not as a little girl, but as a mature young women with developed breasts. While this clearly enhances that aspect of the story in which Ajax rapes the princess, it is one more small step in the development of the female nude in Greek art.[72] Nude or eroticised portrayals of goddesses remained outside of the norm until well into the fourth and third centuries BCE, when nude portrayals of Aphrodite become common, as do versions of the Judgment of Paris showing goddesses standing nude before Paris.[73] Perhaps the best understanding of Aphrodite's iconography is that the goddess *is* erotic, but this aspect of her persona manifests itself only when the artistic milieu is open to erotic portrayals of goddesses.

The concept of the armed Aphrodite is more difficult to address, as the *xoana*, which would have formed the primary data for this subject, no longer exist in any form. The presence of Aphrodite armed and fighting in a gigantomakhy is not to be wondered at, as the motif of the gigantomakhy entails certain actions and attributes that may not be consistent with the rest of the Greek repertoire. Aphrodite's associations with Ares could be understood as a meeting of opposites. However, the combination of image, *xoana*, and a relationship with Ares may, in fact, be emblematic of a certain martial side of Aphrodite otherwise lost to posterity.

In the early literature, then, Aphrodite is erotic, although the early artistic evidence has limitations. In both sources she is a mother (although of exactly what children varies), if not a mother-goddess; possibly a companion to Eros, contributing once again to her amorous nature; and certainly a lover of Ares. Her marriage to Hephaistos may be alluded to on the François vase. She is seen in the Judgment of Paris motif at least five times before 500 BCE, coinciding with one of her greatest roles in the early literature: her contribution to the instigation of the Trojan War. She appears to have some early associations with militarism. And lastly, Aphrodite is associated with doves, which (minimal but extant) epigraphic and iconographic evidence supports.

---

71. Cohen 1992-93: 41.

72. *Ibid.*, 41-43.

73. On the novelty of portraying the goddess nude in (public) sculpture, see Stewart 1997: 100ff.

III.
APHRODITE IN EARLY GREECE[1]

The Indo-European Question

Beyond the schools of thought that argue that Aphrodite is either indigenous to Greece or a fixture of the Greek mentality, it is the Indo-European school of thought that argues for the earliest appearance of Aphrodite in Greece. According to this theory, Aphrodite would have arrived in the Aegean with the Indo-European speakers, either the early denizens of Crete, Greece, and Anatolia—should it be proved that the language(s) showing -σσος and -νθος endings is/are Indo-European—or the first Greek speakers, arriving either in EH III or, according to Drew's theories, at the beginning of LH I.[2] As this would be the earliest evidence for Aphrodite, it is appropriate to begin this chapter with an analysis of the Indo-European question and to determine the extent to which these sources contribute to the quest for Aphrodite's origins.

Looking at Aphrodite exclusively as a linguistic and literary figure, the scholars of the Indo-European school of thought have traced the origins of this goddess through her similarities to other goddesses in the written materials pertaining to the various Indo-European pantheons. The following discussion focuses on the literary parallels between Aphrodite and her so-called Indo-European cognates, to determine the extent to which the argument in favor of an Indo-European origin can be upheld on the basis of literary and linguistic data.

As is traditional in these studies, the term "Indo-European" refers to any society that uses an Indo-European language. For our purposes, the societies examined will be the Greek, Italic, Hittite/Luwian, German, Norse, Celtic, and Indo-Aryan. Although there has been some speculation that the -σσος and -νθος languages of ancient Anatolia, Greece, and Crete might, in fact, be Indo-European,[3] this is as yet not definite, nor is there literature to work from in this endeavor. Thus, the Minoan materials will be handled separately in the section on chronology and archaeology below.

---

1. In this chapter and Chapter Four, the "Greek world" consists of the Greek mainland, Magna Graecia, Greek-occupied Asia Minor, the colonies elsewhere, and the Aegean islands, including Crete, but not Cyprus.

2. Drews 1988: *passim*.

3. Renfrew 1987: *passim*; Finkelberg 1990: *passim*.

From what information is available concerning the deities of these various communities, I would argue that there are no cognates in the Indo-European pantheon to an Aphrodite figure. What might be generalized for a common Indo-European pantheon are:

* sky-father (Zeus, Jupiter, Óðinn or Tyr, Woton, Dyáus)
* earth-mother (Demeter, Dana, Dôn)
* sun-god (Helios, Lugh, Belenos, Surya)
* horse deities (Poseidon, Rhiannon, Macha, Asveni)
* divine twins (the Dioskouroi, the Asveni, Emain Macha)
* dawn-goddess (Eos, Ushas, Saule, perhaps Helen)

DAWN-GODDESS

Scholars such as Friedrich, Boedeker, and Nagy contend that Aphrodite, as an Indo-European deity, emerged out of the last of these, the dawn-goddess, with her closest parallel being Ushas, the dawn-goddess of the *Rig Veda*. So, at this point, it is best to examine the similarities and differences between these two goddesses.

There are approximately twenty-one hymns to the goddess Ushas preserved in the *Rig Veda*, each consisting of both praise of the goddess and appeals for her favor. In all these, she has four major characteristics:

* the temporal/celestial nature of the goddess
* her familial connections
* her role as provider of material wealth
* her beauty

As Dawn, Ushas is related to the cyclical nature of the sky, as are the sun, moon, and night. Thus Hymn 1.113 begins:[4]

> This fairest light of lights has come:
> The bright harbinger has been born effulgent.
> As she, urged on, yields to Savitar's impulsion,
> So Night has yielded up her place to Dawn.
>
> With a radiant calf, brilliant, white she has come.
> Black (Night) has yielded up her seats.
> Akin, immortal, following each other,
> Day and Night travel exchanging their color.

As in all her hymns, Ushas' main function is to yoke her chariot of ruddy bulls/horses, to banish night, and to welcome in the day. She appears consistently in the east, always at the beginning of the day (Hymn 1.123. 8-9):[5]

---

4. MacDonell 1932: 352; Aufrecht 1877: 96. See Appendix B 3.1.

5. MacDonell 1932: 356; Aufrecht 1877: 111-12. See Appendix B 3.2.

Alike to-day and alike even to-morrow.
They follow the wide control of Varuna.
Blameless (they complete) their thirty yojanas:
Each one goes round her circuit in one day.

Knowing the name of the first day, bright, white-hued,
She has been born from the black (region of night).
The maid infringes not the rule of order,
Coming every day to the appointed place.

Unfortunately, this cyclical nature does have a negative connotation. In spite of her general benevolence (see below), Ushas is, nevertheless, the goddess who brings generations to old age and, eventually, death (Hymn 1.92.10):[6]

Being born again and again (though) ancient,
Adorning herself with the self-same color;
A goddess diminishing the throws like a skillful gambler,
Bringing the life of the mortal nearer old age.

Her celestial nature is also clearly defined in her placement within the divine family. She is repeatedly entitled the Daughter of Heaven/Sky, as in Hymn 1.49.2:[7]

With well-decked, lightly running car,
That thou hast mounted, (goddess) Dawn,
Favour, O daughter of the sky,
The man of goodly fame to-day.

She is the sister of Night, the lover of Surya the sun-god, and is closely associated with the Asveni, with whom she shares Hymn 1.92. All of these relations re-enforce her associations with the sky and her exact placement within a divine family (Hesiod-style, perhaps).

When invoked by the poets, she is asked to provide material well-being, most commonly in the form of cattle, horses, and sons. We see this in Hymn 5.79.6–8:[8]

Bestow fame with heroic sons,
Bountiful Dawn, on these patrons,
Who generously have conferred
Upon us abundant treasures,
Thou nobly born, bounteous in steeds.

To those (patrons) bring, bounteous Dawn,
Glory and wide celebrity,
Patrons who lavished upon us

---

6. MacDonell 1932: 351; Aufrecht 1877: 77. See Appendix B 3.3.

7. MacDonell 1932: 349; Aufrecht 1877: 40–41. See Appendix B 3.4.

8. MacDonell 1932: 363; Aufrecht 1877: 387. See Appendix B 3.5.

Treasure in horses and kine,
Thou nobly born, bounteous in steeds.

And bring us an abundance
In kine, O daughter of the sky,
Together with the Sun's (bright) rays,
With (his) shining, brilliant beams,
Thou nobly born, bounteous in steeds.

One can look at Dawn's associations with material wealth either "practically," insofar as dawn is the beginning of the working day, or anthropomorphically, in that, as seems evident, Ushas is a goddess very well disposed to humankind, perhaps in a role similar to that of Hekate. These two interpretations are not mutually exclusive, and one must recognize the goddess as a beneficent being, well-loved by her human worshippers.

Finally, there is Ushas' quality of beauty, even sensuousness. She is, as would be expected for a dawn-goddess, described as "radiant," "lustrous," "golden colored," and "resplendent." In at least five hymns she is said to reveal her breasts, and two hymns describe her as being blatantly erotic. We read in Hymn 1.123.10:[9]

Like a girl, with form resplendent, thou goest,
O goddess, to the god who desires (thee). [Surya]
A maiden smiling in the east toward him,
Shining forth thou displayest (to him) thy breasts.

We see this even more so in Hymn 1.124.7–8:[10]

Like a brotherless maid she goes to meet men,
Like one who mounts a stage for the gain of wealth;
Like a well-clad wife, longing, to (her) husband,
Dawn exposes her breast, like a courtesan.

The sister her place to her elder sister
Has yielded; departs from her to reappear.
Shining forth with Surya's beams, she decks herself
With gems, like women thronging to a meeting-place.

It is in this last quality that Ushas most closely resembles Aphrodite, and it is not difficult to see why scholars of the Indo-European school of thought have traced the two to a common source. Both goddesses are daughters of the sky—Aphrodite is identified either as the offspring of Ouranos in the Hesiodic tradition or the daughter of Zeus in the Homeric. Both are extremely beautiful, sensuous, "golden," and loving.

However, do the similarities outweigh the differences? I would contend that, in the Greek pantheon, it is the dawn goddess Eos, and perhaps Helen

---

9. MacDonell 1932: 356; Aufrecht 1877: 112. See Appendix B 3.6.

10. MacDonell 1932: 358; Aufrecht 1877: 113. See Appendix B 3.7.

of Sparta, who share a common heritage with Ushas, while Aphrodite remains distinct.

To begin, there is the quality of temporality/seasonality. There is nothing cyclical about Aphrodite, no daily or annual patterns or travels. This stands in blatant contrast to Ushas, who cycles with her sister Night; Eos, who leads forth the steeds of Helios every morning; and even Helen, who must, with great effort, be brought back from the east. Even Boedeker's suggestion that Aphrodite, emerging from the sea at her birth, represented the dawn breaking forth from the sea, seems awkward. For as Hesiod described the event, the goddess first went past Kythera before landing on Cyprus, i.e., going west to east, which the highly naval Greeks were sure to realize was inaccurate if this were to refer to the dawn.

Unlike Eos (and Ushas), Aphrodite is not a member of a *family* of celestial beings. Whereas Ushas is the sister of Night, the lover of the Sun, and the friend of the Asveni, Eos the sister of Helios and Selene, and Helen the daughter of Zeus and the sister of the Dioskouroi (cognates of the Asveni), Aphrodite is pointedly an only child (of rather ambiguous parentage at that) who is (in)famous for her relationships with Hephaistos and Ares, neither of whom is particularly stellar. Only in her relationship to Ouranos/Zeus is Aphrodite related to the heavenly regions, and in this she is no different from the earthy Demeter or the sylvan Artemis.

The characterization of the "female who causes life to wane" applies less directly to Aphrodite than it does to Helen and Eos.[11] In the former case, it is evident that Helen, in causing the Trojan War, brought the lives of many men to an untimely end. In the latter, we might look to the myth of Tithonos. Here we have a mortal beloved of Eos, to whom eternal life, but not eternal youth, is given. Thus, Eos is in literature intimately linked to the tragedy of aging humankind. Whereas in the Homeric Hymn to Aphrodite Ankhises expresses fear that the goddess might cause him harm, Aphrodite, in relating the tale of Eos and Tithonos as a worst-case scenario (with the tale of Zeus and Ganymede as a best case scenario), assures Ankhises that the same thing will not occur to him. Quite to the contrary, Ankhises receives a certain measure of eternal life through the son that Aphrodite bears him (however unwillingly).

Nagy claims that the original Indo-European dawn-goddess was a daughter of the original sky-god, to judge from the *Rig Veda*. In the Greek tradition, according to Nagy, this father-daughter relationship between the sky-god and Eos is not expressed due to an awkwardness in meter. However, he claims, as Aphrodite has the title Διός θυγάτηρ, she must be the equivalent of the dawn-goddess. This particular argument seems flawed. First, meter notwithstanding, it is probable that Eos does not command the epithet "Daughter of Zeus" in epic diction because, according to Greek mythology, she is the

---

11. See Chapter Seven for more on this aspect of her persona.

daughter of Hyperion, not Zeus. Second, the argument that Eos and Aphrodite are parallel because Aphrodite is called Διός θυγάτηρ and Eos is not seems a bit stretched. Other goddesses are entitled "Daughter of Zeus," such as the Muses and Ate,[12] who are not necessarily related to Eos, Dawn, or the Indo-Europeans. For all these reasons, it is imprudent to associate Aphrodite with an Indo-European dawn-goddess. However, to examine the Indo-European question more fully, it is also necessary to look farther north, to the goddess Freyja, who is the goddess of sex and love in the Norse pantheon.

FREYJA

Close parallels exist between the Greek and Nordic goddesses and, likewise, parallels exist between both of these deities and the "Great Goddesses" of the Near East, notably Inanna/Ištar. There are three hypotheses to explain these relationships: (1) that similarities exist between Aphrodite and Freyja because they both derive from a common Indo-European tradition; (2) that there are similarities because both derive from a common Near Eastern tradition; or (3) that similarities exist because one or more goddesses were likened to each other in the transmission of the various traditions.[13]

Freyja serves as a far better cognate to Aphrodite than does Ushas. Freyja is specifically a goddess of love and sexuality, in many respects having an even more lustful reputation than her Greek "equivalent." Thus in the Poetic Edda Loki (a fellow deity) accuses her:[14]

> Hush thee, Freya,   I full well know thee:
>   thou art not free from fault:
> all Aesir and alfs   within this hall
>   thou hast lured to love with thee....
> Hush thee, Freya,   a whore thou art,
>   and ay wast bent on ill;
> in thy brother's bed   the blessed gods caught thee.

And to quote the sibyl Hyndla:[15]

> Wert ever eager   with Oth to lie;
>   under thy apron   still others have crept,
> in the night who runnest—thou noble friend—
>   in her heat as Heithrun   the he-goats among.

---

12. For the Muses, see *Theogony* 76 (ἐννέα θυγατέρες μεγάλου Διὸς ἐκγεγαυῖαι). For Ate, see *Iliad* 19.91 (πρέσβα Διὸς θυγάτηρ, Ἄτη, ἥ πάντας ἀᾶται).

13. Much modern scholarship on Nordic goddesses addresses the question of possible Near Eastern cognates (or even origins) of Freyja, such as Ištar and Kybele. See especially Motz 1993 and, *contra*, Näsström 1995.

14. Hollander 1962: 96–97. See Appendix B 3.8.

15. *Ibid.*, 136. See Appendix B 3.9.

The first quotation, with its reference to Freyja as a "whore," calls to mind Aphrodite *Hetaira* and Ištar's role in the literature as both a prostitute herself and the goddess of prostitutes.[16]

Like Aphrodite and Ištar, Freyja is only minimally associated with maternity, having one or two daughters who are merely named in passing within the Eddas. Each of her daughters has the name "jewel" and, considering their general lack of any role, familial or otherwise, in the texts, Motz suggests that they are merely allegorical figures, referring to Freyja's riches and affinity with feminine adornments. No maternal role is indicated.[17]

As Aphrodite has her famous *kestos* (mentioned in Bk. XIV of the *Iliad*), and Ištar her breast ornament (*Ištar's Descent*, ll. 49–50), so, too, does Freyja treasure *Brisingamen*, a necklace (or possibly a belt) that she received in exchange for sleeping one night with each of the dwarves who forged it. As Aphrodite travels through the heavens on a chariot drawn by birds (Sappho I), Freyja travels throughout the nine worlds of Yggdrasil, either in a falcon coat or on a chariot drawn by cats. And, finally, as Aphrodite mourned for the death of Adonis, and the women of the Levant mourned for Tammuz, Freyja shed tears of gold for Óðr, her mortal husband who abandoned her. If Aphrodite were in fact Indo-European, it is this European goddess who would be her closest relative.

There are two arguments against the common Indo-European heritage of Aphrodite and Freyja. The first is that it is not certain that Freyja herself is Indo-European; the second is that many of the resemblances between the goddesses may be due to the Classical training of the transcribers of the Norse traditions.

Whether or not one sees Freyja as Indo-European depends on how one chooses to interpret the relationship between the Aesir and the Vanir deities. Freyja, along with her brother Freyr and father Njord, is classified in Northern tradition as belonging to the Vanir gods, as opposed to the Aesir gods. The Aesir deities are blatantly Indo-European, featuring such members as Thor the thunder-god, and Tyr the sky/war-god (his name linguistically is the cognate of Zeus). The question then remains as to how to interpret the Vanir. According to the Dumézilian tradition, the Vanir represent the deities of the third tier of Indo-European society, while the Aesir represent the first two. Thus, the Aesir are predominantly the gods associated with kingship (Óðinn) and war (Tyr), whereas the Vanir are associated exclusively with fertility. This is certainly possible, as Njord is a sea-god, and Freyr would seem to be some manner of solar deity.

---

16. This role of Ištar's may be overturned if the theories of J. Assante prove true, i.e., the term KAR.KID/ *ḫarimtu* does not, in fact, mean "prostitute," but "single woman." See Assante 1998: *passim*. See also Chapter Eight, below.

17. Motz 1993: 97.

However, unlike many of the Aesir gods, the Vanir do not possess Germanic linguistic equivalents. For example, in Germany, the equivalent of the Nordic Óðinn was Woton, who in England was called Wodan. Tyr's Germanic counterpart was Tiwaz, and Tiw/Tig in England. Thor had the alternate appellations Donar and Thunor respectively, and in all cases these are linguistically associated names. By contrast, Freyr and Freyja, whose names mean "Lord" and "Lady" respectively, do not appear in the Germanic world.[18] They possibly existed as far south as Denmark, where they might have had cognates in the names Frodi (usually applied to mortal kings) and Gefion (not etymologically related to the name "Freyja"). Clearly they are more Scandinavian than Germanic.

Furthermore, Freyja is associated with a very particular form of shamanic magic, known as *seidr*, which consists of the individual (the *volva*) placing herself in a trance, usually with the aid of drum beats or rhythmic chants, and leaving the body to travel to alternate realms. This description closely parallels those given of shamanic practices used by the Finno-Uralic/Lapp populations of Scandinavia, and it appears that the origin of *seidr* magic comes from these regions.

This suggests, then, that Freyja, along with the other Vanir deities, is non-Indo-European, possibly emerging out of the Finno-Uralic culture.[19] When the Indo-Europeans arrived in Scandinavia, the Vanir were recognized as "foreign" deities who were adopted into the Germanic Aesir pantheon, although they continued to be recognized as a separate entity. The titles "Freyr/Lord" and "Freyja/Lady" were given to deities whose names may have been lost or, perhaps more likely, unpronounceable to the Germanic populations (consider the fact that the main hero of the Finnish *Kalevala* is named Väinämöinen).

If, then, Freyja is not Indo-European and does not share a common heritage with Aphrodite, why is it that the two share so many similarities? I would suggest that it was an (un)intentional likening on the part of the Classically trained scribes who recorded the Nordic myths in the Middle Ages. A similar event can be seen in the case of the Irish hero Cú Chulainn, who, for all intents and purposes, is remarkably similar to the Greek Akhilleus. So, too, Snorri Sturlson began his *Gylfaginning* with the statement that the Norse gods originally came from Troy and that Thor was the grandson of King Priam.[20] It is possible,

---

18. It is possible that deities existed that had cognates to whatever their original names had been, assuming this was something other than the titles "Lord" and "Lady." However, as these names no longer survive in the Nordic tradition (assuming that they existed in the first place), this is a futile line of inquiry.

19. The specific titles/names "Freyr" and "Freyja," however, are Norse adaptations, as the /fr/ phoneme does not occur in Finno-Uralic linguistics.

20. Davidson 1964: 25.

although not certain, that a similar mingling of traditions occurred vis-à-vis Aphrodite and Freyja.[21]

ETYMOLOGY OF THE NAME "APHRODITE"

In the final examination of the Indo-European question, one must look not to cognates in alternate pantheons, as this has shown to be fruitless, but to linguistics, for if an Indo-European etymology of "Aphrodite" might be shown, then an Indo-European origin must, to some degree, be accepted. In an argument to show the Indo-European origins of Aphrodite, Boedeker breaks the names down into two parts: "aphro" with a meaning of either "foam" or, more to her liking, "mist," and "dite," which she derives from the Indo-European word for "brilliant." According to Boedeker, "Aphros" derives from the Proto-Indo-European root *n.bh-, which developed later into the forms *n.bhro- and *n.bhr. The former of these evolved into the Greek word *aphros* "foam," whereas the latter allowed for the Doric variant "Aphordita." This much is seldom contested, at least in terms of general linguistics. Concerning the latter part of her name, Boedeker argues that the –*dite* element derives from an Indo-European root **dei-* = "to shine," a root that would also result in the word *deatai* ("to appear"), the adjective *dios*, the name *Zeus*, and even Indic *diti* "brilliant."[22]

This explanation would appear, at least in part, to be a folk etymology. This is notably so with the first element *aphros*, which the Greeks interpreted as "foam," thus, the initial element of the name of the goddess born of the foam. There are, however, problems with the analysis of the latter portion of the name. It is not possible to derive the meaning "shining" from -*dīta*. On the one hand, the stem, which originally meant "sky," was **diw-*, ending with a digamma. While the digamma did drop out of many Greek dialects early, it did not do so in all dialects. Yet Aphrodite's name is never found with a digamma in any Greek dialect. On the other hand, there is, as yet, no parallel for the use

---

21. If this be the case, it opens new avenues of research into the study of Freyja's possible Near Eastern cognates. Opinion here is divided. Motz 1993: 110 argues for a possible link between Freyja and Ištar (or possibly even Kybele), claiming that Freyja is far more similar to the goddesses of the south and east than to those of the north. By contrast, Näsström 1995: 27 asserts that the similarities between Freyja and the eastern goddesses were more imagined than real, especially concerning the motif of the goddess and her dying lover. "Hence, the idea of an influence from the East Mediterranean must finally be laid to rest." It is possible, though, that the links between Freyja and the Near East need not be entirely severed. If, in fact, Aphrodite herself were influenced by Near Eastern deities, and Aphrodite influenced the development or the persona of Freyja as known through the Medieval literature, then there may be a traceable continuum between Mesopotamia and Scandinavia in the mythological literature.

22. Boedeker 1974: 11.

of *-ta/ti* as a feminizing suffix in Greek. One cannot explain how the *-ta/ti* element has become a part of the goddess' name, or how it would relate to the root for "shining."[23]

Furthermore, as W. Wyatt points out in his review of Boedeker's work, neither the name Aphrodite nor any variant thereof appears in any other Indo-European language and, thus, as he argues, it is probably a Hellenized version of some foreign name.[24] This suggestion may be particularly relevant if Aphrodite's origins show a Cypriot influence. Eteo-Cypriot has yet to be deciphered and translated, and so it is not possible to determine if there are Cypriot elements to the goddess' name. Until such time as Eteo-Cypriot is translatable, it is perhaps better to refrain from suggesting etymologies for the word "Aphrodite."

Since the linguistics of the name do not conform to anything openly Indo-European, I would suggest that the name is not Indo-European (despite the folk etymology of the first element). As neither the name of the goddess is Indo-European, nor does she equate to any other goddess in the Indo-European pantheons, it appears that Aphrodite is not Indo-European.

Chronology

As an arrival with the Indo-European speakers cannot be established for Aphrodite, the question remains: When did Aphrodite first appear in Greece? A *terminus ante quem* is, fortunately, easy to determine: The goddess is named in the Homeric and Hesiodic works, dated to the second half of the eighth century,[25] and the so-called Nestor cup from Pithekoussai, dating to 730–720 BCE,[26] mentions the goddess.[27]

> Of Nestor, in this wine cup a pleasant drink;
> who would drink this beverage, immediately
> will desire for fair-crowned Aphrodite seize him.

---

23. Donald Ringe, personal communication.

24. Wyatt 1978: 169–71. For additional commentary on Boedeker's monograph, see Fontenrose 1977: 460–61, and Rebuffat 1977: 324–25.

25. Although some scholars, such as West, now argue that a seventh-century date is more plausible, A.J. Graham (1995: 1–7) has argued quite convincingly that the dates 750–700 BCE should be accepted as correct for the redaction of the Homeric and Hesiodic epics.

26. The *kotyle* was discovered in a grave with items dating it to no later than 720 BCE. Thus, the inscription might be earlier, but clearly not later. See Buchner and Russo 1955: *passim*; Buchner and Ridgway 1993: 219, #168; Russo in Buchner and Ridgway 1993: 745–50.

27. See Appendix B 3.10 and fig. 3a.

This *kotyle* is of East Greek manufacture, and the inscription itself (incised after firing) is in Euboian characters; it now appears likely that the inscription was wrought at some point before the *kotyle* reached the western island.[28] While the *kotyle*, in itself, is not necessarily evidence of a cult of Aphrodite in Magna Graecia at this time (more on this below), it is evidence that by the last quarter of the eighth century BCE, Aphrodite was recognized as a love goddess throughout the Greek world.

Even more significant are Aphrodite's roles in the works of Homer and Hesiod. Although Aphrodite is sympathetic to the eastern Trojans, and is closely associated with a sanctuary and temple on Paphos, Homer, nevertheless, portrays her as a fully integrated member of the Greek pantheon, even casting full blame on her for the inception of the war.

Bronze Age Aegean

Just how long before the Nestor *kotyle* Aphrodite appears in Greek culture remains a difficult issue, for there is no positive evidence of her existence in Greek religion prior to the eighth century BCE. The oldest iconography in the Aegean that is reminiscent of Aphrodite comes from the Cyclades. The schematic-style figurines and the rather "portly" female figurines from the Aegean Late Neolithic period gradually evolve, respectively, into the schematic, Plastiras and Louros images of the Grotta-Pelos culture (c. 3200–2800 BCE). Of these early images the most eroticised are the Plastiras variety, which are

Fig. 3a
The Nestor Cup inscription. See Jeffreys, Plate 47.

---

28. Ridgway 1992: 55–56. That the inscription was rendered before export is now supported by a second piece of evidence: a fragmentary late-Geometric Rhodian bird-bowl discovered in Eretria. The artistic decoration dates the piece to 735–725 BCE. Three lines of verse remain on one side, similar in meter and orthography to the Nestor Cup. As this piece was discovered in Eretria and offers, to date, the best parallel to the Nestor Cup, the evidence suggests that the inscription upon the latter piece was, in fact, incised before export to the west (Johnston and Andriomenou 1989: *passim*).

somewhat more anthropomorphized than the other two and show rudimentary breasts and genitalia.[29]

This Plastiras type, according to Renfrew, evolved during and after the next phase of Cycladic art, the Keros-Syros culture (2700–2200 BCE), into the folded-arm figurines.[30] The four varieties of these figurines—the Kapsala, Spedos, Dokathismata, and Chalandriani (with the original fifth type, the Kea variety, now accepted as a variation of the Dokathismata type)—all show certain basic elements. These are a (mostly) two-dimensional anthropomorphic image with schematic face, painted and/or incised decoration, arms that are held firmly to the torso so that the forearms are crossed at the waist, and legs separated either by molding or incision.[31] The possible associations with an early Aphrodite-deity might be seen in two other common (although not consistent) elements of the figurines' iconography: breasts and genitalia. These sexual attributes have lead some, such as E. Simon, to postulate that these female figurines from the third millennium are, in fact, the earliest representations of Aphrodite in the Greek world.[32]

There are a few problems with this hypothesis. The first, and most obvious, is the problem of chronology. According to both Renfrew and Getz-Preziosi, the folded-arm figurines do not continue either in manufacture or use long after 2200 BCE.[33] This leaves a considerable gap between these images and the next possible Aegean representation of Aphrodite, in the mid-sixteenth century (see below). As it is not probable that there could be a non-visible continuity of iconography or ideology over the course of seven hundred years, it is unlikely that the Cycladic figurines are an early portrayal of the goddess Aphrodite.

The second problem is one of meaning. Are the folded-arm figurines intended to be erotic? Such a meaning for the Cycladic images is unlikely. As Getz-Preziosi notes, many of the figurines have no sexual attributes at all, whereas several are shown to be specifically pregnant or just postpartum.[34] A non-sexual yet often maternal aspect is the antithesis of the Aphrodite studied in Chapter Two. The issues of chronology and iconography, then, argue

---

29. Renfrew 1969: 6–8 and Ill. 4.

30. Getz-Preziosi 1994: 24; Renfrew 1977: 60–67; Renfrew 1969: 9ff. Note that other forms of figurine also existed during this phase, notably the highly schematic Apeiranthos type. However, as these other types can hardly be seen as erotic, they play no real role in this study.

31. Renfrew 1977: 65–67.

32. Simon 1985: 234–36.

33. Getz-Preziosi 1994: 24; Renfrew 1977: 65; Renfrew 1969: 26.

34. Getz-Preziosi 1994: 18.

rather strongly against the possibility of these Cycladic figurines being early predecessors or representations of Aphrodite.

In strong contrast to these is a statuette discovered at the site of Pigadhia on the island of Karpathos.[35] This 65 cm limestone image is schematic in overall design, with a triangular face adorned only with a prominent nose, and stump arms on a simplistic torso ending in rounded hips. The back is flat, suggesting that the image was perhaps intended to be seen only from the front. In contrast to this general lack of detail, however, are the sexual characteristics, which are rendered in great detail. Two round bosses represent the breasts, and a triangle in relief decorated with a vertical incised line indicates the genitalia.[36] This is perhaps the most eroticised (or at least feminized) image from the early Aegean. In general, however, such an emphasis is relatively uncommon in the Aegean, especially in contrast to Cyprus or the Levant, and, due both to chronology and the lack of cognates, is also unlikely to be an early representation of Aphrodite.

No evidence for Aphrodite can be drawn from the Linear B tablets, which would have offered the best positive evidence for the goddess by this name in Mycenaean times. These documents consist predominantly of lists, recording, among other pieces of data, offerings made to the Bronze Age Greek deities. Thus, tablet Fp 1 + 31 from Knossos (= Ventris and Chadwick 200) lists units of oil offered to Diktaian Zeus, Daidalos, *Pa-de*, the augur, the deities of Amnisos, the Erinys, all the gods, and the priestess of the winds.[37] The majority of the deities worshipped in Iron Age Greece do, in fact, appear in the Linear B tablets in these offering lists, including Zeus, Dia/Diwya/Dione (the feminine counterpart of Zeus), Hera, Hermes, Artemis, Poseidon, Eileithyia, Ares, Enyalios (probably an early war-god, later an epithet of Ares), the Erinys (Furies), Athena, a deity named Paiwon, who ultimately may have merged with Apollo, Dionysos, Hephaistos, and possibly Demeter, among others.[38] Aphrodite's name never appears, nor do any of her epithets.

One reference that some have argued might be attributed to her is the mention of a "*Potnia a-si-wi-ja*" in Pylos fragment 1206.[39] If one were to assume that Aphrodite did come from the east, then a title of "Our Lady of Asia" (perhaps more specifically "Anatolia" or "Lydia" as per later terminology) might be appropriate for the goddess. Of course, this makes the assump-

---

35. Melas 1985: 147–48, fig, 62a, b.

36. *Ibid.*; Vagnetti 1991: 148.

37. Ventris and Chadwick 1959: 305–6.

38. Appendix B 3.11; Ventris and Chadwick 1959: 311, 208 = V 52 and Pylos 55 = An 724. *Ibid.*, 125–27.

39. Chadwick 1957: 125ff.

tion that the Mycenaeans themselves thought of Aphrodite as an oriental divinity and would refer to her in common practice as foreign.[40] In his article in *Minos* on the *potnia* goddesses, Chadwick argues that this title might refer to some Asian mother-goddess, perhaps belonging to Anatolia/Lydia.[41] If, already in the Bronze Age, *potnia* refers to a queen as well as a goddess, the title could even suggest a foreign dignitary of some sort. In either case, there is nothing to the title that would clearly suggest Aphrodite.[42]

A second possible reference to Aphrodite occurs in tablet PY Tn 316v, where the signs *pe-re-*82* are present in a list of deities receiving offerings. Although A. Morpurgo recognizes that the signs indicate the name of a goddess, she refrains from attributing any specific name or identity to this deity due to the ambiguity of the sign.[43] The same signs are taken by Palmer to read *Peleia*, a possible name of a dove-goddess, through association with the Πέλεια of Dione at Dodona.[44] As this name does not appear later in conjunction with Aphrodite and as the reading is extremely tentative, I am hesitant to equate this potential reading with Aphrodite. Thus, for the Linear B tablets, I agree with Chadwick when he states quite simply, "There is no trace of Aphrodite."[45]

In the absence of a written record, one must turn to iconography and archaeology in the attempt to locate an Aphrodite-type goddess in the Bronze Age Aegean. However, it is not possible to offer a one-to-one identification of Minoan or Mycenaean goddess representations and the possible names of these deities. Although the figure on the Grain-Goddess fresco from Mycenae may be tentatively identified as Demeter, or the *Potnia Theron* of Cretan iconography as Artemis, these identifications remain speculative and cannot be used as a certain identification of any goddess named in later Greek texts. Instead of attempting to identify the goddess Aphrodite *per se* in the iconographic record, it is perhaps best to consider what iconographic attributes one would expect to identify an Aphrodite-type goddess.

As discussed in Chapter Two, Aphrodite is first and foremost a goddess of sex and beauty. It is probable that were she present in the Bronze Age, Aphrodite would have been depicted nude or in some other erotic manner.[46]

---

40. Chadwick 1980: 85.

41. Chadwick 1957: no. 67.

42. For a counter argument, see J.C. van Leuven 1979: 122ff.

43. Morpurgo 1963: 242.

44. Ventris and Chadwick 1959: 127, PY 172 = Kn02. Through the Dodona connection, the potential dove(s) may, in fact, refer to Dione.

45. Chadwick 1980: 99.

46. This was not the case in the Archaic Age, when there is the absence of any Archaic Greek custom of portraying goddesses nude. Also, this leads to the rather tricky issue

Other attributes of the goddess are birds (doves), the heavens, water/the sea, and, to a certain extent, even gold.[47] Thus, a survey of Mycenaean and Minoan iconography should take these elements into account. Representations depicting at least two of these elements might be taken as evidence for the presence of an Aphrodite-type deity in the Aegean Bronze Age.

NUDE GODDESSES

The most likely candidates for Mycenaean representations of Aphrodite are two small, cut-out ornaments of embossed gold discovered in Shaft Grave III at Mycenae, dating from 1550–1500 BCE. One depicts a nude female "goddess" surrounded by three birds, one by each of her arms, and one above her head.[48] Her hands are at her breasts, and her navel and genitalia are clearly indicated (see fig. 3b).[49] The second is almost identical to the first,[50] except that only one bird is depicted (located above the head), the facial features are more clearly rendered, and the navel is not indicated (see fig. 3c).[51] The nudity, the emphasis on the breast region and genitalia, and the birds suggest Aphrodite and, therefore, these two images are the most probable evidence for the existence of this goddess in Greece as early as the Late Helladic period.

Two points must be borne in mind when considering these two images. The first is that although they both are examples of what some writers have regarded as clear Aegean style and workmanship for the medium, they are

---

of what precisely constitutes "erotic" in a culture. Nudity in the Amazon rain forest, for example, certainly cannot be considered an aspect of sexuality, whereas women's bound, deformed feet in Imperial China were considered to be quite the aphrodisiac. Specifically regarding Aegean Bronze Age iconography, the issue of exposed breasts comes to the fore. The majority of Minoan paintings show women in bodices that reveal the breasts, along with small waists and flounced skirts. Thus, one must argue that either all these women were intended to be portrayed as highly erotic, or one must suggest that, for the Minoans/Mycenaeans, bare breasts were not necessarily considered to be especially erotic. For the purposes of this study, then, I am defining as "erotic" portrayals where *specific* attention is brought either to the breasts, genitalia, thighs, or all the above, through arm positioning or careful delineation in artistic rendering.

47. In this instance, however, gold must be reserved as a secondary characteristic at best. Many "pretty things" were rendered in gold during the Bronze Age, and this medium can no more be used as evidence for the identification of Aphrodite than an object in silver can be used as evidence of Artemis.

48. Athens, Nat. Mus., Inv. 27.

49. Evans 1921: 224; Higgins 1989: 168; Böhm 1990: 14ff.

50. Athens, Nat. Mus., Inv. 28.

51. Böhm 1990: 14ff.

Fig. 3b
Gold foil female image from Circle A, Shaft Grave III at Mycenae.
Athens National Museum, Inv. 27.

nevertheless the product of Near Eastern iconographic influence.[52] Ties to the Aegean might be seen in their iconographic similarity to the Cycladic folded-arm figurines mentioned above, for the pose and genital delineation are almost identical. However, as these images ceased to be produced around 2200 BCE, it is too early to be a direct influence on the Mycenaean figures. The Near Eastern influence can be seen not so much in the individual elements of the images, for both nudity and bird imagery are prevalent in Minoan iconography, but rather in the depiction of the nudity. Female nudes in Minoan glyptic are usually portrayed in some association with the divine, either in the act of ecstatic dance, as in the gold ring from Phaistos (see fig. 3d), or in the act of receiving worship, as the goddess depicted on another gold ring from Phaistos (see fig. 3e). Furthermore, the emphasis on these nudes is on the breasts and thighs, while the genitalia, arms, and occasionally even the heads are rendered as diminutive, if at all. The gold images from Mycenae show a different focus. The breasts, while on one level are brought to attention by the

---

52. *Ibid.*, 15; Higgins 1989: *ill.* 63 and note.

Fig. 3c
Gold foil female image from Circle A, Shaft Grave II at Mycenae.
Athens National Museum, Inv. 28.

placement of the arms, are also not actually rendered on the images; they
show a sharp contrast to the buxom women prevalent in the contemporary
Minoan glyptic. The thighs of the gold images do not show the typical Minoan
fullness, whereas the emphasis is clearly on the genitalia, which are carefully
rendered by engraving. Finally, the gold images have static poses, in sharp
contrast to the Minoan nudes shown in dance or reverence. In the final analysis, the style, while containing Minoan elements, nevertheless shows much
closer parallels to Near Eastern nudes, where emphasis on arm placement,
genitalia, and even navels predominates over breasts and thighs.[53]

_____

53. More detail on Near Eastern iconography in Chapters Eight and Nine.

Fig. 3d
Gold signet ring from Phaistos.
Iraklion Archaeological Museum, Inv. 44.

Fig. 3e
Gold signet ring from Phaistos.
Iraklion Archaeological Museum, Inv. 45.

The second issue to consider is the context in which these images were found. The Shaft Graves of Circle A were filled with all manner of luxuries, many imported, such as amber beads from the Baltic and ostrich eggs from either Africa or the Levant, which served to emphasize the wealth and status of the dead.[54] As such, there is always the possibility that these gold-foil "trinkets" were little more than status symbols for the interred. Perhaps even more importantly, the feminine images in question were located within the same grave as other Minoan gold-foil items, such as a tripartite shrine, a woman in Minoan dress with elaborate headdress, a flying griffin, heraldically set animals, and even an octopus and a butterfly. It appears that all these items were originally used as decoration on a garment that has since disintegrated out of existence, especially as many of these pieces have holes apparently for use as attachment anchors. It is possible, if not probable, that all the images served as some manner of "Minoan" fashion statement for the interred. Thus, the gold-foil females should be seen as decorative elements—glorified sequins—rather than objects imbued with religious (or other) meaning.

Ultimately, it is difficult to determine what relationship these two images bore to Aphrodite. On the one hand, the depiction of a female with strongly emphasized sexuality (in the form of the clearly indicated genitalia) and an association with birds (themselves associated with a tripartite shrine) strongly argues for a Mycenaean recognition of an Aphrodite-type goddess. The quasi-religious context (burial) of the images might indicate that the females in question are goddesses, while their potential use as clothing adornments might lessen that identification, or perhaps even render it insignificant. Their use and meaning are, therefore, extremely ambiguous.

A similar conclusion is to be drawn for the small, ivory figurine from Mycenaean grave 103, excavated by Tsountas in the late nineteenth century, and to be dated from LH II to IIIB.[55] This figurine, 3.2 cm in height, is of a nude female.[56] Neither the head nor the right arm remains. The left arm is close to the body, with the elbow bent and the forearm reaching forward to hold the left breast. The waist is proportionately quite slender, whereas the hips are broad and rounded. The genital triangle is indicated by a V-shaped groove beginning at the upper thighs and meeting below the abdomen and continuing downward to divide the thighs. No feet remain. Although the broad hips and the medium of ivory suggest a foreign, notably Levantine, origin for this image, the slender waist is more indicative of Aegean production and, thus,

---

54. For a full list, see Vermeule 1972: Chapter IV. The ostrich eggs themselves were turned into rhyta in Crete and, thus, are only indirect imports from the Near East.

55. Böhm 1990: 145, M 3.

56. Poursat, by contrast, offers a height of 5.2 cm (Poursat 1977: 16 and Pl. XXXIV 319/4940).

with Böhm, I suggest that this piece is of Aegean manufacture.[57] Once again, while the blatant eroticism is indicative of an Aphrodite-type, the context leaves interpretation ambiguous.

Finally, there are the nude females portrayed in the glyptic from Phaistos (see above), Knossos, Hagia Triada, and Khania.[58] Unlike the gold-foil images from Mycenae, there is no attempt in these representations to emphasize any specific body parts on the females and, thus, one must assume that either the nudity itself was adequate as a representation of eroticism or that the nudity existed apart from notions of explicit sexuality. The images do have as a consistent theme the placement of the nude female in a religious setting, often portrayed dancing by an altar and/or a "sacred" tree or column.[59] It is not clear whether the nude female herself is intended to be portrayed as a goddess, or if she is merely a votary or priestess in a sacred scene.[60]

As it is not possible to determine if the females in question are humans or goddesses, their evidence for an Aphrodite prototype in the Bronze Age Aegean is ambiguous at best. Nevertheless, they do offer testimony that in Crete (NB that all the examples, with one possible exception, come from Crete) the nude female does play a role in the religious ideology. This familiarity with the nude female in Cretan religion may offer some insight as to why the cult of Aphrodite first appears in the Aegean in Crete (see below).

One piece of glyptic that does not feature a nude female, but that is relevant to the examination of possible Bronze Age Aegean Aphrodite iconography due to various hypotheses that have emerged concerning its possible portrayal of that goddess, is a gold signet ring from Mycenae.[61] From left to right of the impression, there is a series of crudely rendered lions' heads along the edge of the ring. To the top left of the scene is a small, vaguely anthropomorphic figure whose head, hands, and feet emerge from behind a figure-eight shield. Beneath this figure are two women, bare-chested, in flounced skirts. The one to the left holds flowers in both of her hands, while the one to the right has her right hand empty, lying next to her hip, and her left hand forward. Beneath the elbow of this female is a girl, also in a flounced skirt, holding flowers in her left hand. To the right of this girl is what would appear to be the central character of the scene, a proportionately larger female seated under a tree, bare-chested and wearing a flounced skirt. One of her arms is upon her stomach, and in her other hand she holds three flowers, possibly

---

57. Böhm 1990: 15.

58. *Ibid.*, 10. A further example, in Geneva, is without provenance.

59. *Ibid.*, 11 and 146–48.

60. *Ibid.*, 13.

61. Athens. Nat. Mus., Inv. 992.

offering them to the woman standing behind the small girl. Behind the tree under which the larger woman sits is another girl with her hands up in the branches of the tree. She wears the same fashion as the other girl. In the center of the scene is a *labrys*; at the top of the seal are a star, a crescent moon, and an inverted rainbow. Simon and Hampe argue that this divinity must be "Aphrodite in the Gardens," whose cult endured from the Bronze Age into the historical period in a city where the cultic traditions of the Mycenaean period were preserved relatively intact.[62] Their arguments concerning the identification of this scene, and this goddess, can be summarized as follows:

- the scene depicted refers to the ritual of the Arrhephoria, for which there is archaeological evidence as early as the Bronze Age
- the figure-eight shield is the Palladion of Athena, whose presence indicates the Athenian Akropolis—the scene of the Arrhephoria ritual
- the ritual of the Arrhephoria was enacted by two young girls—there are two girls behind the goddess on the signet
- the ritual was nocturnal—the moon and star indicate a nocturnal setting
- the star itself may be Venus, a reference to Aphrodite
- the ritual took place during the summer—the mulberry with its ripe fruit on the signet indicates the summer season
- the trees and flowers indicate a garden setting—it is specifically "Aphrodite in the Gardens" who is associated with the ritual
- the scene represents not the ritual itself, but the period the girls spent in service to Aphrodite and Athena just before the ritual[63]

There are several problems with this interpretation. There is no evidence that Aphrodite was associated with the planet Venus before Aristotle.[64] As such, the link with the "star of Venus" is anachronistic in the Bronze Age. All that might be suggested is that a reference is being made to Aphrodite "Ourania" with the star, moon, and rainbow. Trees appear to be endemic in the Minoan iconographic tradition, especially in scenes of ecstatic dance. As such, the tree may serve to intensify the sacred nature of the scene (as does the *labrys*), but in this context it cannot necessarily serve to identify the deity in question.[65] There is as yet no clear evidence from the Bronze Age Aegean that the

---

62. Hampe and Simon 1981: 187.

63. *Ibid.,* 187–88.

64. Heimpel 1982: 22.

65. One might even go so far as to argue that the blooming tree and flowers and the rainbow reminiscent of spring rains might be a good argument for the identification of the deity in question as Persephone.

figure-eight shield is to be associated with Athena.[66] The deity typically shown with such armaments is very minor indeed, to judge from his/her relative size in all his/her portrayals.[67] If there was continuity of cult from the Bronze Age through Classical times (which I believe there was), it does not seem likely that Athena, the possible Linear B "*a-ta-na-po-ti-ni-ja*," would be given such a minor iconography. While the small, armed figure in the background might be Aphrodite's frequent companion, Ares (although with similar problems of iconography and scale), it must be remembered that, to date, in the Aegean, Aphrodite's earliest divine connection is with Hermes, not Ares (see below, Kato Symi). It would, therefore, be anachronistic to use this possible identification of a possible god as a conclusive argument.

Furthermore, the identification of the goddess based on her relationship with the Arrhephoria is quite unsound. The evidence that Aphrodite, in the gardens or otherwise, played any function in this ritual is slight and unsatisfactory. The main evidence, from Pausanias, mentions merely that the girls walk by the temenos of Aphrodite, not that that space, its divinity, or cult personnel has any function in the ritual.[68] Not only is there no good evidence that Aphrodite played a role in the Arrhephoria, there is no evidence that the Arrhephorai worked as servants of Aphrodite preceding the ritual. These girls were in the service of Athena.

Finally, if this scene intended to show the daily life of the Arrhephorai, why is the scene nocturnal? Hampe and Simon argue that the nocturnal setting (as well as the evidence of summer) is appropriate for the nighttime ritual. But if it is not the ritual itself being presented, what meaning does this iconography have? In the end, although the emphasis placed on celestial bodies does perhaps bring to mind Aphrodite Ourania, there is no clear evidence from the iconography that this image is definitely Aphrodite, much less Aphrodite in the Gardens.

GODDESS-WITH-UPRAISED-ARMS

Beyond the gold and ivory images of Mycenae, there are many three-dimensional representations of goddesses in the Bronze Age Aegean, both in Greece and on Crete, stemming ultimately from the Minoan iconographic tradition. The most common representation of goddess(es) is the so-called goddess-with-upraised-arms, a female standing erect, with arms either stretched

---

66. Rehak 1984: 544. When referring to a handful of armed deities in the Bronze Age Aegean corpus, Rehak suggests that "although she possesses some of the attributes later associated with the goddess Athena, it is impossible to ascertain the exact identity of the Bronze Age goddess."

67. *Ibid., passim.*

68. See below, p. 84.

forward or upward, bearing distinctive attributes such as snakes or birds on the arms, head, and waist.[69]

The image originated in Crete as early as the Middle Minoan period. After Late Minoan I, the image is adopted by the Mycenaeans both on the island and on the mainland, and the style changes slightly so that the skirt of the image is wheel-made (the goddess looks as though she is wearing a hoop skirt).[70] This figurine remains most common in Crete and is generally accepted as being essentially indicative of Minoan cult.

The identification of the goddess-with-upraised-arms as a deity is made from the iconography and from the find spots of the images. In terms of location, goddesses-with-upraised-arms come from tombs and sanctuaries: sanctuaries with votive pottery, cult paraphernalia, and architecture, thus ensuring the correct identification of the site's purpose. They are associated with worship, death, and possibly the afterlife. Regarding iconography, their most common attributes are snakes, which wrap around the arms, waist, and/or head, or are borne in the hands of the figurines; tiaras decorated with either snakes, birds, poppies or discoid attachments; and birds, either on the head, shoulders, or hands.[71] The positioning of the arms suggests a stance of benediction or prayer; the divine interpretation of the figurines would support this interpretation.

As these images are understood to be goddesses, their purpose within the sanctuary settings appears to be as cult images, thus as the deities who are worshipped. The presence of either the goddesses-with-upraised-arms themselves or simply the items associated with them, such as snakes and birds, within a sacred complex identifies that complex as being dedicated to at least one female deity. One might, therefore, suggest that the sacred areas of Knossos, Gazi, Gournia, Hagia Triada, Karphi, and Vounous are all goddess-oriented in dedication.[72]

Do any of these images, the most common style of goddess depiction in the Bronze Age Aegean, represent Aphrodite or an Aphrodite-type goddess? Using the stated methodology, for any of these images to be so identified they must include at least one or two of the defining iconographic characteristics of Aphrodite: sexuality, birds, heavens, sea. Of all these elements, only the birds offer any evidence for the goddess. Although Minoan goddess-

---

69. See the bibliography for reference to extensive treatments by St. Alexiou and G.C. Gesell.

70. Further developments occur due to the contact between the Mycenaeans and Minoan goddess iconography, most visible in the development of the Mycenaean *phi, psi,* and *tau* figurines of LHII and later. See French 1971: 103–8 for a full discussion.

71. Gesell 1985: 47–49.

72. Gesell 1983: *passim.*

es (and for that matter mortal women as well) are portrayed with exposed breasts, it cannot be determined if this is intended as a blatant display of eroticism or simply a style of dress. The breasts are not consistently emphasized, and the genitalia (or any aspect of the lower body) are never portrayed. The most common media for the images are either clay or faience; nothing is specifically indicative of the sea; and the heavens, once again, may only be hinted at by the presence of the birds. Thus, there is one element that may suggest an Aphrodite-type goddess in the Bronze Age Aegean, specifically Crete: the bird-goddess.[73]

GODDESS OF KNOSSOS

An alternate image that may offer insight into the presence of an Aphrodite-type goddess in the Bronze Age Aegean is a terra-cotta female statuette from the Sanctuary of the Double Axe at Knossos, excavated by Evans.[74] This figurine, dated stylistically by Böhm to Late Minoan IIIB, is of a seated female. The head is intact; hair is indicated through minimal molding, ears are slightly pinched clay at either side of the face, the eyes are incised dots, and the nose is molded. Three incised dots may indicate a mouth. The neck is long; the shoulders are absent; and the arms extend out from the base of the neck, bend fully at the elbows, and curve back into the body so that the wrists and hands lie fully under the breasts. The breasts themselves are applied clay. A slight curve along the torso is indicative of a waist, and the hips flair out where the image bends to assume a seated posture. There is no navel, but there are two clearly incised dots at the level of the genitalia, although they clearly cannot be intended to represent the vagina. The legs are divided and appear to have been molded separately. The knees bend and the bottom of the legs flair slightly to represent feet. The image is decorated at the neck and along the arms by incision.

That a certain degree of sexuality is implied on this image is evident both in the positioning of the arms and the fact that the only decoration, the incision, is rendered on the arms and around the breasts and, to a certain extent, the genitalia. That the image may be sacred in nature is to be derived from the find context, the Sanctuary of the Double Axe, and possibly by the seated pose (a throne?). Whether a goddess or votary is intended is a more difficult problem. Unlike the goddess-with-upraised-arms, this image has no snakes or birds to adorn it, and thus is bereft of the common Minoan sacred attributes. Nevertheless, although the exact identification is ambiguous, this image does

---

73. Frequently referred to as the "Dove Goddess," especially by Evans. However, as the species of the bird is ambiguous, it is perhaps better to designate this specific portrayal of the goddess as the bird-goddess only.

74. Evans 1902: 52; Böhm 1990: 146.

offer further evidence for a sexual, sacred female figure in the Minoan religious repertoire.

These images, the gold-foil images from Shaft Grave III, the small ivory figurine from grave 103, the glyptic and the statuette from Knossos, all offer testimony that a sexualized feminine figure was known to the Bronze Age Aegean artisans and that this figure had some connection with religion. Only the statuette from Knossos, however, gives any archaeological evidence that this image may, in fact, be the representation of a deity. If one consider that the similar arm positions of the gold-foil images and the figurine from Knossos are indicative of a similar being, then one might argue that the Knossos image is herself associated with the so-called bird-goddess, and thus that this Minoan bird-goddess also had a manifestation as a nude, eroticised goddess, serving as evidence of an early Aphrodite-type in the Bronze Age Aegean. The Minoans had a bird-goddess and recognized the possibility of an eroticised feminine personage in their reli-gious repertoire. Both of these concepts may have contributed to the evolution of Aphrodite.

KATO SYMI

One final datum may argue for the early presence of Aphrodite in the Aegean, and this is the archaeological site of Kato Symi Viannou in Crete. From iconography emerging in the Archaic Age and inscriptions from both the sixth century and the Hellenistic Age, the excavators have determined that the sanctuary was dedicated to the joint worship of Hermes and Aphrodite, although the majority of the cult paraphernalia is associated with Hermes.[75] The sanctuary dates back well into the Middle Minoan period and continues in use into the Roman Age and, thus, is the longest continually functioning sanctuary of Aphrodite (and Hermes) in the Greek world.

There is both continuity and change at the sanctuary of Kato Symi throughout its long existence. Animals (both as votives and sacrifices) play a significant role in the cult throughout its use, as do drinking vessels, and the overall visibility of the ritual.[76] By contrast, there is evidence of frequent, almost continuous, change and evolution at the site in terms of architecture, pottery styles, and, of course, population. Such changes accommodated the transitions in belief, social conditions, and fashion, especially as these changed from period to period and culture to culture throughout the long life of the sanctuary. Such changes occurred not only between Bronze Age and Iron Age

---

75. In the seventh century, especially, over one hundred bronze plaques from the sanctuary depict male scenes, especially hunting scenes, which the excavator associates with male initiation rituals cited in Strabo. Lebessi 1985: *passim*; Kanta 1991: 483.

76. Kanta 1991: 480ff. Note that both animals (as objects of sacrifice and as votive images) and libation vessels are common enough at Aegean sanctuaries in general and may not necessarily point to unique aspects of Kato Symi specifically.

times, but even during the Neopalatial period, and between the Neopalatial and postpalatial periods.[77]

The first significant changes had occurred already in Middle Minoan, when there were no less than four successive building phases between the end of the old palace period and the end of the Neopalatial period, when the entire layout of the monumental structure was radically altered, probably at great expense.[78] Likewise, in Late Minoan IIIB, according to P. Muhly, the type of pottery constituting the cult paraphernalia changes and large, wheel-made animals begin to appear as cult offerings at the site—replacing the smaller, solid animal images of the earlier period—and continuing in use, at least, into the seventh century. This change, believes Muhly, is the result of the Mycenaean influx into Crete at this time.[79] In the Protogeometric and Geometric Ages, anthropomorphic figurines become standard offerings at the site and allow for the earliest study of the deities who were the focus of worship at the sanctuary. Before this time, the only anthropomorphic figurine was of a Minoan male in traditional worshipping pose (standing erect, stomach extended, hand raised to the forehead).

Although it is evident that from the sixth century onward the deities revered at Kato Symi were Hermes and Aphrodite, there is continued debate over whether or not these were the original deities of Kato Symi, or if there were other, unnamed deities at the sanctuary who were, at some unknown later date, assimilated into Hermes and Aphrodite. Lebessi is of the opinion that there is strong continuity of cult at Kato Symi and that a pair of deities, male and female, Hermes-like and Aphrodite-like in attributes, had been worshipped at this sanctuary since the Middle Minoan period. Later, these deities came to be known as Hermes and Aphrodite, whom Lebessi associates with nature and fertility.[80]

Supporting this argument are the continuity of animal images and iconography, and the continuity of pottery types (although pottery styles change and evolve), indicating a continuous ritual at Kato Symi. The animal motif, as mentioned above, begins in the Middle Minoan and continues into the historic period, when the small metal votives found throughout the site represent a male (a god?) returning from the hunt with prey. If prey animals and hunting are, in fact, associated with the god of Kato Symi, then this may be evi-

---

77. *Ibid.,* 485.

78. *Ibid.,* 484.

79. P. Muhly, personal communication.

80. Lebessi 1973: 198. Once again, though, I call into question the automatic association with fertility. Aphrodite's role in male initiation seems logical, as at this point the male is entering a phase of life where sexuality is being directed toward the female sex. As such, it is an appropriate time for an "introduction" to Aphrodite.

dence that a similar male deity was revered from Middle Minoan onward.[81] The continuous use of drinking vessels at the site may indicate a consistent use of libation/feasting/ritual drinking, marking a common cult from Middle Minoan through the historic period.[82]

Nevertheless, there are also arguments against a continuous cult of continuous deities at Kato Symi. Hermes' name is Indo-European, and the presence of his name in the Linear B tablets of Knossos/Crete is somewhat problematic. Tablet D 411 + 511 lists a "di-ko-to / e-ma-a_2-o OVIS^f 60 WE 30[."[83] The e-ma-a_2-o may be interpreted as Hermes in the genitive, indicating that the sheep under consideration belong to him. This is in accord with the role of Hermes in the Thebes tablets, where he is associated also with wool production (TH Of 31[84]). Such evidence may suggest that Hermes was revered in Crete at least in the Late Bronze Age. However, since the name is Indo-European, there is an extremely high probability that he was Mycenaean in origin, a hypothesis supported by the greater representation of his name on the mainland.[85] This leads to the possibilities that either at some period after 1400 BCE a Minoan god worshipped at Kato Symi was assimilated into Greek Hermes, or that the Greeks adopted the Minoan god, named him Hermes, and practiced his cult more so on the mainland than on the island, as is documented in the Linear B records. The former hypothesis, more convincing in my opinion, argues against continuity; the latter in favor of it.

Second, there is the absence of many of the attributes that indicate goddess cult in Minoan iconography. A few *labrydes* were discovered at Kato Symi, but no snakes, birds, or goddesses-with-upraised-arms. Although the absence of the latter may indicate merely that the deities were worshipped in aniconic form at Kato Symi in the Bronze Age,[86] this offers yet another example of change in cult between the Bronze and Iron Ages, for Hermes is frequently portrayed in the votives in the historic period, and female images of the Geometric and Archaic Ages appear to give evidence for the cult of a

---

81. Lebessi 1985: *passim*. Although, as mentioned above, animal motifs are adequately common at Aegean cult sites in general to lessen the impact of this particular manifestation of continuity.

82. Kanta 1991: 482.

83. Nosch 2000: 214.

84. Do-]de *ku* LANA *PA*[
    ]do-de *ku* LANA *PA*[
        e-ma-a_2 re-[.

85. Hägg 1997: 165; Nosch 2000: 211. Hermes appears on the mainland at Pylos in tablets PY Nn 1357, Tn 316, Un 219; and at Thebes in text TH Of 31.

86. Kanta 1991: 481.

goddess. Either there is a change in the deities at Kato Symi, there is a change in method of worship, or both.

Even the feminine images do not offer as much information concerning goddess/Aphrodite worship at Kato Symi as could be desired, either in terms of the identity of the goddess or of the chronology and continuity of the cult. The earliest feminine votive is a terra-cotta female idol (rather aptly described as resembling a *xoanon* by Lebessi, insofar as it is plank-like in shape and barely anthropomorphic) dating from c. 1050 BCE (see fig. 3f). The image is clearly female, with prominently molded breasts and hands that curve toward the genital region.

Although there may be debate as to the proper identification of this image, Lebessi is more certain about applying the name "Aphrodite" to a bronze idol found in the first year of excavation in a context of Geometric pottery and

Fig. 3f
Proto-Geometric anthropomorphic figurine from Kato Symi.
Lebessi, 1972, pinax 187 a.

votive animal figures, all dating to the ninth century BCE (see fig. 3g).[87] It is, in fact, highly unlikely that this bronze image was intended to represent Aphrodite. It is one of a continuum of bronze and clay figurines that emerged in the Greek iconographic repertoire during the ninth century and evolved in a gradual and continual fashion until the end of the seventh century BCE.[88] These small images were dispersed throughout the southern half of the Greek world by the beginning of the eighth century, covering a range from Ithaka to the west, Delphi to the north, Samos and Lindos to the east, and much of Crete to the south.[89] As Aphrodite is not revered at all these sites, nor is any one deity consistently represented at these sanctuaries, such figurines are perhaps better understood as votive figurines rather than as representations of any particular deity.

Nevertheless, the presence of one of these figurines at Kato Symi does offer some evidence of a specifically goddess-oriented cult. The ninth/eighth-century nude-female figurines that appear throughout the Greek world arise

Fig. 3g
Geometric anthropomorphic figurine from Kato Symi.
Lebessi, 1972, pinax 189 b.

---

87. Lebessi 1972: 199 and image 189β.

88. Böhm, *passim.*

89. *Ibid.*

in specific contexts: either within tombs or at sanctuaries. One example from Merenda, one from Fortetsa, one from Knossos, and the four famous ivory examples were all funerary in context. From the sanctuaries, two have come to light near the temenos of Apollo at Delphi, two near and under the Heraion at Olympia, one on the akropolis of Lindos, one at the Heraion at Samos, two within the Diktaian Cave at Psychro, two at the sanctuary at Hagia Triada, two at the Eileithyia cave at Inatos, one at the Aphrodite temple at Axos, and one from the sanctuary at Kato Symi. Other figurines, including three from Crete, come from uncertain contexts.

An examination of the sanctuary find-spots shows a greater concentration in those sanctuaries and temples dedicated to female deities, such as Hera, Eileithyia, and Aphrodite.[90] In fact, on the island of Crete, the only definite, sanctuary find-spot where these images are not associated with a goddess is the Diktaian Cave, dedicated to baby Zeus. As Zeus is not associated with Kato Symi and the figurines are clearly not associated with Hermes, the presence of one of these images signals the worship of a goddess at the sanctuary, in this case (based on the later identification), Aphrodite.

Unfortunately, the Kato Symi bronze figurine is not helpful for the unraveling of the chronology of the cult of Aphrodite. The Kato Symi bronze is one of the earliest of this genre and, as such, its presence at the sanctuary in the ninth century offers more evidence as to when the idols became prominent than to when the cult of a goddess became entrenched. It does, however, offer a *terminus ante quem*—a goddess, possibly Aphrodite, must have been worshipped at Kato Symi no later than the ninth century BCE.[91]

Although there is evidence for continuity of cult at Kato Symi, there is not necessarily evidence for continuity of deities revered. At least one god, possibly associated with hunting, is present at the site from the Middle Minoan

---

90. Böhm 1990: 134.

91. In the seventh century more female images appear that are Daidalic in style. One of these shows typical Levantine/Daidalic goddess iconography (of the so-called Aštart-type) and has her hands by her thighs, pulling back her skirts to reveal her genitalia (see fig. 3h) (Lebessi 1972: plate 190γ). Another, similar figurine shows a Daidalic-style female holding a small child to her chest, suggesting, according to Lebessi, that at Kato Symi Aphrodite was worshipped as a *kourotrophos*, a theory that she believes meshes well with the probable male initiatory use of the sanctuary (*ibid.,* 201-2. Lebessi 1973: 198).

    Once again, though, caution must be used when considering the correlation between these images and Aphrodite, for, as with the ninth/eighth-century idols discussed above, these images also appear throughout the Greek world, found both in mortuary and religious settings, not necessarily associated with Aphrodite (Böhm, *passim.*). Four of the oldest of these, ivory renderings of a nude female standing erect with arms at the sides and wearing a *polos* headdress, come from Tomb 13 in the Athenian Kerameikos. These date to 735-720 BCE (*ibid.,* 156-57). In the religious context,

Fig. 3h
Daidalic mould made plaque from Kato Symi.
Lebessi, 1972, pinax 190 g.

as with the ninth/eighth-century versions, these figurines mainly come to light in the sanctuaries of goddesses, notably Athena at Gortyn, Hera on Samos, Artemis at Sparta and Ephesos, Eileithyia at Lato and Inatos, and Aphrodite at Kato Symi and Axos (*ibid.*, 134–35). These date from the mid- to late-eighth century down to the last quarter of the seventh century, when the style disappears from the Greek repertoire.

These later images have many attributes in common with the earliest idols, such as the one from Kato Symi. The most important elements are the nudity of the females represented (although in later versions they occasionally wear a skirt that is pulled back to reveal the genitalia, thus adding emphasis to that aspect of the image) and the positioning of the arms. There are four poses from the ninth through seventh centuries: (1) arms hanging straight down the sides of the body; (2) arms curved to the body with hands holding the breasts; (3) hanging arms with hands at the genitalia (the pulling back of the skirt appears to be a combination of this and the first type); and (4) images with one hand holding a breast, the other indicating the genitalia. One style that exists only in the earliest phase of these images' existence shows the figurine with arms stretched out forward, as is the case with the example from Kato Symi. As we will see in Chapter Eight, this iconography derives from a Near Eastern prototype, originally most common in the regions of northern Syria, especially in the Orontes valley, that spread to encompass the entire Levantine coast and Egypt. (Badre 1980: *passim*). I disagree here with the interpretation of S. Böhm, who claims that whereas the first and fourth types are Near Eastern in origin, the second and third derive from Minoan/

period, although there are arguments against this god being identified as Hermes during the earliest periods. The evidence for a goddess may be inferred from the feminine images that begin to appear in the Protogeometric period, although, once again, there is no clear evidence to indicate that this was specifically Aphrodite. The Greeks, at some point between the Late Bronze Age and the Archaic Age, may have assimilated the local divinities of Kato Symi

---

Mycenaean proto-types. Whereas similar arm positions did exist in the Minoan/ Mycenaean repertoire, full nudity usually did not, while, likewise, there is a several-century gap between the last of the Aegean versions and these of the Geometric Age. Furthermore, all of these positions are prevalent in the Near Eastern models. The distinctively Greek traits of the Kerameikos figurines indicate that they were made by Greeks as early as the second half of the eighth century BCE (Böhm 1990: 24–27), while Syrian, Egyptian, and Cypriot imports continued to be used at cult sites such as Samos, Kato Symi, Inatos, Lindos, and Kamiros (ibid., passim).

Böhm, in her work on the nude goddess, argues that these images sometimes represent mortal women, especially those that wear the polos, and other times represent goddesses, such as those standing atop lions. When found in graves they are washabti figurines, such as those discovered at the Kerameikos, whereas at sanctuaries they indicate the wishes of the dedicators for children. So, she argues, must one interpret the pointing to the breasts and genitalia (ibid., 134–41).

The problems here are numerous. In identifying many of the figures that come from either funerary or sanctuary contexts as exclusively representations of mortal women, Böhm denies the clearly divine iconography that many of these images possess. While the Greeks did occasionally bury their dead with creature comforts for the next life, such as swords, pottery, and jewelry, neither the evidence from graves nor our current knowledge of the Greek understanding of the afterlife make it likely that substitute wives were buried with the dead (with the possible exception of Polyxena and Akhilleus). The fact that the early female figurine from the tomb at Merenda was buried with a child certainly argues against a washabti interpretation (Böhm 1990: 149, "Kinder Grab 19").

None of the images is of a pregnant woman, an argument against their being votives intended to ask for pregnancy. Another argument is that Athena, Hera, and Aphrodite were not invoked in matters of pregnancy or birth, only Artemis and, later, Asklepios (Demand 1994: 87ff.). Finally, as per the evidence of admittedly later healing shrines, only the part of the body specifically concerned was rendered on the votive, thus eyes for eye problems, ears for ear problems, and, in this instance, breasts for problems with lactation. Of interest here is the shrine of Aphrodite just outside of modern Athens on the way to Daphni and Eleusis, where votive vulvae were discovered within the rock depressions. Entire bodies dedicated to non-fertility-oriented goddesses simply cannot be interpreted as wishes for pregnancy.

I would argue instead that these images have the symbolic meaning of the "Other" and that they embodied Greek conceptions of the exotic. As goddesses specifically were not represented in the nude in Greek art until the fourth century BCE (starting, significantly, with the Knidian Aphrodite), it is evident that a nude goddess image was quintessentially non-Greek. Their presence in tombs and as votives probably conferred a certain élite status to the deceased or the dedicant, indicating her/his access to such exotic items.

with new deities: Hermes and Aphrodite, who may have shared common traits with the original Minoan pair. It is impossible to know when this assimilation took place, or even if both occurred simultaneously.

Conclusions

Based on the current evidence, a number of solutions to the chronology question may be posed. One might argue that Aphrodite did not yet exist in the Aegean during the Bronze Age, but rather entered the Greek pantheon in the early Iron Age. This would be supported by Aphrodite's absence from the Linear B tablets and the infrequency with which Aphrodite-type iconography appears in the Bronze Age Aegean record, an absence made all the more startling by the presence of the gold-foil images from Mycenae, which prove that such iconography was not unknown. Or, one might argue that Aphrodite was present in the Bronze Age Aegean, based on the images from the Mycenaean shaft graves and the birds bedecking the goddess-with-upraised-arms in Crete and, later, Greece. Or, there is the possibility that a goddess of Minoan Crete was assimilated into a new or different goddess in the Iron Age, and this goddess became known as Aphrodite.

This study suggests that at least some elements of the later Greek Aphrodite were present already in the Bronze Age Aegean. This is evident especially in the "nude/bird"-goddess iconography. This character raises two questions:

(1) Was this goddess Minoan or a Mycenaean goddess introduced into the divine repertoire in Crete?

That the goddess in question was, in fact, Minoan and not Mycenaean is supported by three data. The first two are obvious. The sanctuary of Kato Symi, the oldest known sanctuary of Aphrodite in the Greek world, predates the Mycenaean invasion of Crete.[92] Likewise, the majority of the nude-goddess iconography comes from Crete, as does the bird-goddess iconography.

The third datum comes from the evidence of the Linear B tablets. Although Aphrodite herself does not appear in the Linear B corpus, the evidence concerning the Mycenaean versus Minoan divine names that does appear, especially at Knossos, suggests that the Cretans, when they did adopt Mycenaean deities, were more likely to adopt gods than goddesses. This is expressed most clearly in R. Hägg's essay on religious syncretism at Knossos, wherein Hägg compares the deities listed in the Linear B tablets who were worshipped in Crete *and* the mainland to those who were only worshipped in Crete *or* the mainland (data from Knossos, Khania, Pylos, Mycenae, and Thebes).[93]

---

92. Although, once again, it is possible that a new goddess or deities in general may have been introduced into Kato Symi at any point up to the historic period.

93. Hägg 1997: 165.

Hägg notes that the deities shared by both geographic areas are Poseidon, Zeus (Diktaios in Knossos), Ares, Dionysos, Diwya, and Marineus.[94] Save for Diwya (the later Greek Dione), all are male deities. By contrast, the majority of deities worshipped exclusively in Crete were female: Atana Potnija (Lady Athena?), Potnija Dapuritojo (Lady of the Labyrinth), Pade, Qeraija, Pipituna, Eleuthia (Eileithyia?), and Erinus (the Furies?), along with two male divinities: Enyalios and Paiwon (later assimilated into Ares and Apollo respectively). Several more familiar deities were worshipped exclusively on the mainland (e.g., Hera, Artemis, Hermes), including male and female deities.[95] It would appear that whereas a few gods and one goddess passed from the mainland into Cretan cult practice, the majority of the deities were exclusively Cretan or mainland—Cretan goddesses remained entrenched on Crete and mainland goddesses remained in Greece. As the majority of the evidence suggests that an Aphrodite-style goddess was revered in Crete more so than in Greece, it would stand to reason that this goddess was Minoan rather than an adopted Mycenaean.

(2) Was this goddess Aphrodite, a contributing factor to Aphrodite, or did she have nothing to do with the evolution of Aphrodite?

Can one say that this "nude/bird" goddess was, indeed, Aphrodite, i.e., a deity who evolved directly into the Greek goddess of sex with or without minimal influences from the outside world? I am inclined to say "no." Although the iconography and the continuity of cult at Kato Symi may argue in favor of a Bronze Age Aegean Aphrodite, there are too many ambiguities with both sources of evidence. The nude goddess of the Minoan iconography is a rarity, especially in contrast to the strong prevalence of the goddess-with-upraised-arms, who plays such a significant role in Cretan iconography and religion (and later in Mycenaean and even Cypriot iconography and religion; see Chapter Six). Of the two instances (the gold-foil images from Shaft Grave III) in which the nude goddess is depicted with birds, it cannot be denied that: (1) works of art are subject to considerable foreign influence, especially Levantine, thus not necessarily entirely Aegean in conception; and (2) these items are pieces of decoration on clothing, and are not necessarily "icons" in their own right. One cannot easily argue for the presence of an erotic bird-goddess in the Bronze Age Aegean repertoire, which would have offered the best iconographic evidence for Aphrodite. The role of the nude females in the glyptic is likewise ambiguous. It is only the nude female figurine from Knossos that may offer unambiguous evidence for an eroticised goddess in the Minoan pantheon. She is nude, draws attention to her breasts with her arms, sits on

---

94. *Ibid.*
95. *Ibid.*

a throne, and was discovered in the context of a shrine. One very crudely rendered image, then, is the main iconographic evidence for Aphrodite in the Bronze Age.

Also the evidence from Kato Symi is not unequivocal. There is evidence for cult continuity at the site since Middle Minoan times. There is, however, little evidence concerning the deities worshipped there before the Archaic Age. The greatest continuity at the site is the continued use of animal imagery, libation vessels, and prominence of cult site. All of these aspects are common to almost all Aegean sanctuaries, however, and offer little practical information about Kato Symi *per se*. Furthermore, the evidence of the Linear B tablets, especially in light of Hägg's analysis of Minoan-Mycenaean religious syncretisms, suggests that Hermes, by that name, was worshipped primarily on the mainland (Pylos and Thebes), not on Crete.[96] Perhaps, rather than Hermes, an alternate, Minoan god was revered at Kato Symi, a god associated with hunting.

Concerning a female deity at Kato Symi, unlike most other Minoan sanctuaries, the usual iconographic motifs associated specifically with goddesses are mostly absent. There are no snakes, birds, or goddesses with upraised arms at the site. The evidence for a goddess at Kato Symi is, therefore, rather slight, and no evidence whatsoever is available to suggest what type of goddess she may have been had she existed (e.g., snake- or bird-goddess). In short, there is no good evidence to suggest that either Hermes or Aphrodite was originally worshipped at Kato Symi, while the Linear B evidence does suggest that Hermes was not worshipped there. As there is evidence against the hypothesis that Hermes and Aphrodite were the original deities of Kato Symi, the use of the site as evidence for the cult of Aphrodite in the Bronze Age Aegean also becomes less secure.

In the end, I would argue that the Minoans, but not the Mycenaeans, were amenable to an eroticized goddess, possibly even one associated with birds. This amenability probably facilitated the eventual adoption of Aphrodite in Crete and ultimately may have contributed some Aegean influence to her character. Nevertheless, the paucity of evidence suggests that the nude Minoan goddess did not evolve into Aphrodite on her own.

---

96. *Ibid*. Unlike the deities Paiwon and Apollo and the deities Enyalios and Ares, there are no specifically Cretan gods mentioned in the Linear B corpus who come to be associated, even merged, with Hermes.

IV.
THE CULTS OF APHRODITE

The purpose of this survey is to find the earliest evidences of Aphrodite throughout the Iron Age Greek world, following last chapter's consideration of the Bronze Age evidence. For every site considered, only the earliest traces are here recorded and, for the sake of practicality, I have only included arti-factual testimonia earlier than the Classical Age. As such, much of the Greek world does not appear in this survey and the reader will notice that although I include Asia Minor and Magna Graecia in this section, there is little mention of these eastern and western parts of the Greek world, save for Naukratis, Samos, Lesbos in the east, and a small handful of sites in the west (see below). These lacunae are due to the absence of any testimonia to early cult practice rendered to Aphrodite in these regions.[1]

Greek Mainland

Kythera

According to all the ancient literary accounts, the first place where the cult of Aphrodite obtained a foothold on Greek soil was the island of Kythera, ten kilometers off the coast of the Peloponnese. The four primary testimonia come from Hesiod, Herodotos, and Pausanias:

First among the holy Kytherians
she drew near, thence she went to sea-girt Cyprus,
and the reverend fair goddess walked forth, and about
her slender feet grass sprung forth.

Hesiod, *Theogony*, 192-205.[2]

And when they [the Skythians] appeared in Syro-Palestine, Psammetikhos, the King of Egypt, entreating them with gifts and prayers dissuaded them from proceeding farther. Then they, heading back again, appeared in the city Ashkalon of Syria; the majority of the Skythians passed by unharmed, but some of them, seizing the sanctuary of Aphrodite Ourania, plundered it. This is the sanctuary, as I discovered through inquiry, (which is) the oldest of all the sanctuaries of this goddess; for the sanctuary of Cyprus originated there

---

1. For a broader examination of the cults of Aphrodite throughout the Greek world, see Pirenne-Delforge 1994: *passim* for the cult of the goddess on the Greek mainland; Simon 1986: *passim* for Eastern associations; and Schindler 1998: *passim* for Magna Graecia.

2. See Appendix B 2.14.

(Ashkalon), as the Cypriots themselves say, and as for the one among the Kytherians, the Phoenicians are its founders, who are from Syria too.

Herodotos, Bk. I, 105.[3]

Nearby is a sanctuary of Aphrodite Ourania. It was established that the first people to revere Ourania were the Assyrians, and after the Assyrians the Paphians of Cyprus and those of the Phoenicians who dwell in Ashkalon in Palestine; Kytherians worship her having so learned from the Phoenicians.

Pausanias 1, XIV, 7.[4]

Kythera is about ten stades inland from Skandeia. The sanctuary of Ourania, the most holy and sacred, is the most ancient of all the sanctuaries of Aphrodite among the Greeks. The goddess herself is represented by an armed *xoanon*.

Pausanias 3, XXIII, 1.[5]

In his testimony, Herodotos strongly suggests that the cult of Kytherian Aphrodite was the earliest in Greece, and this cult likewise earned the description ἀρχαιότατον from Pausanias. According to the testimonia, it was the Phoenicians, acting as religious intermediaries between Assyria and the Greeks, who first established the sanctuary of Aphrodite Ourania on the island. The connections between Kythera and the Phoenicians are maintained by others authors as well, such as Xenophon, who, in his *Hellenica*, IV, 8, 7, claims that Kythera contained a bay named Phoinikous;[6] and Stephen of Byzantion, who stated that the island was named after its eponymous founder, Kytheros son of Phoinikos.

Contrary to the literary evidence, it is the Cretans, not the Phoenicians, who are attested in the archaeology on early Kythera. The island was originally inhabited by a population who used Early Helladic pottery. In the EM II period this Helladic pottery is replaced by Minoan wares, which remained the dominant pottery on the island through Late Minoan / Intermediate Bronze.[7] Thus, it is clear that Kythera became a Minoan colony, with the Minoans using the site as a port-of-call on the way from Crete to the Peloponnese.[8] Further-

---

3. See Appendix B 4.1.

4. See Appendix B 1.3.

5. See Appendix B 2.15.

6. Of course, it is entirely possible that the association between Kythera and φοῖνιξ has more to do with the island's extensive involvement in the purple-dye industry since Bronze Age times (see Huxley in Coldstream and Huxley 1973: 33–41) than with the Iron Age Phoenicians. Nevertheless, Markoe 1998: 237 sees this as evidence of some early contacts with the Levant.

7. Coldstream and Huxley 1973: 291.

8. *Ibid.,* 35–36.

more, as Sakellarakis discovered, there was at least one peak sanctuary of Minoan type on the island, providing evidence of the transmission of religious ideas.[9] The Minoan colony abandoned the settlement at Kastri on Kythera at the end of Late Minoan / Intermediate Bronze (c. 1450, as most Minoan colonies did in the face of the rival Mycenaeans), and excavators found "no trace of any structures dating from the century immediately following."[10]

Beyond direct relations with Crete, Bronze Age Kythera seems to have had at least superficial contacts with the Near East and Egypt. A vase inscribed in hieroglyphs with the name of the Sun Temple of the Fifth-Dynasty Pharaoh Userkaf (2494–2487 BCE) comes from Kythera, although it is possible that this import came from Egypt via Crete.[11] Likewise, a cuneiform inscription, unfortunately now lost, of Naram-Sîn, king of Eshnunna, is said to have come from a tomb near Kastri (the ancient city of Kythera).[12] This inscription dates from the First Dynasty of Babylon (c.1792 BCE):[13]

> To Mišar
> The land of Dur-Rimuš
> Naram-Sîn,
> son of Ipiq-Adad ...
> for his life ...

It is unlikely that a Mesopotamian king dedicated a votive so far from his homeland. It is far more likely that this small item arrived in Kythera as some sort of souvenir or trinket belonging to the grave inhabitant.[14]

Finally, a column dating from the time of Amenhotep III (c. 1400 BCE) lists several place names, presumably associated with the Ahhijawoi (Mycenaeans). On the front/right are the names of Crete and Rhodes, and on the reverse/left of the column are Amnisos, Phaistos, Kydonia, Mycenae(?), Messenia, Nauplia, Kythera, Ilios, Knossos, Amnisos, and Lyktos.[15]

Whereas Kythera's Bronze Age links to the East are archaeologically visible, those links cease to show up in the Late Bronze/Early Iron Age, precisely when the Phoenicians began their voyages throughout the Mediterranean. Concerning the Phoenicians and the archaeology of Kythera in the Dark and

---

9. No full publication or preliminary publication is yet available.

10. Coldstream in Coldstream and Huxley 1973: 303.

11. W.S. Smith, *CAH* (2), vol. I, ch. XIV: 38.

12. E.F. Weidner 1939: 137–38.

13. Wu 1994: 85. See Appendix B 4.2.

14. That the object in question was in fact originally a votive is evident in the inscription itself, which is dedicated to a god (*ana* [d]DN ...) and contains the standard request "for his life" (*ana balāṭišu*).

15. Cline 1987: 3.

early Archaic Ages, Huxley notes that the supposed Phoenician founders of the cult of Aphrodite mentioned by Herodotos are archaeologically invisible. Of course, it is not possible to argue convincingly *ex silentio* that there were no Phoenician settlers on Kastri (or Kythera in general) during this period. But it may be better to suggest that if there was Phoenician influence on the island in the Geometric and Archaic Ages, it came from trading, not settlement, and that trading may have been in perishable items such as wool and foodstuffs. Only in this way could the excavators reconcile the reports of Herodotos with the (lack of) archaeological evidence.[16]

It is impossible to determine the role of the Phoenicians in the establishment of Aphrodite's sanctuary on Kythera, since the sanctuary has not yet been excavated. Furthermore, as Huxley states, the critical period of time, from twelfth through eighth centuries, shows no signs of settlement at the ancient city of Kastri (once again, though, no such information is yet available for the site of the sanctuary itself). In any event, if Kythera was an early sanctuary of Aphrodite, this cult could have come from many different regions, Near Eastern, Egyptian, Minoan.

Some would argue that Aphrodite has no real historical relation with the island at all. This is predominantly based on the linguistic difficulties raised by the fact that the island itself is Κύθηρα whereas the epithet of the goddess is Κυθέρεια, with no reasonable explanation for the *eta* becoming *epsilon* or vice versa. One possible explanation is that the epithet does not, in fact, relate to the island, but derives from an Indo-European root ghʷedh-/ghʷodh- "desire," "pray."[17] As such, the epithet "Kythereia" does not mean "Kytheran" but rather "Goddess of Desire."[18] The later association made by Hesiod, Herodotos, and Pausanias with Aphrodite and the island were merely attempts to make sense of the epithet, which, apparently by the time of Hesiod, had lost its meaning in Greek.[19]

Argos and the Argolid

> The *xoana* of Aphrodite and Hermes, which they say one is the work of Epeiros, the other a votive offering of Hypermnestra. For Danaos brought her to court, she being the only one of his daughters to neglect his command, and

---

16. Coldstream and Huxley 1973: 36.

17. Morgan 1978: 118ff.

18. *Ibid.,* 120.

19. There are two problems with this theory. First, Aphrodite would, from earliest times, have had an Indo-European epithet, which is unlikely *as per* the argument that Aphrodite herself is not Indo-European (see above). Furthermore, one would expect to find clearer cognates to the epithet with offered meaning elsewhere in the Greek language, whereas it clearly had no close parallel in Greek as early as the writings of Hesiod, otherwise he would not have had to "invent" a meaning relying on the island of Kythera.

the deliverance of Lykeos bringing danger to him, and because her not taking part with her sisters in his plan increased his disgrace. Being tried among the Argives she went free and there dedicated Aphrodite Nikephoros.

Pausanias 2, XIX, 6.[20]

Above the theater is a sanctuary of Aphrodite; before the chamber is an engraved stele of the lyric poet Telesilla. Books are cast there at her feet, while she looks at a helm she holds in her hand and is about to put upon her head.

Pausanias 2, XX, 8.[21]

The (road) to Mantineia from Argos is not the same one that goes onto Tegea, but the one from the gates before the Deras Ridge. Upon this road is a double sanctuary, with an entrance to the west and another to the east. In the one lies a *xoanon* of Aphrodite, while in the direction of the setting sun is one of Ares. They say these are the dedications of Polyneikos and the Argives who fought as his allies to avenge his honor.

Pausanias 2, XXV, 1.[22]

Near the agora of Argos was a temple of Aphrodite, so identified through the writings of Pausanias and through numerous dedications to this goddess found at the site. Although excavations have shown that settlement at this site does go back into Middle Helladic times, there is a definite break between the Bronze Age settlement at Argos and the beginnings of cult practice at the site of this Aphrodision.[23] The cult, to judge from the chronology of the finds, goes back in time further than does the temple itself. Votive offerings in the form of pottery and animal and female figurines of both clay and lead are datable to the end of the seventh century BCE and are most abundant during the sixth and fifth centuries. Many of these were found underneath the architectural remains of the temple, and it is probable that a smaller, older structure was present there before the construction of the Late Archaic/Early Classical structure.[24] Daux has argued that the construction of the sanctuary does not appear to date back further than the middle of the sixth century. If there was a cult building present at the site from the late seventh century, then it could have been no more than a simple oikos, isolated in a summary temenos.[25]

---

20. See Appendix B 4.3.

21. See Appendix B 4.4.

22. See Appendix B 4.5.

23. Daux 1969: 992. "C'est en revanche une period d'abandon extremement prolongée qui s'ouvre avec la destruction de l'habitat mycenien. La campagne de 1968 a en effet confirmé l'absence totale de vestiges des époques protogéométrique et géométrique. Le haut archaïsme même n'est pas representé."

24. *Ibid.*, 996.

25. *Ibid.*, 1002.

Hägg has offered a similar hypothesis regarding the Aphrodision of Argos, while noting that cultic activity in this region, which dates back to the eighth century, is associated only with Hera, Apollo, Athena, and Zeus.[26]

Other than at the Aphrodision itself, Pausanias mentions that there was a joint cult, or at least cult statues, of Aphrodite and Hermes located in the sanc tuary of Lykian Apollo (Pausanias 2, XIX, 6). It is now suggested that this joint cult took place in a small, square, divided architectural structure in the eastern city, wherein were discovered two turtle shells surrounded (ceremoniously?) with rocks.[27] One shell was discovered within each of the divisions of the structure, thus, perhaps separate dedications to both of the deities revered in the structure. One of the shells had four distinct holes drilled into it; Marchetti suggests that this shell was a lyre. As the lyre might be associated with both Apollo (who played the lyre) and Hermes (who invented it according to his Homeric Hymn), it would stand to reason, according to Marchetti, that this would be the perfect dedication to give to Hermes within the sanctuary of Apollo.[28]

If the turtle/lyre shell from the one compartment of the structure was a dedication to Hermes, who, then, would have been the recipient of the other shell? Marchetti argues that the other deity was Aphrodite, basing this asser-tion on the passage from Pausanias that links these two deities in cult at Apol-lo's sanctuary and the fact that Aphrodite, especially in her manifestation as Ourania, was associated with the turtle. This association comes predominant-ly through a sculpture of Aphrodite Ourania in Elis rendered by Pheidias, on which the goddess was depicted standing upon a turtle (Pausanias 6, XXV,1).[29] This image, though, is all that associates Aphrodite with turtles in ancient Greece, and in many respects Aphrodite was far less likely to have the turtle as an attribute than other deities, notably Hermes, Athena at Lindos (where 27 terra-cotta turtle shells were unearthed),[30] Apollo, Artemis, and even Hera at Aphaia.[31] Thus, although the shell, especially prepared to receive potential lyre strings as it was, serves as good evidence for a cult of Hermes in Argos, the potential of the joint cult is based more on the passage from Pausanias and similar joint cults of Aphrodite and Hermes throughout the Greek world than on an intrinsic association between Aphrodite herself and turtles. Nevertheless, the votives do allow for a reasonable theory as to the

---

26. Hägg 1992.

27. Marchetti 1993: 212.

28. *Ibid.*

29. Pirenne-Delforge 1994: 232–36.

30. *Ibid.,* 234.

31. Bevan 1988: *passim.*

location of both the statues of Hermes and Aphrodite mentioned by Pausanias and thus the sanctuary of Lykian Apollo.

According to the testimony of Pausanias, there existed a double sanctuary of Aphrodite and Ares outside of this city. No chronological information is available concerning this cult, as the sanctuary itself has not been discovered. However, Tomlinson sees this joint cult as evidence of a military aspect of Aphrodite at Argos and asserts that, at this city, Aphrodite was a war-goddess as well as a goddess of love. This might be seen in the joint cult and general relationship between Aphrodite and Ares; the previously mentioned statue of Aphrodite *Nikephoros* "Bringer of Victory," and a relief of the poet Telesilla, standing, arming herself before the sanctuary of Aphrodite by the theater.[32]

Troizen

There is a sanctuary of Aphrodite Akraia in Troizen, identified through the description of its location given in Pausanias 2, XXXII, 6. The remains of the sanctuary are located on a northern slope and include the remains of a *peri-bolos* wall and the temple itself, although no trace of the altar remains. The temple, identified as *in antis* and showing Archaic proportions, has been dated by the excavator–Legrand–to the mid-sixth century.[33]

Sparta and Lakonia

There is a sanctuary of Hera Hyperkheiria made according to an oracle when the Eurotas greatly overflowed their land. The old *xoanon* they call Aphrodite Hera; it has been held customary that mothers sacrifice to this deity upon the marriage of a daughter.

Pausanias 3, XIII, 8–9.[34]

Heading not much farther on is a small hill, upon which is an ancient temple and a *xoanon* of Aphrodite Armed. Of all the temples I know only on this one did they build a second storey–a temple of Morpho. Morpho is an appellation of Aphrodite, and she sits and bears a veil [upon her head] and fetters upon her feet. It is said that Tyndareus placed the fetters on her feet to symbolize by the bonds the faithfulness of wives to their husbands. For indeed the other story, that Tyndareus avenged himself upon the goddess, as the disgrace upon his daughters came from Aphrodite, I absolutely shall not admit; for indeed it was absolutely ridiculous to have made an image of cedar and to have given it the name Aphrodite so as to take vengeance on the goddess.

Pausanias, 3, XV, 10–11.[35]

---

32. Tomlinson 1972: 208–9. The theater is, as yet, undiscovered.

33. Bergquist 1967: 51; Pirenne-Delforge 1994: 181–82.

34. See Appendix B 4.6.

35. See Appendix B 4.7.

> To the left of the Bronze House they set up a sanctuary of the Muses, because
> the Lakedaimonians go out to their battles not by trumpet-call but rather to
> the tune of flutes and the stroke of lyres and kitherai. Opposite the Bronze
> House is a temple of Aphrodite Areia; the *xoana* are as old as any in Greece.
>
> Pausanias 3, XVII, 5.[36]

Whereas Pausanias is adamant in his belief that the cult of Aphrodite in
Sparta is of extreme antiquity, with one statue being "fettered" by Tyndareus
himself (the father of Helen of Sparta), and the *xoanon* of Aphrodite Areia
being among the oldest in Greece, the archaeological evidence is not well in
accord with the literary evidence. To date, none of the sanctuaries of Aphrodite in Sparta has yet been discovered and, thus, it is impossible to determine if they do, in fact, support Pausanias' claims. So far, only two archaeological shreds of evidence have come to light that speak of Aphrodite's cult
in Lakonia. The first, from the akropolis of Sparta, is an iron blade with a
bronze mid-rim bearing the inscription "Λύκειος ᾿Αρέ[f]ια[ι]." According to
Woodward, the first word is probably the name of the dedicator, and the second name, in accord with Pausanias 3, XVII, 5, is Aphrodite Areia, whose
shrine would have been near the find site, the "Bronze House" of Athena.[37]
Although the *digamma* suggests an early date for this inscription, its presence within a deity's name easily could cause it to remain "frozen" in epigraphic time; so it should not be used as a chronological criterion.[38]

Somewhat more helpful in determining the chronology of Aphrodite's cult
in Lakonia are the remains of a temple discovered within a cowshed in the
region of Dichova. Here, near the remains of what appears to have been a
Roman villa, were discovered scattered about several Doric column capitals
of "exceptional quality" and of a style that suggests a Late Archaic construction.[39] In the same context as these column capitals were the remains of an
inscription, possibly part of a votive offering, which reads "FIOΣT / EΦANOI
᾿ΑΦΡΟΔΙΤΑΙ" "Violet-Crowned Aphrodite."[40] According to E.I. Mastrocostas,
the inscription dates to around 500 BCE,[41] although G. Saunders suggests that
the date might be closer to 525 at the latest.[42] In either case, the inscription
suggests quite strongly that the Archaic sanctuary in question was dedicated
to Aphrodite.

---

36. See Appendix B 4.8.

37. Woodward 1928–30: 252–53. *SEG* XI, 671.

38. Buck 1928: 45, #53; *SEG* XI, 671.

39. Delivorrias 1968: 153.

40. *Ibid.*

41. Mastrokostas 1970: 427–28.

42. Personal communication.

Once again, as with Argos (and to a certain extent with Kythera), Aphrodite is presented in Sparta as a goddess with militaristic leanings, both in her association with Ares (insofar as she is worshipped as Aphrodite Areia), and as her cult *xoanon* portrays her as armed.

Corinth

> Going up to Akrocorinth is a temple of Aphrodite; the statues are: Aphrodite armed, and Helios and Eros with a bow.
>
> Pausanias 2, V, 1.[43]

Aphrodite is the city goddess and chief protectress of Corinth, watching over the city from her sanctuary on the peak of Akrocorinth. According to Pausanias, she acquired this τιμή from Helios, who was the first lord of Akrocorinth, having been allotted the territory by Briareos during a dispute over the land with Poseidon, who for his own share received the Isthmos.[44] It is possible that within this anecdote lies the history of the religious development of Corinthia from the Protogeometric era.[45] Evidence of cultic activity in the Isthmian region goes back to the tenth century BCE, showing evidence of drinking ritual and a bull cult.[46] This evidence, along with the evidence of the later Isthmian games in honor (at least partially) of Poseidon, suggests that the Isthmian region was sacred to Poseidon from earliest times. Although physical evidence of a cult of Helios does not exist on Akrocorinth, the physical milieu does make the location ideal for the veneration of a solar deity, whose presence in Greece must go back at least to the arrival of the Indo-Europeans, if not to the earliest inhabitation of the land. Helios handing over Akrocorinth as a gift to Aphrodite provides a convenient, mythic explanation for the later replacement of the sun-god by the sex-goddess.

It is possible that historical/political events can help in dating the arrival of Aphrodite at Akrocorinth. According to a theory presented by Williams, the cult of Aphrodite as the patroness of the city could hardly have occurred before the city itself existed as a unified political entity, thus, not before the *synoikismos* of Corinth. This event probably occurred in the eighth century BCE, as determined by archaeological data from the city graves. In the mid-eighth century, the small "family plot" burials around the city were consolidated into a new, common burial ground in the lower plain below the city, and the North Cemetery came into common usage.[47] Thus, one possible date for the introduction of Aphrodite's cult into Corinth is c. 750 BCE.

---

43. See Appendix B 2.17.

44. Pausanias, II, 1, 6, and II, 4, 6.

45. Pirenne-Delforge 1994: 94.

46. Gebhard 1993: 3.

47. Williams 1994: 33–36.

An earlier date may be offered by the remains on Akrocorinth itself, the site of the goddess' sanctuary. Here, conical footed Protogeometric cups were discovered, which may have served as cult items or votives.[48] The temple was originally constructed at the end of the seventh century, to be replaced by a somewhat more elaborate version in the fifth century.[49] It would appear that Aphrodite was worshipped on Akrocorinth at least since the seventh century as Aphrodite Hoplismene, the city goddess of Corinth.

But was this goddess always Aphrodite? Williams notes that normally the ancient Greek *poleis* were protected by an armed Athena. Why in Corinth would it be an armed Aphrodite? Williams, as others, suggests that this break with tradition may be due to early Corinthian contacts with the Phoenicians. As the Corinthians saw their trading partners worshipping Aštart, they adopted this goddess in her perceived Hellenized form—Aphrodite.[50] As such, there is the possibility that the original city protectress of Corinth was, in fact, not Aphrodite, but perhaps some local deity. This local goddess was then assimilated into Aphrodite (Armed, as her *xoanon*) in the Archaic period.[51] While there may be evidence for a cult on Akrocorinth from Protogeometric times, there is also the possibility that Aphrodite was worshipped there continuously only from the eighth or seventh century.

The earliest iconographic evidence of an Aštart/Aphrodite cult in Corinth is a figurine of the seventh century BCE, with Daidalic hair, one hand on a breast and the other apparently indicating the genitalia[52] (see fig. 4a). Although such images do not necessarily refer to Aphrodite in the Greek iconographic repertoire, they often do indicate the cult of a female deity.[53] From nearby Perachora comes one other possible representation of Aphrodite dating to the seventh century. In this case, it is a clay plaque from the Heraion showing a bearded female rising from a bulbous "sack." The female has painted hair and eyes; the beard is rendered by painted dots on the cheeks. Both Payne, the excavator, and Williams have interpreted this image as the Hesiod-

48. *Ibid.,* 36.

49. Williams 1986: 21.

50. Williams 1994: 36–37.

51. If this hypothesis is true, it would offer an extremely interesting insight into early Greek conceptions of the goddess Aštart. Rather than seeing her as a sex goddess, vis-à-vis her identification with Aphrodite, as is common in later centuries, the Corinthians may have originally seen this goddess as she was known by the Phoenicians themselves, as a war goddess. See Chapter Eight below.

52. Davidson 1952: pl. 6, #85. No exact find spot is offered for this image, either in Davidson or in Jenkins, 1936. Davidson claims that the majority of such images derive from the Potters' Quarter, but does not mention this image specifically. See Davidson 1952: 12.

53. See above, Chapter Three, the section on Kato Symi.

Fig. 4a
Terra-cotta mold-made Aštart plaque.
Old Corinth Museum, Inv. 4039.

ic account of the birth of Aphrodite, showing the goddess emerging from the severed genitalia of Ouranos.[54] The beard is indicative of her hermaphroditic nature, strongly associated with Near Eastern connections. According to Williams, this plaque is dated Early Daidalic by style, probably to the second quarter of the seventh century.[55] Finally, there is also a fifth-century sherd inscribed in Corinthian epichoric script with the name "Aštart."[56] This might offer support to Williams' theory that the cult of Aphrodite arose in Corinth due to Phoenician influence.

We have discussed the three sites in ancient Greece where Aphrodite was portrayed as armed in her cult statues: Kythera, Sparta, and Corinth. In no case is the original armed version of the goddess preserved, and it is impossible to know the original purpose and portrayal of the armed Aphrodite.[57]

54. Payne 1940: 231–32; and Williams 1986: 14.

55. Williams 1986: 14.

56. *Ibid.,* 12.

57. They may have been similar to the terra-cotta "Armed Aphrodite" from Mannella in Italy. See below.

In fact, it appears that these images confused even the ancients, as Roman
school boys were asked why the statue of Lakedaimonian Aphrodite was
armed.[58] Although Aphrodite took part in a tradition of bearing weapons in
the Greek iconography, it was not a common, or even necessarily compre-
hensible, practice. The later rendering of these images, as preserved at
Corinth, portrayed the goddess not bearing arms in a belligerent or threatening guise, but in the nude, admiring herself in the inner mirror of the
shield.[59] By Roman times, the nude Venus surrounded by winged Erotes
"playing" with the weapons of Ares was a common artistic motif.[60] Thus,
while Aphrodite is presented as an armed goddess at some of her earliest places of worship, it is, as yet, not possible to do a thorough analysis of the meaning of that specialized iconography, except for how it was interpreted later
by the Roman populations, where the arms were seen as belonging to Ares/
Mars, merely serving as toys for Aphrodite.

Sikyon

> This *peribolos* indeed furnished such things of note; by it is another sanctu-
> ary, of Aphrodite, in which the first statue is of Antiope. For they propose that
> [her] children were Sikyonians and through them that Antiope herself was
> one of them. After this is the temple of Aphrodite. Into this enters a woman
> "neokoros," for whom it is no longer permissible to visit a man, and a maiden
> having the office annually. The maiden is named "Loutrophoros." For the oth-
> ers, they stand seeing the goddess from the entrance and there make [their]
> prayers. Kanakhos the Sikyonian made this statue, and he also wrought the
> Apollo of Didyma in Milesia and the Ismenian Apollo in Thebes. The statue [of
> Aphrodite] is made of gold and ivory, bearing a *polos* on the head, and has in
> her one hand a poppy and in the other an apple.
>
>   Pausanias 2, X, 4–5.[61]

The temple and temenos of Aphrodite that Pausanias mentions have not
been discovered and, thus, no archaeological or chronological data can be
derived. That the original cult statue was rendered by Kanakhos, though, does
give evidence that the cult of the goddess existed at least since the Late Archaic period.

Some have theorized that Aphrodite's cult should have an early presence
in Sikyon due to that city's early contacts with Cyprus, and that in importing
Cypriot bronze they also would have imported Kypris. The origin of this the-

---

58. Quintilian, *Inst. Orat.*, II, 4, 26.

59. Williams 1986: 15.

60. For a general discussion of this motif, see D. Michaelides in *Engendering Aphrodite*,
    forthcoming.

61. See Appendix B 4.9.

ory lies with Stephanus of Byzantion, who claimed that "Golgoi" was "a city of Cyprus, named after Golgos the leader of the Sicyonians away from home."[62] Thus, he claims that Golgoi, an early site of the worship of Aphrodite on Cyprus according to Pausanias,[63] was a Sikyonian colony. This is highly unlikely. A more plausible scenario, suggested by Lippold, is that early metal trade between these two regions, Cyprus and Sikyon, led in later times to theories of a mother-daughter relationship between the two.[64] Gjerstad, in his article "The Colonization of Cyprus in Greek Legend," is even more adamant in his rejection of Stephanus of Byzantion's claims, arguing that it was only the common importance of the cult of Aphrodite between the two cities that caused later authors to speculate upon some manner of connection or relationship between them.[65]

Athens and Attica

Nearby is a sanctuary of Aphrodite Ourania. It is held that the first people to revere Ourania were the Assyrians, and after the Assyrians the Paphians of Cyprus and those of the Phoenicians who dwell in Ashkalon in Palestine; Kytherians worship her having so learned from the Phoenicians. Aigeus established [her cult] among the Athenians, believing himself to be without children—for at that time he had none—and his sisters in duress due to a curse from Ourania. The statue, existing in our day, is of Parian marble and the work of Pheidias. But there is a deme Athmoneos of the Athenians, which claims Porphyrion was king before Aktaios, and that he set up their sanctuary of Ourania. But what they say in the demes is not totally in accord with what they hold true in the city.

Pausanias 1, XIV, 7.[66]

When Theseus lead into one city the demes, he established the worship of Aphrodite Pandemos and Peitho. Now the old image no longer existed in my day, but those that did were not of the worst artists.

Pausanias 1, XXII, 3.[67]

Concerning the location they call the Gardens and the temple of Aphrodite, no word is said among them, nor about the Aphrodite that stands by the temple. For its form is quadrangular in the manner of the *hermai*; the inscription states that Ouranian Aphrodite is the oldest of those called the Fates. The stat-

---

62. Pirenne-Delforge 1994: 151.
63. Pausanias 8, V, 2–3.
64. Lippold 1923: 2530.
65. Gjerstad 1944: 121.
66. See Appendix B 1.3.
67. See Appendix B 4.10.

ue of Aphrodite in the gardens is the work of Alkamenes and one of the most noteworthy sights in Athens.

Pausanias 1, XIX, 2.[68]

And Philomon in "Brothers" narrated as well that Solon first set up in dwellings women for sale, due to the 'crisis' of the young men, and likewise Nikander of Kolophon in the third section of his *Kolophoniakon* relates that he (Solon) also was the first to set up the sanctuary of Aphrodite Pandemos from the revenues received from the house mistresses.

Athenaios XIII, 569, d.[69]

According to Pausanias, the cult of Aphrodite, both of Ourania and Pandemos, was established in Attica by the family of Theseus. It was Aigeus, Theseus' father, who established the worship of Aphrodite Ourania in Athens to assuage the wrath of the goddess, whereas Theseus himself founded the cult of Aphrodite Pandemos to commemorate his *synoikismos* of Attica. As Theseus is a character of the Greek Age of Heroes and, thus, would date back to Bronze Age times, it would seem that the literary evidence from Pausanias supports an ancient cult of Aphrodite in Athens.

However, the chronology of the cult of Theseus himself argues against this proposition, at least in the case of Aphrodite Pandemos. Although Theseus was recognized as a Greek hero, at least since the seventh century, when his exploits are represented on vase paintings and *pinakes*,[70] his role as the unifier of Attica becomes prominent only in the Late Archaic/Early Classical Ages. During this period of political development in Athens, two main trends stand out in the development of Theseus' story: (1) the glorification of Theseus by the addition of fresh deeds of personal prowess; and (2) his idealization as a patriot and national leader.[71] According to J. Neils, it is possible, if not probable, that Theseus became idealized in Athens at the end of the sixth or beginning of the fifth century BCE, when both the Alkmaionidai and Kimon associated Theseus with the glory of their respective families and with their roles in the elimination of the Peisistratids from the city.[72] This would accord well with the resurgence and renaissance of Theseus motifs in Attic vase painting beginning around 520 BCE.[73] At that time, there was special attention upon

---

68. See Appendix B 4.11.

69. See Appendix B 4.12.

70. Ward 1970: 25-33. See Neils 1981: Chapter Two for references to earlier representations of Theseus in the artistic corpus.

71. Ward 1970: 33.

72. Neils 1981: 148-51.

73. *Ibid.,* 144.

Theseus' role as the national leader who oversaw the creation of a unified Attica under the authority of Athens (Thucydides, *Bk. II*), which, in turn, led to
the introduction of Aphrodite Pandemos. If the foundation myth of Aphrodite
Pandemos is intimately tied with the story of Theseus' *synoikismos* and the
tradition of this *synoikismos* only dates back into the late sixth century at the
earliest, then Pausanias' evidence for Theseus and the implementation of Pandemos only dates back into the very Late Archaic Age.

This analysis of the Theseus version of the establishment of the cult brings
it closer chronologically to the alternate version of the foundation myth as
provided by Athenaios, who claimed that it was Solon, not Theseus, who
brought the cult of Pandemos to Athens. In this case, Solon erected the temple
of Pandemos from the funds received from the public brothels. As the archon-
ship of Solon is dated to the early sixth century, the literary evidence for the
earliest cult of Aphrodite Pandemos in Athens is not the Age of Heroes, but
the Archaic Age, not earlier than the 590s BCE.

While the literary evidence for the cult of Aphrodite Ourania technically
dates further back than that of Pandemos (established by Theseus' father, as
opposed to Theseus himself), the archaeological evidence does not support
this claim. The altar of Aphrodite Ourania, as identified by Camp, located in
the northwest corner of the Agora, may be dated only to *c.* 500 BCE on the basis
of pottery found *in situ* about the base of the altar and the use of Pentelic marble in its construction, which only came to be exploited around 490 BCE.[74]

No information can be drawn concerning the cult of Aphrodite in the Gardens who, according to Pausanias 1, XIX, 6, was worshipped by the Ilissos
river, as this sanctuary has not yet been discovered. The statue was sculpted
by Alkamenes, who lived in the mid-fifth century, but this gives no data concerning the age of the cult or sanctuary, as both could function without a cult
image. As for the Aphrodite *hermai* mentioned by Pausanias, their presence
in the Greek repertoire dates back only to the fourth century BCE[75] and, thus,
also offers no chronological data for the cult.

The shrine of Aphrodite and Eros on the north slope of the Akropolis offers
a similar date to that of the altar in the Agora. The earliest material at this site
dates back into the Early Bronze Age, continuing into the MBA when the nearby well within the body of the Akropolis was exploited. So, too, Mycenaean
pottery was present at the site, mostly in the fill discovered in the clearing of
the shrine.[76] All this material, located underneath the structure foundations,
antedates the building of the shrine in question. While the main walls of the
structure are of Roman date, at least one small supporting wall seems to date

---

74. Camp 1986: 57.

75. Delivorrias *et al.* 1984: #10.

76. Broneer 1932: 35.

back into the Late Archaic to Early Classical Age.[77] As such, this shrine, like
the altar of Ourania in the Agora, came into existence around 500 BCE.

The cult of Aphrodite in the Gardens, as seen in the shrine on the north
slope (possibly a "branch" of a more significant sanctuary elsewhere), brings
into question one difficulty in the chronology of the arrival of Aphrodite into
Attica: her role in the Arrhephoria. According to Pausanias,[78] there existed a
rite in Athens whereby two (or four) noble-bred girls between the ages of
seven and eleven were charged with the duty of carrying unknown objects
from the temple of Athena. "There is a *peribolos* in the city not far from the
[area] called of Aphrodite in the Gardens, and beyond this is an underground
passage; the maidens descend there."[79] Here they put down their burdens,
took up new, unknown objects, and brought these back to the Akropolis.
There has been much written as to where this shrine or sanctuary of Aphrodite in the Gardens might have been; one solution offered is that it was the
shrine of Aphrodite and Eros on the north slope.

Of greater concern for this study is the exact relationship between the rite
of the Arrhephoria and the cult of Aphrodite. Specifically, did Aphrodite play
a role in the Arrhephoria? Two pieces of evidence may suggest that Aphrodite
was, in fact, an integral part of the ceremony. One is the passage from Pausanias quoted in part above. The critical issue is the translation of the words
οὐ πόρρω, which may refer either to a region not far outside of the city (ἐν τῇ
πόλει), perhaps referring to the sanctuary of Aphrodite in the Gardens supposedly on the banks of the Ilissos,[80] or to the distance of the underground
passage from the *peribolos*, thus arguing for the shrine of Aphrodite and Eros
on the north slope.[81] However, it must be noted that Pausanias does not say
that the maidens stopped there, nor does this *peribolos* (or its personnel)
serve a function in the rite. Pointedly, Pausanias says that the maidens proceed
past the *peribolos* with their burdens. There is little, if anything at all, to suggest that either Aphrodite or her shrine are part of the ceremony beyond serving as a landmark in Pausanias' description.

The second piece of evidence is a vase fragment that shows, in the center,
a seated Aphrodite (identified by inscription), of whom only the upper body
now remains.[82] To the extreme left of the fragment stands a woman whose

---

77. *Ibid.*, 36. The early wall is designated γ–γ.

78. Pausanias, 1, XXVII, 3.

79. –ἔστι δὲ περίβολος ἐν τῇ πόλει τῆς καλουμένης ἐν κήποις ᾿Αφροδίτης οὐ
    πόρρω καὶ δι᾿αὐτοῦ κάθοδος ὑπόγαιος αὐτομάτη, – ταύτῃ κατίασιν αἱ
    παρθένοι.

80. Pirenne-Delforge 1994: 56.

81. *Ibid.*

82. Delivorrias *et al.* 1984: #1559.

hair is drawn up in a snood/scarf. She is holding some manner of branch or leafy growth. Between Aphrodite and this woman is a young girl who is throwing a ball. On the right side of Aphrodite all that remains is the hand of another girl, apparently about to catch the ball being thrown to her.[83] Langlotz identifies this scene as Aphrodite in the Gardens between the two Arrhephoroi. The identification as Aphrodite is established by the inscription. The specific identification as Aphrodite in the Gardens is based on the goddess' reclining posture, which Langlotz sees as indicative of this manifestation of the goddess; the foliage held by the other woman; and on the association with the Arrhephoroi based on Pausanias (for Pausanias claimed that the Arrhephoroi played ball on the Akropolis during their period of service).[84] However, there is nothing in the fragment that indicates that the scene takes place on the Akropolis, and therefore it does not provide a positive identification for the girls. There is, likewise, as discussed above, no unambiguous evidence that the *peribolos* of Aphrodite in the Gardens is on the Akropolis either. It is thus not possible to prove that the scene occurs on the Akropolis of Athens. As the setting is not certain, it becomes impossible to argue that the girls portrayed are the Arrhephoroi; certainly they are not the only girls in Greece to play ball. Furthermore, as one *pinax* from Locri Epizephyrii shows a young girl dedicating her ball to Aphrodite and Hermes (UM 39-26-3), it is entirely possible that there is another association between Aphrodite, young girls, and their toys. Therefore, there is no cogent reason to identify the girls as the Arrhephoroi or to assume that this scene indicates a link, close or otherwise, between the Arrhephoria and Aphrodite. As neither the literary nor iconographic evidence supports an association between Aphrodite and this ritual, one need not assume that the cult of Aphrodite in Athens is as old as, or related to, the Arrhephoria.

To date, then, our earliest extant evidence for the cult of Aphrodite in Attica, in all her various manifestations, dates back into the Late Archaic Age. If Solon did erect a shrine of Pandemos, then there is evidence to be dated to the early sixth century. Otherwise the current archaeological evidence dates predominantly to c. 500 BCE.

Thebes and Boiotia

> But to Ares
> Shield-piercing, Kythereia bore Phobos and Deimos
> Dread Ones, who drive forth the close-packed ranks of men

---

83. *Ibid.*, 152.

84. Langlotz 1953: *passim*, esp. 11.

in icy war with city-sacking Ares,
and Harmonia, whom high-spirited Kadmos took as a wife.

Hesiod (*Theogony* 933–37).[85]

There are *xoana* of Aphrodite in Thebes that are indeed so old that they say
they were dedications of Harmonia. They were made from the gunwales that
were made of wood for Kadmos' ships. They call the one Ourania, the other
Pandemos, and the third Apostrophia. Harmonia gave these titles to Aphrodite so: Ourania for love that is pure and separated from the body; Pandemos
for sexual intercourse, and third Apostrophia, because she turns the race of
humans away from illicit desire and inappropriate works. For Harmonia
knew of many such things among the barbarians, and as well endured among
the Greeks, such as later were sung about the mother of Adonis, and Phaidra
of Minos, and the Thrakian Tereus.

Pausanias 9, XVI, 3–4.[86]

These quotations from Hesiod and Pausanias are the sole literary evidence
that attests to the antiquity of the cult of Aphrodite in Thebes, although the
evidence from Hesiod speaks more concerning Aphrodite's daughter than of
the cult of the goddess herself. By contrast, the presence of *xoana* and the legend of their dedication at the hands of this Harmonia, according to the ancient
Greeks themselves, would date the cult back before the Age of Heroes, or, for
Symeonoglou in his work on the history of Thebes, back into EH III.[87] A somewhat more conservative estimate, based on the *xoana* and the tradition,
might place the cult back into the Archaic Age.[88] To date, there is no evidence
as to the age of the cult of the goddess from any architectural or artistic
remains. It is possible that a remnant of wall found in the east central part of
the Thebes might have been part of her temple, but even this dates back only
to the Classical Age and is, at the moment, unstudied and unsubstantiated.[89]
As such, it is impossible to determine how old the cult of Aphrodite is in
Thebes beyond the Archaic Age, if it does, indeed, extend further back.

For the rest of Boiotia, Schachter offers two pieces of evidence that may,
tentatively, be offered as evidence of a pre-Classical cult of Aphrodite. One is

85. See Appendix B 4.13.

86. See Appendix B 4.14.

87. Symeonoglou 1985: 78. This is his reckoning of the mythological time frame, and not
his chronology of the history of Thebes by modern standards.

88. "There are also reported to have been three very old statues of Aphrodite made of
wood, which may have been Archaic, although the existence of a sanctuary dedicated
to the goddess is not documented until later," *ibid.,* 109.

89. *Ibid.,* 127 and 299. Symeonoglou has this hypothesis as an oral communication from
the excavator K. Demakopoulou; further analysis of the wall has not yet been carried
out.

a fragment of Hesiod (fr. 70 M–W) that refers to the story of a boy named Argynnos, whose name becomes an epithet of Aphrodite in Argyneion and *Argounis/Argynnis*.[90] However, according to Schachter, this cult comes into prominence, if not existence, only at the end of the fifth century BCE. Thus, in spite of the Hesiodic reference, Schachter does not offer evidence for the cult of the goddess herself in pre-Classical times.[91]

Furthermore, Aphrodite received sacrifice on the great altar at Oropos, based on Pausanias 1.XXXIV.3 and *IG* 7.4253.[92] The cult of Amphiaraos (the deity of Oropos) dates back at least to the sixth century BCE[93] and, thus, if Aphrodite was worshipped at the altar since the creation of the sanctuary, this also may point to a pre-Classical cult of Aphrodite in Boiotia.

Crete

Kato Symi

Although this site is not noted by the ancient authors, it is possible that this is the oldest sanctuary of Aphrodite in the Greek world. Located in southeastern central Crete, the sanctuary was in use from Middle Minoan I until the Late Roman era, with the apex of the sanctuary's prosperity being in the seventh century BCE.[94]

Olous

In the modern hamlet of Sta Lenika is a temple of Aphrodite and Ares, which, on the basis of pottery and architectural style, can be dated to the Geometric, or possibly Protogeometric, Age.[95] Unlike the sanctuary at Kato Symi, this was a relatively poor, rural sanctuary, and votive offerings were few and uninformative.[96] However, the site might nevertheless be identified through inscriptions from the Roman Age, which identify the temple as τὸ ἀρ[χ]αίον Ἀφρ[ο]δισίον.[97] Further inscriptions reveal that the two chambers of the (later) temple were, in fact, used to house two separate deities, and that the other god revered at Sta Lenika was Ares.[98]

---

90. Schachter 1981: 36.

91. *Ibid.*

92. *Ibid.*, 26 and 37.

93. *Ibid.*, 19–26.

94. See above, pp. 57ff.

95. "De l'eschara provienne des tessons Proto-Géométriques, tandis que la chambre rectangulaire est qualifiée tout simplement de <<géométrique>>" (Renard 1967: 576–77).

96. Bousquet 1938: *passim*.

97. *ICr*, XVI, 5, 70 and 27, 8.

98. Bousquet 1938: 404.

Unlike the sanctuary at Kato Symi, it appears that the sanctuary at Sta Leni-ka was originally dedicated to only one deity to judge from its earliest, single *naos* structure (see fig. 4b) and its title: "the Archaic *Aphrodision*." Nevertheless, it is also possible that the original single structure was already dedicated to the two deities, much as the Athenian Hephaisteion was dedicated to both Hephaistos and Athena, and the early single-cella structure at the Samian Heraion accommodated both Aphrodite and Hermes (see below). As such, it would only have been with later reconstruction that both of the deities received their own "rooms," so to speak. However, in the absence of votive remains, it is impossible to determine if a male warrior deity was worshipped during the earliest phases of the temple, or was a later addition.

In 150 BCE, during a renovation of the structure, the orientation was realigned so as to face the sea instead of the mountains, which, according to

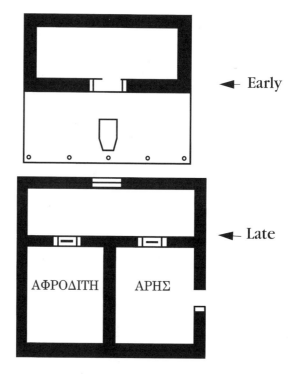

Fig. 4b
Plan of the sanctuary of Olous.
From J. Bousquet, *BCH* 62 (1938).

Bosquet, was to reorient the sanctuary with Hellenic Aphrodite as opposed
to the Minoan mother goddess, whose cult he sees continued in the structure
at Olous.[99] It is otherwise impossible to determine if the cult had previous,
Minoan antecedents. One Linear A [sic] symbol on a second-century BCE stele
is the only evidence of a Minoan presence or influence at the site.[100]

Axos Mylopotamou

Although not as old as the two previous Cretan sanctuaries of Aphrodite,
the temple dates back into the Late Archaic Age, and deserves inclusion in this
survey. The temple itself, as with the others on Crete, was constructed and
reconstructed in three phases: the Late Archaic, Classical, or possibly even
the Hellenistic, and Roman.[101] The earliest phases of the construction are
manifest in remains of porous material in the walls and a few scraps of inscriptions in the same material.[102] So, too, the proportions of the temple, approximately 15 m long by 6.5 m wide, with *pronaos*, *naos* and *opisthodomos*, suggest an early date of initial construction. The excavator, Halbherr, identified
the temple as belonging to Aphrodite through the votive figurines found at
the site, all portraying the goddess, which date from Late Archaic into Classical times. Levi claims that, in all probability, the figurines (as yet unpublished) belong to the cult of Aphrodite-Aštart.[103]

The Islands and the East

Lesbos

The evidence for the cult of Aphrodite from this island is entirely literary,
and, yet, more so than the other sites so far considered, the literary evidence
is valuable for its references to early architectural structures dedicated to the
goddess. The evidence comes from Sappho's poem II, wherein the poet
invokes the goddess:[104]

> Hither to me from Crete to this holy temple,
> Where is your beautiful apple grove
> And altars smoking with incense.
> Cold water gurgles through apple tree branches
> And the entire area is shaded by roses,
> And quivering leaves pour down deep slumber.

---

99. *Ibid.,* 393.

100. Roussel 1939: 275.

101. Levi 1930–31: 51.

102. *Ibid.*

103. Levi 1930–31: 50; although see problems with this interpretation in previous chapter.

104. See Appendix B 4.15.

Therein a horse-rearing meadow has blossomed with spring flowers,
The gales blow gently...
There indeed you, Kypris, take up...
In golden kylikes gracefully pour nectar
Mingled with (our) festivities.

As Sappho was born c. 612 BCE,[105] this poem (presumably written in Lesbos and not during the poet's exile in Sicily) indicates the presence of a temple of Aphrodite on the island of Lesbos no later than the early sixth century. With the lack of archaeological data, however, it is impossible to determine how much older than this reference the structure may be. Nevertheless, with Sappho we may assign a cult structure in an apple grove to Aphrodite no later than the early sixth century on Lesbos, possibly near the city of Mytilene.

Samos

As at Kato Symi, Aphrodite was worshipped in conjunction with Hermes in a temple located within the confines of the sanctuary of Hera on Samos. This is attested in fourth-century BCE inscriptions in which dedications of clothes to these deities are recorded.[106] Hermes may have had the more elaborate cult at the site, for there is a dedication from 346/45 BCE that records clothing dedicated to him that went to his own temple treasury, as well as to his image in the joint temple.[107] Thus, according to Buschor, around the middle of the fourth century there was not only a temple and treasury dedicated to Hermes, but also a double temple dedicated to Hermes and Aphrodite. Statues of Hermes were recorded in both of these.[108]

Until the Roman restructuring of the sanctuary, no building at the sanctuary was constructed later than the sixth century BCE, so the epigraphy and general archaeology provide a rough *terminus ante quem* for the date of the dual cult at the Heraion. Unfortunately, the sources are somewhat vague about the purpose of the different structures at the Heraion, as well as which of these units housed the cults of Aphrodite and Hermes and when. Buschor writes that, in the early sixth century, Rhoikos constructed two individual temples to Aphrodite and Hermes to the north of the great altar that they

---

105. Although any datum for the life of Sappho is debatable, there is one reference in Herodotos (2.134) that refers to the life of Rhodopis as being contemporary with the Pharaoh Amasis (568–526 BCE). Rhodopis was bought by Sappho's brother Kharaxos, and both were rather soundly condemned by Sappho for it. This is as close to contemporary evidence for the date of Sappho's life as is currently available.

106. Michel 1900: # 832.

107. Ohly 1959: 33ff.

108. Buschor 1957: 78.

shared with the temple of Hera.[109] It was only thirty years later, after the destruction of the "Rhoikos level" by flood, that a joint temple to the south of the complex was constructed and dedicated to Hermes and Aphrodite. By contrast, the *Princeton Encyclopedia of Classical Sites* claims that this larger temple, with peristyle and a row of columns along the cella axis, was the Rhoikos temple dedicated to Hermes and Aphrodite. Ultimately, we do not yet know what buildings served what purposes, other than the main temple to Hera and her altar.[110]

While a date at the end of the sixth century is probable for a *terminus ante quem* for the joint cult of Aphrodite and Hermes at Samos, based on epigraphy and archaeology, a more precise date of when the cult arrived and whether both deities were originally worshipped together cannot be determined. The fact that Hermes has both his own temple as well as the joint temple with Aphrodite may (or may not) indicate that he was worshipped here first, to be joined only later by the love goddess (as we shall see below, this may have a parallel in Italian Locri).

Miletos

In 1990, a Late Archaic temple was discovered in Zeytintepe (ancient Miletos), identified through numerous inscribed votives as dedicated to Aphrodite.[111] Whereas excavation of the sanctuary complex shows an early construction in the Late Archaic or early Classical period,[112] the votive terra-cottas date back to the seventh century BCE, as do the terra-cotta, pottery, faience, and metal votives discovered in the sanctuary's *bothros*.[113] Furthermore, at least one "Aštart plaque" was discovered at the site. Since they are present mainly in the Greek votive repertoire in the eighth to seventh centuries, this affords further evidence for cult practice at the Aphrodite sanctuary as early as the seventh century BCE.[114]

Beyond the pottery and terra-cotta votives, metal items were prominent at the sanctuary, including jewelry of bronze, lead, and precious metals, as well as *phiale*, a horse statue of bronze, a votive shield bearing the image of a pegasos, and (of particular interest for Aphrodite) a lead dove originally thought to have been in the hand of a female statuette.[115] The international

109. *Ibid.,* 80–82. There is no clear evidence, however, that Rhoikos was the architect or constructor, *contra* Buschor.

110. Kyrieleis 1981: 21.

111. Graeve 1995: 199 and Abb. 26; Senff und Heinz 1997: 116 and Abb. 2.

112. Heinz und Senff 1995: 220.

113. Graeve 1995: 199; Senff und Heinz 1997: 116.

114. Graeve 1995: 201 and Abb. 4.

115. Heinz und Senff 1995: 223.

popularity of the cult is manifest in the high number of foreign items discovered among the votives. Most prominent were Cypriot terra-cottas, Egyptian faience and stone sculptures, Attic black-figure pottery, Corinthian *aryballoi*, Chian pottery, and Lakonian ceramics.[116] A very high number of oil lamps of the "Punic" variety also came to light at the sanctuary, suggesting a popularity with the western Phoenician populations, as well as the Greek and Cypriot.[117]

Paros

The exact chronology of Aphrodite's cult on Paros is not clear. Although the possible remains of an altar have been found not far from the temenos of Eileithyia in the region of Kounados, its identification as constituting part of a shrine of Aphrodite is only tentative.[118] Furthermore, both the identification of the shrine and its chronology are based on two ambiguous inscriptions. The first of these (*IG* XII, 5, 219 = *SEG* XLII 769 #8) is clearly Archaic in date and is dated by Jeffery to 600–550 BCE. However, only the "ιτης" of the name remains, and so the identification with Aphrodite must remain speculative.[119] The second inscription (*IG* XII, 5, 184) is clearly the name of the goddess "Αφρωδιτη," but in more classically developed letters. In his article containing this inscription, Th. Olympios suggests that the inscription probably derives from an Archaic form, due to the unusual spelling of the goddess' name with an *omega* instead of an *omicron*,[120] a Parian idiosyncrasy datable to this period. However, as mentioned above in the section on Sparta, divine names are often "frozen," and older spellings remain in use long after the dialectical variations disappear (thus the continued use of the *digamma* in Lakonia). As such, while the use of an *omega* for an *omicron* on Paros dates to the Archaic period, it may not be used to date this inscription, which in all other respects appears Classical in date.

Nevertheless, Aphrodite was so prominent that, by the third century BCE, one of Zeus' epithets on the island was Ἀφροδίσιος.[121] This, potentially combined with the inscription from 600–550 BCE, offers some grounds for an early cult of Aphrodite on the island of Paros dating back to the beginning of the sixth century.

---

116. *Ibid.*, 223–24.

117. Graeve 1995: 201.

118. Berranger 1992: 83–84; Leekley and Noyes 1975: 49.

119. F. Hiller von Gärtringen 1902: 9–13.

120. Olympios 1877: 34, no. 31.

121. *IG*, XII, 5, 220.

Delos

Unlike Paros, there is no early evidence for the physical manifestation of a cult to Aphrodite on Delos. There are, however, two pieces of literary evidence of interest not only for their reference to the antiquity of Aphrodite's cult images on the island, but in their references to Crete as the point of origin for these images. According to tradition, as recorded by both Pausanias (9, XL, 3–4) and Kallimakhos (Hymn to Delos, ll. 307–13), it was Daidalos who originally carved the *xoanon* of Aphrodite for Ariadne, who took it with her when she fled Crete with Theseus. Having abandoned or lost Ariadne during his travels, Theseus, unable to bear seeing the statue, as it reminded him of his wife, dedicated it to Delian Apollo. Pausanias describes the image as being small, with a stump or box instead of feet, and a right hand worn away by time. Kallimakhos records that, even in his day, choruses of dancers danced about the image, decorating it with garlands, following in the footsteps of Theseus, who first led the dance about the altar. If such an image existed, it would indicate an old age for Aphrodite's cult on Delos. No speculations are possible in the absence of this datum, however, and we cannot draw any conclusions.

Naukratis

The sanctuary of Aphrodite at Naukratis was constructed on the virgin mud of the site and its earliest phase, of which there were three, dates according to the pottery sequence to the very end of the seventh century BCE or to the first decade of the sixth century. As such, this sanctuary, consisting of a *peribolos* wall, small temenos, and temple, was one of the earliest structures at Naukratis. The fact that it lies on virgin soil is evidence that the structure represented a new cult, as opposed to having been erected on the site of a previous shrine. The geographic specificity of the pottery finds as determined by the recent surveys of Naukratis by Coulson and Leonard serves to confirm that the area of the sanctuaries at Naukratis (including the Aphrodite sanctuary) is located on the earliest part of the city settlement.[122] Thus, at Naukratis there is an Archaic sanctuary constructed by the Greeks at or close to the time of earliest settlement of the city for the worship of their own goddess. This area of earliest settlement at Naukratis is now under water due to a rise in the Delta's water table and the presence of several canals in the immediate area, and no re-excavations of the Aphrodite sanctuary have been possible in recent years.[123]

While Herodotos (II, 178–79) credits the Milesians with the formation of the Naukratis trading station, modern scholarship credits the Chians with the erection of Aphrodite's temenos, due primarily to the large quantity of Chian

---

122. Coulson and Leonard 1982: 372.

123. *Ibid.,* 363.

pottery there, dating to the earliest phase of the temple (c. 600 BCE).[124] Nevertheless, this sanctuary of Aphrodite was clearly frequented by all the residents of Greek Asia Minor who had a stake in Egypt. Beyond the Chian ware, both Milesian and Lesbian ware are extremely well represented.[125] The inscriptions on the dedicated pottery are even more indicative of the goddess's devotees. In his study of the dedicatory inscriptions in *Naukratis II*, Gardner gives examples of two dedicators who identify themselves as Chian,[126] two who identify themselves as Tean,[127] and probably eight who come from Lesbos, two specifically from Mitylene.[128] Several of the dedicatory inscriptions use the epithet "Pandemos," thus, recognizing one of the goddess' more Greek manifestations and, probably, the pan-Hellenic/Pan-Ionian nature of the sanctuary itself.

The votive offerings, all smashed and strewn about the temenos, date predominately from the first phase of the sanctuary (600–400 BCE).[129] The grand majority of the votives are Cypriot terra-cottas, such as were common in East Greek sanctuaries in the seventh to sixth centuries, notably the Samian Heraion and the Athenaion at Lindos, and as well on Rhodes, Amrit, and Al Mina.[130] Gardner, noting the prevalence of Cypriot votives, originally argued for a strong Cypriot/Paphian element to the Naukratite Aphrodite, although in the light of more recent research showing the overall popularity of such terra-cottas in the Greek world, this must now be understood as a bit of an overstatement.

The votives consist of anthropomorphic figurines, either of males, occasionally in the guise of hunters with their game at their backs, or of females, usually standing with one hand at the chest, the other holding an object in front of the body.[131] Whereas Gardner identified the female votives as goddess images, Von Bissing argued that these votives must represent images of the dedicators, literally dedicating themselves to the goddess in the form of per-

---

124. Boardman 1980: 119.

125. Gardner 1888: 38–54.

126. *Ibid.*, 63–64, nos. 706 and 757.

127. *Ibid.*, 64–65, nos. 758 and 779.

128. *Ibid.*, 65, nos. 786–93. These inscriptions are distinctive both for their letter forms and for their distinctively Cretan spelling of "Aphrodite," using the Ἀφροδίτα form instead of Ἀφροδίτη. See Boedeker 1974: 13, esp. no. 1.

129. Venit reports on pottery from these early excavations dating back into the mid-seventh century BCE. Thus, it is possible that the beginning of the earliest phase of the sanctuary should be dated to 650 BCE (Venit 1988: *passim*).

130. Schmidt 1968: 113; Sørensen 1991: *passim*, especially chart LXIV.

131. Gardner 1888: 55–59 and Plates XIII–XV.

sonal statuettes.[132] He added, further, that the presence of male figurines precludes the possibility that these are images of Aphrodite and, thus, he claims,
even the female figures with the names of male dedicators are votives sent by
the proxy of a male relative or connection.[133]

The literary evidence, as supplied by Athenaios (*Deipnosophistai*, XV,
675f–76c), suggests that at least some of the female figurines may in fact have
been of Aphrodite. According to him:

> During the twenty-third Olympiad Herostratos, a citizen of ours, making use
> of trade and sailing about the various lands, arrived at Paphos of Cyprus, and
> purchasing a small idol of Aphrodite, a span in height and of old-fashioned
> craftsmanship, went bearing it to Naukratis. And while approaching Egypt a
> sudden storm fell upon him and he didn't know where on earth he was; all
> the sailors fled to the image of Aphrodite and besought her to save them. And
> the goddess (for she was friendly with Naukratis) of a sudden made the area
> before her full of fresh myrtle and a sweet scent filled the ship, while before
> those sailing despaired of safety being really sea-sick and retching profusely.
> And when the sun appeared they saw their anchorage and arrived at Naukrat-
> is. Herostratos set out from the ship along with the idol, and also bearing the
> miraculously appearing fresh myrtle; he dedicated them in the sanctuary of
> Aphrodite. He sacrificed to the goddess and dedicated the idol to Aphrodite,
> and summoning about the hearth of this sanctuary those who came with him
> and his closest neighbors, he gave them each a crown from this myrtle, which
> he then called "Naukratitis."[134]

That Herostratos purchased an idol of Aphrodite to dedicate at the sanctuary
suggests that the votives might have been understood as representing the
goddess herself. However, evidence from other Greek sanctuaries, such as at
Samos, may make it safer to argue that such feminine figures were merely
icons of feminine divinity, not specifically understood as Aphrodite (or as
Hera), except in the minds of the dedicators.

Magna Graecia

Taras

It would not be surprising to find Aphrodite revered in the daughter colony of Sparta, where, as has been discussed, she had an early cult. Excavations
at Satyrion at Taras have brought to light an urban sanctuary on the slope of
the acropolis, with votive material dating from the mid-seventh century.[135]

---

132. Von Bissing 1951: 64–65. This practice is actually quite common in the Near East,
     dating back to the early third millennium in Mesopotamia in such places as Eshnunna.

133. *Ibid.*

134. See Appendix B 4.16.

135. Schindler 1998: 147–48. A temple was constructed here in the fifth century, but this
     is too late for our consideration.

These votives include a number of terra-cotta female figurines, either seated
or standing, wearing a high *polos*, with arms outstretched; many resemble
Ionic prototypes.[136]

Although the votives themselves are too generic to identify the deity of
the sanctuary specifically, Aphrodite's presence is clearly indicated by an
inscription and a later gloss by Hesychius. Excavators discovered at the sanctuary a black-figure Attic amphora attributed to Exekias and datable to the mid-
sixth century. It was inscribed in a local Tarantine Doric dialect as: Λεοκρά-
τεια ἀνέθεκε τᾶι βασιλίδι "Leokrateia dedicated this to the Queen."[137] Although the "Queen" so indicated could technically be any goddess, Hesychius
informs us that at Taras Aphrodite specifically was worshipped as *Basilis*.[138]
The information from Hesychius combined with the dedicatory inscription
and the general continuity of finds at the site from the seventh century all indicate that Aphrodite was worshipped at Taras-Satyrion from the Archaic Age.

Locri Epizephyrii

There are three areas at this site for possible evidence of the early worship
of Aphrodite: The "Stoa ad U" at Centocamere, the "Sacello" at Marasa Sud,
and the Mannella sanctuary. The first two, 50 m apart and probably functioning together as a single cult site, date from the late seventh and late sixth centuries respectively. However, while these structures do extend back into the
relevant dates for this study, the epigraphic evidence indicates that Aphrodite
came to be the focus of cult attention here only in the mid-fifth century. Before
this, the evidence suggests that the Stoa ad U and the Sacello were dedicated
to Kybele, as is evident in a seventh- to sixth-century sherd inscribed: ... | ς
Χυβαλας. This sherd was discovered in a context of local imitations of Protocorinthian wares in the foundations of the sixth-century city wall near the
gate to the sanctuary.[139] By contrast, epigraphic and other evidence for a cult
of Aphrodite appear only from the early fifth century on, both on a skyphos
inscribed:]ΦΡΟΔΙΤΗΣ found to the east of the Sacello, and a limestone block
from the Sacello inscribed: Παντα[ρης] ανεθ[κε] Αφροδι[ται].[140]

The second major cult site to be associated with Aphrodite at Locri is the
extra-mural sanctuary in Contrada Mannella, located just outside the western
edge of the city's wall. As with the Stoa ad U, the date of early construction

---

136. *Ibid.*, 148.

137. *Ibid.*, 151, note 21.

138. Hesychius s.v. Βασιλίς: Παρὰ Ταραντίνοις δὲ καὶ 'Αφροδίτη Βασιλίς.

139. Schindler 1998: 167.

140. *Ibid.*, 169.

for the Mannella sanctuary has been determined by a gorgon antefix, datable to the late seventh or early sixth century.[141]

The ancient testimonia indicate that this structure was dedicated primarily to Persephone.[142] Evidence for a cult of Aphrodite or, more specifically perhaps, a joint cult of Aphrodite and Hermes is evident in the large collection of *pinakes* that came to light in the large votive deposit found in the valley between the city wall and the sanctuary retaining wall.[143] Of the 156 different scenes that Prückner identified on the 10,000 plus pinax fragments, a full 25 percent represent the goddess Persephone, while only 15 percent show Aphrodite with or without Hermes.[144]

The *pinakes* themselves date, at the earliest, only to the late sixth century, with most deriving from the fifth. As such, as with the Stoa ad U and the Sacello of Marasa Sud, the evidence from Mannella appears to be too late for consideration here. One piece of evidence from Mannella that is of extreme interest, however, is a votive figurine of an armed female. What remains of the figurine is the upper body of a female wearing a heavy garment. The right arm is raised and the clenched fist is pierced through, probably in order to hold a spear. What remains of the left arms suggests that it was held out straight in front of the body. It is possible that this votive is intended to depict Aphrodite Armed, in which case it would be the only remaining iconography of Aphrodite in this guise from the ancient world.[145]

Poseidonia/Paestum

The Santa Venera sanctuary is located just outside of the city of Paestum, approximately 80 m from the south fortification wall and 200 m east of the main city gate. Both pottery and terra-cotta votives at the site date cult activity there to the early sixth century, whereas construction dates from as early as the late sixth century and proceeds primarily in the middle of the fifth century.[146]

Of particular interest at the Santa Venera sanctuary are the large number of nude female votive figurines. According to Ammerman, a total of twenty-one nude female figurines come from this sanctuary, in contrast to the total of fourteen such figures from the rest of Paestum.[147] This suggests that these images were of particular importance for the deity of the sanctuary, which

---

141. *Ibid.,* 172.

142. App. *Sam.* 12.5; Cicero, *De Nat. Deor.* 3.83; Livy 29.8.9–11, among others.

143. Schindler 1998: 172.

144. Prückner 1968: 116–26.

145. Schindler 1998: 174.

146. *Ibid.,* 184–85; Ammerman 1991: 205.

147. Ammerman 1991: 204.

Ammerman identifies as Aphrodite/Aštart (Aphrodite herself may be associated with Hera/Juno/Uni).[148] While the arguments presented in the previous chapter in the section on Kato Symi argue strongly against the possibility of identifying this nude goddess as a specific deity or associating her with any specific deity, further data from the sanctuary do suggest that Aphrodite was worshipped here.

First, there are the faunal remains from the sanctuary, which include sheep, goats, birds, dogs, rabbits, and fish.[149] Although the first three are certainly common offerings in the Greek tradition, the last three are more specific to Aphrodite. Dog sacrifice is particular mainly to Hekate in Greece, although, in Italy at least, this animal might also be offered to Aphrodite.[150]

A second factor is a third-century Latin inscription upon a marble statue base: [–I]us F. CN. Venerei | [d]onavit.[151] Although the introduction of Aphrodite/Venus after the Roman colonization is certainly possible, the general continuity of cult and the faunal remains from the earlier periods do appear to indicate that Aphrodite was present at Santa Venera from the Archaic period.

Gravisca

The sanctuary at Gravisca shows evidence of use as early as the late seventh century. Its history can be divided into three distinct phases. The first phase, from c. 600–480 BCE, is distinctively Greek in character, whereas from 480–400 a more Etruscan character overtakes the site. The final phase, from 400–300, shows a period of massive reconstruction and new building.[152]

During the early Greek phase, there is evidence of the worship of several deities at the Gravisca sanctuary, notably Aphrodite, Apollo, Hera, Demeter, and Adonis. Schindler suggests that although Aphrodite may not have been the earliest deity to be venerated at Gravisca, by the sixth century (the period of the sanctuary's greatest use, as per the pottery) she is clearly the most important, when 84.7 percent of the sanctuary's votives are associated specifically with her sacello.[153] Dedications to Aphrodite, now with her Etruscan name "Turan," continue into the second phase of the sanctuary.

Of special interest at this site are its orientalizing aspects. These include the cult of Adonis; several votives of faience and ivory, including images of Horus and Bes; and a bronze protome griffin from a *lebes* datable to the end

---

148. *Ibid.,* 230.

149. *Ibid.,* 228–29.

150. *Ibid.,* Torelli 1976: 149.

151. Schindler 1998: 193.

152. *Ibid.,* 198–99.

153. *Ibid.,* 200–1.

of the seventh century.[154] Furthermore, a dedication by one Zoilos was uncovered, who may be the same individual who dedicated several artifacts in Naukratis.[155] All this may indicate connections between Gravisca and the east, in general, and Egypt, in particular.

Naxos (Sicilian)

The sanctuary of Aphrodite at Naxos is located in the southwest edge of the city, looking onto the Ionian Sea. Ritual activity is attested as early as the late seventh century. Pottery, including seventh-century Protocorinthian wares, were unearthed in context with animal bones. Sixth-century artifacts include two female Daidalic figurines, one roughly local (from Geloa) and one Greek.[156] As at Gravisca, some contact with the east seems to be suggested by statuettes of Bes found in connection with the sanctuary.[157] Of particular interest is the presence of weapon votives at the site, including daggers and spear points.[158] This might indicate a somewhat martial character for Aphrodite at Naxos, as may have been the case at Kythera, Sparta, and Corinth as well. However, it should be noted that the identification of this sanctuary is questionable. No inscribed votives reveal the name of the sanctuary's deity; the identification is based on the works of Appian (B Civ. 5.454) and Zenobius (3.116). This leaves open the possibility that the site was dedicated to some other deity/ies or to Aphrodite in conjunction with one or more deities.

Monte Iato

A temple dedicated to Aphrodite was discovered at the Sicilian site of Monte Iato. Evidence for the cult dates back into the middle of the sixth century BCE, although the excavator gives a low-end date of 510 BCE for the construction of the actual temple.[159] The altar may be contemporaneous with the temple: a fragment of an Ionic vessel datable to 580–520 BCE was discovered under the altar, once again suggesting a date as late as 510 for initial construction.[160] It has been determined that Aphrodite was the deity revered at Monte Iato on the basis of a single inscribed votive discovered near the temple. This is a fourth-century Attic kantharos inscribed with the letters AΦP, probably short for "Aphrodite."[161]

---

154. *Ibid.*, 201.

155. Torelli 1982: 319.

156. Schindler 1998: 207.

157. Pelagatti 1972: 218.

158. Schindler 1998: 208.

159. Isler 1984: 26; Hollinshead 1999: 197.

160. Isler 1984: 63.

161. Schindler 1998: 217.

The significant question concerning this sanctuary is its "ethnic" origin: Elymian, Punic, or Greek. The close connections with the cult of Aphrodite-Venus-Aštart at Eryx may suggest an indigenous origin with later foreign associations.[162] The excavator is rather of the opinion that the cult was of Greek origin, brought to Sicily by colonists.[163]

Akrai

A Doric-style temple of Aphrodite was located on an acropolis of the city above the agora. Similarities with the sixth-century temple of Apollo at Syracus, the mother-city of Akrai, suggest a late sixth-century construction of the Aphrodite temple.[164] The identification of the temple and sanctuary is based on a number of inscriptions, mentioning both the Aphrodision itself, and votive dedications to Aphrodite extending well into the Hellenistic period.[165]

Eryx

According to Diodorus Siculus (4.83.1) the sanctuary of Aphrodite at Eryx was established by her son Eryx, the eponymous founder of the city. Very little of the early architecture remains due to continued use of the site through the millennia, but the ancient literary sources are quite emphatic not only about the association of the site with Aphrodite, but as well about the (diminished?) wealth of the sanctuary.

> Taking them (the envoys) to the temple of Aphrodite at Eryx they showed them the dedicated items: phials, wine jugs, censers, and not a few other items, which, being mostly of silver, appeared to be more valuable than they were.
> Thucydides, VI, 46.[166]

> The lofty hill of Eryx is also inhabited. It possesses a sanctuary of Aphrodite, which is very much esteemed; in former times it was filled with women hierodules, who were dedicated according to vows by the Sicilians and by many others from elsewhere. But now the region is low in men, and the sanctuary is much missing in sacred bodies.
> Strabo, VI, ii, 6.[167]

As with Monte Iato, there is a certain interest in the "ethnic" composition of the Eryx sanctuary, for the Phoenician presence here is strong and the sanctuary is frequently referred to as the sanctuary of Aphrodite-Aštart.

---

162. Isler 1984: 103.

163. *Ibid.,* 105.

164. Schindler 1998: 210.

165. *Ibid.,* 211–12.

166. See Appendix B 4.17.

167. See Appendix B 4.18. See also Polybius I. 55. 6–8, and Diodorus IV. 83.

The Black Sea Region

Two sites in the Black Sea region offer evidence for cults of Aphrodite before 500 BCE. The first of these is the *polis* of Istros, where sanctuaries and altars to Aphrodite and Zeus were established by the Archaic Age.[168] As a trench (for blood?) ran between the altars of both of these deities, it is probable that the cults were linked, thus a joint cult of Aphrodite and Zeus (such as at Paros, perhaps).[169] Within the *naos* of the Aphrodite temple was discovered a decorated stone basin dated to the third quarter of the sixth century, while to the east of the sanctuary was a stone *perirrhanterion* of the second half of the same century. The *perirrhanterion* was inscribed with a dedication to Aphrodite, either dating to the sixth or fourth century BCE.[170]

Somewhat less evidence comes from the nearby site of Berezan. Here A. Rusjaeva discovered a sherd dated to the sixth century inscribed "Atheno-mandros dedicated me to Syrian Aphrodite."[171] It is of interest to note that this is one of the first sites where the strong connections between Aphrodite and Syria, prevalent in the Hellenistic Age, might be found.

Conclusions

The evidence shows that Aphrodite's earliest cult sites in the Greek world were in Crete, at Kato Symi and Olous. Tradition places her earliest cult statues only slightly farther north, in Kythera and Sparta. With the possible exception of Kato Symi, all evidence for Aphrodite in Greece dates to the Proto-Geometric period or later. By contrast, evidence for her cult in Cyprus dates back to the Bronze Age, concomitant with the early literary evidence of her Cypriot origins. Furthermore, the close contacts between Crete and Cyprus in the centuries preceding the appearance of Aphrodite in the Greek world (see below) suggest that either Aphrodite's cult came to the Greek world from Cyprus by way of Crete, or that her cult was a combination of Cypriot and Cretan elements. It is thus to Cyprus that this study now turns.

A further fact that comes to light in examining the history of the cult of Aphrodite in the ancient Greek world is that, contrary to her literary portrayal (but *not* contrary to her iconography as preserved in the literature), Aphrodite appears to have a martial element to her persona. At three sites, Kythera, Sparta, and Corinth, her *xoana* are portrayed as armed, and it cannot be overlooked that in the former two instances the images are accorded a certain great antiquity (especially at Kythera). At Argos, Sparta, Olous, and (in the lit-

---

168. Vianu 1997: 21.

169. *Ibid.*

170. *Ibid.*, 22 and note 37.

171. *Ibid.*, 15.

erature) Thebes, Aphrodite is joined in cult with Ares, either being Aphrodite Areia herself or simply worshipped in a joint sanctuary.[172] With the slight exception of Thebes, Aphrodite's early military characteristics are concentrated in southern Greece and Crete. If Crete was important in the early evolution and dissemination of the cult of Aphrodite, it is possible that militarism was a very early aspect of the goddess' persona, one that disappeared as the goddess evolved in the Greek pantheon. Regardless of the role of Crete, though, these references to Aphrodite's belligerent aspects confirm the possibility that military goddesses, and not just erotic goddesses, may have contributed to the evolution of Aphrodite.

---

172. Some, taking a literary structuralist approach, have and do continue to argue that this pairing of Aphrodite with Ares should be seen as a pairing of opposites, war versus love, and thus a confirmation of Aphrodite's non-military character. Based on the more extensive evidence offered here and in Chapter Five, where the Paphian goddess may be associated with some manner of male, military deity, it may be prudent to reconsider the "passive" origins of Aphrodite's associations with Ares.

V.

APHRODITE AND CYPRUS:
THE CHALCOLITHIC TO
LATE PREHISTORIC PERIODS

The archaeological evidence suggests that Aphrodite first appeared in the Greek world in Crete and the literary evidence indicates that she arrived there from her much older home on Cyprus. As these next two chapters will make clear, Aphrodite's cult site on this eastern island does predate those in the Aegean by some 400 years. What, then, is Aphrodite's relationship to Cyprus? Is she Cypriot? Was she indigenous to the island of did the Cypriots themselves adopt her from a foreign culture? When did the goddess emerge in Cyprus, and how is she related to the various deities who populated the Near East and the Aegean? Was this goddess always a goddess of sexuality, or did her character change over the centuries or millennia, and under what impetus?

To address these questions, we need to explore the evolution of the artistic and, eventually, literary evidence for Cypriot religious belief. This will involve changes in iconography throughout the ages, the distribution of cult paraphernalia and architecture, and the literary testimonia concerning Aphrodite and other goddesses in Cyprus. The various civilizations that held influence over Cyprus throughout its (pre)history will also be examined and considered in this context. As such, we might see how the eventual Aphrodite developed, and what factors contributed to her final form.

Cypriot Chronology

The chronological subdivisions of Cypriot (pre)history and the circumstances that accompany the progression of the divisions are extremely difficult topics, since many new ideas concerning Cypriot chronology have emerged during the last fifteen years as a result of new excavations. Neither the chronology nor the transitions are well established.

Specific terminology has been formulated for identifying the different phases of Cypriot history. Following the Neolithic (aceramic and ceramic) are:[1]

---

1. Peltenburg 1989, xvi.

Chalcolithic	
Early Chalcolithic	3800–3500
Middle Chalcolithic	3500–2800
Late Chalcolithic	2800–2300
Philia	2500–2300
Early Bronze Age	
Early Bronze I	2300–2075
Early Bronze II	2075–2000
Early Bronze III	2000–1900
Middle Bronze Age	
Middle Bronze I	1900–1800
Middle Bronze II	1800–1725
Middle Bronze III	1725–1600
Late Bronze Age	
Late Bronze I	1600–1450
Late Bronze II	1450–1200
Late Bronze III	1200–1050

In 1994, Knapp, Peltenburg, and others offered more fine-tuned under-standings and new terminologies for these early phases of Cyprus. According to Knapp, the early periods of Cyprus can be divided roughly into Early Pre-historic and Late Prehistoric–Protohistoric; the former dating from 10,000–2400 BCE and comprising the periods from "pre-Neolithic" to the end of the early Chalcolithic, the latter dating from 2400–1000 and comprising periods from Middle Chalcolithic through the end of the Late Bronze Age (PreBA 1 and 2 and ProBA 1–3).[2]

Within these periods both Knapp and Peltenburg identify specific sub-phases. Knapp recognized particular chronological periods within the Neo-lithic and Chalcolithic based on type sites. The aceramic Neolithic he labels the Khirokitia culture (KCU), the ceramic Neolithic as the Sotira culture (SCU), and the early Chalcolithic as the Erimi culture (ECU).[3] Peltenburg divides the Chalcolithic into three phases (instead of the original I and II): Early, Middle, and Late, which extend from 3900–2400 BCE.[4] At the site of Kissonerga-*Mosphilia* this chronology is further revised into five periods: Period 1 reach-ing from the late seventh millennium into the Late Neolithic; Period 2 com-prising the early to mid-fourth millennium; Period 3 comprising the mid- to

---

2. Knapp *et al.* 1994: 381.

3. *Ibid.*

4. *Ibid.*, 409–10.

late fourth millennium through 2900 BCE; Period 4, spanning from 2700 to 2400; and Period 5, which exists only in 2400 BCE.[5] The end of Period 4 and Period 5 overlap with the Philia phase of Cypriot prehistory.[6]

The transition from Chalcolithic to Early Bronze Age is one of the most vexing issues in current Cypriot studies. It is generally now accepted that the Philia phase is the transitional period between Chalcolithic and Bronze Age Cyprus. This transitional phase is well recorded in the archaeological record; sites classified as the Philia phase are Bellapais-*Vounorouthkia*, Dhenia-*Kafkalla*, Episkopi-*Bamboula*, Khrysiliou-*Ammos*, Kissonerga-*Mosphilia*, Kyra-*Alonia*, Kyra-*Kaminia*, Marki-*Alonia*, Marki-*Davari*, Marki-*Vounaros/Pappara*, Nicosia-*Ayia Paraskevi*. Philia-*Drakos* B, Philia-*Laksia tou Kasinou*, Philia-*Vasiliko*, Philia/Vasiliko-*Kafkalla*, Sotira-*Kaminoudhia*, Vasilia-*Alonia*, Vasilia- *Kafkallia & Kilistra* and Vasilia-*Loukkos Trakhonas*.[7]

The continuity between the two phases (Philia and EC), even extending into the early Middle Bronze Age, is clearly visible at the well-published site of Marki-*Alonia*.[8] The Philia presence at the site is identifiable through the presence of Philia-style pottery (red polished, red polished coarse, white painted, and black slip and combed),[9] although no architectural remains have survived from this period. The earliest architectural remains (coming from level D) were largely demolished to make way for later structures, designated levels C and B, and dated by the associated ceramics to EC III–MC I.[10] Both the minimal structural remains from level D and the presence of earlier pits, postholes, pebble-lined plaster emplacements, and pre-EC III ceramic finds show that there was habitation at the site between the Philia phase and the later EC II period, thus from EC I through II.[11]

What brought about the transition from Chalcolithic to Bronze Age (via Philia) is still a matter of debate.[12] One theory, espoused by Webb and Frankel, is that the transition was instigated by the arrival of a new population into Cyprus from southern Anatolia. The new pottery indicative of the Philia phase (red polished) is clearly distinct in color and formation from the earlier Chalcolithic wares, and the majority of Philia metal instruments are also without

5. Peltenburg *et al.* 1998: vii.

6. *Ibid.*, 14–17; Knapp *et al.* 1994: 414; Webb and Frankel 1999: 40.

7. Webb and Frankel 1999: 6.

8. Frankel and Webb 1996: *passim*; Webb and Frankel 1999: *passim*.

9. Frankel and Webb 1996: Chapter 7; Webb and Frankel 1999: 14ff.

10. Webb and Frankel 1999: 37.

11. *Ibid.*

12. See Knapp *et al.* 1994: 420 *versus* Webb and Frankel 1999: 38ff.

earlier, local antecedents.[13] By contrast, red polished ware has precedents in Anatolia, specifically in the Tarsus region of Cilicia.[14] Thus, Webb and Frankel suggest that the origin of the Phila "facies" (as they call it) derives from the intrusion into western Cyprus by communities from the Anatolian mainland around 2500 BCE. These Anatolian communities adapted to their new habitat, adjusting their material culture, and eventually intermarrying with the native Cypriot population. The Philia facies might then be seen to migrate outward from the area of original Anatolian settlement to the areas of cultural intermingling of the Anatolian and Cypriot populations The mixture of Cypriot and Anatolian cultures led first to the Phila culture itself, and eventually to the Early Cypriot Bronze Age.[15]

By contrast, Knapp and others suggest that the transition from Chalcolithic to Bronze Age was not dependent upon immigrants from Anatolia (although trade with Anatolia seems clear), but rather through changes in the Cypriot economy, which had their heaviest impacts in the subsistence economy, notably in the introduction of new animals and ploughing technologies, and the increasing importance of copper mining and trade. This latter innovation led to the formation of an élite class who demanded foreign prestige items, thus increasing demand for the export of copper products.[16] In either hypothesis, two things are clear: (1) there is a distinct difference in the physical remains from the Chalcolithic culture and those from the Philia: rectilinear structures replaced circular, funerary goods were placed in graves, and graves themselves became more elaborate and often contained metal weapons;[17] (2) some manner of contact with Anatolia is apparent, commingled to one extent or another with indigenous developments.

The primary change distinguishing the EC III/MC I phase from the preceding period is the emergence of white painted ware at the beginning of EC III.[18] The wares, which Samuelson defines as white painted IA and white painted IB, are endemic to the EC III period, while "transitional" and white painted II wares are more typical of the very late EC III and MC I eras.[19] Except for a change in the appearance of figurines (more below), there is little other marked difference between the later Early Cypriot period and the beginning of the Middle Cypriot.

---

13. Webb and Frankel 1999: 39.

14. Swiny, 1985b: 20–21; Peltenburg 1994: 159.

15. Webb and Frankel 1999: 43.

16. Knapp *et al.* 1994: 420-21.

17. Peltenburg 1994: 158–59. Peltenburg attributes these changes to the emergence of a new élite society in Cyprus during the Philia phase.

18. Samuelson 1993: 111-14.

19. *Ibid.*, 122-25.

By contrast, there is a decisive break between Early – early Middle Cypriot and Middle Cypriot III and the ensuing LC I. Knapp considers these two latter phases together and names them the Protohistoric Bronze Age (ProBA I) dating from 1700–1400 BCE.[20] Perhaps the most important defining characteristic of this period is Cyprus's increased contacts with the other powers of the eastern Mediterranean. To the west, the end of EC III is corroborated with the discovery of only a MM Ia spouted jug in a tomb at Lapithos, while the beginning of MC is marked by the find of a single MM II Kamares cup in an MC I tomb at Karmi.[21] In the LC period, there is the emergence of writing in Cyprus with the creation of the so-called Cypro-Minoan script, appearing between 1550–1500 BCE.[22] The similarities between this syllabary and that of Minoan Crete offer yet further evidence for close contacts between Crete and Cyprus at this time.

The growing contacts between Cyprus and the Near East are manifest both textually and archaeologically. To date, ten Akkadian-language texts have come to light that bear the name Alašiyah, the Bronze Age/Near Eastern name of Cyprus.[23] Eight of these come from the Syrian city of Mari and are dated to the Old Babylonian Empire (middle chronology). While fragmentary, they all concern the importation and use of copper from Alašiyah.[24] The two documents from Alalakh that may be dated to the eighteenth century are prosopographical in their evidence. The first, a ration list, names Arammu the Alašiyan, whereas the second mentions the following:[25]

> 15 shekels of silver received
> from Alašiyah
> the son of Iripa
> supervisor of Kuwen, son of Am...

Archaeologically, the trade between Cyprus and the Near East is evident primarily in the dispersal of Cypriot pottery throughout the Levant. While MC I ware never leaves the confines of Cyprus,[26] MC II ware appears at Ras Sham-

---

20. Knapp *et al.* 1994: 424.

21. Karageorghis 1982: 52.

22. Woodard 1997: 46–49.

23. See both Muhly 1972 and Knapp 1996: Introduction, for the relevant arguments concerning this identification.

24. J.M. Sasson in Knapp 1996.

25. D.J. Wiseman in Knapp 1996: 20. In this instance it seems clear that the word Alašiyah refers to the personal name of an individual. However, it is possible that the personal name reflects the place name, much as Kimon of Athens named his son Lakedaimonios.

26. Åström 1957: 204ff.

ra (Ugarit), Megiddo, and El-Lahun.[27] The presence of Cypriot pottery in this region increases in MC III. In Palestine, MC ware has been found at Tel el-'Ajjul, Megiddo, Ashkalon, Tanturah, Tel el-Far'ah, Gezer, Lachish, Tel el-Jerisheh, and Akko, and during the same period Tell el-Yahudiya ware makes its way to Cyprus.[28] In Syria, MC wares have been found at Ras Shamra, Qal'at el-Rus, Tell Sukas, Kassabine, and Tell Atchana/Alalakh.[29]

Beyond foreign relations, there are internal changes that mark the passage from Prehistoric to Protohistoric Cyprus. Public and ceremonial architecture begin to appear frequently in urban centers; the social stratification that begins in the Early Cypriot Bronze Age becomes increasingly apparent in mortuary practices and remains; copper mining and smelting increase significantly; and both fortifications and a new interest in weapons indicate a growing need for defense.[30] In general, there appears, at this time, to be an economic boom based on control of the copper supply and export of this material to the high civilizations of the Near East and, to a certain extent, the Aegean. Foreign prestige items begin to appear in greater numbers on the island as the latest élite affirms its place in the hierarchy. That this hierarchy was important not only on the island but within the eastern Mediterranean community is supported by the correspondence between Cyprus and the Levant during this time.

According to this textual evidence, Cyprus was not only well connected with the various political powers of the Near East, but the Cypriot king was recognized as one of the peer kings of the Bronze Age international milieu. In the Akkadian-language letters discovered at Amarna from the king of Alašiyah to the pharaoh of Egypt, the king of Cyprus addresses the pharaoh as "brother," the form of addressed used between peer kings in the Late Bronze Age. Thus, a letter from the fourteenth century begins:[31]

> To the king of Egypt, my brother: message of the king of Alašiyah, your brother. For me all goes well. For you may all go well. For your household, your wives, your sons, your horses, your chariots, and in your country, may all go very well.

By contrast, Ugarit, the trading station between Cyprus, Egypt, and the Near East in general, was the political inferior of Cyprus, with the king of Ugarit referring to the king of Cyprus as "father." Thus, a royal letter from the Ugaritic king to Cyprus dating to the end of the thirteenth century begins:[32]

27. Catling 1971: 44. Åström, 1957: 204ff.

28. Åström 1957: 138.

29. *Ibid.* See also Knapp *et al.* 1994: 426.

30. Knapp *et al.* 1994: 424–25.

31. Moran in Knapp (ed.) 1996: 21; Mercer 1939: 190.

32. Beckman in Knapp (ed.) 1996: 27.

> Say to the king of Alašiyah, my father: Thus says the king of Ugarit, your son: I fall at the feet of my father. May my father be well! May your palaces, your wives, your infantry, and everything that belongs to the king of Alašiyah, my father, be very, very well!

Finally, as will be important for this study, foreign iconography begins to appear on Cyprus at this time, indicative of a new religious ideology and/or a new means of justification and stability for the upper classes. This culture will remain in place through the end of the Bronze Age on Cyprus.

The Chalcolithic Age (3900–2300 BCE)[33]

The earliest evidence for a possible feminine presence in Cypriot religious thought occurs in the Chalcolithic, specifically in the Middle (3500–2800 BCE) and Late Chalcolithic (2800–2400). Before this, small figurines of either gender or, occasionally, genderless are present at various sites in Cyprus during the Neolithic. J. Karageorghis has suggested that these figures belong to a cult of ancestors more so than to a cult of divinity.[34] Furthermore, both Le Brun and Vagnetti have noted that, in terms of gender, there is a much greater tendency in the Neolithic to portray images of the phallus, suggesting a male, as opposed to female, concern in the early iconography.[35] By contrast, it is in the Chalcolithic that small, female figurines begin to appear in contexts that suggest some manner of public ritual.

This period of Cypriot pre-history, as well as the Neolithic before it, is well documented in modern archaeology. Scientific excavations have been carried out at Cape Andrea-*Kastros*, Khirokitia-*Vounoi*, Kalavasos-*Tenta*, Kalavasos-*Ayios*, Kissonerga-*Mosphilia*, Kissonerga-*Mylouthkia*, Lemba, Ayios Epiktitos-*Vrysi*, Souskiou, Alaminos-*Zorzakis*, Khirokitia, Sotira-*Teppes*, and Erimi-*Pamboula*, among others.[36] The feminine figurines that form the core of the evidence concerning Cypriot ritual practice during this period all come from the southwest of the island, notably from Souskiou, Lemba, and Kissonerga, although further data also derive from Erimi, Kalavassos-*Ayious*, Kalavassos-*Tenta*, and Alaminos-*Zorzakis*.[37]

---

33. For both this section and the following sections on Early and Middle Bronze Age figurines, I refer the reader to A Campo for an updated reference.

34. J. Karageorghis 1977: 17.

35. Le Brun, "Like a Bull in a China Shop," delivered at the "Transmission and Assimilation of Culture in the Near East" Conference, Feb.–March 2000. Publication forthcoming. Vagnetti 1991: 139–40.

36. Bolger 1994: 10.

37. Bolger 1988: 103. Bolger 1994: 15.

FEMININE IMAGES

There are three styles of the feminine image that are of particular interest: (1) the rough anthropomorphic figurines from the Erimi region in southern Cyprus; (2) the picrolite figurines from the Paphos region; and (3) the terracotta images from Kissonerga-*Mosphilia*.

The region around Erimi has brought forth an assortment of anthropomorphic figurines that are rather crude and of indeterminate identification and intent. There is some debate as to whether these images were ever intended to represent the female, as many are fragmentary and show no indications of gender.[38] As such, they could be likened to the Neolithic "pebble" figurines, which represent both sexes as well as neither. By contrast, Dikaios, in his early assessment of these images, pointed out that the torsos are either genderless or specifically female, and that whereas the surface treatments might be extremely crude, a clear effort existed on the part of the artist to render recognizable breasts (see fig. 5a, from Alaminos). So, too, at least one lower body fragment depicts a steatopygus figure with incised feminine genitalia (see fig. 5b).[39] One might argue that the images are either genderless or female, or that they are all intended to be female, with only a few actually portraying sexual traits.

Fig. 5a
Anthropomorphic figurine from Alaminos.
Cyprus Museum, Inv. 1933/XII - 13/6.

---

38. *Ibid.*, 106.

39. Dikaios 1936: 56–57.

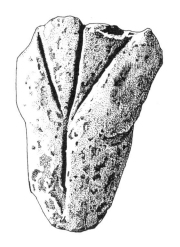

Fig. 5b
Steatopygos figurine from Erimi.
See Dikaios, "The Excavations at Erimi, 1933–1935." *RDAC* 1 (1936).

A possible symbolic significance of these images may be expressed in two relatively intact clay figurines portraying women squeezing milk (?) from their breasts into bowls. On the one unprovenanced example (Louvre AM 1176) a women is seated bearing a large bowl on her lap. Her torso is cylindrical and leans backward, as does her upward-looking head. Her rather crude arms curve out and return to the body with the hands upon the breasts, which are highly decorated with incised designs. The thumbs are on the upper surface of the breasts, with the remainder of the fingers below, suggesting the action of squeezing, probably into the bowl on the legs. The second figurine, found at Alaminos, shows the same overall pose, although the legs (which would have borne the bowl) are missing. In all other respects the figurines, in posture and decor, are so similar that A Campo suggests that they could have been made by the same artist.[40]

The two potential explanations for these images, as suggested by A Campo, are fertility rite or mourning ritual, whereby either the recent maternity, hence fertility, of these females is expressed through their obvious lactation, or mourning is expressed in the gripping of the breasts. As the bowls suggest that lactation is occurring, the former explanation seems more probable.[41] Nevertheless, there is little or nothing in these images that would suggest either divinity or cult ritual.

---

40. A Campo 1994: 55.

41. *Ibid.*

    There is less gender ambiguity in the picrolite images from the southwest
of the island.[42] Here, the figurines were found predominantly in mortuary settings, particularly from the necropolis of Vathyrkakas-*Souskiou*, but also from
Kythrea, Salaminou, and Ayia Irini.[43] These images are cruciform in shape,
and, as one figurine from Yalia shows, were potentially worn as pendants (see
fig. 5c). Although these figurines are occasionally "genderless" or, more accurately, depicted without specific sexual attributes, many of them are rendered
as specifically female. Approximately 14 percent have breasts (see fig. 5d) and
many wear jewelry. Some of the cruciform images are doubled, whereby the
cross is formed by two anthropomorphic "individuals" being sculpted at right
angles to one another and meeting at chest level. One such example comes
from Salaminou, one from Souskiou, and another two are unprovenanced.[44]
J. Karageorghis sees these as possibly a mother-child image, where the upright
figure is holding the child in her arms. Or, it is possible that image is yet one
more example of the Cypriot love of reduplication, evident in many of its early
pottery forms.

Fig. 5c
Chalcolithic cruciform figurine from Yalia, Cyprus.
Cyprus Museum, Inv. 1934/III-2/2.

---

42. Vagnetti 1991: 140ff.

43. J. Karageorghis 1977: 22.

44. A Campo 1994: 137.

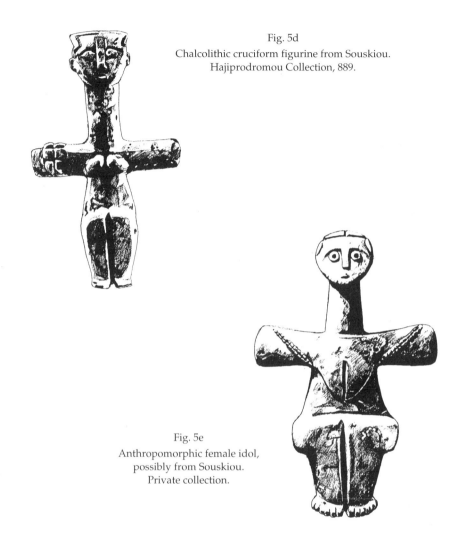

Fig. 5d
Chalcolithic cruciform figurine from Souskiou.
Hajiprodromou Collection, 889.

Fig. 5e
Anthropomorphic female idol,
possibly from Souskiou.
Private collection.

A Campo has conducted an intensive study of these images in an attempt to determine their symbolic significance through computer analysis of their various attributes. In this way, she has determined what attributes were critical in the shaping of these figurines and, thus, essential for the symbolic role they fulfilled. She has also determined which attributes were of secondary importance, either because they were of less symbolic significance or because they were pre-assumed by the culture that made use of the figurines. The most important attribute that A Campo calculated was the bent knees of the figurines. Every example studied, regardless of size, has this one, basic characteristic.[45] Other attributes of primary importance are the outstretched arms and the long neck. Secondary attributes are a backward-tilted head, facial features (be they schematic or anthropomorphic), jewelry, and breasts.[46] This apparent lack of emphasis on breasts should not cast doubt on the female identification of the figurines. Although it is possible, as with the images from Erimi, that both female and genderless entities were intended, the overwhelming consistency of posture and dominant attributes suggest that a similar, if not identical, image was intended in all renderings of the cruciform image. They must be either *all* genderless or *all* female. As a considerable number *must* be female, this argues strongly in favor of the hypothesis that they are all female. Furthermore, as A Campo mentions, on such schematic figurines, it is to be expected that certain aspects are to be understood as present even in their apparent absence. Thus, even though not all the picrolite figurines have mouths, mouths are to be understood as part of the natural facial structure. The fact that breasts are only present on 14 percent of the study's figurines suggests that the Chalcolithic population that made use of these images already understood their inherent "femaleness," and breasts were only purposely depicted on the more elaborate versions of the figurines.[47]

Further information concerning the purpose of these images is derived from their find contexts. The majority of provenanced picrolite cruciform figurines come from inhumations, either single burial, or multiple burial in shaft graves (as at Souskiou) or chamber tombs (Kissonerga-*Mosphilia*).[48] At Kissonerga, Lemba, and Souskiou these figurines were found exclusively in the graves of women and children. The four tombs at Kissonerga that had both picrolite pendants and skeletal remains were of children. At Souskiou the wealthiest grave (tomb 3) contained the bodies of at least three adult females and an eight-year-old child. To date, no such pendant has been found in context with an adult male at any site.[49]

Of special importance is the fact that pendants and the dentilium shell necklaces of which they were frequently a part were too heavy to have been worn by the infants with whom they were buried. This, coupled with the well-worn surface of some of the pendants, has lead Kissonerga-*Mosphilia* excavators Peltenburg, Bolger, and Goring to the conclusion that these pendants were originally worn by adults, probably women, and only placed with children upon their burial.[50]

---

45. *Ibid.*, 131.

46. *Ibid.*

47. *Ibid.*, 134.

48. Bolger 1996: 368.

49. *Ibid*; Peltenburg 1992: 33.

50. Peltenburg 1992: 32–33.

Two larger figures show similar features to those of the smaller picrolite figurines and may perhaps be used to uncover the meaning or purpose of these images. The first is a statuette (see fig. 5e; h. 39.5 cm) that is in all respects a larger version of the cruciform figurines. It comes from illicit excavations and, thus, while it is attributed to Souskiou, there is no information concerning precise context.[51] The hair-lines are rendered by incision, whereas face, brows, eyes, nose, and mouth are rendered by molding. The neck is long and cylindrical; the arms are outstretched. Breasts are indicated by a combination of incision and molding. The figure is seated; the legs are separated by a groove, as are the individual toes. Molded lines across both arms might indicate jewelry, by comparison with the necklaces and bracelets prevalent on many of the smaller picrolite figurines.

The second is a figure from Lemba-*Lakkous*. Although it is qualitatively different from the cruciform images in some respects, its find spot and similar iconography so clearly identify it as supernatural in character that it must be included in any examination of Chalcolithic religious belief. Its find spot, according to Peltenburg, was believed to be one of the more elaborate dwellings of the site, being adequately large and with enough space around it that it was originally identified as a shrine.[52] This opinion has since changed in the light of additional buildings at Lemba of equivalent dimensions. However, what is of extreme interest is the location of the figure within the walls of the dwelling.[53] The figure was located under a more recent layer of dirt floor in a sector of the dwelling that, as recent research by Peltenburg shows, was symbolically significant to the inhabitants of Chalcolithic Cyprus with the past and with the dead. In one case a child burial was set here; while a dwelling in Kissonerga (see below) was specifically oriented so that an older deposit was situated under this part of the floor.[54]

The figurine itself (see fig. 5f; h. 36 cm) is almost violin-shaped. The head is squat and rounded, with eyes and nose in relief. The neck is long and cylindrical, and the arms are outstretched in the cruciform fashion albeit rather stumpy. The hips are extremely broad, and the legs are separated by a short, incised groove. Breasts and genitalia are indicated by incised lines, and a round belly (possibly pregnant?) is rendered in relief. Thus, we have an explicitly feminine figure, with emphasis on feminine attributes such as hips and genitalia, and possible fertility associations through the potentially pregnant belly.

---

51. Morris 1985: 129.

52. Peltenburg 1989: 122.

53. Peltenburg, personal communication.

54. *Ibid.*

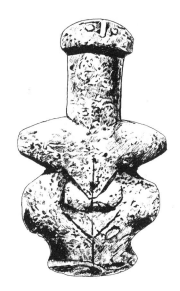

Fig. 5f
Anthropomorphic female idol from Lemba.
Cyprus Museum Inv. 1976/54.

Both of these larger figures show that the cruciform style (as well as a possible steatopygus form) could exist not only as a small personal adornment,
but as what could almost be identified as a cult image. The precise purpose
of these larger figures is not yet known.

The final datum concerning the function and meaning of the cruciform figurines, as well as the possible role of the feminine in Chalcolithic Cypriot ritual belief, comes from excavations led by the Lemba Archaeological Project
under Peltenburg at Kissonerga-*Mosphilia*.[55] This is a deposit known as Unit
1015, comprising about fifty objects dated to the *Mosphilia* Period 3 (Middle
Chalcolithic, c. 3000 BCE).[56] The deposit consists predominately of terra-cotta
figures, the most notable of which is what Peltenburg and others call a "shrine
model," the only one of its (or any other) kind from the Cypriot Chalcolithic
to date. Included with this shrine, buried either within the model itself or
around and on top of it, were terra-cotta female figures, stone figurines, a
model stool, some pottery, and several stones cracked due to apparent severe
temperature shifts.[57]

55. Peltenburg *et al*. 1991: *passim*. Peltenburg and Goring 1991: *passim*; Goring 1991:
    156ff.

56. Peltenburg and Goring 1991: 17.

57. *Ibid*., 20.

The so-called shrine model is in the form of a bowl and shows a round structure with an arched entrance at one side. The floor is decorated with a painted radial pattern, and the walls are covered with painted geometric designs. A door, formed of a separate piece of terra-cotta, was broken off but remained next to the model itself; originally it was attached to the bowl structure through a hinged apparatus. Breaks above the door are all that remain from external protomes above the lintel. The entire model was decorated with red and orange painted design, including zigzag, checkerboard, and linear designs on the interior, and stepped motifs and wavy bands on the exterior.[58] The door and the round shape (similar in all respects to the architectural dwellings discovered at Kissonerga) support the hypothesis that this is a model of an inhabitable structure.

The eight terra-cotta figurines found with the model are all female, and all appear to be in various stages of pregnancy or parturition.[59] They all have breasts, a recognizable fat roll and emphasized buttocks; the majority (where preserved) also have swollen bellies and emphasized hips.[60] One figurine has the head of an infant appearing between her legs, and a cruciform figurine is painted upon her neck. All (where preserved) are rendered in a seated or squatting pose. The stone figurines are not as clearly feminine in gender, although what few sexual traits do remain (X's upon the chest and pubic triangles) suggest that they, too, were female.[61]

The three-footed, terra-cotta model stool is understood to be a birthing stool.[62] The exact function of the heat-fractured stones is unknown, although Peltenburg suggests that they may have been used for steaming, such as in a sauna.[63] The pregnant and laboring figurines and the birthing stool suggest that the collection of objects was related to childbirth.

In its original context, the pit containing these items was extra-mural and located among several of the largest structures of Kissonerga-*Mosphilia* in the Middle Chalcolithic.[64] It lay to the east, where it formed an irregular space bounded by Buildings 2, 4, 206, and 1000. This area is regarded as being ceremonial/ritualistic due to its public setting and the ritual nature of the acts that were apparently performed here.[65]

---

58. Peltenburg *et al.* 1991: 12.

59. Goring 1991: 156ff.

60. Peltenberg *et al.* 1991: 39.

61. *Ibid.*

62. Peltenburg and Goring 1991: 25.

63. *Ibid.*, 20.

64. Peltenburg *et al.* 1991: 1–12. Peltenburg and Goring 1991: 17ff.; Goring 1991: 156.

65. Peltenburg *et al.* 1991: 1.

As there was no indication of mortuary remains within the context of the find, Peltenburg theorizes that this deposit marks the material remains of a sacred, non-mortuary, public ritual.[66] It was only later, during the Late Chalcolithic, that a new structure's dwelling was built on top of the deposit. At this time, the dwelling was oriented so that the deposit would "peek out" above the floor level in that same area as that in which the "Lemba Lady" was found, that is, in the area specifically associated with the past.[67]

The condition of the find suggests that it was deliberately "killed" before burial. Red ochre was smeared on several of the objects. The shrine model was deliberately broken (notably the protomes above the door), as were the terracotta female images. Many of the objects show signs of burning, although the surrounding matrix makes it clear that none of them was burned *in situ*.[68] Why the deposit was deliberately destroyed and buried remains a mystery. There is no sign of site-wide destruction that would indicate a need to hide precious objects.[69] It is possible that this collection, with its emphasis on feminine creativity, may have been destroyed during a general trend toward new social organization and stratification at Kissonerga, whereby control over production and fertility, including women's fertility, was taken over by a new élite at the site. The destruction of the older sacred artifacts would herald in a new dominant power.[70]

What do all these data mean concerning religion, cult, and ritual in Chalcolithic Cyprus? There are cruciform figurines all rendered as female, squatting, with arms outstretched. All were discovered in context with women and/or children, and all showed signs of wear before burial. One such image was painted upon the neck of a terra-cotta female figurine shown in the act of giving birth, rendered in a squatting posture similar to that of the picrolite images. Two larger versions of these cruciform figurines have been discovered, one almost identical to the picrolite versions, and one clearly portrayed as pregnant with a similar posture to the preceding images. Finally, these images themselves might be stylistically linked to several terra-cotta images (one, once again, depicted as wearing a picrolite figurine) all associated with birth and associated with a possible shrine model deposited in a public place of possible ceremony.

66. Peltenburg and Goring 1991: 18.

67. I am most grateful to both E. Peltenburg and D. Bolger for sharing their thoughts on this with me.

68. Peltenburg and Goring 1991: 17ff.

69. *Ibid.*, 19

70. Bolger 1990: 365–69. Peltenburg, "Ethnography, Egalitarian Society and Kissonerga c. 3,000 B.C." Delivered at CAARI in March 1998, at the Engendering Aphrodite Conference. Publication forthcoming.

Two hypotheses, non-contradictory, might be surmised. The first is that the image of the squatting, outstretched-armed female in Chalcolithic Cyprus is intimately linked with the concepts of pregnancy and birth. The second is that there may have been some manner of public or semi-private (females only?) ritual associated with both human female procreation and these images, possibly even occurring in a birthing hut/shrine. It is also possible that this public ceremony surrounding female fertility was suppressed by the end of the Chalcolithic either by a general change in culture or by the emergence of a new, patriarchal élite in southwestern Cyprus.

What is clear, though, is that there is nothing in any of these images, the picrolite, limestone, or terra-cotta that might be identified as a goddess, much less as Aphrodite. Rather, in her interpretation of these figurines, A Campo suggests that they are not deities but charms intended to promote successful pregnancy through sympathetic magic.[71] The focus of all these items is, in fact, on human fertility, giving very little evidence for a society-wide cult or religion, much less one that involved men as well as women.

Furthermore, at the end of Chalcolithic, the cruciform images cease to be produced or used, possibly due to the change of society hinted at by Peltenburg and Bolger that accompanied the transition from the Chalcolithic to Bronze Age. This clear break in the picrolite/fertility-figurine tradition at the end of the Chalcolithic shows that there can be no continuity between these earliest feminine images and the eventual Aphrodite.

The Philia Facies and the Late Prehistoric Period (2400–1700 BCE)

The main sources for ideological data in the Chalcolithic cease to exist in these later periods. The picrolite figurines disappear after the Late Chalcolithic whereas the deposit at Kissonerga-*Mosphilia* was a unique find. By contrast, an entirely new symbolic vocabulary appears at the dawn of the Bronze Age possibly, if not probably, imported by the immigrants from Anatolia hypothesized for the Philia facies.

To date, no clear evidence of symbolic representation has derived from the Philia period of Cypriot (pre)history. In the Early Bronze Age, red polished ware figurines and models form the basis of modern understandings of (possible) Cypriot religious beliefs of that time. The areas under consideration are those originally referred to as the Vounous culture, named for the original type-site at Bellapais-*Vounous* excavated by P. Dikaios. Other sites falling into this category are Lapithos-*Vrysi tou Barba*, Karmi-*Lapatsa*,[72] and, to a certain extent, Marki-*Alonia*.

71. A Campo 1994: 162.

72. Swiny 1986a: 30.

The finds from Vounous are divided chronologically into two phases: Vounous A = Early Cypriot II and Vounous B = Early Cypriot III plus the beginning of Middle Cypriot I.[73] The chronology of objects is determined both by context and style, with the most significant distinction between the two styles being the rise of anthropomorphism in Vounous B. Before this, the early Vounous representational imagery was zoomorphic in character. In its earliest phases, the Vounous religious iconography was dominated primarily by the bull and the snake, animals associated both with fertility and, especially in the case of the snake, with chthonic powers.[74] So, too, horned animals such as deer appear with frequency on pottery of a possibly sacred nature. Thus, they, too, seem to belong to the early Vounous sacred tradition. In EC II, corresponding with Vounous A, birds become prominent in the religious iconography, frequently perched on the edge of ritual vessels. Dikaios suggests that these birds were doves, due to the later association of that animal with Aphrodite, but for the moment it is perhaps best to refer to them simply as "birds."[75]

It is in the later phase of the Early Cypriot Bronze Age and the earliest stirrings of the Middle Bronze Age that anthropomorphic images appear that might have religious significations. As with the earlier Chalcolithic, these images consist of figurines and "shrine" models. The figurines, utterly distinct from the Chalcolithic cruciform figurines, are generally referred to as "plank-shaped," a shape that Des Gagniers and Karageorghis argue might derive from associations or identifications with *xoana*.[76] In their simplest forms, these images are extremely stylized (see fig. 5g). They have flat-topped heads decorated with incisions; the eyes and mouths are rendered either through incised circles or incised points. In most cases, the ears are slightly molded and pierced for the insertion of clay or metal earrings, and the nose is consistently a molded lump. The necks are long and usually decorated with incised necklaces. Arms were originally shown by incision, if at all, but, as the style developed, arms were rendered by molding, extending out from the body, occasionally even holding a baby. No legs or feet were rendered on the cruder models, but some of the more complex, rounded models show molded legs and feet. Incised geometric designs on the body may indicate tattoos

---

73. Des Gagniers and Karageorghis 1976: 1. See Knapp *et al.* 1994 for revised terminology for this chronology.

74. J. Karageorghis 1977: 36–37 and Des Gagniers and Karageorghis 1976: 4. The religious nature of these images is based predominantly on their appearance on cult vessels that are adequately complex and elaborate to allow for no practical application, and in the "shrine" models discussed below As with the female images, the role of the snake and bull in fertility is subject to debate.

75. Dikaios 1932: 350–51.

76. Des Gagniers and Karageorghis 1976: 8.

Fig. 5g
Cypriot EC plank figurine.
Cyprus Museum, Inv. 1963/IV-20/12.

or clothing.[77] Alternate forms of these figures are two- or three-headed versions and *kourotrophos* images.

Concerning context, the earliest examples of these figurines came from burials in the north of the island; it was originally assumed that their role was predominantly funerary. More recently, these images have come to light in settlements, about eight from Marki-*Alonia*, a handful from Alambra-*Mouttes*, and at least one from Ambelikou-*Alteri*.[78] The presence of these figurines at settlements, the evident ware on their surfaces, and mend holes on two examples (Marki AP8 and Lapithos Tomb 21.A25) provide convincing evidence that these images were used by the living before being placed with the dead.[79] Smaller versions of the "plank-shaped" images were used as decorative elements on vessels, either forming the handle of composite vessels or appearing as decorative elements along the rims of bowls.

There is an ongoing debate as to the exact nature and function of these figurines in Early (and as we shall see Middle) Bronze Age Cypriot religion. The first question is whether or not one might even recognize the plank-shaped figurines as being inherently female, for, as Merrillees points out, many anthro-

---

77. Lubsen-Admiraal 1989: 112. But see below on A Campo's theories.

78. Frankel and Webb 1996: 188.

79. *Ibid.*

pomorphic images from this period are either male or genderless.[80] L. Talalay and T. Cullen in their paper "Sexual Ambiguity in Early Middle Cypriot Plank Figures" refer to one such image that has breasts, a phallus and holds a baby, so constituting an entire nuclear family all in one.[81]

Whether these images are to been seen as deities or, for that matter, even religious is a matter questioned by Frankel, Webb, and A Campo. The former two note that their battered state and domestic associations suggest that they were not accorded special status or used in designated ceremonial or ritual areas.[82] A Campo, in her analysis of the figurines, noting that the decorative emphasis of these figurines rests not on the body, but on the incised "clothing" on the body and "tattooing" on the face, surmised that it is not the similarity of the images that is important, but the decorative differences. As A Campo does identify the majority of these figurines as female, she argues that the figurines represent not one "goddess" figure (as there is no emphasis on similarity), but different women, with differences in decoration possibly indicating different clans or social groups.[83] Continuing in this vein, A Campo suggests that these images might have been used as a part of a marriage ceremony, whereby the transfer of the female image reflects the transfer of the human female.[84]

The identification of these images as exclusively female, especially in the light of plank images with phalloi, is tenuous at best and, thus, they should not be interpreted based upon gender. As Talalay and Cullen have argued, it is possible that gender ambiguity is an important aspect of the role of these images and that the automatic identification as female would cloud alternate meanings. Contrary to Dikaios' and J. Karageorghis' interpretation of these images as mother goddesses, there is no good evidence that these plank-shaped figurines were ever intended to have a religious component, much less be representations of any manner of goddess.

Two "shrine" models to be examined are said—they had been excavated illegally—to come from Kotchati, yet there is a lack of an Early or Middle Bronze Age site at Kotchati. In fact, the models may have come from Marki, 3 km distant.[85] The third model comes from the eastern part of the island at Kalopsidha. All three are dated to c. 2000 BCE.[86]

---

80. Merrillees 1980: *passim*.

81. This paper was delivered on 21 March, 1998 at the Engendering Aphrodite conference in Nicosia. Publication forthcoming.

82. Frankel and Webb 1996: 188.

83. A Campo 1994: 166.

84. *Ibid.*, 168.

85. J. Webb, personal communication.

86. Karageorghis 1970: 10; Åström 1988: 5.

In these images, a wall is portrayed that stands atop a floor, or possibly a ground line, that also serves as the base of the image. From this ground line three vertical ridges rise to the top of the model along the wall, where they are topped by horned animal heads. The center and right head have curved horns and clearly indicate bulls. The head to the left on one of the models has straight horns and might represent a deer or goat, or may just be the result of accident—all animal heads on the other models are clearly bulls.[87] On the upper part of the model, between the vertical ridges, are projecting horns (snakes, phalloi?). At the base of the wall of the best preserved model (although not on the version from Kalopsidha) stands a human female (indicated by molded breasts) beside an amphora; the woman's short arms are extended to her sides.

The meaning and purpose of these models have come under considerable debate. In the earliest interpretations, V. Karageorghis and J. Karageorghis argue that these scenes are shrines.[88] The horned animals represent the deities, possibly in the form of crude *xoana*, while the woman at the base of the model pours a libation to these deities into the amphora before her.

Frankel and Tamvaki have argued that these scenes are intended as representations of funerary chambers and mortuary cult.[89] This is based upon the similarities between these three-dimensional images and the low-relief portrayals of humans on the *dromoi* of Early Cypriot funerary chambers, notably those of Tombs 6 and 2 in the Palaealona cemetery at Karmi.[90] As such, what is represented is a funerary cult; the bull heads are indicative of sacrificial animals and not deities. There are no gods portrayed or intended in this interpretation.

In a more recent interpretation, Åström analyzed the individual elements of each of the models in the context of Cypriot tradition and in comparison with Aegean cult practices.[91] He contends that the raised border separating the "platform" from the vertical panel suggests a deliberate enclosing on the Kalopsidha model, while the women standing before the amphora should be seen as engaged in the act of an offering, be it of the amphora itself or a libation into said amphora. Both of these data argue in favor of a religious interpretation of the scene, hence a shrine. The ambiguity lies in the interpretation of the animal heads. In comparison with Aegean practice, Åström suggests,

---

87. Åström 1988: 11.

88. Karageorghis 1970: *passim*; J. Karageorghis 1977: 43.

89. Frankel and Tamvaki 1973: *passim*.

90. *Ibid.*, 40.

91. Åström 1988: *passim*.

as Frankel and Tamvaki, that the heads are indicative of sacrifice and that the bulls are no more than sacrificial animals in the Cypriot repertoire.[92] It is highly probable, then, that these models do refer to early Cypriot cult practices, possibly, although not necessarily, associated with the dead. They do not, however, offer evidence of a bull or caprid cult in Early Cyprus, nor do they offer information concerning any deity in this early period.

More important for the understanding of (possible) early Cypriot cult practice is a sanctuary scene uncovered at Vounous, Tomb 22, which is also dated to 2000 BCE (see fig. 5h).[93] Here is a bowl that has one arched entrance; within stand several human or humanoid figures. That some manner of initiatory or exclusive event is taking place is manifest by the one "person" who looks over the rim/wall but who, it would seem, is not allowed to enter. One humanoid figure stands directly within the entrance. To either side of the arched entrance are small, enclosed areas where bovines are kept. Standing directly before one of these corrals is a humanoid, *kourotrophos* figure, identified as female. In the other corral stands one humanoid figure. Opposite the entrance the "ritual" scene takes place. To one side of the central area stand five humanoid figures, of which two or three have phallic bulges, and the others are without sexual characteristics. Beyond these, on a bench at the edge of the bowl, sit four humanoid figures, of which two are clearly male. They sit apparently watching the standing figures before them; they all have crossed arms. Just past these seated figures another figure stands/kneels facing the side of the bowl; before him/her, on the side of the bowl, is a small architectural structure containing an unidentifiable image. The most significant figures in the bowl, to judge from their size, are three seated figures in the last quarter of the bowl. One, male, is larger than all the other figures in the scene; he sits on an enormous chair-throne, and faces the shrine on the side of the bowl. The two other figures, almost as large as the first, sit on the side of the bowl.

Traditionally, a ritual interpretation of the model is inferred through the exclusive nature of the scene, the three greater-than-life-sized figures seated opposite the entrance, and the "shrine" area before which the individual kneels. The oversized figures are understood as deities, or possibly cult officials, who preside over ritual, their larger size intended to portray their status. The bovines kept on either side of the entrance are interpreted as sacrificial victims. The exact activities of the five standing and four sitting figures is uncertain, although a sacred dance has been suggested by Dikaios.[94] The sex of the participants is a matter of debate, for only some of the figures show phalloi, while the others are devoid of any sexual characteristics. It is possible that

---

92. *Ibid.*, 8 and 10.

93. Dikaios 1932: *passim*; Dussaud 1932: 223.

94. Dikaios 1932: 347.

they are younger members of the community, not represented with sexual characteristics.[95] Only one character has breasts, and she also holds a child.

A recent interpretation of this model has been offered by Peltenburg. Opposing the traditional interpretations of the scene as based on religious assumptions and focus on gender, Peltenburg bases his analysis on a less ambiguous aspect of the model: the relative size and placement of figures. In so doing, he has determined that not cult activity, but "order and sacred legitimization are two overtly signified aspects of the bowl."[96]

Sectors, or thematic units, are defined as having their own internal dynamic focus. In C (see fig. 5h), near the entrance, are penned bulls with their keepers, and observing the cattle, the only female, holding a child. In the next sector, B, is a self-contained group of standing males, with arms folded, looking at one another. There is no hint of movement, suggestive of dance or singing, and, in the group's inward-looking stance, no contact with adjacent sectors. In A are seated and kneeling figures engaged in some rite before and to either side of bucranial pillars. The largest male, seated on an elaborate chair, presides over the proceedings and he is directly opposite the iconographic devic-

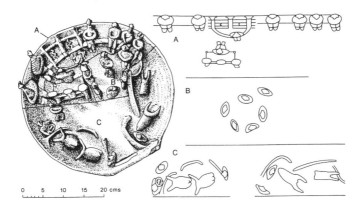

Fig. 5h
Peltenburg analysis of the Vounous model.
Op Ath XX: 10 (1994), 157–162.

---

95. For more on this theory, see E. Ribeiro, "Altering the Body: Representations of Pre-Pubescent Gender Groups on EC/MC 'Scenic Compositions,'" forthcoming in the "Engendering Aphrodite" publication.

96. Peltenburg 1994: 160.

es on the wall. Viewed in this manner, it may be seen that the compositional structure of the bowl was deliberately designed as a hierarchy, one perhaps expressive of a general social ideology. Thus, at the base of this hierarchical construct (C) are bulls, symbols of new wealth/status resources and a female with child, also suggestive of vitality, fertility, and prosperity. The woman/child figure is intentionally associated with the cattle by her position and the direction of her face. Next (B) is the adult world of decision-making males. Beyond that (A), sacred rites before symbols of transcendent powers that, if conceptually related with sectors B and C, effectively legitimate the whole social structure.[97]

This interpretation, especially that of the placement of the female, accords well with Bolger's views concerning the changing roles of women in the development of early Cypriot (pre)history. She argues that one important distinction between the portrayal of females in the Chalcolithic and that of the Early Bronze Age is that the former focuses attention on the birthing process, whereas the latter emphasizes the postpartum relationship between woman and child. Put simply, the female transforms from *genetrix* to *mater*.[98] As the female is no longer viewed as a producer but as a care-taker, her status within the community falls. Thus, the one evident female in the scene is in sector C, the "have-nots," grouped with the cattle and away from the males who form the dominant majority in the scene. In any respect, it appears that this model says far more about the mortals of early Cyprus than of their deities.

CHANGES IN FIGURINES IN THE EARLY MIDDLE CYPRIOT PERIOD

As discussed above, the Early Cypriot III and the Middle Cypriot I periods form a continuity, observable in settlement at Marki-*Alonia* and in the ceramic record in the development of white painted ware. One important development during this period is the transformation of the plank-shaped anthropomorphic figurines.

The predominant change in the anthropomorphic figurines is the Cypriot potters' attempts at three-dimensional representation. Beginning with the rather two-dimensional plank-shaped images, the figurines slowly grow more three-dimensional, becoming more cylindrical in shape, as the incised decoration becomes increasingly replaced by relief decoration.

Beyond the tendency toward three-dimensions, the other significant change is the prevalence of nudity and gender in the MC figurines. Whereas the plank-shaped images of the EC period traditionally have bodies decorated with incised "clothing", the more modeled MC figurines have no such decoration on their bodies and it is probable that the later artists meant to portray

97. *Ibid.*

98. Bolger 1996: 369–71.

them as nude. As more of the body becomes, technically, visible, greater emphasis is placed on the sexual characteristics of the figurines, such as the breasts and, possibly, the navel or vagina. Nevertheless, a certain degree of gender ambiguity remains in this latter period. Karageorghis notes at least two white painted ware anthropomorphic figurines that are male.[99] These are clearly in the minority in comparison to the female images, but their presence precludes hypotheses based on an exclusively female identification of this corpus.

Unlike the transition between the Chalcolithic cruciform figurines and the EC plank-shaped figurines, the evolution from the Early Cypriot to the Middle Cypriot forms is gradual and observable. One unprovenanced example from MC I shows all the typical features of an Early Cypriot figurine. The top of the head is flat, and the ears are molded and pierced. The eyes are incised points; the nose is molded, prominent, and proportionately large. Necklaces are incised at the neck, and incised lines on the body may represent either clothing or tattoos. New, MC elements are also present in this image. Eyebrows are molded, as is the nose, indicating a first step toward fully rendered facial characteristics. Arms are rendered in molding and, rather than just holding a baby, are extended to the sides of the figure. Finally, breasts are indicated by molding on the figure's chest, possibly indicative of nudity.

Another figurine from the same period (and also unprovenanced: see fig. 5i) shows the further development of the Middle Bronze Age female figurines in Cyprus. Here is a cylinder-shaped figurine of white ware. The head is no longer flat at the top, but has a bump that might indicate some manner of crown. The ears are highly schematic but still multiply pierced. The eyes are incised in an almost rosette design, and both the prominent nose and mouth are rendered by molding. The breasts are molded on the chest, as are the arms, of which only one remains, curving out to the side akimbo-style with the hand resting on the stomach. The body is decorated with incised dots, and midway down the figure's body is a relatively large, pronounced hole, which may either represent the navel or an extremely awkwardly placed vaginal opening. Although legs are not indicated, a slight incision in the bottom center of the figure shows the beginnings of rendered legs/feet.

What role did these images play in the lives of the Middle Bronze Age Cypriots? Once again, the frequently disturbed contexts and the lack of provenance for so many of the figurines makes this a difficult question to answer. In the majority of cases, as with the EC figurines, the MC figurines were discovered in tombs, although this is to be expected when the majority of excavated sites are tombs and, thus, offers little insight as to the actual function of the images. These images have come to light also in settlement contexts, both

99. Karageorghis 1991: 178–79, Ea10 and Eb1.

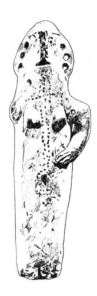

Fig. 5i
Cypriot MC plank figurine.
K. Severis Collection, Nicosia, Inv. 1539.

at Alambra-*Mouttes*[100] and Marki-*Alonia*.[101] In the former instance, the figurines, eleven fragments in all, were discovered scattered in various rooms of
the settlement, many coming from unstratified contexts. Looking randomly
dispersed, or treated as rubbish, the excavator rather doubted that they were
religious objects at all, stating that it seemed unlikely that these so poorly treated figurines were objects of veneration.[102] The examples from Marki show
both signs of wear and mending, suggesting that they were used "in life" as
well as being laid to rest with the dead.[103] Frankel and Webb concur with
Coleman's findings that the battered and mended states of the figurines pre-
clude their having special status or use in ritual or ceremony.[104]

Both V. Karageorghis and J. Karageorghis claim that it is in the Middle Cypriot period that the Cypriot artisans incorporated many elements of Levantine

100. Coleman *et al.* 1996: 202–3.

101. Mogelonsky 1988: 138–41.

102. Coleman *et al.* 1996: 200.

103. Frankel and Webb 1996: 188.

104. *Ibid.*

iconography into their own renderings of the "goddess."[105] This might be logical if one were to consider the Middle Cypriot Bronze Age as a coherent unit and, thus, the changes in figurine production would accord with the new, strong contact between Cyprus and the Levant as described above. However, the changes in the early MC figurines occur before the increase in contacts with the Levant in the later Middle Cypriot Bronze Age, making this hypothesis anachronistic. Furthermore, the style of rendering of female images is quite different between the two traditions. It is only the rendering of the navel or vagina on the MC figurines that might cause one to look to the Near East for inspiration. But, although the Near Eastern goddess figurines do place emphasis on both navel and genitalia, the means of rendering these attributes are quite different from the Cypriot style. The Levantine style makes use of a large triangle over the pubic region, usually cross-hatched for emphasis, to display the female genitalia. By contrast, the MC figurines that display this attribute have merely a deeply incised hole, possibly surrounded by incised dots or lines to represent the pubic triangle. Rather than arguing that the Cypriot artists adopted the Levantine method of displaying sex in a figurine, it seems more likely that the Cypriot artists, in attempting to create a female figurine in the nude, sought some way to portray all the feminine/sexual attributes, breasts as well as genitalia.

In the end, there is no convincing evidence for the cult of a female deity, specifically Aphrodite, in Cyprus during either the Early or Middle Cypriot Bronze Ages. The plank-shaped images prevalent during the Early Bronze Age do become more feminized, and even sexual, during the Middle Bronze Age, but just as the former could not clearly be identified as deities, neither can the latter. There is no evidence of Aphrodite's presence in the Chalcolithic that remained continuous during this early phase of the Bronze Age, nor of her introduction into the Cypriot repertoire through contact with alternate cultures, such as Anatolia, in the Early Bronze Age or the Levant in the Early Middle Bronze Age.

---

105. J. Karageorghis 1977: Chapter Three, and V. Karageorghis 1975: *passim*. I should distinguish between my use of the terms "goddess" and goddess, here. Both V. Karageorghis and J. Karageorghis believe that the female images in Cyprus, dating back as far as the Chalcolithic, are representations of goddesses. Thus, when considering their arguments, I put this term in quotation marks, as I ultimately do not think that these images portray deities. There is far greater evidence that the female figurines of the LC period do, in fact, portray goddesses, and, as such, I refer to them as goddesses without the quotation marks.

VI.
APHRODITE AND CYPRUS:
THE PROTOHISTORIC AGE

Middle Cypriot III (1725–1600 BCE)

Regarding this period, we may speak reasonably about foreign, specifically Levantine, influences in Cypriot anthropomorphic art. One specific image serves well to show the transition from the white painted ware figurines of the early Middle Cypriot Bronze Age to the bird-faced idols of the LC Bronze Age (see fig. 6a). This is a figurine of dark-slip III ware dating from the final phase of MC III.[1] The most important innovation in the image is the "spindle" shape, whereby the figurine has a small head, pointy feet, but is excessively broad at the level of the hips. This silhouette is almost identical with the idols of the Levant, specifically Syria, during the Late Bronze Age, and well predicts the arrival of the bird-faced figurines in Cyprus in the LC II period. The positioning

Fig. 6a
Cypriot MC spindle shaped figurine.
Metropolitan Museum of Art, Inv. 74.51.1537.

---

1. Sjöqvist 1940: 153–54, figure 16, no. 12.

of the arms, molded on either side of the body, extending out from the sides and curved inward so that the hands are resting on the chest, possibly meant to be holding breasts, is also strongly reminiscent of the Syrian bird-faced figurines, and this, too, may be the result of foreign influence.

Nevertheless, this image also shows a strong continuity with the female figurines of the earlier periods. The top of the head is flattened and the ears are molded, pronounced, and pierced. The facial features—eyes, nose and mouth—are all molded in typical Early Middle Cypriot style. This is clearly a period of transition. Otherwise there is little relevant data from this period.

The Late Bronze Age (1600–1000 BCE)

LATE CYPRIOT I (1600–1450 BCE)

The feminine figurines and ceramic models that provided evidence for Cypriot ideology for the previous millennia find no counterparts in LC I, nor are there sanctuaries from which to draw information concerning religious beliefs. Nevertheless, the period between MC III and LC II is of extreme importance in the history of Cypriot religion. By LC II, Cypriot idols and votives had become strongly orientalized, and it would seem that during these two centuries the increasingly common contacts with the Levant had a strong effect on Cypriot iconography and, most probably, ideology.

In the opposite direction, Minoan Crete and Mycenaean Greece make their first forays into the Cypriot sphere. The Minoan presence is most visible at *Toumba tou Skourou* in the northwest, where the circular shaft grave, Tomb I (1550/1525–1450 BCE), contained several fragments of Minoan pottery datable to c. 1525–1475. Early examples of Cypro-Minoan script have also come to light at *Toumba tou Skourou*, c. 1500.[2] Contacts between Cyprus and Greece increase during LC IB, when, LH IIb and IIIa pottery appears in significant quantities in Cyprus at Milia and Enkomi in the east; Nicosia in the center; and Maroni, Hala Sultan Teke, and Arpera in the south. Such finds might be correlated with similar finds in the Levant and Egypt.[3]

It is, therefore, not surprising that a certain degree of Aegean iconography comes to be seen in Cyprus during LC II– the so-called normal-faced figurines (see below). Both Levantine and Aegean religious influence (among others), then, might be understood in the ensuing period.

LATE CYPRIOT II (1450–1200 BCE)

After the relative "dark age" of the Cypriot coroplastic arts in LC I, new types of Cypriot figurines, artistic motifs, and religious architecture appear in abundance in LC II, strongly influenced by both Near Eastern and Aegean styles.

---

2. Vermeule 1974: the book has no page numbers.

3. Catling 1979: 199.

Trade with the Near East and the Aegean flourished. To the east, a previous intense trade with Syria changed to a new interest in Palestine, where quantities of LC fine wares peaked in the fourteenth century.[4] Although the diagnostic LC II wares—base-ring II and white slip II—appear in Ugarit to the north, much of this ware has come to light in greatest numbers farther south, notably in Megiddo, Gezer, Beth Shan, Tell Beit-Mirsim, Tel el-Deweir/Lachish, Tel el-'Ajjul/Gaza, and Ashkalon.[5] Almost no pottery flows in the reverse direction, most likely due to the LC II fondness for Aegean pottery types. Instead, the Cypriots imported luxury goods from the East, including gold, cylinder seals, and glass.

For imported pottery one needs to look to sources in the west. It was during LC II that the Cypriots began importing Mycenaean wares with a passion. The tombs of such sites as Enkomi, Pyla, Hala Sultan Teke, Maroni, Kourion, and Morphou-*Toumba tou Skourou* have revealed large quantities of Mycenaean pottery, most notably such large vessels as *amphorai* and kraters decorated in the Pictorial Style.[6] Chemical and neutron analysis of these wares has established that they were made in the Peloponnese and then exported to Cyprus and, possibly through Cyprus, to the Levant, as well.[7]

For the reconstruction of Cypriot religion in the Late Bronze Age, the opening lines of a LC II letter from an Ugarit official to a king deserve special attention:[8]

> To the king, [my] lo[rd],
> speak thus:
> From the officer of the one hundred, [your servant]
> At the feet of my lord, [from afar,]
> seven and seven times [I have fallen.]
> I myself have spoken to Baal...
> to eternal Šapš, to 'Aṭtart,
> to 'Anat, to all the gods of Alashiyah...

This text is significant, as it is the earliest written evidence concerning the possible identity of the deities of Cyprus. In this instance, it would appear that the deities Baal, Šapaš, Aštart, and Anat are named as at least a sub-set of the gods of Alashiyah (the addition "and all the other gods" is a typical add-on for such expressions). It is probable that the names given do not record the true names of the Cypriot deities, but rather the Ugaritic version of their names (much as the Romans claimed that the Gauls worshipped Jupiter, Ares, and

---

4. Bergoffen 1990: 211.

5. Sjöqvist 1940: 168–180; Bergoffen 1990: 202.

6. Vermeule and Wolsky 1978: *passim*; Karageorghis 1982: 78.

7. *Ibid.*

8. PRU V.8. Walls in Knapp (ed.) 1986: 36.

Minerva, as opposed to Taranis, Teutates, and Epona). By comparison, though, one might suggest that the Ugaritic official who wrote the letter recognized in Cyprus a chief male deity, perhaps associated with storms, a sun-goddess,[9] and a goddess or goddesses associated with warfare and hunting.[10]

The physical remains of the Cypriot cult show that contacts with the Near East (and to a lesser extent with the Aegean) had a profound effect on Cypriot religion in this Protohistoric period. This is partially evident in the sanctuaries that begin to take prominence in the LC Bronze Age, and assuredly so in the figurines and the glyptic art that become prominent throughout the island at this time.

The Sanctuaries[11]

Ajios Jakovos-*Dhima*

One of the earliest of the Cypriot shrines is located at Ajios Jakovos-*Dhima*.[12] Here, Sjöqvist discovered a floored area, circular in plan, divided into two unequal parts by a poorly preserved stone wall. In the eastern section of the circle were two round podia, both of equal height, but the northern of the two being over twice the size of the southern. Below the floor, to the south of the podia, was a circular rock-cut pit containing pottery remains found *in situ*.[13] The western section of the circle contained a terra-cotta, bath-shaped basin located within a shallow pit in the rock floor. On either side of the basin were rock-cut pits. From this area, especially around the basin and pits, came all the Late Bronze Age votive goods from the site.[14]

---

9. Whereas male solar deities are the norm in both Mesopotamian and Hellenic cultures, a female solar deity is common to both the Ugaritic and Hittite pantheons, the latter venerating the sun-goddess of Arinna as the head of their pantheon. As such, it would not be unusual for a female solar deity to be venerated in Cyprus and so recognized by an Ugaritic visitor.

10. As it would appear that in the last centuries of the Bronze Age the goddesses Anat and Aštart began to merge (eventually resulting in the Hellenistic Atargatis) the mention of both Anat and Aštart here could result from the presence of one goddess to be identified as either or both by the Ugaritic official.

11. More detail concerning sanctuary and temple structure and votives will be offered in this chapter than in those concerning Greece and the Levant for the sake of examining issues of continuity, foreign relations, and possible identifications of relevant deities.

12. Some might argue that the LC Ia-b site of *Phlamoudhi*-Vounari offers an example of a Cypriot religious structure before the LC II period. However, as the evidence at the site only offers proof of religious use starting in the Cypriot Archaic Age, I am discounting it as evidence for evolution of cult in Bronze Age Cyprus.

13. Sjöqvist 1927–31: 356.

14. *Ibid.*, 357.

Sjöqvist had been under the impression that this shrine had been in use since the MC III period. He based this assessment on the pottery from the rock-cut pit in the eastern section of the shrine—the oldest material present at the site—dating back to late MC III, which he felt certain were fragments of earlier votive offerings from an older sanctuary on the same ground.[15] As no LC I items were present at the shrine, Sjöqvist concluded that the shrine was abandoned during the LC I religious "dark age" and reused during the renaissance of the LC II period. However, it is now apparent that the pit that contained the pottery predates the shrine level by at least two centuries. As there is no indication of any activity during this hiatus, it is perhaps safer to say that ritual activity began at Ajios Jakovos-*Dhima* only in LC II, with no relationship whatsoever to the 300 odd MC pottery sherds located at the site.[16]

In the LC II period, the podia that Sjöqvist interprets as altars and the terracotta basin (in which the shrine's votive offerings were discovered) were erected. The finds discovered at the site consisted of (*inter alia*): gold and silver jewelry, silver funnels (six with gold mountings), several bronze weapons including six arrowheads, a stone axe, a small bronze lion figurine, several shards of pottery including Mycenaean wares, a ring bearing the cartouche of Thutmosis III of Egypt, and four cylinder seals.[17] Two of these seals, identified by Sjöqvist as Babylonian but by Webb as Cypriot,[18] show images of nude individuals with hands clasped before the chest, and one was inscribed in cuneiform with the word/name *Milatawaya*.[19]

The remains of this shrine suggest two developments. First is the importance of foreign goods as votive offerings, due most probably to their luxurious and exotic nature. Second, the shrine appears to have been dedicated to *two* deities, probably male and female.[20] The high quantity of jewelry possibly suggests a female deity, especially since jewelry had played such a prominent role in the imagery of female figurines in Cyprus for the past millennia. Weapons are a new addition to the Cypriot religious repertoire, and the high number of weapons dedicated at the shrine suggest that they were an important attribute or aspect of the deity/deities there adored. Although it is certainly possible that weaponry, like jewelry, might be dedicated to a female deity, especially if she was a war-goddess such as Anat or Ištar, parallels both

---

15. *Ibid.*, 360.

16. J. Webb, personal communication.

17. Webb 1992a: 95; Eriksson 1993: 41.

18. Sjöqvist 1927–31: 357–58; J. Webb, personal communication.

19. Webb 1992a: 95.

20. This is following the standard interpretation of this site as a shrine. For a counter argument in favor of identification as a funerary site, see Webb 1992a, 94ff.

to the east and west of Cyprus, especially with the Ugaritic Baal mentioned in the text discussed above, suggest, rather, that the weapons were intended for a male deity. As an armed male deity does become prominent in the Cypriot glyptic iconography at this point, as well as in the three-dimensional iconographic repertoire in LC III, the dual nature of the shrine at Ajios Jakovos-*Dhima* and the weapons found there argue that this male deity entered the Cypriot religion as early as LC II. However, the glyptic also shows a goddess bearing arms and, thus, the weapons could be interpreted as belonging to either deity, or both.

Kition

The idea of dual deities in Cypriot religion, as recognized at the shrine at Ajios Jakovos, is also present at the LC II sanctuary of Kition. Excavation at the northern tip of the city (Area II) revealed a complex containing two structures attributable to floor IV (LC IIC period). These are identified by Karageorghis as temples 2 and 3, separated by a garden and bordered to the north by the city wall.[21]

Temple 3, the smaller of the two temples, is located on the north-central sector of Area II. It consists of two rooms of unequal size, with the larger room to the east appearing to be the main hall of the temple. While no column bases were discovered associated with this level of occupation, the excavator— Demas—believes that the space was small enough that the area could have been roofed without the use of columns.[22] In the southeast corner of this room was located the entrance to the temple, giving the temple a bent-axis approach.[23] At the eastern end, in front of the entrance, was altar E, possibly consisting of both a hearth and a table of offerings. The hearth itself was filled with a 10 centimeter-thick layer of ash, whereas the area around the hearth contained disturbed patches of ash and carbonized bone.[24]

No objects were found within Temple 3, probably due to extensive reconstruction on and around the temple in subsequent years.[25] However, objects were discovered in several of the large pits that separated Temples 3 and 2, and Demas suggests that two or three of these pits contained objects originally located in Temple 3, including several Mycenaean figurines and two stone anchors.[26]

---

21. Karageorghis and Demas 1985: 24ff., Chapter IV.

22. *Ibid.*, 25.

23. *Ibid*; Webb 1999: 38.

24. Karageorghis and Demas 1985: 25.

25. *Ibid.*, 26.

26. *Ibid.*, 30.

Temple 2 lay 16 meters southeast of Temple 3 and was more than three times as large. Like Temple 3, it was oriented east to west, with an entrance on the southern side and consisted of a large main hall with a small room adjoining it to the west, although in the case of Temple 2 there was also an entrance hall to the east.[27] As with Temple 3, a bent-axis approach is present. Two rows of column bases were present in the main hall of Temple 2, dividing this hall into three parts and giving it symmetry and a focus on the hearth. For these reasons—greater size, extra room, more monumental construction—it appears that Temple 2 is the more significant of the two temples.

Unlike Temple 3, several objects of the LC IIC period did come to light from Temple 2. In room 24B (the entrance hall to the temple providing access to the main hall) were found two stone anchors, two fragmentary base-ring bowls, a bronze pin, a white shaved-ware jug, a weight, and two LH III stirrup jars.[28]

The main hall of Temple 2 (Room 24) contained a hearth similar to that of Temple 3 at the western end of the room. The ashy remains from this hearth are attributed to the later reoccupation of the temple, but a pit at the eastern end of the hall contained ashy soil, bones, a fragmentary cooking-pot, and a bronze ring. These may indicate a use for the hearth similar to Temple 3 at this time.[29] Finds from this room include (*inter alia*): a stone anchor; faience beads; LH IIIB chalices, a stirrup jar, bowl, and rhyton; Cypriot wares; scrap metal; a bronze arrowhead; a gold ring; and a lead sling-bullet.[30] The final room of the temple, Room 24A, appears to have been a storeroom, containing beads of faience and carnelian, gold and bronze jewelry, a bronze votive "kidney," base-ring ware, a spindle whorl, and scrap metal.[31]

Between the two temples was a complex of pits and channels that the excavators believe represents the remains of a sacred garden.[32] It is important to note that although the gardens are located between and, thus, associated with, both temples, it is Temple 3 specifically whose entrance opens onto the garden, whereas that of Temple 2 faces away from the garden.[33] One could argue, then, that it is specifically Temple 3 that is linked to the garden.

Who "lived" in the temples at Kition is a difficult issue. It is important to note that the two temples form a unit, suggesting the cult of a pair of deities. If the objects found in the pits are, in fact, the votives from Temple 3, then

---

27. *Ibid.*, 26.

28. *Ibid.*, 27.

29. *Ibid.*, 28.

30. *Ibid.*

31. *Ibid.*, 29.

32. *Ibid.*, 32.

33. *Ibid.*, 37.

the Aegean figurines may indicate that Temple 3 was dedicated to a female deity, as does the close link between the temple and the sacred gardens (in later times strongly associated with Aphrodite). The remains from Temple 2 would, at first glance, appear to go either way: the bronze arrowhead and lead sling-bullet could indicate a male deity, even a war-god (although see possible links between weapons and goddesses under "Ajios Jakovos"), whereas the gold jewelry and spindle whorl would seem to be indicative of a female deity. However, the more "masculine" items, such as the arrowhead, derive from the main hall of the temple, whereas the more "feminine" items come from what the excavators believe was a storage room. One might suggest that the votives from the main hall are more indicative of the nature of the deity than the cult paraphernalia from the storage room and, thus, lend greater weight to the hypothesis that Temple 2 was dedicated at least to a male deity, if not the joint cult of a male and female.

Athienou

Athienou extends over four periods, ranging from MC III/LC I through the Iron Age. However, the remains from the earliest phase (Stratum IV)—pits and small huts—suggest a secular use of the area and the significance of the site as a religious center does not begin until Stratum III = LC II. At this time, a large court area was constructed flanked to the northeast by a large building measuring approximately 20 meters by 20 meters.[34] In the court area were pits containing votive deposits, most notably over 10,000 pottery fragments, both of normal size and miniature, which the excavators estimate were of votive rather than practical intent.[35] Beyond the pottery, the court brought forth a wealth of significant finds. In the central courtyard of the building were several copper nodules, along with a large quantity of votive vessels. Also in this area were unfinished, finished, or broken copper objects. These, along with the copper nodules mentioned previously, suggest the presence of a copper workshop at the site. In nearby pit 543 were discovered bone, ash, shells, and sea urchins, which the excavator believes may have been involved in the metal-working process, although they may also be votive in nature. This pit also yielded LH IIIC pottery along with the brow and horns of a bull.[36]

Whereas the LH IIIC pottery from this stratum seems to be an intrusion from Stratum II, both LH IIIB and Minoan wares are prevalent in the Stratum III finds.[37] It is clear that both ox remains and copper are important aspects of cult practice during the LC II phase.

---

34. Al-Radi 1983: 67.

35. Dothan and Ben-Tor 1983: 20.

36. *Ibid.*, 140.

37. *Ibid.*, 46–52.

Myrtou-*Pigadhes*

Similar in many respects to Athienou and Ajios Jakovos is the last sanctuary dating to the LC II period, Myrtou-*Pigadhes*. Once again, while this site has elements that date back into the MC period, the architecture associated with cult ritual appears only during the LC II phase. *Pigadhes* was clearly of great significance as a cult spot during the LC II period, for no less than five phases of construction and reconstruction are identified as belonging to the period between c. 1400 to 1175.[38]

The first architectural structures associated with *Pigadhes* as a cult spot are several rooms constructed during the sanctuary's Phase III (early LC IIA). In some respects, the area might be likened to a rectangular version of the Ajios Jakovos structure.

To the west is a small room in which the excavators discovered a pit in the floor that contained a small stone axe and pottery shards.[39] Although hardly equal to the sumptuous finds at Ajios Jakovos, it does suggest a tendency toward *bothroi* for votive offering apart from the altar/podium room. To the east of this antechamber of sorts is a longer, rectangular room in which it is possible (although not entirely certain) that a podium existed as early as the Phase III structure. Entrances into this room (CD3) appear to have been at openings in the eastern corners of the room, suggesting, as with Kition, a bent-axis approach.[40] The presence of Base-Ring and White-Slip wares, as well as early wheel-made pottery, date this level to the early LC II.[41]

During the next phase of occupation, Period IV, little occurred at the site, to judge from the paucity of remains.[42] But in Period V, dating to LC IIC, the sanctuary is expanded to become a large cult complex, with its central features being a large court to the west of a stepped altar constructed of limestone and topped by what the excavator believes to be horns-of-consecration.[43] Discovered on top of the remains of this altar was a bronze figurine of a bull, which may have some symbolic association with the large quantity of animal horns found throughout the sanctuary.[44]

Many of the votives dedicated at the sanctuary remained at the site, so something might be determined about the cult of the deity there worshipped. The most noticeable dedications are animal bones. In the earlier phases of the sanctuary, starting in Phase III but significant as well in Phases IV and V, are

---

38. DuPlat Taylor *et al*. 1957: 113–16.

39. *Ibid*., 9.

40. Webb 1999: 36.

41. DuPlat Taylor *et al*. 1957: 10.

42. *Ibid*.

43. *Ibid*., 10–18; Al-Radi 1983: 81–82.

44. DuPlat Taylor *et al*. 1957: 13.

animal horns, particularly deer antlers and goat horns.[45] Other, scattered bones from these species, as well as from sheep and oxen, were present at the site, and so one might think of animal sacrifice. However, no burnt remains or signs of burning were present in the court or by the altar; it is, therefore, difficult to determine the role played by these animals in the cult.[46] Nevertheless, it must be noted that incised ox scapulae formed an important percentage of the items discovered with the votives. The presence of the horns, antlers, and incised ox bones points to a cult of a deity associated with horned animals, a matter to be considered further in our section on glyptic.

Incised ox scapulae were found with other votive deposits within storerooms at the easternmost edge of the sanctuary (Rooms 15, 16, 17, 20a, and 20b), where it would seem that old votives were collected during periods of reconstruction.[47] Here the excavator found shards of local pottery, shards of Mycenaean ware, bronze, and a quantity of copper slag.[48] It would seem that, although there is no evidence of copper smelting at this site, the products of that industry are appropriate for the deity in question.

Figurines

A second source for reconstructing Cypriot religion in the LC II period are the female figurines prevalent throughout the island. As in the Chalcolithic, Early, and Middle Bronze Ages, LC II figurines come frequently from tombs, when any provenance for them is available at all. It must be remembered, however, that this provenance has more to do with the preponderance of funerary contexts excavated than on any intrinsic relationship between female figurines and mortuary practice, as Webb has argued.[49] The new LC II figurines have a common style and iconography throughout the island, appearing in Yialousia in the north, Bamboula in the south, Enkomi in the east, Linou in the west, and throughout the central island.[50] Furthermore, unlike their predecessors, the LC II images show clear derivation from Near Eastern images that are explicitly divine. It is during this period that a new religious ideology appears to have entered Cyprus, an ideology of a deity who could be represented in anthropomorphic form (as opposed to the bull and snake images of the preceding centuries). Thus, for the first time, we might discuss these female images as true goddess figurines.[51]

---

45. Zeuner in DuPlat Taylor *et al.* 1957: 97–100.

46. Cornwall in DuPlat Taylor *et al.* 1957: 101.

47. DuPlat Taylor *et al.* 1957: 20. Webb in Karageorghis and Demas 1985: 320.

48. DuPlat Taylor *et al.* 1957: 20–21.

49. Webb 1992: 88–90, 97–99.

50. Merrillees 1988: 55.

51. For the full explanation and identification of these figurines, see Chapter Eight.

The LC II figurines are of a style considerably distinct from the MC variety, although they evidently began their emergence in the Cypriot repertoire at the very end of this latter period. This is evident in the MC III dark-slip-style figurine described above. Although this figurine dates to the end of the Middle Cypriot III period and shows a close affinity with the earlier terra-cotta female figurines of the Middle Cypriot period, she nevertheless shows the earliest developments of what will be one of the dominant characteristics of at least one style of LC female figurines. This is her overall form, a form that has been described as "spindle-shaped," and is typified by a relatively small head, arms curving onto the chest or abdomen, extremely broad hips and thighs, and small, rather pointy feet (see fig. 6a).

The female figurines, all terra-cotta, that become prominent in the LC II period are of two similar, though distinct, types. The first of these is the so-called bird-faced figurine, a style typified by the spindle-shaped silhouette described above (see fig. 6b). They exist in two iconographically identical types: hollow and solid-bodied. The top of the head is generally rounded and on either side of the face are large ears with two or three piercings each. The face itself has a prominent, beak-like nose and round eyes of molded clay. The mouth is seldom indicated. The neck is long and decorated with incised

Fig. 6b
Cypriot Bird-faced figurine.
British Museum, Inv. A 15.

bands, possibly indicating a necklace, and incised lines crisscross between the breasts. In almost all cases, these breasts are rendered by molding. The most prominent aspect of these figurines is the pubic triangle. This is indicated by incised lines over the pubic region, one to three lines at the waist and on either leg. The region within the triangle is filled in with incision, either dots, lines, or cross-hatching. In some examples a navel is indicated. The legs are always rendered separately and, in some cases, knees are rendered by molding. The arms, also molded, are found in various poses. In some figurines the arms extend from the shoulders away from the body, curving back to rest on the torso or under the breasts. In others, the arms lie akimbo on the hips or have one arm on the chest, stomach, or holding an object, such as a child, bird, or musical instrument.

The second type of figurine has a "normal" face, with a flat head, molded eyes, eyebrows, nose, and an incised mouth (see fig. 6c). Unlike the bird-faced figurines, these figurines are decorated not by incision, but with paint, particularly on the face, neck, and pubis. They are never shown carrying children or other objects; otherwise, they make use of the same arm positionings. In all other respects, the normal-faced figurines are similar to the bird-faced figurines and appear to be an attempt to "Aegeanize" the more avian style.

Fig. 6c
Cypriot normal-faced figurine.
Cyprus Museum, Inv. A 51.

These LC II figurines show some continuity with the female figurines of the preceding ages on the island as well as considerable novelty. Certain motifs remain just as important in the Late Bronze Age in Cyprus as they were in the Chalcolithic and the earlier Bronze Ages. Dating back even into the Chalcolithic is the importance of jewelry bedecking the figurines, as well as the stress on a specific pose or posture highlighting the feminine attributes of the figurines (the birth pose in the case of the Chalcolithic figurines and the arms indicating breasts, belly, and hips in the case of LC II figurines). Continuous from the Early Bronze Age is the emphasis on incised decoration, prominent nose, and ears (the latter consistently pierced and bearing earrings), and the tendency toward a *kourotrophos* motif. Finally, the LC II figurines show the ultimate fulfillment of the MC tendency toward three-dimensionalism and emphasis on sexual attributes. Both periods of figurines show molded breasts highlighted by the placement of the arms. The MC sub-waist pierced hole, indicating either navel or vagina, is represented on the LC versions through the incised pubic triangle and the frequently incised navel.

These figurines are distinctive in their over-all shape, the emphasis on the legs and, most importantly, the emphasis on the pubic triangle and hips. While the MC figurines show a growing tendency toward three-dimensional representation, their cylinder-shaped bodies hardly foretell the spindle-shaped bodies of the LC II period. Only one figurine from MC III begins to show this silhouette, possibly the result of an extensive influx of Syrian iconography. While the feet of the MC figurines were occasionally divided by a small, incised line, the legs of the LC II images are wrought individually, each being added to the torso separately.[52] Finally, whereas the MC figurines occasionally made use of a single incised hole on the lower abdomen, representing either navel or vagina, the LC II figurines emphasize these attributes, often representing the navel on the mid-abdomen and always portraying the genital area with strongly incised lines in the case of the bird-faced figurines, and with paint in the case of the normal-faced figurines.

These novelties are due to a heavy influx of iconography during the LC Bronze Age, both in (probably) LC I and LC II. The bird-faced figurines, which are the older of the two styles, derive from Near Eastern figurines prominent in northern Mesopotamia and Syria since the third millennium. These figurines exist in three distinctive types throughout three separate regions of the Near East: the Littoral region, the Orontes region, and the Euphrates region.[53] The figurines from the Littoral region, which includes Ugarit and Byblos offer little information concerning the origins and meaning of the Cypriot figurines. Very few terra-cotta figurines come from the Littoral region, possible due to the availability of bronze and ivory in this area. Further-

52. Orphanides 1983: 30–33.

53. Badre 1980: *passim.*

more, mass produced, mold-made figurines are more common in this region, thus rendering a style quite distinct from the handmade Cypriot versions. To the east, in the Euphrates region, the figurines are also different in many respects from the Cypriot version. It is in the Orontes region, especially at Hama, Ebla, Selemiyeh, Alalakh, and Tel Judaidah, that figurines almost identical to the Cypriot images appear.[54] According to Badre, these images are most common during the middle of the second millennium, at approximately the time that pottery trade between Cyprus and Syria is at its peak. Thus, it would seem that the Syrian figurines entered the Cypriot repertoire during the MC III–LC I phase, when contacts between these two regions were strong. This would also account for their sudden emergence island-wide at the beginning of LC II.

These Orontes-style figurines, like the Cypriot versions, have spindle-shaped silhouettes. The heads are rounded and frequently bear a hairstyle consisting of curls on either side of the face.[55] They wear molded necklaces decorated with incised lines. Two crisscrossed incised lines appear over the chest. The majority of the figurines have molded breasts, although this is not as consistent as in the Cypriot figurines. The navel is either rendered as a molded bead with one incised dot on the belly or is entirely incised. The pubis is indicated by incised lines, either in the form of a filled in triangle as in Cyprus, or by two parallel lines at the top of the legs running perpendicular to the line separating the legs. The legs are straight, with knees occasionally being rendered by molding. The toes are indicated by incision. There are four styles of arm-positioning. They might extend straight out from the body (similar to Mycenaean *tau* figurines); extend out from the shoulders and bend back to support or cover the breasts; hang straight down the sides of the body; or one arm might curve to cover a breast while the other hangs down the body. Whereas the attributes of breasts and navel are common throughout the Near East on female figurines, the pubic incisions and the crossed lines between the breasts are common to the Orontes region.[56] The most important difference between the early Syrian figurines and those from Cyprus is that the Syrian versions never have a child in the arms.[57]

There is also a minimal amount of influence from the west in these LC II images, particularly in the case of the normal-faced figurines. It is generally believed that these figurines are a later evolution of the bird-faced figurines,

---

54. *Ibid.*

55. I find it quite possible that these hairlocks were re-interpreted by the Cypriots as pierced ears, according to their own long-standing tradition.

56. Badre 1980: Chapter Two.

57. *Ibid.*, 136. Later versions, found in Palestine only, show *kourotrophos* imagery, possibly due to influence from Cyprus.

but heavily influenced by Aegean-style figurines. Thus, the use of paint, the more "human" dimensions, and the flat head, all recall the decorative motifs of Mycenaean *tau, phi* and *psi* figurines.

Finally, a purely Aegean style of figurine must be mentioned, although these images become far more common in the ensuing LC III period. These images are typical Mycenaean *psi* figurines, with *polos*-style headdresses, schematic bodies with upraised arms, and semi-conical bases. They are relatively unpopular in the LC II period: the small hoard at Kition, one figurine at Enkomi, one at Kourion-*Bamboula*, and one at Maroni-*Tsaroukas*.[58] It is evident that the Aegean is beginning to exert some iconographic (possibly ideological?) influence on Cyprus at this time, evident both in Aegeanizing architectural motifs as at Athienou and the *psi* figurines, although this influence appears to pale in comparison to the Levantine.[59]

Glyptic

Another important source of data for the Cypriot pantheon is the glyptic art. There are certain difficulties in dealing with this particular medium: the uncertainty as to the actual use of cylinder seals in Cyprus (no impressions have been discovered);[60] the difficulty in determining the extent to which the Cypriots adopted *in toto* the iconography of their neighbors (Mesopotamia, the Levant, Anatolia, and the Aegean); and the extent to which they adapted the glyptic to portray their own worldview. The creative mixing of styles—Syrian, Mittani, and Aegean—have lead some to argue that the Cypriot glyptic is, in fact, distinctive, and that the iconography presented might serve to reveal information concerning Cypriot religion.[61]

The majority of cylinder seals on Cyprus have come to light at Enkomi, others from Kourion, Hala Sultan Teke, Iaysos, Kameiros, Klavdia, Maroni, and Dhima.[62] As might be expected, a certain percentage of these are imports, approximately 20 percent at Enkomi.[63] In terms of chronology, the seals appear to have been in use from the LC IIB period up through LC IIIB.[64]

---

58. Begg 1991: Appendix III.

59. French 1971: 106 suggests that the popularity of these Mycenaean figurines in Greece may be due to Levantine influence. Here, we may be seeing a similar development, or even contribution to that development, by way of Cyprus.

60. Webb 1992b: 113–17.

61. Webb 1988: *passim*; Porada 1991: *passim*.

62. Kenna 1971: 39.

63. Courtois and Webb 1987: 26.

64. Porada 1948: 178; Courtois and Webb 1987: 26. This flatly contradicts the dates assigned by Schaeffer-Forrer to the cylinder seals from Enkomi as published in 1983,

A handful of seals represent deities, both male and female. In typical Cypriot fashion, the deities are strongly influenced by both Syrian and Aegean styles. Thus the "Master of Animals" on the hematite seal from Enkomi (Enkomi-Alashia 1.002) is strongly Minoan in imagery, wearing a Minoan style kilt and "petting" heraldically placed lions with faces turned away from the god.[65] By contrast, cylinder seal no. 1900.5-21.1 from the British Museum shows a god of Near Eastern type, with horned mitre, upraised mace in one hand and a variety of weapons in the other, in striding posture atop a seated bull (see fig. 6d).[66]

The glyptic preserves three goddess types: a goddess, possibly armed, shown opposite a god; a *potnia theron* goddess; and a nude goddess, possibly winged. These categories overlap and, thus, may not be viewed as pointedly distinct. That the females in question are, in fact, goddesses can be determined by either the presence of horned mitres (as in the Near Eastern style), their presence upon thrones of a divine style (also as per comparison with the Near Eastern glyptic), and their possession of certain non-human attributes, most notably wings.

An example of the first category, an armed goddess, is MMA 74.51.4308 from Kourion, a member of Porada's Group I.[67] Here is a female deity wearing a tall, conical cap. In her left hand she wields a flail above her head; in her right hand she holds a spear with its butt upon the ground. She is winged and wears a fringed gown similar to those of the Syrian style, except that such items of attire never adorn a female in the Syrian glyptic.[68] In the composition she faces a male deity (with horned cap). Between them are a lion and a genie with the head and wings of a bird and the lower body of a human. In this particular instance, the goddess carries a spear that is similar in style to Aegean Bronze Age spears. Furthermore, the motif of a god and goddess fighting the same creature is not a Levantine motif, but has its closest parallels in Greece. As such, Porada suggests that, in this instance, one might regard the "Armed Goddess" as being Aegean in inspiration.[69] Nevertheless, an armed-winged-*potnia theron* goddess appears in the Syrian repertoire, and the Aegean origin of this motif should not be exaggerated.[70]

---

who dates some seals up into the nineteenth century. Cylinder seals from this text will be considered here, but the dates offered by Schaeffer-Forrer will not be accepted.

65. Schaeffer-Forrer 1983: 56.

66. Kenna 1971: Pl. IX, no. 36.

67. Porada 1948: Pl. VIII, no. 8.

68. *Ibid.*, 182-83.

69. *Ibid.*

70. More on this motif in Chapter Eight.

Fig. 6d
Cypriot cylinder seal.
BM 1900.5.21.1.

A similar motif is evident on the cylinder seal mentioned above, BM 1900.5-21.1 (see fig. 6d). While the striding god stands to the left of the image, there is a seated goddess to the right of the scene. She wears a horned mitre and is facing left. Her left hand is raised in a gesture of greeting; in her right hand she holds two objects that Kenna identifies as grain but that bear no resemblance to grain as typically presented in Near Eastern glyptic.[71] The goddess sits upon a throne with her feet resting upon a footrest. In the middle of the composition is a votary (?), who faces the goddess and offers her a bird that is trying to fly away.[72]

The *potnia theron* motif appears predominantly with lions and caprids. An excellent example of the *potnia theron* motif is cylinder seal MMA 74.51.4315 from Ayia Paraskevi, categorized as belonging to Group VII.[73] Here is a goddess presented *en face* but with the head turned to the side (although a damage in the cylinder seal upon the face makes this difficult to make out entirely). This goddess is surrounded to the right and left by animals, including a caprid, an ox, and a fantastic-looking bird that she is touching on the beak. In this instance, the goddess appears to be associated with several different groupings of animals.

---

71. Kenna 1971: 22.

72. Kenna identifies the bird as a dove, but with little supporting evidence (*ibid.*).

73. Porada 1948: 190–91 and Pl. X, no. 35.

Cylinder seal 1898.12–1.64 in the British Museum, from Maroni, though faint, shows at least one if not two females in full dress gripping caprids by the horns.[74] The females have schematically rendered heads with no facial features. The dresses are reminiscent of Minoan clothing: there is a full upper garment with what, in modern times, would be regarded as shoulder pads. The skirts, while also faintly rendered, appear to be flounced, as there are horizontal lines descending down the length of the skirts, parted by a vertical line in the center. The caprids are portrayed as rearing upon their hind legs; each is facing away from the female who holds the caprid's horns. As with the "Master of Animals" described above, there is a strong Aegean flavor to this representation of the *potnia theron*.

A full collection of cylinder seals portraying a goddess dominating caprids is offered in Webb's 1988 publication.[75] In one example, Louvre AO.4500, a goddess sits upon a throne that is itself set upon the back of a lion (see fig. 6e).[76] A procession of individuals (the last having the face of a bird, possibly representing a genie or priests/priestesses in a mask) walks toward this goddess, each carrying a caprid by the horns. The person standing before the goddess holds the caprid to her, which the goddess takes with her right hand. On seal Louvre AO. 450, a goddess sits upon a throne facing a procession.[77] In her right hand she holds a sickle. The procession itself appears, once again, to consist of fantastic creatures/cult personnel, each holding one or two caprids. Of particular interest are two winged goddesses portrayed *en face* holding two caprids by the lowers paws.

From Enkomi Quarter 3 comes a cylinder seal in two registers. In the upper register is a goddess upon a simple throne wearing a long gown.[78] In her left hand she holds a knife, while in her right hand she holds a caprid by a leash(?) at the animal's neck. To the right of this goddess is a lion-hunt scene, with a chariot chasing three lions. In the lower register are two heraldically seated goddesses, each seated upon the back of a seated lion. These two goddesses are holding a caprid between them and each has the other arm raised as if to strike. Beneath the chariot, in the lower register, are two individuals, one in a long skirt carrying a spear and a stick, and one in a kilt carrying just a stick. The heraldically seated goddesses motif occurs on a seal from Kition (Cyprus

---

74. Kenna 1971: 30, no. 84.

75. Webb 1988: 276ff.

76. *Ibid.*, Pl. XXXVIII, no. 2.

77. *Ibid.*, Pl. XXXVIII no. 3.

78. Terms such as "upper" and "lower" are somewhat misleading, as the registers are inverted from each other, and one or the other side appears right-side-up when the cylinder is held either way.

Fig. 6e
Cypriot cylinder seal.
Louvre AO.4500.

Museum T.9/16), where the enthroned goddesses each hold a caprid by the horns.[79]

In the majority of cases, the goddess is shown either sitting upon a caprid or lion (or upon a throne with the feet of such animals) or holding a caprid by the horn (as described above) with a weapon of some sort in her opposite hand. In such instances, she might be understood as dominating the creatures in question. When the imagery portrays the goddess with a weapon in conjunction with the living or dead bodies of caprids, we may be seeing references to animal sacrifice associated with her cult and/or ideology.[80] It is highly probable, then, that the Cypriot pantheon had a goddess strongly associated with animals, in general, and caprids and lions, in particular. Perhaps caprids were associated with the goddess through their prevalence as sacrificial animals in this goddess's cult (although in some instances, as seen above with Myrtou-*Pigadhes*, the bones may be present at a sanctuary with no other evidence of sacrifice).

---

79. *Ibid.*, Pl. XXXVIII, no. 8.

80. *Ibid.*, 277-78.

Fig. 6f
Cypriot cylinder seal.
Chypre A9, Schaeffer-Forrer 1983.

Finally, there is the nude goddess prevalent in Cypriot glyptic iconography. One excellent example of this goddess is shown on seal A9 from Enkomi
(see fig. 6f).[81] The image in question is a nude, winged female, shown *en face*
but facing to her right and with feet pointing to the right. She wears an elaborate headdress; the breasts are not rendered, but both the navel and the
pubic triangle are emphasized by incision. One of her hands is at her waist,
the other holds some object above what appears to be an altar. Behind the goddess in an *ankh*, behind which is a striding male figure, probably a god, who
holds some manner of weapon in his right hand. Standing before the goddess
and facing her over the altar is another male deity, wearing an *atef* crown. His
left hand, like her right, holds an object above the altar, and his right hand,
raised behind his head, wields a weapon. A small lion is behind this god, surrounded top and bottom by a guilloche.

A second example of the nude goddess is shown on seal MMA, 74.51.4310
from Kourion.[82] In this case, the nude goddess does not have wings. She
wears a small cap and faces to her right, although otherwise she is portrayed
en face. Her arms bend at the elbows and curve in to clench at the waist. The
pubic triangle is rendered by incision and the thighs are large. Before her
stands a striding male in a kilt who holds what appears to be a lamp or highly
stylized tree in his hands. On the opposite side of the lamp and facing the pair
is a genie with the head, wings, and feet of a bird but the torso and legs of a
human. Behind the goddess is a guilloche; above the guilloche are two lions
couchant; below are two heraldically placed caprids facing each other over
a small, stylized plant.

---

81. Schaeffer-Forrer 1983: 62.

82. Porada 1948: Pl. VIII, no. 2.

Another example (Chypre A 2) shows a nude goddess standing upon a striding lion's back, holding a caprid in both hands—one by the leg and one by the horn.[83] The goddess wears some manner of headdress (schematic) and has a Hathoric hair-do. The face is minimally rendered. There is some patterning upon the chest (not breasts) and the genital triangle is rendered by molding. The goddess herself stands *en face*, but her feet point toward the right. On either side of the goddess are gods. The one to her right wears an Egyptian-style white crown and holds a shepherd's staff in his right hand. The god to the left wears an Egyptian-style *atef* crown, holds a similar staff, and in his other hand grasps a caprid. On either side of the goddess's head are small, winged sphinxes. The goddess appears to be smaller than the two gods, because of her placement upon the lion. All three have heads at the same level (isocephaly), indicating that they are to be understood as being the same height.

One further example of a nude goddess in Cypriot glyptic is British Museum 99.12–29.35, from Klavdia.[84] It includes a nude goddess with wings standing *en face*. She wears a highly schematic horned mitre and, once again, the arms are bent so that the hands reach the breasts. No sexual characteristics are shown. To the left of this goddess is a caprid facing toward the goddess; to her right is a griffin, apparently striding toward the goddess. In this instance, a winged, nude goddess is clearly being portrayed as a *potnia theron*.

In all these examples, the goddess is the same size as the god(s) and is shown in context with him. This is in contrast to other portrayals of the nude goddess that show her on a much smaller scale than the other figures within a scene. One excellent example of this is on British Museum seal 1900.5–21.3.[85] To one side is a fantastic creature with the head of a bull, wings, and the body of a human in a full gown. One "hand" reaches behind the creature to hold the tail of a rampant lion, the other "hand" is extended upward in an apparent sign of greeting. To the right of this creature and facing it is a goddess with upraised arms. She has a cap from which horn-like protrusions emerge. She faces to the left, and a hair knot is visible at the nape of her neck. Both of her arms are raised and she is clad in a full-length gown. Between these two figures is a floral motif, beneath which is a winged, nude goddess. She stands *en face*, although her feet point to the right. Her cap is similar to that of the goddess to her right, marking her as divine. She holds her hands to her breasts. In height she is about three quarters the size of the other two divinities. To the rights of this group are two rampant lions on either side of a sacred tree, at the base of which are two juxtaposed caprids (? no horns are visible). A

83. Schaeffer-Forrer 1983: 59.
84. Kenna 1971: no. 28.
85. *Ibid.*, 29, no. 77; Porada 1948, no. 11.

small male figure is shown squatting under the tail of the farther lion. Aegean elements are evident in both the apparent goddess-with-upraised-arms motif and the three-quarter rotation of the bull-creature's head.[86]

In some examples the nude goddess is shown equal in size to the other members of the composition; in other instances she is considerably smaller, and even looks as though she was added as an afterthought (although this category is clearly in the minority). She may be winged or not; she may be a *potnia theron* or not. She is usually portrayed with lions or caprids, thus strongly associating her with the *potnia theron* type.

There appears to be considerable interchangeability between the *potnia theron* and the nude goddess. It is possible that they represent the same entity, or that there is a strong commonality between the different goddesses of Cyprus at this time. In at least some instances, the nude goddess is portrayed as strongly resembling the figurines mentioned above in this section: nude, *en face*, with hands to breasts or waist, and emphasis on the genital region. It is, thus, possible that the nude goddess in the glyptic represents the same entity as the figurines, but, as well, offers a fuller picture of this goddess, insofar as the element of the *potnia theron* is added into her character.[87]

In all instances of the latter two goddess types, *potnia theron* and nude, the similarities with the Levantine glyptic are overwhelming, especially in light of the motif of the winged, nude goddess, which is quite common in the Near Eastern repertoire. These motifs will be examined in greater detail in following chapters, but, as with the figurines themselves, the glyptic provides yet one more piece of evidence that the significant contributors to the evolution of the Cypriot goddess came from the east.

Ultimately, what might be gleaned from the texts, the architecture, and the art is that Cyprus played a significant role in the eastern Mediterranean in the LC II period, and that the island absorbed a considerable amount of Near Eastern and Aegean influence at this time. In terms of religious development/evolution, the LC II period marks a point where what existed of Cypriot tradition merged with Levantine, and some Aegean, influences and from this confluence a new manifestation of cult, visible both in the places of worship and the depiction of the deities, emerged.

A strong Levantine influence can be seen in Cypriot architecture with the rectangular structures located within the city walls using bent-axis approach, such as at Kition and Myrtou-*Pigadhes*.[88] Such temples are composed of long, usually bent-axis rectangular halls complete with benches or platforms and a back room for the storage of cult paraphernalia. Similarly styled structures

86. Porada 1948: 185.

87. Wiggermann 1998: 50 discusses the possible interchangeability between nude goddess and *potnia theron* in Mesopotamian and Cypriot glyptic.

88. Wright 1992 (Vol. I): 507.

appear in LB II–IA I Palestine at such sites as the Fosse temple at Lachish, the Wayside shrine at Tel Mevorakh, and the temples at Tel Qasile. This style appears also in thirteenth-century Greece, contemporaneous with those structures in the Levant and Cyprus.[89]

The direction and order of influence is, of course, a matter of some debate. Negbi has postulated that an original Palestinian design, best expressed at Tel Mevorakh, was adopted in the west, notably at the cult center at Mycenae and the sanctuary at Phylakopi. This style of architecture was then brought back to the Levant by the Philistines, recognizable in the shrine at Tel Qasile.[90] As the LC II temples pre-date the movements of the Philistines (and the end of the Bronze Age in general), it is evident that the influence must come from the east. Ultimately, influence from both east and west merge in Cyprus in LC III sanctuaries such as at Paphos (see below), resulting in an architectural style that both Burdajewicz and Maier recognize as essentially Cypriot in nature.[91]

This merging of cultures is also evident in the new figurines, where, as mentioned above, aspects of the earlier Cypriot artistic tradition, dating even as far back as the Chalcolithic, were retained. This is most evident in the Cypriot LC II *kourotrophos* figurines, a motif that does not occur among the Syrian bird-faced images, but that is common in Cyprus since, at least, EC III. Evidently, the Cypriots, while importing a new image whose iconography must have embodied many of their own beliefs, needed to add an aspect of their own conception of the supernatural missing from the traditional Syrian version so as fully to answer their own worldview and spiritual needs.

The glyptic offers yet one more source of religious data. The mere fact that Cypriots adopted cylinder seals shows a considerable influence from the Near East, even if the actual function of the seals was not adopted on the island. These seals show some of the greatest mixing of Near Eastern and Aegean motifs in Cypriot art of the time and also shed light on the nature of the deities revered.

It appears evident that oxen are associated with male deity/ies in Cyprus, based on the glyptic (see fig. 6d, e.g.) and both Near Eastern and Aegean comparanda. As such, the presence of ox bones (especially incised) and horns at a sanctuary may indicate that the sanctuary-temple was dedicated to a god. However, the glyptic argues very strongly for the association of horned animals, especially caprids, with a goddess. Thus, not all animal horns can be said to be indicative of a god and, in fact, it may be safer to argue that only oxen might be seen in context with a god, and that other horned animals can be regarded as belonging to the cult of a goddess.

---

89. *Ibid.*, 515–16.

90. Negbi 1988: *passim*. For counter arguments, see Gilmour 1993: *passim*.

91. Burdajewicz 1990: 105–11; Maier 1979: *passim*.

Faunal remains of both oxen and caprids were discovered at Myrtou-*Pigadhes* and Athienou in context with copper slag and copper-working. This would suggest that copper-working (the national industry) was associated with at least a god or a goddess, if not both.

Finally, the goddess associated with animals, according to the glyptic, may be identified with the nude goddess who often functions in the glyptic as a *potnia theron*. The similarities between the nude goddess as she appears in the glyptic and the bird- and normal-faced figurines are adequately strong to suggest that the two images indicate the same entity. There would, therefore, appear to be an island-wide cult of a goddess associated with (horned) animals and nudity/eroticism and probably copper. This goddess (or goddesses) exist(s) alongside the cult of at least one male deity, possibly more.

Summary

Unlike the previous eras of Cypriot prehistory and protohistory, in the LC II there is a unified religion throughout the island, as can be seen in the island-wide use of similar sanctuaries, similar votives, similar female figurines, and a common glyptic tradition. The twin sanctuaries of Ajios Jakovos and Kition suggest that at least two deities were revered in Cyprus at this time, and that it was not uncommon to worship these two together. To judge from the votive remains at Ajios Jakovos and the glyptic, this pantheon consisted of at least a god and a goddess.

Beyond the sanctuaries, the female figurines were associated with the grave, suggesting at least one role as the protector/guide of the dead, possibly, although this is speculative, to rebirth. The iconography as a *kourotrophos* suggests, also, either associations with maternity, guardianship of children, or care over new life. All three are certainly possible. What is significantly novel in the representation of this goddess (or goddesses) in the LC II is her prevalence throughout the island and a strong sexuality, as her iconography heavily focuses on the sexual attributes of breasts, hips, genitalia, and, occasionally, navel. The combination of sexual attributes, the significance of jewelry in both the figurine iconography and in the votives (as at Ajios Jakovos), and the occasional association with children all emphasize the extremely feminine nature of this deity. In many respects, the sole distinction between this deity and Aphrodite is the association with children, an association that is minimized in subsequent centuries.

It is during the LC II period that a female divinity appears that may, in fact, be the earliest known version of the eventual Greek Aphrodite. She is heavily influenced by Levantine, notably Syrian iconography and probably ideology.

LATE CYPRIOT III (1200–1050 BCE)

The Late Cypriot III period shows a remarkable degree of cultural continuity during what was for the entire eastern Mediterranean a period of chaos and extensive change. What is particularly significant about these tribulations for the aims of this study are the facts that (1) in c. 1190 settlers from Greece established residence in Cyprus where (2) they came into extensive contact with a deity at Paphos who, through archaeological continuity and literary tradition, appears to be an early form, if not the actually progenitress, of the later Greek Aphrodite.

Figurines

One major change that occurs in Cypriot cult practice between LC II and LC III is the style of the cult images. The bird-faced and normal-faced figurines that dominated the LC II iconographic repertoire vanish almost entirely. These are replaced in part by bronze idols, sometimes measuring up to half a meter in height, representing both female and male, thereby showing yet another change from the LC II practice in which the male was only minimally portrayed. Another great innovation of the LC III figurines is their anthropomorphism. Unlike the figurines of previous eras, the LC III images are rendered with natural proportions, especially hip-to-height ratios, ear size, and general hair styling. The faces, while admittedly rather crude, are far more naturalistic than the bird-faced, or even the normal-faced, figurines of LC II.

All these innovations might be attributed to Near Eastern influence. In the Littoral region, including Ugarit, Tell Sukas, and Byblos, a highly anthropomorphized style of divine images came to be common by around 1500 BCE.[92] In general, human images were wrought of terra-cotta, whereas bronze, ivory, and other precious materials were used for creating divine images.[93] This style reached its pinnacle in the first millennium in the gold foil "Aštarte" plaques that were widespread throughout the Phoenician and Greek worlds in the eighth and seventh centuries. Before this, however, this style probably reached Cyprus from Ugarit around 1200 BCE, when the city was destroyed and refugees fled to the island.[94]

Unlike in previous eras, very few cult images remain from the LC III period, possibly due to the rather precious nature of the material involved. Only five bronze images show the stylistic development of goddess iconography: a tiny votive figurine from Enkomi, the unprovenanced Bomford Figurine, the Nicosia Figurine, the Paphos Figurine, and the "Ladies at the Window" upon a stand from a tomb in Enkomi.

---

92. Badre 1980: 128.

93. *Ibid.*, 109.

94. Sanders 1987: 153.

The figurine from Enkomi (perhaps the most dubious in terms of identification as a goddess image), 5 cm in height, is intact from the top of the head
to mid-thigh. The top of the head is flat and is covered by what looks like a veil
but is probably hair. The face has a very slight forehead with no eyebrows, and
the eyes are rendered as circular beads. The nose is extremely prominent, and
the mouth is a slight incision underneath the nose. The figurine's arms arc
close to the body, bent at the elbows so that the forearms cover the breasts,
and the hands are just below neck level, grabbing what appears to be tresses
of hair. The body is nude, with clearly incised navel, pubic delineation and a
groove separating the legs. J. Karageorghis notes that a similar, small, double-
headed female figurine came from a tomb context in Enkomi dating to the LC
II period.[95] As such, this image might show part of the transition of iconographic media from the LC II to LC III periods.

The unprovenanced bronze statuette, the so-called Bomford figurine, is
closely associated with the Ingot God statue of Enkomi (see below) as she
stands upon an ingot-shaped base. The figure is 9.9 cm in height and depicts
a nude female (see fig. 6g). The top of the head is rather flat, and the hairstyle
has four tresses, two long and two short. The shorter tresses lie on either side
of the figure's face just before the ears, whereas the larger tresses fall behind
the ears and then come forward to lie on the figure's shoulders just at breast
level. The statue's ears are relatively large and turned forward. The eyebrows
are lightly incised; the eyes are large and molded as is the nose; the mouth is
a vaguely incised gash. The neck has small, molded ridges that Catling interprets as setting off the tight necklace that the figure wears, below which is a
cord from which hangs a pendant descending down to the statue's abdomen.[96] The breasts are unusually highly set and are composed of "lumps" of
metal. The pubic triangle is prominent, rendered in strongly incised lines
filled in with slighter gashes. The legs are straight and separated by a groove.
The arms extend out from the shoulders and curve back in to rest akimbo on
the waist. The back of the figurine, although showing slightly molded buttocks, is, nevertheless, less fully wrought than the front, and so the image was
probably intended to be viewed from the front exclusively.[97]

This statuette, both stylistically and iconographically, is very similar to a
bronze statuette that was unearthed in Nicosia. The figurine, intact from the
head to just above the ankles, measures 10 cm in height and might have
attained a height of 12 to 13 cm when fully intact, especially if it, too, stood
on a base.[98] The top of the head is more rounded than that of the Bomford fig-

---

95. J. Karageorghis 1977: 103.

96. Catling 1971: 19.

97. *Ibid.*

98. *Ibid.*, 20–21.

Fig. 6g
Bomford figurine.
Ashmolean Museum, Inv. 1971.888.

urine, and the Nicosia statuette has only two large tresses descending from the head behind the ears to the shoulders. The ears stick out at a 90-degree angle from the side of the face. Eyebrows and mouth are minimally incised; the eyes are large molded dots; the nose is quite prominent. The Nicosia statuette shows no indication of a tight necklace around the neck, but she wears a pendant similar to that of the Bomford figurine: a thick cord around the neck descending down between the breasts and terminating in an unidentifiable pendant just above the navel. The breasts themselves are prominently molded dots. The pubic triangle is rendered with strongly incised outer lines, slighter incised lines within the triangle and, unlike the Bomford version, the vulva is also clearly incised. The arms arch out at the shoulders, but hang down the length of the body.

Both of these figurines, on the basis of style, can be dated to the early twelfth century BCE. This is due both to their evolved form from the bird-faced and normal-faced figurines of the LC II period, and to their resemblance to the "Ladies-at-the-Window" stand from Enkomi. This stand is dated by both Gjerstad and Catling to the first half of the twelfth century, which is consistent with the other objects discovered in the same tomb group, including pottery of the decorated LC III-style.[99] This bronze stand, although badly corroded,

---

99. *Ibid.*, 22–23.

has cut-out "windows" along all four panels, which supposedly represent building façades. Within each of these windows are two female heads modeled in the round. Although it is difficult to discern exact features, these females have large noses, prominent ears turned out 90 degrees from the side of the face, and large tresses, which descend from the head down to the shoulders.

A final version of this figurine style comes from an excavated tomb at Palai-paphos. This figurine was discovered in Tomb 104, Chamber K at Kouklia-*Ter-atsoudhia*. It lay face down on a bench by the hole that linked Chamber K with its adjoining *dromos* L, and the excavator suggests that, in fact, the fig-urine may have fallen into the chamber through this opening during the loot-ing, which was apparent in the chamber.[100] As such, it is not practical to assume an intended mortuary context for the image.

The figurine itself (K.5) stands 9.5 cm high and is fully intact except for some corrosion at the feet. The top of the head it flat; the hairstyle consists of two broad tresses descending from the top of the head passing behind the ears, coming forward of the shoulders and finally resting on the figurine's wrists. The eyes resemble coffee beans, the nose is prominent, as are the ears, and the mouth is not indicated. Two bands encircle the neck (visible as only one band from behind), and a further band descends from the neck between the breasts down to the navel. The arms extend away from the body, bend at the elbows and curve back to the body, where the hands grasp the breasts. According to V. Karageorghis, the hands are squeezing the nipples.[101] The pubic triangle is both molded and incised, making it quite prominent, while a line of "flesh"(?) lies directly above the pubic triangle. The legs are rounded and separated by an incised groove. The feet are mostly corroded away, but it is evident that they rested upon some manner of base, still present.[102] The back of the image is minimally worked, and it would appear that, once again, it was intended to be viewed from the front only.

All these images—the two-faced female figurine from Enkomi room 11, the Bomford figurine, the Nicosia figurine, the Paphos figurine, and the "Ladies-at-the-Window" from Enkomi—show certain consistent traits. They all have large noses (reminiscent of the bird-faced figurines) and hair tresses that descend down to the chest. Except for the Enkomi figurine, all have promi-nent ears and were meant to be viewed only from the front. All the free-stand-ing figurines are portrayed nude and emphasize the pubic triangle (absent on the Enkomi stand for the obvious reason). Many of these attributes show a clear sense of continuity with female figurines of the previous eras: the flat-tened heads, the large noses, and the out-turned ears. Perhaps even the new

---

100. Karageorghis 1990: 11.

101. *Ibid.*, 29.

102. *Ibid.*, Plate XXI.

pendants of the bronze idols hearken back to a tradition of rendering female figurines with abundant jewelry.

Nevertheless, these bronze idols and figurines also show strong inspiration from the religious iconography of the Levant, most notably Ugarit. Levantine coastal goddess images, commonly mold-poured for mass production,[103] are predominantly frontal figures, and their pose is almost exclusively *en face*.[104] They are portrayed nude, with careful attention to the breasts and pubic triangle. The bodies are rendered in human proportions, with arms either hanging to the sides, resting on the body, or holding attributes, such as flowers, on either side of the body. The treatment of the hair is important. Two styles, one Mesopotamian in origin and one Egyptian, coifed the goddesses of the Levant. The Egyptian version, known as the "Hathor-style," shows the hair parted in the center, curving around the face, and descending to the shoulders, where the end of each tress curls outward. The hair of the double faced figurine from Enkomi might be inspired by this style. The Mesopotamian style shows the hair divided into braid or cork-screw-like tresses, usually curling toward the front of the body to lie on the shoulders or chest.[105] This style was particularly common on molded, terra-cotta female figurines, but was also employed on the mold-poured, metal versions. This tressed style is the inspiration behind the new hairstyle on the Bomford, Nicosia, and Enkomi-stand figures, showing a definite, continued contact with and inspiration from Near Eastern iconography.

Sanctuaries

Further information about Cypriot religion in the LC III phase may be derived from a study of the sanctuaries. Continuity of cult is evident in the continued use of the same sacred areas through and beyond the transition of LC II to LC III. Although significant changes occur in the layout and orientation of these early sacred sites, their overall use remains fairly constant.

Athienou

The shrine of Athienou continues in use from its earliest foundation in the sixteenth century into the mid-twelfth century BCE. The only two elements of the shrine that alter between Stratum III (LC II) and Stratum II (LC III) are the nature of the pottery and the focus of the industry. As the LH IIIB pottery is replaced by LH IIIC, the forms of the vessels change as well. Instead of the smaller, votive vessels common in the LC II period, the LC III remains are practical in nature, suggesting use by humans rather than gifts to gods. So, too, the

---

103. Catling 1971: 19.

104. The exceptions to this will be examined in Chapter Eight.

105. Badre 1980: *passim*.

metal-working component of the shrine is expanded in LC III, thus increasing
the level of copper-smelting associated with the shrine. The excavators attribute these changes to the arrival of the Achaeans in Cyprus.[106]

Nevertheless, one should remember that the LC II shrine of Athienou was
associated with copper-working, and the association between metal-working
and religion was a theme in the religious evolution of Cyprus through LC III
throughout the island. As such, the greater emphasis of Athienou as a foundry
rather than as a shrine should not be seen as a radical change at the site, but
rather as a relatively natural progression of use.

Kition

Even more radical continuity-in-change occurs at Kition. The two significant changes at the turn from LC II to LC III (corresponding to levels IV and
III at the site) are: (1) the arrival of Achaeans at the site as indicated by far greater quantities of Mycenaean wares than earlier (especially LH IIIC:1b), the
wide-scale use of ashlar masonry in constructions and reconstructions of Area
II,[107] and corresponding data of Achaean migration around the island, most
noticeable at Paphos beginning c. 1190; and (2) extensive reconstructions in
Area II, including the erection of three new temples and the development of
the copper foundries. Continuity is evident in the tendencies of the builders
to have later structures, especially Temples 1 and 2, correspond to the structures of the LC II period.

The most significant change that occurred in Area II was the general
expansion of the sanctuary complex, evident in Floors IIIA and III. Temple 3
was dismantled (or at least not reconstructed), and Temple 1 was erected in
its stead. This temple was much larger than either Temples 2 or 3, and was
probably intended to be the main focus of the sanctuary complex. As this temple was entirely reconstructed by the Phoenicians in the ninth century, the
remains of the LC III temple, both in terms of architecture and votives, are
scanty.

Temple 1 stood to the south of Temple 2, which was reconstructed but in
most respects similar to the Temple 2 of the LC II period. The main difference in construction is the use of ashlar masonry (as in Temple 1 and the new
city walls).[108] Objects found associated with the LC III level were, *inter alia*,
several pieces of Aegean-ware (LH IIIB and C), coarse-ware, and plain-white-
ware vessels.[109]

---

106. Dothan and Ben-Tor 1983: 140.

107. Karageorghis 1976: 59. In Area II, a new Cyclopean wall was constructed similar in
    style to those at Enkomi, Sinda, and Maa-Palaiokastro.

108. *Ibid.*, 49.

109. *Ibid.*, 106.

Beyond these two main temples, the sacred precinct of LC III Kition contained two temenoi. Temenos B was the focal point at the western end of the precinct, communicating with Temple 1 to the west, Temenos A to the north, Temple 2 to the south, and possibly with some manner of piazza to the east.[110] The temenos was an enclosed courtyard with a portico along its southern side[111] and may have served as a monumental entrance or processional route to/for Temple 1. North of Temenos B (and much smaller) is Temenos A. The north wall of the temenos is the city wall, and its south wall comprises the northern limit of Temple 1. At the western end, the temenos had direct access to the copper workshops in the northern sector of Area II.[112]

Proceeding east from Temenos A, through an empty courtyard, was a completely new structure: Temple 4. Unlike the previous two temples, Temple 4 was first constructed for Floor IIIA. It is located in the eastern sector of the sacred precinct and abutted the northern city wall at its eastern end.[113] The temple was constructed of ashlar masonry and, as the other temples, consisted primarily of a large hall (Room 38) to the west and two small rooms and a vestibule to the east (Rooms 38A–C). Room 38C may have been the temple's storage room. Discovered within it at the level separating Floors IIIA from III (but attributable to Floor IIIA according to the excavators) were objects of (1) ivory: a plaque of a lion, a plaque of the Egyptian god Bes, and an engraved rod and a pipe;[114] (2) bronze: a nail, a tool, a disk, and a fragmentary dagger; (3) ceramic: ten plain white wheel-made bowls, LH IIIB wares, decorated Late Cypriot wares; and (4) miscellaneous materials: a lead weight, faience and paste beads, and a bone spindle-whorl.[115]

The final innovation in the sacred architecture of Area II at Kition was Temple 5, lying obliquely to the south of Temple 4. Like Temple 4, it was first constructed for Floor IIIA. It comprised a large rectangular hall (Room 58) extending to a courtyard to the east and a narrow inner chamber (Room 58A) to the west. A worked ashlar block on the southern wall may have been the base of a niche constructed in the south wall for the display of cult objects.[116] This is the only such construction so far seen at Kition.

There was an altar/table of offerings located along the western wall and associated with Floor III / IIIA, and a stone anchor that projects southward

---

110. *Ibid.*, 55.

111. *Ibid.*, 59.

112. *Ibid.*, 61–62.

113. *Ibid.*, 107.

114. Both the plaque of Bes and the pipe were inscribed with Cypro-Minoan characters.

115. Karageorghis and Demas 1985: 71.

116. *Ibid.*, 75.

from Room 58A was incorporated into this altar. In the Floor III phase the most important change to Temple 5 was the addition of a built altar.[117] Also of particular significance at this level is the discovery of deer antlers.[118]

To the north and west of the temples proper in the sacred precinct were workshops containing slag, burnt materials, and signs of copper-working.[119] Since the northern workshops, in particular, were directly connected to Temple 1, it appears that there had been some manner of temple control over the copper foundry, possibly even over the entire copper-working industry. Or, as B. Knapp suggests, the "aura of divinity" was used to legitimize the ruling class, who maintained their control and monopoly over the island's most important natural resource (excluding food and water, of course).[120]

During the second quarter of the eleventh century, a wave of destruction, either natural or human, hit Cyprus, and the site of Kition was destroyed. Unlike Enkomi, which was totally abandoned during this period, Kition was rebuilt over the remains of the previous structures, and the temples of Area II were reconstructed according to their original plans.[121] It is during this brief period, at the very end of the Cypriot Bronze Age, that Minoan religious influence becomes apparent at Kition. The evidence is slight but highly significant for the study of religious connections throughout the eastern Mediterranean. Excavations of the later, Phoenician construction in the area of Temple 1 revealed a *bothros* at the front of the temple containing terra-cotta images of a goddess-with-upraised-arms and three clay *naiskos* models of a sub-Minoan type.[122] Evidently, these were buried in the sanctuary complex by later settlers who intended to reconstruct the temple but showed respect for the former temple's votive remains. That these objects were buried in front of Temple 1 suggests that either all votives from the LBA were collected from throughout the site and buried together before the largest temple or, more likely, these figurines came from the wreckage of Temple 1.

The identity of the deities revered at Kition remains speculative in spite of the extensive archaeological evidence. The presence of two temples at the earliest phase of Area II would indicate that at least two deities were worshipped at Kition since the LC II/Floor IV period at the site. That Temple 2 continued in use and that Temple 1 was clearly and carefully placed on top of Tem-

---

117. *Ibid.*, 110.

118. *Ibid.*, 244. In the Floor II phase of Temple 5 the number of skulls of horned animals increases considerably, suggesting quite strongly that these animals were of continuing relevance to the deity or deities revered within this temple.

119. Karageorghis and Demas 1985: 77–84.

120. Knapp 1986: *passim*.

121. Karageorghis 1976: 91.

122. *Ibid.*

ple 3 suggest that the same two deities were worshipped during both LC II and LC III. The deity worshipped in Temple 3 was probably the divinity of the sacred gardens between the two temples, as that temple was constructed to open onto those gardens, whereas Temple 2 opened away from them. In the reconstruction, Temple 1 overlays and absorbs those gardens. In the LC III period, the deity of Temple 1 came to exert control over the copper industry, to judge from the close relationship between Temple 1 and the city's copper foundry. Further data from throughout the island (such as the bronze statues, discussed above in the case of the female images and below for the male) suggest that at least a male and female deity were revered throughout the island at this time, possibly a divine couple. Karageorghis suggests that it was this pair/couple which was worshipped at Kition.[123]

The evidence supports the hypothesis that Temples 3/1 were dedicated to a female deity: the close association between Temple 3 and the sacred gardens (not difficult to link with Aphrodite in later periods), Temple 1, and Temple 1's associations with goddess-with-upraised-arms in its later phase (but *before* the abandonment of the site). Furthermore, comparable evidence from Palaipaphos shows that a temple associated with a copper foundry could belong to a goddess (in the case of Paphos specifically Aphrodite) and, thus, the close connection to metal-working does not rule out a goddess. If this is the case, then it is also possible that Temple 2 was dedicated to a god, at least in the LC II period.

Who may have been revered in Temples 4 and 5 is another, and just as difficult, issue. Most likely, new gods were introduced, on the basis of the newness of these temples and the continued use of the older ones (i.e., they do not function as new homes for old gods). These "new" deities arrived probably from the Levant, either through close contacts or actual immigrants. The presence during this and subsequent phases of anchors, especially in the construction of the altar, suggests that Temple 5 may have been dedicated to a male deity. This usage of boat anchors has parallels in the Near East, notably at Ugarit and Byblos, and may reflect possible Near Eastern associations of this deity.[124] This temple (and associated deity) came into prominence during a period of strong ties with the Levant. If anchors are an aspect of the cult, for example, of Baal at Ugarit, then in Temple 5 we might see either evidence for the importation of the cult of Baal into Cyprus, or, more likely, the importation of a Baal-type deity, with some of this god's iconography, transformed into a deity appropriate to the worldview and spiritual needs of the Cypriots.

Karageorghis had originally believed that two deities were worshipped in Temple 4, having identified the vestibule and storeroom at the eastern end of

---

123. Karageorghis and Demas 1985: 261–62.

124. Frost 1982: 164; Karageorghis and Demas 1985: 282.

the hall as twin *adyta*. Although the presence of charred remains may in fact support this conclusion, the absence of cult idols argues against such an identification of these rooms. The image of Bes discovered among the finds may be slight evidence for either the cult of a goddess or a deity of either gender who was nevertheless associated with women, as Bes himself was associated with women and childbirth in Egypt.[125]

In the end, it appears that at least four deities were worshipped in Area II of Kition in the Late Bronze Age. Two of these (the deities of Temples 2 and 3) were older at the site than the other two, and it is likely that they were a god and a goddess. A goddess was probably worshipped in Temples 3/1; a god in Temple 2. A god was worshipped in Temple 5 (discussed above) and perhaps a goddess in Temple 4.

Enkomi

Enkomi is extremely important for the study of LBA religious development at Cyprus, as the site contained at least two well-preserved sanctuaries[126] and produced the most iconographically distinctive and informative idols of the LC III period. As with Kition, the transition from LC II to LC III at Enkomi suggests the arrival of a new population around 1200 BCE, most demonstrable in the discovery of LH IIIB pottery and the Cyclopean architecture of the new city wall.[127]

However, unlike at Kition and at Paphos, where large-scale sanctuaries yield evidence for the cult of a Cypriot goddess or goddesses, Enkomi has, as of yet, produced extremely meager evidence for the cult of a female divinity. By contrast, the two sanctuaries and the two idols to be discussed offer further evidence for the growing polytheism of LC III Cyprus, particularly in the growing number of possible male deities. Although the apparent absence of a female divinity in the current data might seem to make Enkomi rather irrelevant to this study, much current scholarship attributes a goddess cult to the excavated regions of this site, and the site, therefore, does become enmeshed in the study of Aphrodite's origins. I do not think that the current evidence supports this hypothesis.

The two identified sanctuaries of a male deity/deities, the "Ingot God"[128] and the "Horned God,"[129] are consistent with all other sanctuaries associated with Cypriot gods from both LC II and III, in terms of votive remains if not

---

125. Drioton and Vandier 1984: 77.

126. The identification of the House of the Columns and the Tower sanctuary as cult sites are debatable. See Burdajewicz 1990: 39–45.

127. Karageorghis 1976: 59.

128. Courtois 1971: *passim*.

129. Dikaios 1969–71: 194–205.

architecture. The first of these, the temple of the Ingot God (so named for the statue of a warrior deity mounted upon a stand in the form of an ox-hide ingot) is located in sector 5E of the city, and is dated to the LC IIIB period.[130] The structure consists of a walled-in rectangular area divided along its long axis by a short, central wall.[131] The temple was entered by a single entrance on the southern, shorter wall from a paved courtyard, thus giving a bent-axis approach.[132] Along the eastern wall was a bench on which were discovered votive remains.[133] In the western end of the main cella, just to the west of the wall that divides the cella into its northern and southern components, are three monoliths. Courtois identifies two of these as altars, probably for use in the sacrifice of animals, and the third stone, punctured with a "tethering" hole, as the tethering stone used to keep the animals until sacrifice.[134] Just to the south of these was located a large hearth structure.[135] Along the northern wall is evidence of small columns, which led the excavator to suggest that this wall was originally covered by a portico, while the wall itself was lined with an offering bench whereon were discovered two centaur figurines and considerable pottery.[136] In the northeastern corner of the structure was a small room entered from the south in which was discovered the statue of the Ingot God; for this reason the excavator suggests that this may have been an *adyton*.[137]

Although this structure is unique in many ways from what we have so far seen of Cypriot sacred architecture, the commonalties are quite strong. The plan consists of a rectangular space that is entered by a bent-axis approach. The internal space is divided into two sub-divisions, one of which, being possibly covered by a portico, is reminiscent of the temple of Aphrodite at Paphos (see below).

Votive remains of pottery and faunal remains were discovered strewn all over temple floor, with the slight exception of the southeastern corner. The finds were most heavily concentrated along the northern wall and along the western bench.[138] The faunal remains consisted mainly of ox skulls and in-

130. Courtois 1971: 308; Courtois, Lagarce and Lagarce 1986: 32; Burdajewicz 1990: 42.

131. Courtois, Lagarce et Lagarce 1986: Fig. 5.

132. *Ibid.* Courtois 1971: Figure 2.

133. *Ibid.*

134. Courtois 1971: 178-90.

135. *Ibid.*, 211ff.

136. *Ibid.*, Figure 2; Courtois, Lagarce and Lagarce 1986: 33.

137. Courtois 1971: 308; Courtois, Lagarce and Lagarce 1986: 36. But see Karageorghis and Demas 1985: 250 for arguments concerning the identification of an *adyton* in Cyprus.

138. Courtois 1971: Figure 2, 223ff., 240ff.

cised ox scapulae, thus offering simultaneously comparanda to the remains from both Kition[139] and Myrtou-*Pigadhes*.[140]

The *adyton* is so identified not so much by its position within the structure, but by the discovery therein of the cult idol—the Ingot God. This bronze idol depicts a male deity standing upon an ox-hide ingot-shaped base (35 cm in height).[141] On his head he bears a horned helmet; in his right hand is an upraised spear; his left hand carries a round shield. He is dressed from shoulders to knees in what appears to be a light-weight robe. The bottom of the base has a tang evidently intended for insertion into some manner of socle.[142] The armaments appear to associate this deity with warfare, while the ingot-shaped base supports connections with metal-working.

It is evident that this sanctuary remained in use through the LC IIIC period in the other finds discovered in the temple's *adyton*, notably numerous goddess-with-upraised-arms figurines that had been ritually broken or "killed" and set to the west of the sanctuary's main hall. Such images indicate broad contacts with Crete in the eleventh century, as well as the continuous cult at Enkomi.[143]

All the discoveries at this sanctuary point to the worship of a male deity associated with horned animals, especially oxen, and, through the ingot iconography of the cult idol, some aspect of metallurgy.[144] A similar situation is present in the sanctuary of the Horned-God.

This sanctuary is especially distinctive since it was incorporated into a pre-existing complex rather than being an independent structure.[145] Nevertheless, it appears that the builders attempted to conform to a specific ritual arrangement. The sacred area of the complex consists of three rooms, 45, 9, and 10 in the LC IIIB phase, and 13, 9, and 10 in the LC IIIC phase.[146]

---

139. Webb in Karageorghis and Demas 1985: *passim*. Two incised ox scapulae from the LC III period came to light in Courtyard C, south of Temple 1, and three fragments from Well 7 to the east of Temple 4. Later, Cypro-Geometric scapulae and skulls were associated with Temples 4 and 5 only.

140. DuPlat Taylor *et al.* 1957: 21, 99–100; Courtois, Lagarce and Lagarce 1986: 33.

141. Schaeffer 1965: 56–57.

142. Courtois, Lagarce and Lagarce 1986: 36.

143. *Ibid.*, 37.

144. The Minoan goddesses-with-upraised-arms are a later intrusion, as discussed below.

145. Dikaios 1969–71: 171–90. This arrangement may seem similar to the sanctuary/metallurgy complex at Kition. But whereas at Kition these elements were constructed contemporaneously, with the primary emphasis being on the layout of the sanctuary and the industrial quarter just fitting in between the temple walls and the city wall, at Enkomi that entire complex was already in place by LC II, with the sacred rooms being re-adapted into a pre-existing design.

146. *Ibid.*,194–201; Courtois, Lagarce and Lagarce 1986: 16–18; Burdajewicz 1990: Figures 16–18.

Room 45 (called the West Megaron by Dikaios)[147] was a rectangular structure oriented north–south. The megaron was entered through three smaller rooms to the south (I, IA, and 34, of which IA had access to the street).[148] By the entrance was a, perhaps sacred, well flanked by stone slabs.[149] Three stone bases (A–C) embedded in the floor presumably supported wooden pillars, which supported a roof.[150] Two separate levels of floor existed in this room: Floor III and Floor II. Between pillar bases A and B was an ashy area 0.5 m across, which apparently served as a rudimentary hearth.[151] To the west of this was an ox skull found lying face up. Near the western wall were a stone mold for gold (?) ornaments and a hematite weight.[152] Southwest of pillar base B was a shallow rectangular pit lined with stones. By the entrance to Room 9 were discovered (*inter alia*) miniature gold-leaf models of horns and a miniature bronze spearhead. Animal bones were found all over the floor.[153]

On Floor II, just beyond the passageway to Room 9, the excavators found an area covered with carbonized materials and ashes, evidently a hearth. Upon the ashes were two fragmentary ox skulls. Three more such skulls and other animal bones were found in the northern portion of the room, and in the northwestern sector of the floor was a quern and a shard of LH IIIC:1b ware.[154]

Room 9 was located between Rooms 45 and 10, and was clearly intended as the passageway between these two chambers. Like Room 45, two distinct levels (III and II) are discernible.[155] Floor III yielded little material. In the northeastern portion of the room was an overturned trough containing a few bird and mammalian remains. Also discovered on this level were two gold pendants and additional animal bones.[156]

Floor II was far richer. Here Dikaios discovered a juglet of plain wheel-made ware, a gold pendant, a rosette of lead covered with gold, a gold nail, a miniature gold-leaf ox horn, bronze pins, a nail head of bronze, and animal

---

147. Dikaios 1969–71: 194.

148. *Ibid.*, 195.

149. *Ibid.*, 199.

150. *Ibid.*, 194.

151. *Ibid.*, 195.

152. *Ibid.*

153. *Ibid.*

154. *Ibid.*

155. *Ibid.*, 197.

156. *Ibid.*

bones.[157] Mixed in with the pisé of the upper level (Floor I) but probably deriving from Floor II were also deer antlers, an ox horn, and animal legs with joints still articulated.[158]

Finally, there is Room 10, identified by Dikaios as the *adyton*. Dikaios mentions no clear distinctions between Floors III and II for this room. The most important find from this room is, of course, the cult idol—a god in bronze wearing a horned helmet and a short kilt around the waist (55 cm in height). Unlike the Ingot God, there is nothing particularly martial about this idol. Instead, the god has his left hand pressed to his chest, and the right arm is extended, palm down, possibly in a gesture of benediction. This image was discovered in a depression in the southeastern corner of the room, where the excavator suggests it may have been placed for protection from raid or pillaging.[159] Also present in Room 10 were several pieces of pottery representing a total of 276 bowls of LH IIIB and C, white painted wheel-made and white slip II wares.[160]

In the LC IIIC phase, Room 13 came to replace Room 45 as the main hall of the sanctuary of the Horned God. Originally serving some more mundane purpose, the room was refloored and rededicated in purpose at the end of the Bronze Age. On the renewed floor the excavators discovered metal objects and ox skulls.[161]

According to Diakios, the worshippers would have first entered by way of room 45, probably from one of the three rooms to its south. Here they would have performed rites such as the offering of ox skulls and, possibly, the sacrifice of animals (as per the burnt remains found on Floors III and II). Then the worshippers would proceed to Room 9 where there was a trough and where further rites were enacted, possibly including dedication of more ox-skulls or even stag antlers. Found in the remains were also bull-head rhyta with gold-leaf covered horns, indications of Minoan influence. The last stage of the worshippers' peregrinations took them to Room 10, where the bronze cult idol stood. The ritual here seems to have been played out with another trough, bowls, and more sacrificed animals, once again as per the remains found in the excavations.[162]

Whether one or two different deities are represented in these two sanctuaries is difficult to determine. The iconography of the cult idols is quite distinct and suggests that a war-god is worshipped in the one, whereas some other deity without immediately identifiable attributes was worshipped in

---

157. *Ibid.*

158. *Ibid.*

159. *Ibid.*

160. *Ibid.*, 196; Webb, personal communication.

161. *Ibid.*, 201.

162. *Ibid.*, 199.

the other. The horned helmet that they both wear is not indicative of a single deity, as horned headgear is common to all the deities of the Near East and, thus, might not be used as a distinguishing factor. Nevertheless, the common votives may lend weight to the argument that these are the same god. Different interpretations have been offered over the years as to the identity of this deity, ranging from an Apollo *Kereatas* or *Alasiotas* for an Aegean orientation to Rešef or Nergal from the east.[163] Most probably, this deity (or deities) is of Near Eastern extraction and strongly altered to fit the spiritual needs and worldview of the Cypriots. Syrians, Phoenicians, and Achaeans would have recognized in him their own closest equivalent.

It is in the rooms east of the sanctuary of the Horned God that the main argument for the presence of a cult of a female deity in Enkomi lies (at least Dikaios believed so). In this arrangement, two rooms created the sanctuary, with Room 12 serving as the main hall or megaron, the equivalent of Room 45, and Room 11 serving as the *adyton*, the equivalent of Room 10 for the male deity. Room 12 was roughly square in shape, running 7 m north to south and 6.2 m east to west.[164] To the northwest was the hearth, circular in form and roughly central to the layout of the room. It is evident that this hearth was actually burning when the roof collapsed over Floor II.[165] On the platform of the hearth and in the immediate vicinity were numerous LH IIIC cups and wares and, most importantly, a terra-cotta figurine on the eastern wall of the room.[166] This was a Minoan style goddess-with-upraised-arms with a disc-shaped head; from its size, it appears more likely to be a votive than a cult idol.

Room 11 communicated with Room 12 by an entrance in the eastern wall.[167] Three shallow pits were found in this room, two near the south wall and one by the west wall. The Janus-faced female figurine mentioned above was found in one of the southeastern pits. Other items from this room consist of a paste bead, a piece of gold leaf, a bronze nail of mushroom shape, a bronze pin, and a few other scraps of bronze.[168]

Whether this room complex might be regarded as a sanctuary to a goddess is difficult to determine. In contrast to the two sanctuaries to the male deities, this complex has neither a clear cult image (the Janus-faced figurine, at 5 cm of height, is too small to serve this function) nor any remains of sacrificed offerings. It might be argued, though, that the goddess did not receive "bloody" sacrifices (as was recorded of the Paphian cult of Aphrodite), but that the

---

163. See Courtois and Lagarce 1986: 17; Catling 1971 and Hadjioannou 1971.

164. Dikaios 1969–71: 200.

165. *Ibid.*

166. *Ibid.*

167. *Ibid.*

168. *Ibid.*

hearth was used for burning such items as incense. This would account for the lack of faunal remains in Rooms 12 and 11. The many examples of pottery found on the Floor of Room12 would then be indicative of the dedications offered to the goddess of Enkomi.

Nevertheless, the arguments against the identification of a goddess sanctuary in Rooms 12 and 11 are strong. What might be identified as votives, a scrap of gold leaf, and a few nails could easily be the remains of a small workshop or the left-over of the annual inventory and house cleaning. No jewelry, ivory, Near Eastern imports, or precious stones were found that would show a continuum of votives between this "sanctuary" and those at Kition and Ajios Jakovos. This is especially significant in light of the sudden disaster that struck Rooms 12 and 11 seen on Floor II, where the room clearly caught fire while in use. One should assume that either any votive remains (and idols) were cleared out of the room entirely and moved to a completely new part of the city or these items had never been present in the room. As votive remains rather consistently appear in floors of reconstructed rooms in the other two sanctuaries mentioned above, the latter option is more convincing.

This leads to a second argument against the sacred character of Rooms 11 and 12. The Minoan figurines commonly associated with goddesses, notably the goddess-with-upraised-arms, were discovered in the western part of the sanctuary of the Ingot God, including a larger figure that could have functioned as a cult idol.[169] If, as is likely at Kition, there had been a sanctuary of a female deity, these figurines would most likely have been deposited there. Instead, only one such figurine comes to light from Room 12. Perhaps, in the absence of a goddess sanctuary, the newly arrived Minoans adapted the sanctuary of a god to accommodate their own goddess-oriented religion.[170] Thus, around 1075 BCE, shortly before the abandonment of the city, a goddess-with-upraised-arms cult idol stood beside the Ingot God and there received Aegean figurine votives. I will not go so far as to say that there was no goddess worship in Enkomi in the Bronze Age, as the Minoan-style figurines already argue against that. Furthermore, the site has yet to be entirely excavated and published and, thus, no definitive assertions can be made. Nevertheless, to date, the evidence speaks mainly for a foreign (Minoan) goddess cult in Enkomi, giving no clear data for the cult of an indigenous goddess.

Paphos

Whereas the evidence from Enkomi is apparently negative and that from Kition somewhat positive, the archaeological and literary evidence from Paphos indicates that an individual goddess of Cyprus had a sanctuary there,

---

169. Courtois 1971: 326ff. Courtois, Lagarce and Lagarce 1986: 37.

170. See especially Gesell in the bibliography for evidence on Minoan religion.

that the Achaeans adopted the cult of this goddess, and that this goddess came to be known as Aphrodite.

Finds throughout the city's cemeteries and wells indicate that there was an affluent settlement at the site as early as the fifteenth century, growing in prosperity especially during the LC II–III periods.[171] Although trade and contacts between Paphos and the Near East (notably Syria and Egypt) were long standing, the exchanges between these areas increased considerably during the LBA, when an increase in Near Eastern luxury goods such as faience, precious stones, and cylinder seals made their way into the graves of the city's rich.[172] To the west, intermittent contacts with the Aegean began as early as LC I, as is evidenced by a fragment of a Late Minoan IA cup discovered in one of the *Evreti* wells.[173] Trade relations with the Aegean, in general, and Mycenaean Greece, in particular, increase during the later fifteenth and early fourteenth centuries when the number of imported Aegean vessels rises considerably. The LH IIIA:2 style is represented by 86 vessels and shards, mostly remains of closed vessels.[174] Connections increase further in the LC III period; several LM IIIB "oatmeal" stirrup-jars and no less than 343 examples of LH IIIB-style pottery were discovered throughout the remains of the old city.[175] Around 1200–1190 Achaean Greeks themselves settled at Palaipaphos, initiating the ultimate Hellenization of the island.

It is during this last phase, c. 1200 or, more generally, at the transition between LC II and LC III, that the remaining architectural elements of the Paphian sanctuary were erected.[176] Unfortunately, the later construction of the Roman temple to Aphrodite at the same site, as well as a Medieval sugar refinery, has mostly obliterated all but the westernmost remains of the LBA structure and, thus, all reconstructions are tentative at best. Nevertheless what does remain allows for a fairly accurate chronology of the structure and an interpretation of the deity venerated there.

The LBA archaeological remains consist of two well-defined areas: an open court to the south and a covered hall to the north. The court is defined on its western side (the only remaining side of the sanctuary) by a wall composed of large, ashlar orthostats. A break in this wall serves as at least one entrance into the court. Directly before this entrance is a limestone slab with a low nar-

---

171. Maier and Karageorghis 1984: 51 and 71.

172. *Ibid.*, 71.

173. *Ibid.*

174. *Ibid.*, 55.

175. *Ibid.*, 55 and 71.

176. As the sanctuary was constructed toward the end of the LC II phase and as it is most significant in the LC III phase, I introduce the Paphian sanctuary in the LC III section instead of the LC II.

row rim set into the floor, which the excavator identifies as shallow basin for ritual ablutions.[177] Just to the north of this basin, between it and the enclosed portion of the sanctuary, is a limestone block that might have served as a base for votives. To the north of this is another wall running east to west, separating the court from an area containing two rows of six column bases. There are slight remains of a northern wall, indicating the extent of this hall/colonnade.

One interesting object discovered *in situ* within the colonnade portion of the sanctuary is a LC II *pithos* decorated with wavy lines and the impression of a cylinder seal on one of its handles. The style of the seal, although Levantine in origin, shows clear iconographic influence from the Aegean and, thus, could be dated to the fourteenth century, when Aegeanizing features were fashionable in Levantine artistry.[178] The *pithos* is intact except for its upper neck, which was probably destroyed during one of the rebuildings. It appears that the jar was buried within the hall so that only its uppermost portion emerged above floor level, and that it served as a repository for votive offerings, as several fragments of LC II and III vessels were found within it.[179] The style of the cylinder seal, the pottery within the *pithos*, and the fact that it was discovered *in situ* under the sanctuary floor all indicate that at least this portion of the sanctuary was constructed in LC II.[180] This is confirmed by the discovery in the sanctuary of a LC II goddess figurine (headless, but probably of the normal-faced variety to judge from the ratio of shoulders to hips).

Extrapolating only from the western end, it appears that the LBA sanctuary at Paphos follows the general pattern of sanctuary planning as the other LC II and LC III sanctuaries within Cyprus. As at Kition and Enkomi, the sanctuary consists of two primary areas: an open court and a covered area, in this case an elaborate hall extending beyond the court along the (remaining) sanctuary's long axis, as opposed to the portico on the northern portion of the sanctuary of the Ingot God at Enkomi. A small basin and possibly a votive base stand between the entrance and the covered portion of the sanctuary, as at Kition, Temple 1. Whether the colonnade might be regarded as the sanctuary's *adyton* is difficult to speculate due to the paucity of remains. In accordance with the arrangement at Kition, Temple 1, the *adyton* should be located past the court at a right angle from the entranceway (a bent-axis approach) and the colonnade would conform to this plan. However, the temple of the Ingot God at Enkomi has both an open court and covered portico before reaching a

---

177. Maier and Karageorghis 1984: 91, who credit Webb for this interpretation.

178. *Ibid.*, 96.

179. *Ibid.*

180. The style of the cylinder seal could, of course, pre-date the construction of the temple by generations, as these objects could easily be kept as heirlooms. However, in conjunction with the other evidence, it does strengthen the argument for a date of construction before 1200 BCE.

smaller room containing the cult idol, identified as the sanctuary's *adyton*. If the tradition recorded by Tacitus (*Historiae*, II, 3) concerning the sanctuary's altar is true—that it stood in open air and yet was never wet by rain—then perhaps being located within the colonnade would be the most logical explanation.[181]

Furthermore, in keeping with other Cypriot sanctuaries in the LBA, there is evidence for a connection between metal-working and the Paphian temple.[182] To the immediate west of the temple in a stratified context containing Mycenaean pottery the excavators discovered a quantity of copper slag.[183] In the *Evreti* sector of Paphos, copper slag from a well, along with other implements of the trade, suggests that metal-working was practiced here as well, perhaps offering evidence that the industry was not totally controlled by the sanctuary.[184]

While the Paphian sanctuary is extremely similar to the other Cypriot sanctuaries discussed so far, there are also numerous indications of Aegean, notably Mycenaean, influence in the temple's construction. These elements, combined with the generally accepted construction date of the sanctuary as 1200 BCE, have led some to the conclusion that it was, in fact, the Achaeans, and not the Cypriots, who constructed this sanctuary.

Evidence for Aegean influence in the sanctuary are an Aegean-style *larnax*, discovered *in situ* within a rock-cut trench in the southwestern portion of the colonnade, whose purpose is unknown;[185] stepped limestone capitals; and two horns-of-consecration, both Aegean in style and both, unfortunately, not found *in situ*.[186] Furthermore, many Mycenaean sherds dating from the thirteenth and twelfth centuries were discovered at the sanctuary, although these sherds, too, were unstratified.[187]

Although these elements might argue that it was the Achaeans who constructed the sanctuary, as the chronology of the sanctuary's construction and the arrival of the Achaeans is so close, comparative evidence from throughout Cyprus suggests rather that these elements were used or borrowed and incorporated into Cypriot religious architecture well before the arrival of the Greeks. For example, a *larnax* located within a sanctuary and used for the

---

181. It is actually quite reminiscent of the death of Pryderi at the hands of Bloedeuwedd in Welsh mythology, whereby the youth could not be killed either indoors or outdoors. He was eventually murdered under a portico with a covering but no walls.

182. Burdajewicz 1990: 63.

183. Megaw 1951: 258.

184. Maier and Karageorghis 1984: 70.

185. *Ibid.*, 96.

186. *Ibid.*, 99.

187. *Ibid.*

reception of votives has a clear parallel at the Ajios Jakovos-*Dhima* sanctuary of LC IIA (see above). There is the presence of horns-of-consecration from the altar portion of the sanctuary at Myrtou-*Pigadhes*.[188] As the remains from the Myrtou-*Pigadhes* sanctuary date to Periods V and VI of the sanctuary's use, i.e., from the LC IIC through early LC III period, it is evident that the horns-of-consecration motif was used in Cyprus before the arrival of the Achaeans. So, too, the stepped capitals appear to be more Cypriot than Aegean in character, thus offering no evidence for Achaean influence.

As the Paphian sanctuary conforms so closely to the other LC III sanctuaries both in overall arrangement and in association with metallurgy, and as the Mycenaean Greeks had no tradition of monumental temple architecture before the Early Iron Age and, finally, as the pottery and *pithos* found *in situ* within the colonnade show the establishment of the sanctuary in the LC II period, when Aegean motifs were imported but the Achaeans themselves had not yet arrived in numbers, we can conclude that the Paphian sanctuary was constructed by the Cypriots and only afterward adopted by the Achaeans. This, in turn, should lead to the conclusion that the sanctuary was dedicated to a Cypriot deity and that, once again, the Achaeans adopted this deity.

Unfortunately, the paucity of remains from what is left of the sanctuary do not offer any clues as to the identity of the deity—pottery remains, but no bones, horns, gold, or ivory. In general, it appears that only one deity was adored in the sanctuary, since there is no archaeological evidence for the worship of dual gods, as is evident in either twin temples at Kition in the LC II period and the dual nature of a single sanctuary, as at Ajios Jakovos-*Dhima*.

A number of arguments indicate that this deity was a manifestation of the Cypriot goddess whose cult became visible in LC II, specifically the one who would eventually become the Aphrodite of the Greeks. Although none of them alone necessarily proves the exact identification of the deity of Paphos, combined they form an extremely convincing argument in favor of the Paphian deity as Aphrodite.

The main argument is the continuity of settlement and population at Palaipaphos from the LBA through the Cypro-Geometric I period. Such continuity is visible at the necropolis of *Lakkos tou Skarnou*, where three tombs produced remains of both proto-white painted and white painted I/II pottery, thus linking the Late Bronze and Early Iron Ages. Similar data also derive from the tombs at Skales. Such findings from both regions make it clear that there was continuity of occupation at Palaipaphos from at least the beginning of the Late Bronze Age to the end of the Proto-Geometric period.[189] While later Aegean settlers did arrive in the eleventh century, there is no evidence for a radical change of population as at Kition between the Bronze and Iron Ages.

---

188. DuPlat Taylor *et al.* 1957: 15–17.

189. Maier and Karageorghis 1984: 126.

Thus, one might expect the cult established at Paphos to have been continuous at least from 1200 to 950/900 BCE.

As stated in Chapter Three, the earliest known evidence of the cult of Aphrodite in the Greek world was on the island of Crete at the sanctuary of Kato
Symi Viannou. If a transfer of cult did occur between Cyprus and Crete or, perhaps more likely, an assimilation, then the critical dates of contact and transfer are during the period of continuous settlement at Paphos. The chronology
of this transfer will be discussed more thoroughly in the following chapter.

The next argument in favor of a goddess being worshipped at Paphos is
the overwhelming evidence provided by the later literature. The identity of
the deity adored at Paphos is preserved in the records and nomenclature that
the newly arrived Achaeans and later Greeks and even Romans kept regarding
the deity of Paphos, for the cult remained very much alive through the Roman
era. In Homeric Hymn V, ll. 58–59, Aphrodite prepared for her seduction of
Ankhises:[190]

> Going to Cyprus she entered the sweet-smelling temple
> in Paphos, where are her temenos and fragrant altar.

Similarly, in the Song of Demodokos, after being caught by Hephaistos in her
tryst with Ares (*Odyssey*, VIII, ll. 362–66):[191]

> Then smile-loving Aphrodite went to Cyprus
> To Paphos, where are her temenos and altar of sacrifice;
> The Charities bathed and anointed her with ambrosial oil
> Which adorns the ever-living gods;
> About her they draped a garment, a wonder to behold.

Even in later literature Paphos is recorded as being one of the earliest of the
goddess' cult places:

> Nearby is a sanctuary of Aphrodite Ourania. It is held that the first people to
> revere Ourania were the Assyrians, and after the Assyrians the Paphians of
> Cyprus and those of the Phoenicians who dwell in Ashkalon in Palestine;
> Kytherians worship her having so learned from the Phoenicians.
>
> Pausanias, 1, XIV, 7.[192]

In Roman times, the mythic history of the sanctuary and cult's creation is
preserved in two, apparently contradictory, stories handed down by Pausanias and Tacitus.

---

190. See Appendix B 6.1.

191. See Appendix B 6.2.

192. See Appendix B 1.3.

Agapenor of Agkaios the son of Lykourgos, being king after Ekhemos, lead the Arkadians at Troy. After seizing Ilion, the storm that arose during the return sail home forced Agapenor and the navy of the Arkadians to Cyprus, and Agapenor both became the founder of Paphos, and he built the temple of Aphrodite in Palaipaphos; before this time the goddess was worshipped by the Cypriots in a region called Golgois.

Pausanias, 8,V, 2.[193]

The founder of the temple was the king Aerias, according to an ancient tradition, but some report that that is the name of the goddess herself. A more recent opinion claims that the temple was consecrated by Kinyras and that the goddess herself, born of the sea, had landed on this spot; but the science and art of haruspices was imported here and that it was the Cilician Tamiras who introduced them. They thus believe that the descendants of the two families preside over the ceremonies.... It is forbidden to spread blood on the table of sacrifice; they honour the altar with prayers and pure fire; and the altar, even though it is out in the open, is never rendered wet by rain water. The statue of the goddess does not have human form; it is a circular block, larger at the bottom and growing smaller to the top, as a cone; the reason for this is obscure.

Tacitus, *Historiae* II, 3.[194]

Whereas Tacitus claims that it was a native of Cyprus, the mythical founder of the Kinyraid dynasty, who established the temple of the Paphian and was its first priest, the account of Pausanias suggests, rather, that it was a Greek, blown off course on his return to Greece from Troy, who founded the cult. The archaeology and the later history of the cult show that, in fact, both of these accounts are correct. The sanctuary itself is clearly pre-Greek and, thus, supports Tacitus' account of an indigenous origin to the cult and temple. The tale of Pausanias, by contrast, reflects the arrival of the Achaeans (post-Trojan War and, thus, quite accurately, in the final centuries of the Bronze Age) at the site and their adoption of the Paphian deity.

The population at Paphos remains constant until 950/900 BCE, which would indicate that the deity of the sanctuary was consistent as well, and by 750 BCE Homer clearly equates Paphos with Aphrodite. It is unlikely that the Achaeans brought an Aphrodite-like goddess with them to Paphos, as all the Aegean images that may be indicative of such a deity are Minoan. Achaeans form the highest population of immigrants at Paphos and, obviously, the cult

---

193. See Appendix B 6.3.

194. Loeb translation by C. H. Moore. See Appendix B 6.4. Although Aphrodite's name is not explicitly mentioned, the description of her aniconic stone fits the description of this idol on the Roman coins depicting her sanctuary and, thus, confirms the identification. Karageorghis 1998b: 128 suggests that Kinyras was also the lover of Aphrodite, and that his position was justified through some manner of *hieros gamos*.

was not taken over by any clearly Achaean goddess, such as Hera or Athena. Thus, even if a change of cult could have taken place in the two-century (or less) gap during the Dark Ages, between 900 and 750 BCE, one would have to conclude that this change over would be to an Achaean goddess, which did not occur. We are, therefore, left with the conclusion that the original deity of Paphos was a goddess, and it was this goddess who became, over the next few centuries, the Greek Aphrodite.

The Kyprian

I would argue that it is only in LC II that the cult of this goddess might be said to have begun, that the "Paphian" or even "Kyprian" came into her earliest identifiable manifestation. Before this period, the evidence for possible religious beliefs on Cyprus are the birthing/mothering figurines of the Chalcolithic Age and the sexually ambiguous plank-shaped figurines of EC III, which become, over time, the more three-dimensional figurines of the earlier MC period. While the former images clearly played some role in the ideology of birth in the Chalcolithic Age in the southwestern corner of the island, it would be rash to identify them as "goddesses" *per se*, and they certainly could not, considering their limited geographical scope, constitute a goddess of Cyprus as a whole. The purpose and meaning of the plank-shaped figurines is still far from clear, and it would be overly hasty to assign to them the title of "goddess" (or, for that matter "god" in the case of the masculine or asexual versions).

By contrast, as of LC II there existed throughout the island the iconography of a strongly eroticised goddess, whose earlier, bird-faced imagery showed her with exaggerated sexual characteristics, and whose later, LC III iconography preserved those emphases while rendering her more human and associating her with bronze (both material and ingot based). In contrast to the LC II versions, this goddess never shows kourotrophic imagery, thus divorcing the goddess from the ideology of motherhood. This goddess was worshipped in conjunction with a male deity at Kition, Pigadhes, and probably Athienou, while worshipped alone at Paphos(?). The eroticism (nudity and exaggeration), the association with gods linked to bronze and warfare (Hephaistos and Ares), and the long-standing relationship with Paphos, "home" of Greek Aphrodite, all indicate that the goddess revered throughout Cyprus since LC II was, in fact, an early form of Aphrodite.

Minoan Influence

One final but important element presents itself in the evolution of Aphrodite on Cyprus in the Late Bronze Age: the addition of Minoan iconography into Cypriot goddess' repertoire. As is evident in the cult idols from Cyprus during the early Geometric Periods I and II (1050–850 BCE), this Aegean influence had a profound effect on the Cypriot iconographic repertoire.

For centuries, beginning in 1075 BCE, the goddess-with-upraised-arms was the dominant form of idol throughout the island, from Paphos to Enkomi to Lapithos, and the earlier nude bronze or terra-cotta idols all but disappeared. This process began in the last days of the Cypriot Bronze Age, when a new style of female figurine became popular in Cyprus. These are known as the "bottle-shaped" figurines, as they are, in fact, pouring vessels in the shape of the female body. These figurines, originally in proto-white painted ware and eventually in white painted ware, show a clear combination of Aegean and Cypriot styles.[195] In the tradition of Cypriot female figurines, they have rounded, bead-like eyes, prominent noses, and flap ears. The breasts are prominently molded and the arms, much as the bird-faced and normal-faced images of LC II, lie to the side of the body, curling back to have the hands rest under the breasts. Much as the normal-faced figurines of LC II, which were themselves inspired by Aegean iconography, they are bedecked with painted jewelry, especially necklaces in the typical Cypriot tradition. Quite new to the iconographic repertoire is the shape, whereby the legs are hidden behind a "skirt," much like the bell-shaped female figurines of Crete, such as those at Karphi and Gortyn. These bottle-shaped figurines were discovered predominately at Salamis, although they also appeared briefly at Enkomi.[196]

This new style was the forerunner in Cyprus of the goddess-with-upraised-arms. This image showed the ultimate "occidentalizing" of Cypriot goddess iconography, for in this image almost all the distinctive attributes of the previous iconography were abandoned in favor of a purely Cretan style. Like the bottle-shaped figurines, they are typified in their earliest manifestations by a bell-shaped bottom, which is identified as a skirt, often elaborately painted. The breasts are molded in relief; the arms, rather than accentuating the breasts or other sexual attributes, rise vertically on either side of the figurine's head. The head itself is decorated with paint with careful attention paid to the eyes and hair. The top of the head is often flattened in the style of a *polos* headdress. Thus, the strong emphasis on the sexual/genital attributes of the Cypriot goddess iconography, prevalent since the Late Middle Bronze Age in many respects, all but disappears from the iconographic repertoire. Nevertheless, the strong erotic elements of this Paphian goddess were not lost in spite of the more "conservative" Minoan iconography, for Aphrodite emerged both on Crete and in Greece as the goddess of sex and love.

Although the recently arrived Cretan populations might have continued to identify this image as a representation of one of their own Cretan deities, it is

---

195. J. Karageorghis 1977: 121.

196. *Ibid.*

apparent that the Cypriots identified this figure with their own Cypriot goddess(es) and, thus, the image appeared in long-standing cult centers associated with this goddess, as at Paphos, Ajios Jakovos, Amathus, and Kition.[197] Especially noteworthy in this context is the image found at Kition, which portrays the city goddess even after the Phoenicians colonized the area and established their cult to Aštart in Area II (see Chapter Nine). As such, although it is clear that the Levantine elements were the dominant element in the evolution of Aphrodite, the importance of the Minoan iconographic influence should be noted as well, giving the goddess her earliest Aegeanization at the very beginning of the Iron Age.

By LC II, there existed in Cyprus a strongly sexualized goddess and a horned god, both associated with metallurgy and horned animals. This pairing of deities once again calls to mind Aphrodite's earliest cult site in the Greek world, Kato Symi, and offers perhaps the final explanation as to why the cult of the goddess was adopted there at the beginning of the Iron Age. As was discussed above in Chapter Three, the earliest evidence for worship at Kato Symi shows the adoration of a deity associated with animals, starting with the animal votives of the MM period and continuing with the images of Hermes returning from the "hunt" in the Archaic Age. Based on continuity of cult, one might suggest that it was the male deity at Kato Symi who was specifically associated with (horned) animals. So, too, it is entirely probable that a goddess was worshipped alongside this god-of-animals, although nothing of the votive remains allows for any speculation as to the character and identity of this goddess. However, if the Cretans saw in the god of Cyprus a parallel to their own god of Kato Symi (or, conversely, the Cypriots saw the Kato Symi god as a parallel of their god), then it would be logical that as Cypriot influence spread to Crete, the "new" Paphian goddess became merged or associated with the older Minoan goddess through her identification as a goddess of (horned) animals and as the consort of this god. Thus, the Paphian would find a home at a cult site that shows continuity far earlier than any of the evidence would suggest for the presence of Aphrodite in the Aegean.

---

197. Karageorghis 1998c: 1–17 and Pl. I–X. Karageorghis also lists Late Geometric and Archaic goddesses-with-upraised-arms deriving from Marion, Idalion, Arsos, Ayios Tychonas, Kythrea, Kazaphani, and Saittas-*Livadhia*.

VII.
CYPRUS BETWEEN OCCIDENT AND ORIENT

It is important to account for the transmission of iconographies and ideol-ogies among the Aegean, Cyprus, and the Near East in the Late Bronze Age and Early Iron Age, especially the exchange of goods and ideas between these regions. The Late Bronze Age is marked by extensive interaction among the "Great Powers" of the ancient world: Babylonians, Hittites, the kingdom of Mittani, Egyptians, Assyrians, and the Ahhijawoi, generally understood to have been the Mycenaean Greeks. So, too, the sea power, possibly even "thalassocracy," of an-cient Crete has received partial confirmation through the presence of MM pottery as far afield as Italy, Greece, Asia Minor, Egypt, and the Levantine coast.[1] Textual documentation from Ugarit shows the close relations be-tween this city state and Mari to the east, Cyprus to the west, and the Hittites to the north, while Aegean pottery appears throughout Egypt, the Levant and Cyprus, attesting to a thriving international trade.

To date, however, the finest evidence for the extent of international trade and contacts throughout the Bronze Age eastern Mediterranean comes from the excavations of sunken trading vessels along the southern coast of Turkey.[2] These excavations attest to substantial trade and contact between the Levant, Cyprus, Egypt, and the Aegean.

The style of pottery from the Ulu Burun wreck suggests that the ship sank between the end of the fifteenth century and the beginning of the four-teenth,[3] although current dendrochronologial data reveal an exact date of the wreck to be 1306–1305 BCE.[4] The goods aboard the ship included ele-phant and hippopotamus ivory; gold, silver, faience, and amber jewelry; Mycenaean, Cypriot, Canaanite, and Ugaritic pottery; glass ingots and beads; copper and tin ingots; bronze weapons; Mycenaean seals; an Ugaritic-style gold chalice; and a (possibly) Syrian finger cymbal.[5]

---

1. Bass 1972: 20; Lambrou-Phillipson 1990: *passim*; Cline 1994: *passim*; Betancourt 1998: 5–12.

2. Those of Ulu Burun and Gelidonya were conducted by G. Bass and the Underwater Archaeological Museum of Bodrum; that of Point Iria by Yannis Vichos and Yannos Lolos of the Hellenic Institute of Marine Archaeology in Athens. Further evidence derives from the excavations at Marsa Matruh off the coast of Libya by Donald White.

3. Bass 1986: 270.

4. Institute for Nautical Archaeology (http://nautarch.tamu.edu/INA/ub_main.htm).

5. Bass 1986: 274.

Bass notes that the Cypriot pottery on board was of the sort commonly exported to the Levant, such as Bucchero jugs, white shaved juglets, white-slip II milk-bowls, and base-ring II bowls.[6] So, too, fifty-two of the Syro-Palestinian amphorae excavated were of a style that is commonly found at Ugarit (possibly a site of production) but that have their best parallels on the Greek mainland—one in a Mycenaean chamber tomb and the other in a tholos tomb at Menidi.[7] According to the excavator, the glass discovered was of Syro-Palestinian origin but was chemically identical to Egyptian cored vessels and to Mycenaean glass amulets.[8] The Mycenaean seal may attest to the presence of an Aegean merchant on the vessel, as does the presence of the very few Mycenaean *kylikes* (although Bass believes that the ship was ultimately of Levantine origin, probably with a Levantine crew). The amber beads attest to trade as far afield as the Baltic, and the ivory points to trade either with Egypt to the south or, more probably, Palestine.[9] To the extreme east, the presence of tin ingots may attest to trade with Elam or even Bactria (although the possibility of an Anatolian source of tin remains open).[10]

In the end, Bass argues that the abundance of Near Eastern materials, the paucity of Aegean pottery, and the east–west orientation of the vessel suggest that the ship was proceeding east to west and that a circular route from the Levant to Cyprus to Greece ran along the southern coast of Anatolia, then proceeding to Egypt, back to Cyprus, ending up again in the Levant.[11]

The material from the Cape Gelidonya shipwreck offers similar data for the late thirteenth century BCE.[12] According to the original publication of the finds, the pottery from the vessel was predominantly Palestinian, Syrian, and, most extensively, Cypriot.[13] The large quantity of Cypriot pottery correlates well with the other item found in high quantities on the ship: ox-hide ingots of copper.[14] The evidence of the pottery and the style of the ingots themselves offer a date of c. 1200 for the final voyage of the ship.[15] In contrast to

---

6. *Ibid.*

7. *Ibid.*, 277.

8. *Ibid.*, 282.

9. *Ibid.*, 284–86.

10. *Ibid.*, 294.

11. *Ibid.*, 296.

12. The Institute for Nautical Archaeology arrives at a date of 1200 BCE +/- 50 based on the radio carbon dating of the brushwood in the wreck (http://nautarch.tamu.edu/INA/capegelidonya.htm).

13. Bass 1967: 125.

14. *Ibid.*, 52ff.; Bass 1973: 29–33.

15. *Ibid.*

the ship at Ulu Burun, the Gelidonya wreck offered very little by way of Aegean artifacts or pottery, either in terms of trading commodities or personal possessions of the crew. Based on these findings, the high concentration of Cypriot and Levantine goods and minimal Aegean finds, Bass surmised that the Gelidonya ship was Cypriot, possibly manned by either a Cypriot crew or a combination of Cypriots and Syrians, as per the personal items found aboard the ship, such as seals and amulets.[16]

The possible destination(s) of the Gelidonya ship might be surmised from the collection of weights found in the wreckage. According to Bass, the weights show that the ship was capable of trading with Egypt, Syria, Palestine, Cyprus, the various civilizations of Anatolia, Crete, and probably the Greek mainland.[17] The ship's last major port-of-call was Cyprus itself, where the ship acquired substantial amounts of pottery and metals. From Cyprus the ship travelled west, although the final destination is unknown.

Further evidence comes from the recent excavations of a shipwreck off the coast of Point Iria in the Argolic Gulf in southern Greece.[18] Whereas the Gelidonya excavations have pointed to connections between Cyprus and the Levant, the data from this excavation offer equally strong proof of the close connections between Cyprus, Crete, and Greece during the LBA.

The pottery salvaged from the sunken vessel is predominantly Cypriot (LC IIC/IIIA) and Mycenaean (LH IIIB2), accompanied by eight Cretan-Mycenaean stirrup jars of the LM IIIB2 style.[19] All these offer a date c. 1200 BCE for the wreck. Based on the typology of the pottery found on board, the excavators derived a possible trade route for the ship's final passage, beginning at a harbor on the southern coast of Cyprus and heading first to the north coast of Crete, then to the west of the island. From here, in decent weather, the ship would have probably passed by Kythera on its way to Cape Malea and the Peloponnese. There it probably stopped at harbors, such as at Tiryns and Asine, continued its trading, and then continued on to Herminone or the Argosaronic islands, such as Hydra or Aegina. In all cases, the primary cargo was probably foodstuffs, such as fruit and oil.[20] This trade route is, of course, hypothetical. Nevertheless, it does accord well with the route taken by the spread of Aphrodite's cult as determined in Chapter Three, proceeding from Cyprus to Crete and finally the Greek mainland.

---

16. Bass 1973: 36. This revises his earlier view that the ship and crew were of Syro-Palestinian origin.

17. Bass 1967: 142.

18. Lolos 1995: 72–76.

19. Vichos and Lolos 1995: 324; Lolos 1995: 73.

20. Vichos and Lolos 1995: 328–29.

Finally there are the data from Marsa Matruh in northern Africa to consider. Over the course of two excavations in 1985 and 1987, White uncovered a broad stretch of LBA remains on the island, including architectural remains (minimal), metal objects, and pottery. Once again, it is the pottery that offers the best data concerning foreign contacts and trade. According to Linda Hulin, who analyzed the combined pottery of the two seasons, the majority of LBA pottery is Cypriot in origin, constituting no less than 80 percent of the total number of shards.[21] Second in number to the Cypriot material are the Pharaonic wares from Egypt, attesting to trade between Egypt and her Libyan neighbors.[22]

Only slightly less significant in the pottery finds were many Canaanite storage vessels, almost outnumbering the Cypriot storage vessels on the island.[23] For the Aegean, only twenty shards of combined Minoan and Mycenaean finds wares were discovered during the two seasons of excavation. As such, the Aegean is only minimally represented in the pottery assemblage from Marsa Matruh.[24]

In terms of chronology, the Cypriot pottery found on the island dates from the fourteenth to the very early thirteenth centuries BCE. The architectural remains show three distinct levels of settlement, which come (abruptly) to an end in the thirteenth century.[25] Although Aegean wares are infrequent among the finds, White suggests that perhaps Marsa Matruh played an important role in Cypriot trade, with the island serving as a convenient port-of-call and watering-hole on the way from Egypt to Crete.[26] Thus, one might be able to interpret the low percentage of Aegean wares as a sign that ships traveling from the Near East would reach Marsa Matruh before heading up to Crete, whence they would travel homeward by a more northerly route. As such, the finds from the island, like those of the wrecks off the coast of Turkey, attest to an extensive east–west trade and contacts between Cyprus, Canaan, northern Africa and, possibly, the Aegean.

The excavations at Ulu Burun, Gelidonya, Cape Iria, and Marsa Matruh indicate extensive contact among the Levant, Africa, Cyprus, and the Aegean during the Late Bronze Age. This archaeological evidence reflects the con-

---

21. Hulin 1989: 120. Of these, 31 percent were Cypriot fine wares and 69 percent were flat-bottomed plain white and painted white wheel-made jars and storage vessels.

22. White 1989: 113.

23. Hulin 1989: 124.

24. *Ibid.*, 121.

25. White 1989: 112.

26. White 1986: 83.

tacts mentioned by Homer in the *Odyssey*.[27] In Book IV Menelaos recounts his *nostos* (*Odyssey*, Bk. IV: 82–85):[28]

> Seven years at sea,
> Cyprus, Phoenicia, Egypt, and yet farther
> among the sun-burnt races.
> I saw the men of Sidon and Arabia
> and Libya too.

Later, in Book XIV, Odysseus relates a similar itinerary to Eumaios the swineherd, Odysseus beginning as a Cretan pirate, traveling to Egypt, leaving Egypt with a Phoenician to travel to that man's homeland before heading out toward Libya and Crete. Thus, the contacts of the late Bronze Age are recorded not only in the archaeological record, but in the literature as well.

Whereas these excavations have presented evidence for general eastern Mediterranean trade in the Late Bronze Age, it is important to scrutinize the connections between Cyprus and the Aegean in the Late Bronze Age and Early Iron Age, so as to determine how each may have affected the iconographic and ideological traditions of the other.

Although the exact chronology (and even methodology) of Greek-Cypriot relations from the Bronze Age into Iron Age times remains a topic of lively debate, it is generally agreed that the earliest Aegean imports found on Cyprus date from the Early and Middle Bronze Ages. Lambrou-Phillipson lists a handful of pre-LBA Minoan items found on Cyprus at the sites of Lapithos, Vounous, Karmi, Kourion, and Paraskevi.[29] By contrast, no Helladic wares or items appear on the island before the LBA, when they begin to appear in the LC IB (c. 1450 BCE) period. Mycenaean IIB and IIIA1 wares have been found at Hala Sultan Teke, Maroni, Arpera, Enkomi, Milia, and Nicosia—put simply, throughout the island.[30] At this same time, a greater quantity of Cretan wares also become prevalent on Cyprus, notably at Morphou-*Toumba tou Skourou*, Phlamoundi, Enkomi, Ayia Irini, Hala Sultan Teke, Kouklia, Limassol, and Maroni.[31]

The presence of Greek and Cretan potteries on Cyprus is most pronounced in the LH IIIA2 to IIIB periods.[32] This is indicative of increased contact between these two cultures from c. 1375 to 1200 BCE and, thus, some would see it as the first possible date of Aegean settlement in Cyprus. There

---

27. Bass 1997: 72–74.

28. See Appendix B 7.1.

29. Lambrou-Phillipson 1990: 87.

30. *Ibid.*, 92.

31. *Ibid.*, 87.

32. Åström 1973: 123; Lambrou-Phillipson 1990: 87 and 92; Cline 1994: 60–67.

are two main arguments against this hypothesis. First, analysis of the pottery reveals that this Mycenaean ware was produced in the Aegean and not at Cyprus, thus not local production by Greek colonists.[33] Second, no alternate evidence exists for the arrival of an Aegean society in Cyprus—there is no indication of new burial customs.[34]

It is generally accepted that a first wave of Aegean settlers in Cyprus arrived c. 1190 BCE, at the transition from LC IIC:2 to LC IIIA:1, when large quantities of locally produced LH IIIC ware began to appear in earnest in Cyprus at the sites of Enkomi, Sinda, Kition, Hala Sultan Teke, Athienou, Maa-*Palaeokastro*, and Palaipaphos.[35] These Mycenaean wares included both cooking implements and Aegean loom weights, suggesting the arrival of entire families with their household goods.[36] This LH IIIC ware appeared alongside native Cypriot styles, such as Decorated LC III, and even merged with these styles to form a style designated by Iacovou as Cypro-Mycenaean IIIC.[37] As Iacovou pointed out, the LH IIIC styles never appear in separate clusters in either settlements or graves (with one exception in a tomb at Palaipaphos). Furthermore, ceramic analysis has shown that both wares (Decorated LC III and the Cypro-Mycenaean III) could have been from the same fabrics, even from the same workshops.[38] In addition, the native Cypriot style of burial was maintained throughout the first three quarters of the twelfth century.

Apparently, then, that Aegean settlers arrived at Cyprus as early as 1190 BCE, bringing their own pottery styles, looms, and cuisine with them. However, this new Aegean population was not politically dominant on the island. It appears that for over a half century the new immigrants lived in relative

---

33. Catling 1973: 37.

34. The arrival of Aegean populations in force is therefore dated down into the twelfth century, although the current understanding of the arrival of the "Achaeans" has changed considerably in the past twenty years. Up through the 1970s the hypothesis was that, c. 1190 BCE, Achaean war lords arrived in force, their first stronghold on the island at the sites of Maa-*Palaeokastro* near Paphos and Pyla-*Kokkinokremos*. This initial presence lead to the ultimate Hellenization of the island. Later hypotheses have suggested, rather, that the Hellenization of the island—including Greek language, funerary architecture, and the like—is actually a product of the eleventh century, and resulted from the arrival of refugees, not warlords (Karageorghis and Demas 1985: 276).

35. *Ibid.*, 272; Karageorghis and Demas 1988: 259; Iacovou 1989: 53; Burdajewicz 1990: 6.

36. Bunimowitz and Yasur-Landau, "Women and Aegean Immigration to Cyprus in the 12th Century B.C.E.," presented at the "Engendering Aphrodite" Conference, 1998. Publication forthcoming.

37. Iacovou 1989: 53.

38. *Ibid.*

peace, side-by-side with the native Cypriot population and, possibly, even immigrants from the Levant.[39]

The real evidence for discontinuity and destruction in Cyprus, then, comes not c. 1190 with the arrival of the "Achaeans," but at the transition from LC IIIA and LC IIIB, c. 1125 BCE, with implications lasting well into the middle of the eleventh century BCE. Up through 1125, both settlements and cemeteries on Cyprus continue in use, as excavated at Maa-*Palaokastro*, Palaipaphos, Kourion, Idalion, Athienou, Hala Sultan Teke, Kition, Sinda, and Enkomi.[40] Of all these sites, only Palaipaphos, Kition, and Enkomi show any signs of continuity after 1120–1100 BCE, that at Enkomi only lasting up to c. 1050 before being totally eclipsed by Salamis.[41] Meanwhile, the sites of Amathus, Salamis, and Alaas first come into being at this precise moment when the older Cypriot sites are dying off, indicating a break with the Bronze Age Cypriot settlement patterns and the establishment of the *poleis* that were to prove politically dominant on the island during the Iron Age and beyond.[42]

During this period, and especially into the eleventh century, new, Mycenaean-style burial chambers, with long *dromoi* approaching squared chambers, come into use on Cyprus, notably at Palaipaphos, Lapithos-Kastros, and Marion.[43] This new style of burial, which accompanied the new settlement pattern, was itself accompanied by a new style of pottery called proto-white painted ware (PWP), which begins to appear in Cypriot grave contexts in LC IIIB (1125–1050), erratically at first, but with increasing frequency beginning in the early eleventh century. Karageorghis is of the opinion that this PWP ware shows evidence of inspiration from Crete.[44]

It is during this period, LC IIIB—between approximately 1125 and 1050—that Cyprus became Hellenized. The continuity observable at sites such as Alaas and Salamis, later seats of Greek power on the island, emphatically suggest this, as does the establishment of the "Eteo-Cypriot" site of Amathus, where, according to Aupert and Hermary, the indigenous population of Cyprus fled when overwhelmed by Aegean immigrants.[45] So, too, the new, Aegean-style tombs, supposedly containing an Aegean population, increasingly came to hold greater percentages of the wealth and status markers of Cyprus.[46]

---

39. Catling 1994: 133.

40. Vanschoonwinkel 1994: 110.

41. *Ibid.*

42. *Ibid.*

43. Coldstream 1989: 328–32.

44. Karageorghis 1968: 183.

45. Hermary 1987: 376–77; Aupert 1997: 20–21.

46. Coldstream 1989: 333.

How exactly this transition from Cypriot to Aegean came about is still not entirely understood. That at least one second wave of Aegean immigrants arrived in the late twelfth century seems entirely plausible, although whether these were peaceful colonists or Homeric-style pirates is debatable.[47] That only one further immigration was necessary to Hellenize the island is also a matter of further consideration.[48] What does appear to be acceptable on the basis of the current data is that the eleventh century was a significant period of change on Cyprus, and that the ultimate outcome of that change was the metamorphosis of the island from indigenously Cypriot to essentially Greek.

Of special significance for this study, however, are the specific examples during the eleventh century of the influx of Minoan cultural artifacts into Cyprus, and the fate of Paphos during this period of tribulations on Cyprus and throughout the Mediterranean in general.

Karageorghis enumerates three significant elements of Minoan artistic or iconographic style that become incorporated into Cypriot art forms at this time.[49] One of these is the proto-white painted ware mentioned above, which is indicative of the second wave of Aegean immigrants into Cyprus. Karageorghis argues that proto-white painted pottery is based on a Cretan style and, thus, evolved in Cyprus due to strong Cretan influence. Another Minoan influence is the iconography of idols. For example, centaur figurines come to be produced in Cyprus at this time, and Karageorghis sees the style of these figurines as once again indicative of Minoan inspiration.

Finally, the goddess-with-upraised-arms makes her first appearance in Cyprus in the eleventh century, with her earliest Cypriot examples coming from Enkomi, Kition, and Ajios Jakovos. As the Minoans settled in Cyprus, they apparently brought this aspect of their religious customs with them. Then, the Cypriots, gradually at first, would have come to adopt this new icon, especially during and after the eleventh century.[50] Once the Cypriots adopted this "goddess" or, more specifically, her iconography, she remained in the Cypriot iconography into Archaic times, spreading over the island so that she is found from Kition to Lapithos to Palaipaphos, where she evidently became identified with the Paphian goddess. As will be discussed below, this Cypriot

---

47. Catling 1994: 136–37. Maria Iacovou, in her paper "Cyprus at the Dawn of the First Millennium BC: Cultural Homogenisation versus the Tyranny of Ethnic Identifications" delivered at the "Transmission and Assimilation of Culture in the Near East" Conference in Jerusalem, Feb–March 2000 (publication forthcoming), argues against any massive influx of any social group visible in the eleventh to tenth centuries, but rather for a gradual homogenization of the Cypriot culture throughout this time period.

48. Vanschoonwinkel 1994: 126.

49. Karageorghis, "Αι Σχεσεις Μεταξυ Κυπρου και Κρητης Κατα Τον 11ον Αι. π.Χ."

50. Karageorghis 1977: 13.

adoption of Minoan iconography may help to explain the early acceptance of the Cypriot goddess in Crete.

Concerning the second issue, as mentioned above, Paphos was one of the greater sanctuaries of Bronze Age Cyprus, which continuity and tradition suggest was the sanctuary of the Cypriot goddess who was adopted by the Greeks as Aphrodite. As also mentioned briefly above, Paphos, along with Kition and, to a lesser extent, Enkomi endured throughout the period of transition from LC II through LC IIIB and even beyond, well into the tenth century BCE.[51] If, as the current arguments suggest, an Aegean population first appeared in numbers on Cyprus c. 1190 BCE (at Maa, geographically close to Paphos) and lived in relative harmony with the indigenous population for at least sixty-five years (1190–1125 BCE), this would afford an opportunity for the Aegean population to come into contact with the Cypriot goddess of Paphos during a period when she was still venerated by her native constituents. The continued occupation of the site and, apparently, use of the sanctuary during the Hellenization of the island suggest that this cult weathered well the transformation of the population from Cypriot to Aegean. Thus, in spite of the obvious and radical changes that affected Cyprus at the end of the Bronze Age, there was stability at that one site where this study suggests that the Greeks were most likely to have first encountered and adopted the goddess who would become for them Aphrodite.

From Cyprus to the Aegean[52]

Having established the ways immigrants from Greece and Crete made their way to Cyprus and to the cult of the Paphian, we need to examine how this "new" cult of a Cypriot goddess wended its way to the Aegean and to discover the reason that this cult first manifested itself in Crete.

GREECE

Between the years 1050–975/950 BCE there is a bit of a dry spell in relations between Greece (including the eastern Greek islands) and Cyprus.[53] The extensive contacts, even emigration, that typified relations between Greece and Cyprus for the preceding two centuries was now replaced by a far more limited type of contact. Later, beyond certain commonalities of a newly emerging élite class, such as cremation, the use of iron implements, and a cer-

---

51. Iacovou 1994: 157-58; Vanschoonwinkel 1994: 110; Karageorghis and Demas 1988: 259; Karageorghis and Demas 1985: 272.

52. For a full catalogue of objects and aspects of trade between these two regions, see Demetriou 1989: *passim*.

53. Demetriou 1989: 83; Kourou 1997: *passim*.

tain fondness for antiques,[54] the primary evidence for contacts between the Greek mainland and Cyprus from the tenth through eighth centuries is discernible through imports of Greek pottery to Cyprus. The pottery is inevitably either Euboian or Attic.[55] The earliest find site for post-Bronze Age Greek pottery, exclusively Euboian, on Cyprus is Amathus, an Eteo-Cypriot site that probably served as a port-of-call for east–west trade between Euboia and the Levant.[56] This Euboian monopoly on the markets of Cyprus (and the Levant) is maintained throughout the Sub-Protogeometric period, and it is only in the Middle Geometric period that Attic imports begin to appear throughout Cyprus.[57]

In the opposite direction, both Cypriot and Phoenician artifacts appear in Greece.[58] This is evident in Euboia possibly as early as the tenth century, where there is evidence for trade with the Levant via Cyprus in the Heroön of Lefkandi. The most notable direct import from Cyprus here is an antique bronze krater with direct parallels to two such kraters from Kalorizki Tomb 40.[59] So, too, a grave in the Toumba cemetery, dating (according to the pottery) to 950–900 BCE, contained a set of bronze wheels of Cypriot character, four vases of faience, and an animal plaque and a ring of the same material. In nearby graves were discovered two incised metal Near Eastern bowls, one decorated with sphinxes and the Tree-of-Life, the other with a divine-procession scene. Also in the Toumba cemetery was found a little centaur figurine—ritually "killed" and buried in two separate graves—that shows clear Cypriot influence. At the same time, a grave in Palia Perivolia produced a Cypriot bichrome flask. A Near Eastern pilgrim flask came from a tomb in the Skoubris cemetery.[60]

In the following century luxury goods from the East increased—gold was even more plentiful at Lefkandi than in the previous generation. There is an abundance of broad finger-rings, solid enough to have been worn in life, and those from Skoubris cemetery are Cypriot in character (ribbed and plain convex). Gold earrings were found decorated with granulated pendants similar in style to Levantine models. There are also four gold diadems of oriental character: one has a lively frieze of assorted animals, which is probably an import

54. Crielaard 1998: 187–81; Matthäus 1998: 140.

55. Coldstream and Bikai 1988: 42.

56. *Ibid.*, 35.

57. *Ibid.*, 42.

58. Kourou 1997: 220ff. For more on Aegean-Phoenician contacts at this period, see Chapter Eight.

59. Crielaard 1998: 190 with references.

60. Popham *et al.* 1980: 217–64.

from the Levant, whereas the others have zigzag and dotted designs similar to Cypriot work.[61]

The Athenian Kerameikos begins to show evidences of eastern contact in many of its wealthier graves in the tenth and ninth centuries.[62] Imitations of Cypriot white painted pottery were buried with the dead, as were artifacts of Levantine goldsmiths.[63] So, too, Cypriot-style weapons began to appear also in Attica in the ninth century, notably a Protogeometric spearhead (c. 875 BCE) and LPG shield bosses dating to c. 850 BCE.[64]

To the east, in the Dodecanese, renewed contact with the Near East is evident as early as the Late Protogeometric (c. 925) period with the appearance of Cypriot materials in Kos.[65] These materials, catalogued by Demetriou, include various types of pottery, including bird vases, pilgrim flasks, and barrel-jugs, as well as at least one sword.[66] There is, as yet, no evidence for Dodecanese artifacts in Cyprus between the years 1050–700 BCE[67] and, thus, Coldstream suggests that the Dodecanese probably served as one of the main ports-of-call on the trade routes between Cyprus and the western Mediterranean.[68] It would seem that the new connections between Cyprus and Greece occurred originally between Cyprus and Euboia-Attica, probably passing through the Dodecanese.

CRETE

Starting in the mid-tenth century, there is a reversal in the previous two centuries of relations between Cyprus and Crete, whereby Cyprus becomes the source of several imports and artistic innovations in Crete. Tombs 200 and 201 at Knossos contained both jewelry and weapons with close parallels to burial goods discovered at contemporary Palaipaphos-*Skales*, *Kaloriziki*, Amathus, and Salamis.[69] Tenth- and ninth-century iron *obeloi* of Cypriot man-

---

61. *Ibid.*, 217–30.

62. Kourou 1997: 221; Tzedakis 1979 points to one lentoid flask found at the Kerameikos that might show contacts as early as 1075 BCE. However, Tzedakis himself claims that these relations were not direct, but probably through Rhodes. Furthermore, until the ninth century this flask remains in relative isolation as an eastern Mediterranean import.

63. Coldstream 1977: 55–68.

64. Demetriou 1989: 75.

65. *Ibid.*, 77–78; Coldstream 1998b: 255.

66. Demetriou 1989: 77–78, 85.

67. *Ibid.*

68. Coldstream 1998b: 260.

69. Crielaard 1998: 190.

ufacture came to light both at the Fortetsa cemetery near Knossos and at the site of Kavousi.[70] Also discovered at the Fortetsa cemetery, specifically in Teke Tomb J, was a hemispherical bronze bowl of Cypriot type with a Phoenician graffito dated to c. 900 BCE.[71] Even earlier Cypriot bowls were discovered in the Idean Cave. These bronze bowls with handles decorated with lotus blossoms are of a style typical of the Cypro-Geometric I and II periods.[72] Similar bowls have been found at the Iron Age site of Arkadhes in southern Crete, along with faience beads similar to those discovered both in Cyprus and the Dodecanese.[73] This same site has produced light pottery and metalwork either of Cypriot import or, at least, direct inspiration and, thus, gives evidence of close contacts between Crete and Cyprus in non-cosmopolitan regions of the island.[74] Finally, three shards of Phoenician wares were discovered at the southern Cretan site of Kommos, datable to sometime between the end of the eleventh through the ninth centuries.[75]

In the second half of the ninth century, small ribbed juglets of Cypriot style were placed in some of the more affluent tombs of Knossos. While the style is distinctively Cypriot, analysis of the clay showed it to be of east Cretan manufacture, prompting Coldstream to suggest that there may have been at least one immigrant Cypriot potter plying his trade in Crete by the end of the Dark Ages.[76]

Concerning the adoption and adaptation of Cypriot artistic motifs into the Cretan repertoire, some objects, such as tripods, display a continuation of Cypriot styles prevalent in (and apparently maintained since) the Late Bronze Age.[77] Concerning Iron Age imitations, however, certain Cypriot traits are absorbed into the Cretan repertoire at the end of the tenth century.[78] By about 950 the Cypriot style lip-handled amphora, the "sigynna" spearhead, and the spearhead with long blade and prominent midrib all appear in Crete. Later came the metal, hemispherical bowl, the bird vase, the trefoil-lipped oinochoe, the comb motif, and the bracket ornament. By 850, the Cypriot-style beaded fibula made its appearance in Crete.[79]

70. Matthäus 1998: 141.

71. Coldstream 1979: 257; Catling 1977: 12.

72. Matthäus 1998: 134.

73. Kanta and Karetsou 1998: 168.

74. Ibid., passim.

75. Shaw 1998: 18.

76. Coldstream 1998b: 256.

77. Kanta and Karetsou 1997: 160ff.; Matthäus 1998: 129.

78. Coldstream 1979: 257; Demetriou 1989: 84.

79. Demetriou 1989: 85–86.

These motifs, pottery, and even weapons reveal a definite reversal of cultural influence in the tenth through eighth centuries throughout the eastern Mediterranean. At the end of the Late Bronze Age, as discussed above, Aegean immigrants arrived in Cyprus over the course of LC IIIA–B, bearing new styles of pottery and new types of religious iconography, of which the goddess-with-upraised-arms is one example. In the Early Iron Age, Cypriot styles and artifacts became more common in the Aegean, especially in Crete and the Dodecanese, somewhat less so in Euboia and Attica. Thus, it is at this time that Cypriot influence on Aegean culture should be sought.

How, then, does this accord with our earliest evidences of Aphrodite in the Aegean? As discussed above, in our survey of the Greek world, the two oldest known cult sites of Aphrodite are located in Crete, the older being at Kato Symi Viannou, followed by the sanctuary at Olous. It is extremely difficult to use the chronology of Kato Symi to determine an "arrival date" for Aphrodite, as the sanctuary dates back well into the MM and it is possible that a female deity was worshipped there alongside the male hunting-god. When this goddess came to be assimilated into Aphrodite (and the god into Hermes) is indeterminable. However, the chronological data do accord well with the foundation of the sanctuary at Olous, which dates from Late-Protogeometric to Early Geometric. If we combine this with the general trend of Cypriot influence on Crete in the tenth to eighth centuries BCE, it would seem likely that this is the appropriate date of the arrival of the cult of Aphrodite-as-Aphrodite in the Greek world, when Cyprus is exporting concepts both artistic and, evidently, religious to Crete.

Both Crete and mainland Greece maintained some level of contact with Cyprus during the Proto- and Geometric periods. Part of the difference is the nature of the contacts between these two regions. It appears that Greece, specifically Euboia and then Attica, was an exporter to Cyprus and the Levant during the Dark Ages. Pendant semi-circle skyphoi and dishes made their way to Amathus and Salamis as Greek traders made their way to the Levantine coast. In return, the Greeks in Euboia and Attica received luxury items, such as the gold jewelry discovered at Lefkandi. Thus, it was primarily élite goods that traveled from Cyprus to Greece. It can be noted that, according to the chronology of Aphrodite's cult described in Chapter Three, neither Euboia nor Attica showed early evidence of the cult of Aphrodite. This strongly suggests that the trade between Greece and Cyprus did not result in the importation of a new deity.

By contrast, there is a greater emphasis on importation of Cypriot culture into Crete during this period. Luxury items, grave goods, votive offerings, and even weapons and dining paraphernalia from Cyprus appear on the island from Knossos to Mt. Ida to Arkadhes. Thus, while Greece is exporting to Cyprus, Crete is importing from Cyprus. This offers one explanation as to why the cult of a Cypriot deity might first appear in Crete.

A further difference lies in how each of these cultures, Cretan versus main-land-Greek, perceived the Cypriot goddess. The Greeks, coming from a pre-dominantly Indo-European religious tradition, had no (pre)history of a god-dess of love and sex.[80] A goddess whose primary attribute was one of sexu-ality, but not maternity, would have had no easy cognate in the minds of the Greeks. The goddess' associations with water would only serve to make her even more foreign to a culture that originated on the Eurasian plains.[81] Thus, while the Greeks came to recognize Aphrodite as a deity, they nevertheless did not welcome her with open (or "upraised") arms. She was identified as a foreign deity and frequently entitled as such. Even the later Greek literature, beginning with the works of the Homeridai, betrays a lack of trust in this god-dess; what other deity is pointedly insulted in his/her Homeric Hymn?[82]

By contrast, the goddess of Cyprus was not entirely foreign to the Cretans. As discussed in Chapter Three, there is some minimal evidence that a nude, possibly eroticised goddess was revered in Crete in the Bronze Age, the best evidence coming from Knossos. Some scholars, beginning with Evans, even suggested, based on such evidence, that Aphrodite was derived from some manner of Minoan dove-goddess. It is really only in the matter of degree that Cyprus serves as a more probable region of origin for the goddess than Crete. Crete, and even Mycenae, had only a handful of nude female/goddess repre-sentations, in contrast to Cyprus, where heavily eroticised female images had been prevalent throughout the island for centuries.

That the goddess of Cyprus may have been familiar (or at least not wholly alien) to the Cretans is also suggested by the Cypriot adoption of the goddess-with-upraised-arms. From Middle Minoan times the Cretans used this image in the worship of (one of) their goddess(es) (be that a "Great Goddess," the "dove-goddess," the "snake-goddess," the "opium-goddess" or whomever). Approximately fifty years after the introduction of this figure into Cyprus she becomes a standard image in Cypriot religion as well, being found in sanc-tuaries from Enkomi to Lapithos to Palaipaphos. The use of the goddess-with-upraised-arms continued in Cyprus into Archaic times, and one should con-clude that whatever connotations the Cypriots had of her suited their per-ception of the Paphian deity. Thus, a common iconography was suitable to two cultures' views of feminine divinity.

---

80. See Chapter 3.

81. Mallory 1989: *passim*. Even Poseidon was originally a horse deity, who was adapted to a new environment rather dominated by θάλασσα.

82. The fact that the *Homeric Hymn to Aphrodite* (V) begins with high praise for the goddesses immune to her power and then proceeds to tell the tale of Aphrodite's humiliation with Ankhises does not suggest a hymn intended to honor. Many thanks to Sheila Murnaghan for this insight. So, too, see Aphrodite's role in the "Song of Demodokos."

Furthermore, to judge from the iconographic and Linear B evidence, goddesses were more common in Minoan religion than gods, rather in contrast to the more patriarchal nature of the Greek/Indo-European pantheon organized under Zeus. A powerful, feminine deity who maintained her sexuality—as opposed to the most prominent of the Greek goddesses, the virgins Athena and Artemis—would strike less of a contrast among the Cretans than among the Greeks, and would, therefore, lead to easier assimilation/identification.[83] As it is quite probable that a Minoan goddess contributed to the evolution of Aphrodite through the iconography of the goddess-with-upraised-arms, the Cretans would be adopting a goddess who was far from new or unusual into their own cults.

Another argument offered for the ease of Aphrodite's assimilation into Cretan religion is the possible presence of oriental versions of this goddess already in the Minoan pantheon, as determined by her name in the Linear A corpus.[84] The name A/JA-SA-SA-RA-ME, identified as a deity in the Minoan Libation Formula, has been tentatively identified as a Minoan version of the Hittite Išhara or Levantine Aštart. This possibility is unlikely at best. First, we do not yet know enough about Linear A to conduct a linguistic analysis to see if the closest parallel, Išhara, is in fact a cognate. Second, if Owen's suggestion is correct, i.e., the name derives from Hittite *Isassaras* "Lady,"[85] then it refers to a female deity in general and not to a specific goddess, such as Išhara or Aštart.[86] In point of fact, as Išhara was more commonly revered farther east and Aštart, to judge from the Ugaritic texts, was not as significant in the Bronze Age as in the Iron Age, then the title "Lady" would better fit some other, more prominent goddess, such as Ašerah or Ḫepat. Finally, there is no later evidence for this goddess in Crete. As such, until our knowledge of both Linear A and the Minoan pantheon is increased, we should not consider the name A/JA-SA-SA-RA-ME to be evidence for the cult of an oriental love/sex goddess in Crete in the Bronze Age.

A final piece of somewhat ambiguous (and somewhat late) evidence concerning the early arrival of Aphrodite into Crete is the sacred site of Kommos,

---

83. One might be tempted here to think of Ariadne and her joint cult with Aphrodite at Amathus. However, as there is little evidence for the Minoans at Amathus and the literature concerning their joint cult there is of Roman date, this identification would be tentative at the very best.

84. Owens 1996: *passim.*

85. *Ibid.*, 209.

86. Neither of whose names means "Lady." Aštart derives from the Semitic Attar, Venus-god (see Heimpel and Roberts). Išhara, while no clear etymology is yet evident, potentially derives either from a pre-Semitic name, or from the Semitic *šeru*, meaning "morning" (see Haas 1994: 393). The name Freyja, of course, means "Lady," but this would be quite a stretch.

the port of Phaistos, where Phoenician pottery dating back as far as the late tenth century has come to light, dating to the earliest architectural phase of the site's temple (Temple A).[87] According to the excavator, Phoenician contact with Kommos peaked during the ninth century, c. 875–800 BCE, as determined by the amount of Phoenician wares there discovered.[88] It was perhaps due to this Phoenician influence that, when the temple of Kommos was reconstructed in the ninth century (Temple B), there were strong Phoenician elements to it, notably a shrine of three upright baetyls in the center of the temple. It is this so-called "three-pillar shrine," which is of interest concerning the spread of Phoenician religion into the west, for the closest parallels for such objects occur in Phoenicia's western colonies, particularly at Nora, Sousse, and Lilybaeum.[89] Thus, Kommos may represent one of the earliest extensions of Phoenician religion and cult practice into the Aegean.

Unfortunately, the precise meaning of these pillar-shrines is uncertain. If the meaning of their name—baetyls = *beth el* ("house of god")—indicates their cult significance, then such baetyls would have served as aniconic representations of the deities, deities who would literally be "housed" within them. Thus, as in typical Near Eastern cult practice, the baetyls might be served as were the cult statues of the ancient Near Eastern temples, before whom offerings were laid and prayers made.[90] In later Greek tradition, especially for the aniconic representation of Aphrodite at Paphos, this was certainly the case. Such a speculation is supported by the presence of the benches on the northern and southern walls of the temple, a hearth directly in front of the shrine, and what may have been a libation bowl behind the shrine, providing the means for rendering offerings both before and around the three baetyls.[91] Both hearths and offering benches were of use in the Aegean since Bronze Age times and, in this respect, Kommos shows a combination of Aegean and Near Eastern religious elements.

The identity of the deities worshipped at this shrine is a matter of debate. Concerning the identity or, perhaps better stated, the *Phoenician* identity of the deities venerated at Kommos, such Punic-Phoenician triads as Baal, Ašerah, and Aštart or Tanit, Ašerah, and Aštart are possible, although not certain.[92] This, of course, does not answer the question of which Cretan/

---

87. Shaw 1989: 181–82.

88. *Ibid.*, 182.

89. *Ibid.*, 176–78 for pictures and references. Other sites in the Phoenician world may have produced such structures, such as at Moyta, Sicily, and Malta, but the archaeological evidence from these sites is uncertain.

90. The aniconic form might also relieve some of the usual burdens associated with cult statues, such as the laundering of the image's clothing.

91. Shaw 1989: 165–72.

Aegean deities the natives would have recognized at Kommos. Further, in the later history of the cult at Kommos, it is the deities Zeus, Athena, and possibly Poseidon who are mentioned in inscriptions, and the offering of bull figurines at the temple would easily support an association with either of these male gods, although it should be noted that a gap of two hundred years divides the "Phoenician" Temple B from the later, classical Temple C.[93]

However, although the Phoenicians may have established a cult place to Aštart at Kommos, it would be imprudent to translate this immediately into a cult of Aphrodite and to consider this as evidence for why the cult of Aphrodite emerged in Crete before the rest of the Greek world. Unlike the sanctuaries of Kato Symi, Olous, and Axos, it is clear from the epigraphic evidence that no later cult of Aphrodite remained at the site. Furthermore, it would be rash to equate Aphrodite and Aštart, assuming that the cult of the latter would inevitably translate into the cult of the former.[94] For both of these reasons, the shrine at Kommos should not be used as an explanation for the early arrival of Aphrodite in Crete.

As we have seen the connections that linked Cyprus and Crete at the end of the Bronze Age and Early Iron Age, it is now important to turn to the other important source of influence in the evolution of Aphrodite, the Levant, to see what evidence exists for contact and trade between Cyprus and her eastern neighbors, and then to determine what goddess (or goddesses) of the east was behind the bird-faced figurines and other Late Cypriot divine iconography.

92. *Ibid.*, 182–83.

93. *Ibid.*, 165.

94. This will be addressed further in Chapter Nine.

VIII.
LEVANTINE CONTRIBUTIONS TO APHRODITE

Aphrodite did not originate in the Aegean, and she has no counterparts in the Indo-European pantheons or adequate parallels in the Minoan iconography. It is, therefore, most logical that it was stimulation from the East, from the Levant, that affected the evolution of the Cypriot/Paphian goddess who eventually became the Greek Aphrodite. This chapter deals with the various Levantine sites that were in contact with Cyprus during the crucial MC III – LC II periods, and examines their cults and pantheons, in order to see what deities were exposed to the Cypriot imagination at the time when a proto-Aphrodite was coming into being (i.e., the bird-faced and normal-faced figures). Furthermore, as it is the bird-faced figurines that are the predominant archaeological evidence of this new iconography, possibly ideology, in Cyprus, the meaning of these images in their Levantine homeland must be considered if we are to come to some understanding of what they meant to the Cypriots who adopted them.

Bronze Age Levantine Contacts with Cyprus

Beginning as early as the MC III period and increasing steadily through the fourteenth century, there was a significant increase of Cypriot ceramic wares in the Near East. This occurred both in the northern Syrian territories and in the area designated southern Canaan, where the proportion of Cypriot wares at individual sites increased exponentially.[1] This is also a period when new religious ideas, at least in terms of architecture and iconography, must have entered into the Cypriot consciousness for them to have been so widespread throughout the island at the dawn of the LC II period.

Opinions are somewhat divided concerning the nature of the trade that occurred during this phase of Near Eastern history. Some scholars contend that only certain areas within the Levantine sphere had contact with the Cypriots, and that the Cypriot pottery that was imported into cities such as Ugarit was then passed on both eastward and southward to more distant markets such as Egypt.[2] Points of contact between Cyprus and her Near Eastern neigh-

---

1. Bergoffen 1990: *passim*. There appears to have been a brief break in Cypriot imports c. 1600 according to recent excavations at Tell Arqa/Irkata (H. Charaf, pers. comm.). C. Bergoffen's upcoming publication of Alalakh will, it is hoped, shed more light on this issue.

2. *Ibid.*, Chapter Seven.

bors would have occurred at a few specific sites. Others scholars see a more "grass-roots" approach to the nature of Cypriot-Levantine relations, whereby the Canaanite culture as a whole had considerable influence on Cyprus (and *vice versa*). Thus, one could not so much say that Tel el-'Ajjul had influence on Cyprus, but rather southern Canaan did, and thus was born the Cypro-Levantine culture that permeated the eastern Mediterranean during the Late Bronze Age.[3]

In either event, it is evident that aspects of Levantine religious ideology had a profound effect on Cyprus, notably in the form of the (new) goddess/es and in the introduction of the horned, male deity/ies into the Cypriot pantheon.

According to Sjöqvist, Gittlin, and Bergoffen certain sites in the Levant show particular importance in the trade with Cyprus, as based on the vast array of Cypriot pottery that these sites have revealed. Trade with Cyprus during the LC I period occurred mainly with Ugarit and Alalakh in the north and Tel el-'Ajjul and, to a lesser extent, Tel Mevorakh in the south. Tomb types common at Megiddo and Beth Pelet made their first appearance on Cyprus at this time, suggesting close links, possibly even familial, between Cyprus and these two regions. Trade between Cyprus and the Levant expanded even further in the LC II period, and quantities of LC II wares appeared in the east at Ugarit, Megiddo, Beth Shan, Tel el-'Ajjul, Ashkalon, Gerar, Lachish/Tel ed-Duweir, Gezer, Beth Shemesh, and North Sinai.[4]

Regional Cults

Ugarit

Since this city-state was Cyprus' closest trading partner in the east, Sjöqvist and Sandars speculate that there may have been a colony of Ugaritic settlers on Cyprus in the Late Bronze Age.[5] Contacts with Cyprus are also evident in the written sources from Ugarit. Already mentioned are the letters passed from an Ugaritic king to the king of Alašiyah and the Ugaritic LC II text that invokes Baal and Aštart and the other various gods of Alašiyah (see above, Chapter Six). It is clear from both the archaeological and historical records that Ugarit was an important presence in the history and development of Cyprus.

In the Middle Bronze Age the Semitic Ugaritic population was joined by an influx into the general area of non-Semitic populations, such as the Hittites

3. Bikai 1994: *passim*.

4. Sjöqvist 1940: 164–65; Bergoffen 1990: 202, Chapter Eight *passim*. Tel el-Far'ah (South) also shows extensive Cypriot influence in its funerary architecture, notably in the 900-series and 500-series tombs. The first of these date to c. 1550 BCE, and the later to the period of Philistine penetration. For details, see Gilmour 1995: 155–61.

5. Sjöqvist 1940: 165; Sandars 1987: 153 and 199.

and the Hurrians.[6] Relations with Mesopotamia at this time can be document-ed by correspondence with Mari and the discovery at Ugarit of cylinder seals dating from the Old Akkadian[7] and First Babylonian dynasties.[8] Strong ties with Egypt were established at this time, while relations with Crete are rec-ognizable in finds of Cretan pottery, including an egg-shell cup found within a tomb of Level II.[9] Finally, in the Late Bronze Age, some Mycenaean-style short swords appear in tombs at Ugarit, implying contact with Greece.[10] Ulti-mately, the religion of Ugarit is essentially West Semitic. Nevertheless, early contacts with Mesopotamia had a profound effect on the nature of some of its deities, and early contacts with Egypt affected the spread and interpretation of some of the Ugaritic mythology.[11]

According to the texts, the two most authoritative deities in the Ugaritic mythological literature were El ("god") and his wife Aṯirat (Ašerah).[12] The most "active" members in the Ugaritic mythological literature are Baal (a title meaning "Lord," applied to the West Semitic god Hadad, known in the eastern Semitic pantheons as Adad or Addu) and his companion Anat. Anat is the bat-tle maiden and huntress, similar in persona and some functions to both Ath-ena and Artemis in the Greek pantheon. It is she who aids and supports Baal in his epic roles, and she who brings Baal back to life after his harrowing encounters with Death (the god Mot).[13]

---

6. Curtis 1985: 35–36.

7. Caquot and Sznycer 1980: 3–4.

8. Curtis 1985: 36.

9. *Ibid.*, 36–38.

10. *Ibid.*, 39.

11. This is especially so after the Hyksos interlude, when many West Semitic deities and concepts were adopted into the Egyptian pantheon.

12. One is faced with a veritable embarrassment of riches when it comes to the docu-mentation of Ugaritic religion, for much of it has been preserved both in the literature and in the archaeology of the ancient city. As several books and monographs have already emerged concerning this topic, it is not possible here for me to express fully all aspects of Ugaritic religion and mythology, and thus the reader must content herself with a quick overview of the principle deities of Ugarit and their most basic iconog-raphy. A good, general book on the topic for the non-specialist is Lowell K. Handy's *Among the Host of Heaven.*

13. Other deities important in the Ugaritic pantheon are Kothar-wa-Hasis, the crafts god; Šapaš, the sun-goddess; Mot, the god of death; Yamm, the god of the sea; Athtar, one of the "sons of Athirat"; Dagan, who seldom appears in the literature, but is the father of Baal; Pidray, Talay, and Arsay, the goddesses of dew and moisture; and Rešef, the god of war. Many other deities are mentioned in sacrifice lists, such as Išḫara (Ugaritic Usharay) and Dadmis, but they play no role in the literature (Prechel 1996: 135).

Appearing often as a companion to Anat is the goddess Attart (Aštart), who shares Anat's martial nature, is a huntress in her own right, and who, according to the later Egyptian texts, is also a goddess of horses and chariots (no doubt through their association with battle). Several other deities are present in the Ugaritic corpus, such as the sun-goddess Šapaš and the smith Kothar-wa-Hasis. Some deities, such as Išḫara, appear in offering texts, but not in the mythology *per se*.

The iconography from Ugarit—the stele and idols of the deities discovered through archaeology—add a further level to our understanding of Ugaritic religion. Deities are identifiable through various iconographic techniques. As in Mesopotamia, gods wear horned crowns, most notably the gods El and Baal and, possibly, the goddess Atirat. Unlike Mesopotamia, however, these horned crowns are not consistently portrayed, nor do the number of horns indicate the rank of the deity, and thus images of El and Baal have only one pair of horns apiece. Attributes also accompany deities in their iconography, such as Baal with a lightning bolt.

Another prominent, and relevant, type of iconography from Ugarit is the so-called "Aštart plaque." These items, often rendered in gold, show a nude female *en face*, often with a Hathor-style hairdo (parted in the center and extending down to the shoulders, where the tips curl upward), her arms are either at her breasts or to either side of her body, holding either animal or floral motifs. The female may be portrayed standing atop a lion's back.

Alalakh

Alalakh was the second-most important trading post between Cyprus and the Levant during the LC I phase, when the bird-faced figurines were first making their way into the Cypriot consciousness.[14] The name "Alašiyah" appears in texts from Alalakh as early as the eighteenth and seventeenth centuries and continues even into the archival material of the fifteenth century, suggesting long-standing contacts between the two regions. Likewise, the eighteenth-century Mari texts refer to a trade in copper between Mari and Alašiyah/Cyprus, thus indicating a long-distance network of trade and communications during the early Late Bronze Age. The proximity of Alalakh to Cyprus and its location between Mari and Cyprus would make it difficult to believe that Alalakh did not form an important link in this network, an argument only strengthened by the references to Alašiyah in the Alalakh texts. Finally, as will be explained below, Alalakh is one of the sites with the most long-enduring use of bird-faced figurines in the ancient Levant, figurines identical to those that appear in Cyprus in LC II. The similarity of these items alone justifies an examination of contacts between these two neighbors.

---

14. Sjöqvist 1940: 162.

As these bird-faced goddess images are such a crucial aspect of the changes perceived in the Cypriot iconography, it is not amiss to begin with a study of their presence in Alalakh. Wooley describes these hand-made terra-cotta female figurines as:[15]

> a nude female figure, generally flat behind..., the hips very wide, the pubic triangle strongly accentuated, the navel rendered by a holed pellet, the arms outstretched and reduced to short pointed stumps, the legs, often very short, ending in a point with no indication of feet, the nose pinched out into an exaggerated beak, no mouth, the top of the head flattened and carried up into a square or domed form pierced by two or three holes (perhaps for the attachment of a thread wig?), the ears large and projecting, pierced with holes for ear-rings, the eyes and breasts rendered by pellets, while a necklace is generally shown by an applied roll of clay sometimes enriched by roulette-incised lines.

Such images are represented from levels XII to I at the site, and thus show a continuous presence at Alalakh for over one thousand years without considerable stylistic change.[16] The only significant stylistic variation in these figurines is a version in which the arms, rather than projecting to the sides, curve around so that the hands support the breasts, as in many of the Cypriot models.

Along with the hand-made images were mold-pressed female figurines, prevalent from Levels VII through II at Alalakh. The earliest example of these formed the decoration on a brazier from the temple of Yarim-Lim, testifying to the sacred nature of their use.[17] As with the mold-pressed nude goddesses from Archaic Greece, these figurines are prevalent in three styles: with hands under the breasts, with one hand under the breast and the other at the side, or with both arms hanging down the sides. Of these, the first is the most common, whereas only one example of the last has come to light at Alalakh.[18] The find contexts for these images are also of interest for their relation to the Cypriot versions. Many of the figurines come from temple complexes, such as the molded images on the incense burner from the Yarim-Lim temple. At least eleven figurines come from within the walls of temple complexes, while fragments of at least nine more come from rubbish pits associated with the temple complex of Level V.[19] A few fragments come from households, and four from mortuary contexts, one buried with an adult, one with an adult/child pair and two buried with infants.[20] As with the female figurines from

---

15. Wooley 1955: 244.

16. *Ibid.*

17. *Ibid.*, 246.

18. *Ibid.*

19. *Ibid.*, 249.

20. *Ibid.*, 248.

Cyprus, these images clearly have associations with both the religious world of the living and with the dead.

We are quite fortunate in that many texts from Alalakh have been pre-served from Level VII (eighteenth to seventeenth centuries)[21] and Level IV (fifteenth to fourteenth centuries).[22] According to the political texts from Level VII at Alalakh, the three most prominent deities were Addu (Hadad, Adad, Baal, or ^{d}IM), Hepat (the sun-goddess of Arinna of the Hittite pantheon, which played a considerable role in the Alalakh pantheon), and IŠTAR.

The actual identity of this last goddess is rather difficult to determine, for the cuneiform sign for the goddess' name was used fairly consistently throughout texts of both periods and possibly hid the name of a more local but similar goddess, such as Ištar, Aštart or Išhara.[23] This IŠTAR deity was clear-ly of considerable importance in the religious life of Alalakh. One text from the reign of Yarim-Lim casts an interesting light on the power and nature of this goddess:[24]

> When his brothers rebelled against Abbael, their lord, king Abbael, with the help of the gods Hadad, Hebat and the spear [of IŠTAR] went to Irride, conquered Irride and captured his enemy. At that time Abbael, in exchange for Irride which his father granted, gave Alalakh of his free will. And at that time, Yarimlim s[on of Hammu]rapi and servant of Abbael, brought up [his statue to the temple] of IŠTAR. [If(?) the offspring(?) of Ab]bael shall take what he (Abbael) gave to Yarimlim—he will give him city for city.

> Whoever shall change the settlement that Abbael had made and do evil against Yarimlim and his descendants—may the god Hadad dash him into pieces with the weapon which is in his hand; May Hebat-IŠTAR shatter his spear; may IŠTAR deliver him into the hands of those who pursue him; may IŠTAR...impress feminine parts into his male parts.

Two further documents from this period, Al 126 and 127, refer to the tem-ple of IŠTAR and the payments made thereto, while Al 126 refers also to an agreement made between Yarim-Lim and a "brother" (a peer king), sworn before IM and IŠTAR.[25] Thus, we know that in eighteenth-century Alalakh there was a temple to this IŠTAR goddess and that she was called upon to guar-antee oaths. According to the above-quoted text, she may have had a hand in

---

21. The palace of Level VII is generally attributed to Yarim-Lim of Yamhad, who was a contemporary of Hammurapi I of Babylon, thus placing a beginning date in the eigh-teenth century. Thus, the level was destroyed by Hatushili I no later than 1620 BCE.

22. Associated with Niqmepa, and thus dated to the fifteenth century.

23. Wiseman 1953: 16–17.

24. Translation according to Na'aman 1980, with one adaptation: I have placed IŠTAR in capital letters. Based on this textual evidence, Na'aman has suggested that the fortress temple near the palace of Alalakh VII was dedicated to the IŠTAR-deity.

25. Wiseman 1953: 63.

military affairs, as she might hand the traitor over to his enemies, while she is also concerned in matters of sexuality, as it is she who "makes eunuchs" and might attack the traitor in his genitals. These last two elements speak strongly for the character of Ištar.

Nevertheless, it is possible, if not probable, that the ideogram for IŠTAR actually conceals the name of a similar goddess: Išhara. The prosopography from the Level VII tablets at Alalakh shows names formed with the ideogram IŠTAR but syllabically with the name Išhara.[26] Furthermore, Išhara serves as a guarantor of oaths throughout Bronze Age Syria.[27] Finally, as a member of the Hittite pantheon as well as the Mesopotamian/Levantine, the strong Hittite influence upon the cults of Alalakh makes it somewhat more likely that it is Išhara, as an Ištar-like goddess, who is intended in these documents and names.

By Level IV, when Alalakh had come under the control of the Mittanian empire, Išhara had become one of the dominant members of the Alalakh pantheon. Although the ideogram for IŠTAR was still in use, it was far less common, and only one name from the census lists contains it, in contrast to the six names bearing the syllabic writing of Išhara.[28] One of these census lists, Al 180, names one Tulpiya (l. 2), who is listed as a SANGA-priest of Išhara.[29] During this period, Išhara still has an important role as guarantor of oaths.[30] In a treaty concerning the extradition of slaves between Idrimi of Alalakh and Pilliya of Kizzuwatna(?), the oath ends with the interdiction "May the gods IM, UTU, Išhara and all the gods destroy whoever transgresses (the words of this treaty)."[31]

From Level VII to Level IV, when Alalakh goes from being independent and under Hittite influence to dependent under the rule of Mittanian/Hurrian influence, certain aspects of the city's religion remain constant. One of these is the adoration of a storm-god as represented by the ideogram IM, although whether this orthography refers to Addu in Level VII and to Teššup in Level IV is difficult to determine. Another continuous aspect is the cult of an Ištar-type goddess, be she Ištar herself or her close cognate Išhara. As the prosopography from both levels shows the name of Išhara, and as both levels have IŠTAR/Išhara as the guarantor of oaths, one must see that either both goddesses were revered at Alalakh throughout the second millennium or that at least Išhara was worshipped, appearing in the texts either as IŠTAR or as Išhara.

---

26. Prechel 1996: 42.

27. *Ibid.*, *passim.*

28. *Ibid.*, 69–70.

29. *Ibid.*, 69.

30. This is, in fact, her most common function in Hittite mythology. See G. Frantz-Szabó.

31. ^{d}IM ^{d}UTU ^{d}Iš-ha-ra DINGIR.MEŠ *ka-li-šu-nu li-hal-li-[qú-šu]*. Translation, Wiseman 1953: 31–32, Al. 3, l. 46–47.

The nude-female figurines are consistently associated with the cults of goddesses, as in Crete. As such, if we are to link them with a goddess worshipped in Alalakh throughout the period of the use of the figurines, then we must associate them with Išḫara or, possibly, Ištar.[32] It is thus possible that during the LC I phase, corresponding in time to Levels VI through IV at Alalakh, aspects of the cult and persona of Išḫara/ Ištar were introduced into Cyprus.

Megiddo

This Palestinian site shows considerable contact with Cyprus during the LC I and II phases. In LC I a new tomb type appears in Cyprus, one that has a forerunner at Megiddo,[33] and in LC II Megiddo becomes one of the major recipients of Cypriot pottery. Sjöqvist suggests that not only must this site have been a major port of trade between Cyprus and the Levant, but it might even have had political and familial relations with the island.[34]

Megiddo shows continuous habitation from the Chalcolithic into the Iron Age, with continuous reconstruction of the sacred precinct upon the same area. A group of stone etchings comes from High Place 4008, dating to the Chalcolithic and Early Bronze Age phases and offers some of the earliest testimony concerning the nature of the cult. The majority show hunting scenes and animals, and a few also show representations of "defeated enemies," possibly having a sympathetic magic effect. One rough image shows what Kempinski suggests might be a female deity holding a spear and facing a plant. She wears a headdress, possibly similar to a *polos*, and a long robe, in contrast to the male figures shown nude or in loincloths. Kempinski suggests that this might represent some manner of "proto-Ištar" deity.[35]

From EB III to MB I (2650–2000/1950 BCE) a new population inhabits Megiddo, and with it new sacred structures come into being, most notably a large altar (4017) around which, toward the end of the era, were set three small temples. As there was a high proportion of Hurrians in this new EB–MB population, it is possible that the three temples were dedicated to the three primary Hurrian deities: Teššup, the storm-god; Ḫepat, his consort; and Šarruma, their son.[36] The Israeli Archaeological Service suggests that the three deities were the West Semitic El, Baal, and Ištar.[37]

---

32. See below, pp. 231ff.

33. This is the corbelled-vaulted tomb 21 at Enkomi, discussed by Sjöqvist 1940: 164. The north-Syrian antecedents, as opposed to Aegean, are argued in Gilmour 1995: 163–65.

34. Sjöqvist 1940: 164.

35. Kempinski 1989: 173.

36. *Ibid.*, 175–77 and note 21.

37. As based upon the explanatory literature present at the site itself.

During MB II (1950–1650 BCE = Strata XIII to XI) the large altar 4017 fell into neglect, being replaced first by a small offering area (4009) and then by a *bammah* (high place) in the southeastern corner of square M-13, probably indicating a dramatic change in cult practice at Megiddo.[38] The cultic architecture and orientation of the *bammôt* remain essentially the same from Stratum XIII through Stratum X (Temple 2048), indicating continuity of cult throughout this period.[39]

The anthropomorphic votives from these high places are exclusively female, some armed, some seated, and some of the variety of nude figurines holding their breasts that have been discussed throughout this study. Votive remains from the rubbish pits associated with the temple areas at this time (Strata XII to XI) shed some light on the cult and deities of this period. Of particular relevance for this study are bronze figurines of, what Epstein calls, a "fertility goddess," a small bull figurine, and a chalice and lid decorated with applied bulls' heads and snakes of clay.[40]

The votive remains from Strata X and IX show a certain continuity with those of the previous era. Both bronze and lead female figurines are prevalent, although now accompanied by a lead image of a male deity. Chalices are still in use, and, most interesting for this study, terra-cotta birds occur.[41]

In other respects, however, there is a clear change in cult, not only in Megiddo, but throughout the Levant c. 1650 BCE, heralding in a phase of uniformity in religious architecture and, probably, cult practice and belief that endures until the end of the Bronze Age. The style of architecture manifests at Megiddo shows a monumental square (or rectangular) outline with thick walls probably indicative of tower-like height. In the interior is one hall, at the end of which is a niche, possibly serving as the holy-of-holies. Before the entrance to the large sacred room with the niche is a small antechamber. This new style of temple, with variations in orientation, is to be found at Alalakh, Ebla, Ugarit, Hazor, Shechem, and even Avaris in Egypt.[42]

Within the temple were found four images of male deities. Two figures are of seated gods, one hand holding a cup, the other raised in benediction. The other two figures from the temples are of warrior-gods, one dating from the sixteenth or fifteenth century, the other clearly datable to the end of the Bronze Age by its *atef*-crown and use of a figure-eight shield.[43]

---

38. Kempinski 1989: 178.

39. *Ibid.*, 180.

40. Epstein 1965: 213.

41. *Ibid.*, 210–11.

42. Mazar 1992: 211.

43. Kempinski 1989: 184–85.

During this period the temple "houses" what appear to be two male deities, possibly El as the seated god and Baal as the warrior. Nevertheless, the continued use of the female votives appear to indicate a popular cult to goddesses, concomitant with the official cult of the gods.[44] Unfortunately, no texts have survived from Megiddo that might suggest a name for the goddess or goddesses worshipped for so long at this site and associated with the distinctive Nude Goddess iconography.

Beth Shan

Archaeological data on the cult and religion of Beth Shan derive mainly from the period when the city was under Egyptian control, whereas the primary textual references to the city and its cults come from the Bible, which refers to the city, during the wars of Saul and David, as being a Philistine stronghold.[45]

The earliest temple from Beth Shan, discovered by Mazar in 1989–1990, dates to LB I, preceding the period of Egyptian occupation (early fifteenth century BCE).[46] This temple is of the "non-monumental, irregular" types, also called a "wayside" shrine. This structure at Beth Shan is roughly rectangular, being 11.7 × 14.6 m, with a tripartite arrangement, including an entrance hall, a central hall, and an inner room/holy-of-holies. The latter two were lined with benches, and all the walls, platforms, and benches were coated with white plaster.[47] Unlike the more typical temples of the day, the passage from the entrance hall into the central hall was to the side of the dividing wall between the two, giving the "indirect or eccentric" access referred to by Wright.[48] Cylindrical pottery stands and a bath were discovered in the chambers of the west wing. Other than these few objects, however, the temple was cleaned out and abandoned, and offers little insight as to which gods were worshipped there.[49] Only the leg of an image of a "striding god" found within may suggest that a male deity was worshipped.[50]

According to Rowe, there were four temples in ancient Beth Shan that derive from the period of Egyptian hegemony.[51] Very few inscriptions come from these structures that permit a (tentative) identification of the deities

---

44. *Ibid.*, 184.

45. E.g., 1 Sam 31:8–12.

46. Mazar 1990: 611.

47. Mazar 1997: 151.

48. Wright 1992 (Vol. I): 507; Mazar 1997: 151.

49. Mazar 1997: 151–52.

50. Mazar 1990: 615.

51. Rowe 1940: *passim*.

worshipped there. One such inscription is a stele dedicated to the god Mekal, about whom little is known.[52] Another inscription comes from the Northern Temple of Ramses III. This image, on a rather corroded stele, shows a female deity wearing an Egyptian crown bedecked on both sides by plumes. Her silhouette is long and slender, and it is difficult to determine whether or not she is dressed. She holds what appears to be a weapon in her left hand, and she is turned (paratactically) to face a smaller individual who strides before her. The inscription at the top of the stele by the goddess reads: "Antit, the queen of heaven, the mistress of all the gods."[53] Above the smaller, striding figure reads: "An offering that the king gives to Antit, that she may give all life, prosperity and health to the double of Hesi-Nekht."[54]

The temple of Seti I was identified by the excavator as a temple of Mekal and Aštart. However, the one inscription from the building (a door socket), according to Rowe, reads "Praises be to thee, O beautiful one [the sun-god], who possesseth everlastingness ... thou didst fashion the Nile."[55] If the identification of this deity as a sun-god is correct, then it is somewhat more probable that it is Amun/Re, the solar-deity, who is venerated here. The presence of a female deity is suggested only by one pottery figurine fragment and a gold-covered female figurine with outstretched arms. In the face of this evidence, it is perhaps safer to see this temple as dedicated to an Egyptian deity, probably male.

Rowe suggests that the southern temple of Ramses III is dedicated to a male deity, either Rešef or possibly some Egypto-Canaanite combination of Rešef and Seth.[56] The identification of the temple's deity/deities is based exclusively on the iconography, of which very little remains. One piece of evidence is a serpentine cylinder seal from the lower level of the temple, which depicts on one side the pharaoh, Ramses II, in full battle gear and on the other the image of the god Rešef.[57] The other piece of evidence is a small bronze statuette of a seated male deity who wears a conical cap and holds a spear or scep-

---

52. Although see Thompson 1970: *passim* for further information.

53. Rowe 1930: 33.

54. *Ibid.* Rowe identifies this Antit with the goddess Aštart due to the goddess's apparel, which the excavator claims is typical of the Egyptian cult of Aštart (see below). Rowe's identification, however, may be an attempt to identify the temple as a "Temple/House of Aštoreth," thus, to embody the temple wherein the armor of Saul was laid according to the Biblical text. As the inscription identifies this goddess as Antit, and as the figurines found within the temple do not conform to those seen at Alalakh or Megiddo, it is perhaps better simply to see this deity as "Antit."

55. Rowe 1940: 19.

56. *Ibid.*, 22–23.

57. Rowe 1930: 31–32.

ter.[58] Rowe simultaneously identifies this image as Baal, Rešef, and Mekal,[59] although the image has closer parallels with the iconography of El in Ugarit. In any event, it does appear that the temple was dedicated to a male deity, even if the precise name (or names) of that deity currently eludes us.

It is only in the fourth temple, the temple of Amenophis III, where a preponderance of nude-female figurines suggests that a female deity was worshipped.[60] The goddess orientation of the temple is especially supported by the discovery of a limestone stele in the inner sanctuary that appears to depict a goddess. Unfortunately, the inscription on the object cannot be read, and thus we have no inscriptional evidence for the name of the goddess, who in all other respects is similar to the image of Antit discussed above. From at least the time of Thuthmosis III, this temple was dedicated to the local deity Mekal and, thus, it is possible that at Beth Shan this pair formed some manner of divine couple. If Mekal is a local version of Baal, then the pairing of Aštart with Baal/Mekal is consistent with the literary evidence from both Ugarit and Emar. If this deity is Antit, then the pair should be the primary deities of Beth Shan.

Smaller objects of faience and metal also offer some insight into the cult at Beth Shan. Locally made Egyptianizing items show representations of Hathor, Bes, Tawert, and Sekhmet, as well as a more Levantine-style god and goddess. This suggests a rather syncretic Egypto-Levantine religion in the popular cult, comprised of the more significant Egyptian deities and a Levantine god and goddess.[61]

Tel Mevorakh

To judge from the quantities of white slip I, base-ring I, and monochrome wares found at the site, there were commercial contacts between Tel Mevorakh and Cyprus during the LC IA through LC II periods, contacts that decreased at the end of LC IIA only to resume again in the LC IIB2 period.[62]

During excavation of the Late Bronze Age period at Tel Mevorakh, three successive levels of temple construction were discovered (Levels XI–IX), dating from approximately 1550 to 1280 BCE.[63] Although in structure the temple is of the typical "irregular" Canaanite style, the excavator notes the sacred area is unusual in that it offers no representations of the deities ven-

---

58. *Ibid.*, 32.
59. *Ibid.*
60. Rowe 1940: 6.
61. McGovern 1992: 694.
62. Kromholz in Stern 1984: 20.
63. Stern 1984: 39.

erated, either in clay or in metal.[64] It is fortunate, then, that two items from Stratum X offer some insight into the temple's deity. The first is a bronze snake figurine, which has a twisted body and a deteriorated head on which eye markings are still visible. It was discovered in pieces in Locus 185 on the surface of the temple's platform.[65] As images of snakes are commonly associated with portrayals of female deities in the Levantine iconography (not to mention Minoan and Mycenaean), appearing both on Levantine and Egyptian goddess plaques, its presence here offers evidence of the cult of a goddess at Tel Mevorakh. The second item of note, coming from Locus 194 just west of the temple, is a bronze pendant on which an eight-rayed star is represented with a central boss and eight smaller bosses between the star's rays.[66] Stern suggests that the star emblem on the pendant is a sacred symbol, probably attributed to the goddess Ištar.[67] The other votive items found at the temple's various strata are typical of Canaanite cults, and thus offer no information concerning the nature of the recipients. The excavator speculates that the bronze snake (as well as the star pendent) hints at the identification of the temple's deity as an Ištar-like goddess, possibly in combination with Baal.[68]

Lachish

The earliest evidence for the Lachish pantheon in the Late Bronze Age is an inscribed shard found in the fill of Palace A (c. 1500 BCE).[69] The name deciphered is *b'lt*, possibly *l]b'lt[*, indicating a dedication to Baalat, referring either to the goddess Aštart or Hathor.[70] Later, in the fourteenth century, a censer lid found in Tomb 216 was painted in red letters with the name *b'l*(=Baal).[71]

An inscription from Fosse Temple II also sheds some light on the Lachish pantheon. The so-called Duweir ewer bears an inscription on the shoulder in

---

64. *Ibid.*, 35.

65. *Ibid.*, 22.

66. *Ibid.*, 23.

67. *Ibid.*, 24. Note that this astral symbol is the Mesopotamian symbol for Ištar, specifically used to indicate this goddess on the *kudurru*'s of the contemporary Kassite Era. They appear in portrayals of the goddess on cylinder seals as early as the Old Akkadian period (see fig. 8g).

68. Stern 1984: 35.

69. Puech 1986: 13.

70. *Ibid.*, 13–14.

71. *Ibid.*, 17.

red paint that refers at least to one deity entitled Elat (literally: "goddess").[72] This may indicate the feminine counterpart of the Semitic god El ("god"), possibly Ašerah. Puech contends that the inscription is longer than previously thought, and he sees a possible reference to the god Rešef as well.[73]

Finally, and rather late, is a bowl fragment with a Proto-Canaanite inscription discovered in Pit 3867 of Level VI, Area S. The first line of the three-line dedication mentions the god *l'b*(=Ilab), a deity known also from Ugaritic sources. It is possible that a barely legible [*š*]*m* following the Ilab refers to Šamaš, the sun-god.[74]

Iconographic evidence is rather late, deriving from the late Late Bronze Age temple on the acropolis (Level VI=1200–1150 BCE).[75] Whereas the general layout of the acropolis temple shows close affinities with Egypt, the ico-

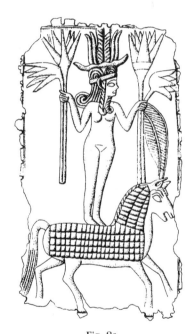

Fig. 8a

Drawing of gold foil image from Lachish. Israel Museum.
From C. Clamer, "A Gold Plaque from Tel Lachish."

72. *Ibid.*, 17.

73. *Ibid.*, 18: *mtn. šy r[b]ty 'lt r[š]p* or *šy l(?)[b]ty 'lt r[š]p*.

74. *Ibid.*, 21–22.

75. Ussishkin 1992: 117; Ussishkin 1978: 12.

nography discovered within, while somewhat Egyptianizing, is essentially Levantine in character.

The most significant iconographic evidence for the Lachish pantheon is the so-called "Lady Godiva" plaque found in Locus 3323.[76] This gold-foil image (see fig. 8a), originally some 19 × 11 cm, was discovered ripped into five pieces within the remains of the temple. The image is of a nude female standing on the back of a horse. Upon her head is an elaborate headdress consisting of a feather flanked by four horns, two to a side. All these rest atop a curving but unidentifiable base (horns?). The hair is bound by a headband and is awkwardly arranged; above the band two upward curved tresses indicate the typical Hathor-style coif. The female's head is facing sideways, contrary to the arrangement of the upper hair. Below the headband the hair falls to the female's right, landing below the shoulder, while two chest-length tresses fall on either side of the face. As stated above, the face looks sideways to the female's left; otherwise the body is portrayed *en face* except for the feet that also turn to the left. The female's arms extend to either side of the body and she holds in each hand very large lotus flowers. Both the breasts and the pubic triangle are incised. The horse upon which she stands is facing left and has a quilting pattern upon its body and neck. What appears to be a large feather emerges from between the horse's ears up to the level of the female's left hand. Additional Nude Goddess plaques, both of metal and terra-cotta, come from Bronze Age strata at the site.[77]

In most respects, this image from Lachish is strongly reminiscent of the Nude Goddess figurines from Ugarit and Alalakh. The primary differences are the paratactic positioning of the head and feet, the headdress, and the fact that the female stands upon a horse instead of a lion. Both of these differences might be attributed to Egyptian influence. As will be discussed below, this image is a depiction of the Levantine goddess Aštart and, thus, is evidence of her presence in Lachish.

Somewhat less elegant are graffiti incised onto the slabs upon the floor leading to the side entrance of the main hall (Locus 3161).[78] One of these depicts what appears to be a male deity, depicted from waist up, facing left, holding a spear in both hands. He has large eyes, a long beard, a cap with a streamer, and a belt with double baldric.[79] It is possible that this may represent either Baal or Rešef. A second graffito, very rough, shows the faces in profile of a male and a female. The conical cap on the male betrays Egyptian influence, but otherwise little might be made of the image.

---

76. Ussishkin 1978: 22, who really does call it "Lady Godiva."

77. Tufnell 1940 and 1958.

78. Ussishkin 1978: 18.

79. *Ibid.*

THEORIGIN OF APHRODITE

Egypt

The Cypriots (as well as the Greeks, Minoans, and all other members of the Eastern Mediterranean community) had contact with the Egyptians and, thus, were exposed to the full panoply of Egyptian deities. Unlike the Levant, where deity iconography is still a difficult matter of debate, Egypt offers a simpler interpretation of divine iconography through epigraphy, where images of gods and goddesses might be identified by name. As such, rather than review all the goddesses (and gods) who may have been known to the Cypriots, in the case of Egypt it is simpler to determine which goddess or goddesses were associated with a relevant iconography, so as to determine which goddess/es might have served as a forerunner of the Paphian.

Unlike the Levant, nudity is not a common iconographic motif in Egypt. There is only one goddess for whom such iconography is typical, and this the goddess Qudšu, who is herself Levantine in origin. She, as several other Levantine deities, entered the Egyptian pantheon during the Eighteenth Dynasty, during/after a period of extensive Levantine influence in Egypt under the Hyksos. This goddess, whose name means "Holiness," was portrayed nude, *en face*, standing atop a lion, and often in association with the gods Min and Rešef. Concerning the epigraphy that accompanied her, she was commonly identified as or associated with Aštart and Anat, and, like Hathor, she possessed the title "Queen of Heaven."[80]

Unfortunately, it is next to impossible to comment on the cults and pantheons of the other sites relevant to the study of Cypriot-Levantine relations due to a paucity of evidence. Beth Shemesh is clearly associated with the sun-god, but little more can be gleaned from the site's texts or archaeological remains. Tel el-'Ajjul has brought forth gold-foil, nude-female images in abundance, but they come from hoard contexts that offer no information concerning their use or meaning at the sites. At Gezer, the one image that might fit into the "goddess" typology came from a household context with no further supporting evidence concerning the city's cult. Not even the Amarna letters offer insight, as there is quite a lack of references to deities of the Canaanite pantheons in the Amarna correspondence from that region.[81] Perhaps in deference to the divinity of the Egyptian pharaoh, the subject Canaanites made little reference to their "other" gods. One minor exception is reference to *Bēltu ša Gubla* (Baalat Gubal) of Byblos,[82] although it is possible that this goddess was a local form of the Egyptian Hathor. In general, so far south, one must imagine that

---

80. Stadelmann 1967: 114–17.

81. Hess 1986: 162.

82. *Ibid.*, 151, 162–63.

the pantheons were a mix of Canaanite and Egyptian deities, much as at Beth Shan.

Leaving aside southern Canaan, the evidence from Ugarit, Alalakh, Megiddo, Beth Shan, Lachish, and Egypt shows that Cypriot/Levantine trade in the LC I and LC II periods would have exposed the Cypriots to the deities El, Ašerah, Anat, Aštart, Baal, Mekal, Išḫara, Šapaš, Rešef, Antit, Qudšu, and Ištar. The Cypriot iconography suggests that at least two of these deities became integrated into the Cypriot pantheon by the dawn of LC II, as is manifest in the dual sanctuaries, the adoption of male cult idols such as the Ingot God from Enkomi, the female figurines such as the bird-faced figurines of LC II, and the female cult idols of LC III such as the Bomford figurine.

The Literary Personae of the Near Eastern Goddess

Important to this study is the identification of the goddess or goddesses who contributed so much to the Cypriot iconography and, presumably, religion during the Late Bronze Age. Of the possible candidates, Anat, Antit, Ašerah, Aštart, Išḫara, Ištar, Qudšu, and Šapaš, the goddesses Ašerah, Aštart, Išḫara, Ištar, and Qudšu are the most likely to be the Near Eastern progenitresses of Greek Aphrodite. Šapaš is improbable as she is most definitively a sun-goddess. Antit is also unlikely as her cult appears to be localized exclusively in Beth Shan with no evidence of Nude-Goddess iconongraphy. Although Anat has in the past been considered to be a sexually active goddess, favoring her brother Baal as her partner, recent work by N. Walls has argued that, in fact, Anat was and remained a virgin battle goddess in the Ugaritic corpus.[83] Displaying no aspects of a sexual character, and having no associations with the other attributes indicative of Aphrodite (gold, sea, birds), Anat does not present herself as a possible element in the evolution of Aphrodite.

What follows is an examination of the literary evidence for the characters of the other goddesses, so as to determine whether or not they have parallels with the Greek goddess of sex. After this, we may consider which of these deities may have been represented by the bird-faced figurines and so-called "Aštart" plaques.

Inanna/Ištar

In Mesopotamia, Inanna and Ištar are essentially the same goddess, these being simply the Sumerian and Semitic forms of her name respectively. Both make descents to the underworld; both are married to Dumuzi or Tammuz (once again, Sumerian and Semitic forms of the same name); and they share common ideograms in the orthography of their names. As one of the most

---

83. Walls 1994: *passim*. Although Anat is entitled "Mistress of High Heaven," showing celestial affiliations, the differences far outweigh this one possible similarity.

prominent members of the Mesopotamian pantheon, extensive work on the persona of Inanna/Ištar has already been done, and thus I shall not attempt to present a full analysis of the goddess here. Three qualities of the goddess do stand out for recognition in this study. One is that Inanna/Ištar is a goddess of sex and love. This is made manifest in a section of an Old Babylonian hymn to Ištar, written during the reign of Ammiditanna:[84]

> She of joy, in loveliness she is clothed
> She is adorned in sexuality, beauty and charm.
> Ištar of joy, in loveliness she is clothed
> She is adorned in sexuality, beauty and charm.
> [Her] lips are sweet, life is in her mouth
> On her features blooms delight.
> She is glorious, loveliness covers her head
> Beautiful are her colors, her eyes are many-colored and iridescent.

Another important element of Ištar's persona is her martial character, well expressed in the following hymn of self-praise:[85]

> I rain battle down like flames in the fighting,
> I make heaven and earth shake (?) with my cries,
> I..., I make my feet ...
> I, Ištar, am queen of heaven and (?) earth.
> I am the queen, ...
> I constantly traverse heaven, then (?) I trample the earth,
> I destroy what remains of the inhabited world,
> I devastate (?) the lands hostile to Shamash.
> I am the most heroic of the gods,
> she who slays the inhabited world,
> I draw back on its bridle (?), he who slays ...
> The [Mo]on-god begot me, I abound in terror!

Finally, there is Inanna/Ištar's association with the sky. This is most notable in her role as the Venus deity, the personification of the morning/evening-star. As one of her many Sumerian hymns praises her:[86]

> The one come forth on high,
>   the one come forth on high,
>   I will hail!
> The [h]oly one, come forth on high,
>   I will hail!
> The great [queen] of heaven,
>   Inanna,

---

84. My translation of AO 4479 ll. 5-12 (Thureau-Dangin 1925: 170-71): see Appendix B 8.1.

85. Foster 1993: 74.

86. Jacobsen 1987: 113 (quoted with the permission of Yale University Press)

> I will hail!
> The pure torch lit in the sky,
> the heavenly light, lighting like day,
> the great queen of heaven Inanna,
>   I will hail!
> The holy one,
>   queen awe-laden
>   of the Anunnaki,
> noblest one in heaven and earth,
>   crowned with great horns,
> oldest child of the Moon,
>   Inanna,
>   I will hail!
> Of her grander, of her greatness,
>   of her exceeding nobility,
> of her brilliant coming forth
>   in the evening sky,
> of her lighting up in the sky,
>   a pure torch,
> of her stepping up onto the sky
>   like Moon and Sun,
> noted by all lands from south to north,
> of the greatness of the holy one of heaven,
> to the young lady I will sing!

Inanna/Ištar is simultaneously a goddess of love, sex, war, and the celestial sphere. The two former characteristics certainly make her an excellent parallel to Aphrodite, as do her associations with the sky, complementing Aphrodite's identification as *Ourania*. It is only in Inanna/Ištar's military aspects that one might pause in contemplating the parallels. However, if Ištar does show to be one of the earliest elements of Aphrodite, then perhaps we have here an understanding of Aphrodite's associations with both arms and Ares in many of the earliest aspects of her cult in Greece. (I refer especially here to the *xoana* in Kythera, Sparta and Corinth portraying the goddess as bearing arms.)

Išḫara

The extent to which Ištar and Išḫara are the same goddess is a matter of dispute. In one Old Akkadian love incantation, the speaker invokes the beloved, grasping her by both "mouth and vagina" and summoning her by the names of Ištar and Išḫara.[87] As such, these goddesses might be viewed as separate entities, each of whom is concerned with matters of love and sex. This idea of separate identities is reenforced by the fact that the two goddesses have dif-

---

87. Leick 1994: 195.

ferent symbols on the Kassite-age *kudurrus*: a star for Ištar and a hydra or scorpion for Išḫara.[88] However, in the *Epic of Gilgameš*, Gilgameš and Enkidu first meet and wrestle in a wedding context, where: "a bed is set up for Išḫara; Gilgameš lies by the maiden in the night," possibly taking part in some manner of *droit du seigneur*.[89] Likewise, in the myth *Atrahasis*, the poet claims that in the context of a wedding: "they shall call Ištar 'Išḫara'."[90] Thus, Išḫara is identified specifically as a bride. She is not a separate entity from Ištar, but an aspect of her: the portrayal of Ištar as the young bride. This would account for the possibility that in Alalakh the ideogram for IŠTAR, in fact, refers to the goddess Išḫara. There is a potential for the goddesses to be viewed as one and the same.

D. Prechel gives an excellent general interpretation of this goddess in her summary section on the epithets of Išḫara. According to her titles, Išḫara served many functions in the Mesopotamian spiritual domain. Like Ištar she bears the title *bēlet rāmi*, "Mistress of Love" and is, thus, a love goddess. With the titles *iltum rēmēnītum*, "Merciful Goddess" and *ummu rēmēnītum ša nišē*, "Merciful Mother of Peoples" she partakes of a protective character.[91] With her title *šarrat nīš ili* "Queen of Oaths" she is an oath goddess, just as her epithet *ša muna(b)biāti* "She of Prophecy" associates her with divination.[92]

Išḫara is a goddess of love and sex, a goddess who protects oaths and treaties (as seen above in the section on Alalakh), and is concerned with matters of prophecy. The first of these attributes likens her to the Greek Aphrodite, while her associations with proper rule and governance, as manifest in the role in oaths, might relate her more closely to both Phoenician Aštart and perhaps the Kyprian, both of whom were concerned with the royal households of their respective domains (according to later literature).

Ašerah

The cult of the goddess Ašerah[93] (Ugaritic *aṯrt*) extended throughout the Near East in the Bronze Age, from Southern Arabia to Mesopotamia to

---

88. Lambert 1980: 176–77; Wiggermann 1998, 51. In the third- and second-millennia glyptic, Išḫara is occasionally shown in amorous scenes with these creatures, thus, reaffirming her associations with sexuality. *Ibid.*

89. Prechel 1996: 58.

90. Tablet I, vi.

91. *Ibid.*, 185.

92. *Ibid.*, 186.

93. Much recent scholarship has been produced on this goddess, most notably by Perlman in 1978, Hadley in 1989, Wiggins in 1993, and Binger 1997. I shall not attempt to (re)cover all the material presented by these scholars, but enough to provide a basic

Ugarit.[94] It is mainly the textual documents from Ugarit, such as the *Keret Epic*, that provide any considerable information concerning the character of this goddess.

In the *Keret Epic* Ašerah is identified as El's consort, has maternal instincts, and is associated with the sea. Ašerah appears in the *Keret Epic* when the hero of the story, Keret, is making his way to Udm in the hopes of acquiring a wife who will bear him heirs. On the way:[95]

> they went a day, and a second,
> after sunset the third (day)
> he came to the sanctuary of Athirat of
> the two Tyres,
> even to (the sanctuary of) the
> goddess of the Sidonians,
> there noble Keret vowed a gift,
> 'O Athirat of the two Tyres,
> and goddess of the Sidonians,
> If to my house Huray I take,
> cause the maiden to enter my court,
> twice her weight of silver I will give,
> and thrice her (weight) of gold.

Later, it appears that Keret had forgotten his vow:[96]

> and Athirat remembered his vow,
> and the goddess [   ]
> and she lifted her voice and [called out]
> Look, I beg you, has Keret then [broken(?)]
> or has [(?)] changed [his] vow?
> I will break......

Beyond her anger with Keret over the forgotten gift, it does appear that Ašerah had a hand in the rearing of Keret's heir, Yassib:[97]

> he [Yassib] will suck the milk of Athirat,
> drain the breasts of the virgin [Anat]
> wetnurse(s) [   ]

Ašerah also has a significant role to play in the Baal Cycle, specifically when Baal must convince El to allow him to build his own house. When

---

understanding of this goddess. The reader is encouraged to look to these works for more in-depth information.

94. Wiggins 1993: *passim*. The many biblical references to Ašerah will not be considered here, as the relevant data derive from the Bronze Age.

95. Translation Wiggins 1993: 21–22.

96. *Ibid.*, 25.

97. *Ibid.*, 26.

Anat's attempts at tactful persuasion to intercede on her brother's behalf do not succeed, the young deities try a different approach, entreating El's consort Ašerah to approach El for them. The original complaint voiced by Baal is that he has no house of his own:[98]

> Groaning indeed he calls out to Bull El his father,
> El the king who begot him,
> he cries to Athirat and her children,
> to the goddess and the gathering of her company,
> "Now there is no house for Baal like the gods,
> (nor) a court like the children of Athirat,
> the dwelling of El
> is the residence of [his] so[n],
> the dwelling of Lady Athirat of the Sea
> the dwelling of [the perfect brides]...
> is the dwelling of [Pdr]y, daughter of mist,
> [the residence of] Tly [daughter of] rain,
> the dwelling of [Arsy daughter of ?]."

Baal and Anat go to find Ašerah, bringing with them a present made by Kothar-wa-Hasis. They find her at her chores:[99]

> to the stone [   ]
> She grasps her spindle [in her hand,]
> her spindle whorl in her right hand.
> Her garment of covering she let loose,
> she carried her clothes to the sea,
> her two garments into the river.
> She placed a cauldron on the fire,
> a pot on top of the coals.
> She fluttered her eyelids (at) Bull El the Compassionate
> she winked (at) the Creator of Creatures.[100]

Athirat reacts to their approach:[101]

> Athirat indeed perceived the approach of Baal,
> the approach of Virgin Anat
> the swift arrival of Ybmt [Limm],
> at this (her) feet [stamped,
> beh]ind her loins [broke
> on top] her [f]ace sweated,
> [the joints of] her [lo]ins convulsed,

98. *Ibid.*, 30.

99. *Ibid.*, 44–45.

100. M. Smith in Parker (ed.) 1997: 122 translates the last two lines differently: "All the while she is servile before Bull El the Beneficent, Deferential to the Creator of Creatures."

101. Translation Wiggins 1993: 48–51.

those of [her] back became weak,
she lifted up her voice and cried...
"Why is mighty B[aal] approaching?
Why is Virgin Anat approaching?
(are they) my smiters, or the [sm]iters of my children,
or (are they) the destroyers of my gathered kin?"
The [plating] of silver [Athirat] indeed saw,
the plating of silver and [   ] of gold,
Lady Athirat of the Sea rejoiced...
Moreover to her squire indeed [she called]
"See the cunning work, moreso[   ]
Fisherman of Lady Athir[at of the Sea].

Ašerah agrees to intercede with El on Baal's behalf. She summons her servant
Qodeš-wa-Amruru to saddle a donkey for her to ride to El's abode. Upon her
arrival:[102]

She uncovered the tent of El,
and she entered the room of the King, Father of years,
at the feet of El she bowed down and fell,
she prostrated himself and she honoured him.
Behold, El indeed saw her,
he parted the throat and laughed,
he placed his feet on the footstool,
he twirled his fingers,
he raised his voice and shou[ted]
"Why has Lady Athirat of the Sea arrived?
Why has the Bearer of G[ods] come?
Are you indeed hungry and journey [worn(?)]?
Or are you indeed thirsty and weary?
Eat, indeed, drink!
Ea[t] food from the tables!
Drink wine from the carafes!
From a cup of gold the blood of trees,
or does the hand of El the King tempt you?
The love of the Bull arouse you?"

In the end, her intercession succeeds and Baal is permitted to build himself
a home on Mt. Sapon.

In the Baal Cycle, when Baal is overwhelmed by Mot (Death), Ašerah plays
a meaningful role.[103]

"now Athirat and her sons will rejoice,
the Goddess and the company of her kin,
for dead is mighty Baal,

---

102. *Ibid.*, 57–58.

103. *Ibid.*, 63–64.

for perished is the Prince, Lord of the Earth."
El cried aloud,
"Hear O Lady Athirat of the Sea,
Lady Athira[t] of the Sea,
give one of your son and I will make him king."
And Lady Athirat of the Sea answered,
"Shall we not make him king who knows (and is) intelligent?"
And Benevolent El the Compassionate answered,
"One who is small of vigour cannot run,
(compared) with Baal he cannot release the spear
(compared with the son of Dagon he is weak."
And Lady Athirat of the Sea answered
"Shall we not make Athtar the Terrible king?
Let Athtar the Terrible be king!"

These quotes present the Ugaritic Ašerah at her fullest. The characteristics dominant in her persona are her relationship with the head of the Ugaritic pantheon, her maternal status, and her association with the sea.

A reference to Ašerah's possible erotic nature comes from a myth preserved only in the Hittite corpus. In the tale *Elkunirsa and Ašertu*, Ašerah, the wife of El, attempts to seduce Baal:[104]

> Elkunirsa looked at Baal and asked him: "[Why] have you come to?" Baal said: "When I came into your house, Ashertu sent young women to me, (saying:) 'Come sleep with me.' ...Ashertu is rejecting you, her own husband. [Although she is] your wife, yet she keeps sending to me: 'Sleep with me.'"

When he refuses her, she goes to El and accuses Baal of having propositioned her.[105] In the end, Baal is saved by his sister, named in the text by the IŠTAR ideogram and translated by Hoffner as Anat-Aštart.[106] The text makes clear that El and Ašerah are husband and wife. The blatant reference to the attempted seduction may also point to erotic overtones inherent in Ašerah's character that would liken the goddess to an Aphrodite prototype.

Ašerah is referred to as *qnyt.ilm*, the "bearer of the gods." She is mentioned in conjunction with her children in several instances: when she fears for their safety at the arrival of Baal and Anat; when Anat claims that Ašerah and her kin will rejoice at the death of Baal; and when El, needing a replacement for Baal, asks Ašerah to provide one of her children. This maternal role extends beyond just Ašerah's relationship with her own children and serves as well as a theme in the Keret story. Here, not only does Keret invoke Ašerah's aid in acquiring the wife who will provide him with an heir, but it is Ašerah who suckles the infant upon his birth.

---

104. Hoffner 1998: 91; Laroche 1965: 140, ll. 8–10, 17–19.

105. Hoffner 1998: 90.

106. *Ibid.*

Ašerah's most common epithet is *rbt.aṯrt.ym*, "Lady Ašerah of the Sea."[107] Some contend that the title could even be taken as "She who treads on the sea," with the name Aṯirat being a participial form of the verb "to tread."[108] One of Ašerah's attendants is *dgy* "Fisherman,"[109] and she plies her household tasks, such as spinning and washing, by the side of the sea where Baal and Anat find her. Thus, even if Ašerah originally was not closely associated with the sea, especially in her more land-locked places of reverence, it is apparent that her cult in Ugarit had strong maritime qualities and, thus, to some extent, one can consider her to be, among other qualities, a sea-goddess.

Ašerah had another servant, *qdš-(w)-amrr*, either to be rendered "Sacred (qdš)-and-Amruru" or simply "Sacred Amruru," depending on whether or not the conjunctive-*w* is used. This connection leads to an aspect of Ašerah's persona in the Mesopotamian corpus (far more limited in scope than the Ugaritic). According to a cylinder seal, the goddess Ašratu (Ašcrah) was paired with the god Rammanum, known to be the deity Amruru, a West Semitic storm-god.[110] This relationship is further expressed in the god list AN = Anum, in which culticly associated deities are presented in a hierarchy formulated as a family with its entourage: ^dAš-ra-tum is listed as a spouse of ^dAN.MAR.TU in AN = Anum.[111] It was only later, when Ašerah was transplanted to the coast and, according to Perlman's theories, made consort of El that her relationship with Amruru was changed from one of marriage to one of mistress and servant.[112]

Another source for the nature of Ašerah in Mesopotamia is a Sumerian-language votive inscription composed during the reign of King Hammurapi of Babylon:[113]

---

107. By contrast, Binger translates *ym* as "day" rather than "sea," thus making Ašerah a solar/celestial deity rather than a sea-goddess.

108. Perlman 1978: 73ff. Alone this would simply render "she who treads." Within the epithet (*rbt.atrt.ym*) it renders "Great lady who treads upon the sea," and some have even extended the appellation to "She who walks on the sea dragon," thus offering an explanation for associating Ašerah with snakes (see below, under Qudšu). Perlman argues against this interpretation, suggesting instead that the name Aṯirat is a nominal form referring to a "place (of worship?)" (Perlman 1978: 73–78, esp. 77–78). The goddess was probably originally revered by a population that did not dwell along the coast, and her strong connections in the Mesopotamian material with the steppes, may argue against interpreting the goddess' name as "She who treads upon the sea."

109. Wiggins 1993: 40–41.

110. *Ibid.*, 142, esp. n. 71.

111. Tablet VI 257–62 (see Litke 1998: 218–19). For the possible reading of the divine name AN.AN.MAR.TU, see Richter 1998.

112. Perlman 1978: 83. Cross 1973: 59, suggests that "Amruru" may be the name given to El in Mesopotamia; thus El and Amruru are one and the same and Ašerah's relationship with him is consistent.

113. Translation Frayne 1990: 359–60, also quoted in Wiggins 1993: 136.

For [the goddess Aš]ratum, daughter-in-law of the god An, the one suitable for ladyship, lady of voluptuousness and happiness, tenderly cared for in the mountain, lady with patient mercy, who prays reverently for her spouse, his lady, for the li[fe] of Hammu-r[api], king of the Amo[rites], Itur-ašd[um]. Chief of the [S]ilakku canal (district), son of Šuba-il[an], the servant who re-[verences her, set up] as a wonder a protective genius befitting her d[ivi]-nity, [in her] beloved residence.

According to this text, one might surmise several qualities about Ašerah. She is listed as the daughter-in-law of An, suggesting that she is indeed married, presumably to Amruru. She is the "Lady of the Mountain," which rather dis-associates her from the predominantly flat Mesopotamia. As her name is West Semitic,[114] it stands to reason that she comes from the west of Mesopotamia as opposed to the mountainous district of Elam. She is a beneficent goddess, shown in her titles "Lady of Voluptuousness and Happiness" (which may also denote certain erotic characteristics of the goddess) and "Lady with Patient Mercy." Finally, Itur-ašdum mentions that he set up his "wonder" in Ašerah's "beloved residence," giving evidence that Ašerah did, in fact, have a temple in Mesopotamia in the second millennium BCE.

What might one deduce from these data about the character of Ašerah in the Bronze Age? Her West Semitic name shows that she was originally a West Semitic deity—Amorite according to Perlman and Wiggins—whose cult spread east to Mesopotamia and west to Ugarit. In Mesopotamia she was the wife of the storm-god Amruru, while in Ugarit she was the wife of El and "Sacred Amruru" was her servant. In either case, she was married to a prominent celes-tial god. According to the Ugaritic material, she was the queen of the gods, as well as their mother, with the epithet "sons of Aṯirat" being a normal appel-lation of the deities. Upon the death of the champion-god, she was not only invoked to help decide who should be the next champion, emphasizing her role as queen deity, but specifically one of her sons was to be put onto the now vacant throne. Her maternal aspect extended even past the realm of the dei-ties, as seen in the *Epic of Keret*, where she is invoked by the king to provide him with a wife who would give him heirs, and Ašerah herself nursed the prince. She had some associations with the sea, as indicated in her appellation "Lady Ašerah of the Sea" (*rbt.aṯrt.ym*) and in her servant *dgy*, the Fisherman.

Several of these attributes may have been significant in the evolution of Aphrodite. Ašerah, as queen of the gods, may foreshadow the Paphian's title *wanassa*, "Queen." Ašerah's links with the sea might have given rise to Aph-rodite's interest both in the sea and, later, sailors and their safety. By contrast, Ašerah's important role as the chief mother-goddess of Ugarit may speak against her as a possible cognate for Aphrodite, who has only minimal asso-ciations with maternity.

---

114. Perlman 1978: 74-78.

Aštart

Aštart assumes several roles in Ugaritic literature.[115] In the Baal Cycle, Aštart stands besides Baal when he faces potential rivals for his throne, notably the sea-god Yamm.

In the *Epic of Keret*, Aštart is mentioned in conjunction with Anat, being presented as a standard of loveliness to which Keret's prospective fiancée is compared:[116]

> What is not in my house you must give to me:
> You must give me Lady Huraya,
> The Fair One, your firstborn child!
>
> Who's as fair as the goddess Anath,
> Who's as comely as Astarte.

Perlman suggests that, in fact, it is not relevant whose names were placed in this context, arguing instead that comparison to any pair of goddesses was actually an Ugaritic cliché for beauty.[117] Nevertheless, the names of Anat and Aštart were used, nor does it seem unfitting that they might serve as standards of beauty, being, as they were, young goddesses. As such, I argue that this expression in the *Epic of Keret* may, in fact, indicate that Aštart was seen as a lovely goddess.

The next portion of the text shows a slight ambiguity between the goddesses Aštart and Ašerah:[118]

> She will bear you the Lad, Yassib,
> Who'll draw on the milk of Astarte,
> And suck at the breasts of the Maid [Anath]
> The wet-nurses [of the gods].

Later, when Keret's life is crumbling about him, he curses his son, this time portraying Aštart as a violent deity:[119]

> May Horon crack, my son,
> May Horon crack your head,
> Aštart-named-with-Baʿal, your skull!
> May you fall at the peak of your years,
> Be subdued while you still make a fist!

---

115. For a complete listing of all references to Aštart in the Ugaritic corpus, see Perlman 1978: 129ff. For biblical references to the goddess, see Chapter Nine.

116. KTU 1.14, Tablet I, iii, 38–42. Translation by E.L. Greenstein in Parker (ed.) 1997: 17.

117. Perlman 1978: 141.

118. Tablet II, ii, 25–28. Translation by Greenstein in Parker ed. 1997: 25. This is probably a acribal error.

119. Tablet III, vi, 54–58. *Ibid.*: 42.

The myth *Aštart the Huntress* is the longest piece of surviving Ugaritic literature concerning the goddess Aštart.[120]

> Ashtarte, the Huntress [scoured the fields]
> she went off into the desert [of Kuthan].
> [The stars(?)] were renewing themselves
> and Hcl[al(?)   ].
> The flood ab[ove] inundated [the desert],
> the produce of its marshes [Ashtarte] desired,
> her nostrils she [set to] the largest one.
> [Thereupon] Ashtarte cowered in the marsh.
> [At her right side] she put "Mosquito,"
> at [her] left side [she put] "Locust."
> She lifted up her eyes [and saw:]
> a doe was espying a bull,
> the eye [of the bull ...] the cow.
> She took her spear [in her hand]
> her club in her right hand.
> She thr[ew it at] the bull(?),
> knocked off the gobbling animal.
> [She re]turned to [her] house.
> (For the Bull, her father El, she set the table
> [and ga]ve him to eat.
> Yarikh, the attendant she gave to eat,
> [she gave to eat] Kothar, the smith,
> and Khasis [   ].
> [   ] ... Ashtar[te   ]
> [   ] Bull, [her father El]

There is a break in the tablet, with a few lines missing. When we return to the tale, Aštart has apparently cleaned up a bit:

> [An he saw Ashta]rte with the watchman of the vineyard,
> [the most graceful of the daughters] of her father in the vineyard of Ari.
> [She had covered] her [body?] with a chemise of linen,
> [over] it she [had placed] a coat of cypress-wooden mail.
> [And] her [beau]ty wore a sheen like the male stars,
> [a sp]lendor(?) like the female stars of Kuthan.
> [The] virgin(?)–Baal coveted her,
> he wanted to possess her beauty, Demaron.
> Before her face descended Almighty Baal.
> In order to please the awe-struck (girl),
> he wanted to lo[ve her?] limbs(?).
> He brandished his horns against thc watchman.

---

120. KTU 1.92. Originally published by Herrmann in 1969, in 1994 Dijkstra found an additional portion of the broken tablet. Our citations from this text are from Prof. Dijkstra's most recent edition, which he has most kindly shared with us. See Appendix B 8.2.

[but] Pidru [answ]ered him: 'Be careful, [O Baal]!
Should you not give [the ... of your bo]dy on the co[uch!]
[the ... not] give for a prepared bed(?)!
[Now if the desire] of Baal craves for [a living being],
[or the lust of the Ri]der on the Clouds,
[here are ... of wi]ne and portions(?) of fish.
[Let a table be set(?)] for Almighty Baal,
let the Rider on the Clouds be [pleased].

Two specific elements of this tale merit our attention. First, Aštart is clearly portrayed as a huntress: "Aštart, the Huntress [scoured the fields]... She took her spear [in her hand], her club in her right hand. She thr[ew it at] the bull(?)." The second element is that, in agreement with her role in the Keret epic in which she is compared to Huriya in terms of beauty, Aštart is portrayed as a most desirable young goddess, so much so that Baal can hardly keep his hands off her:

[And] her [beau]ty wore a sheen like the male stars,
[a sp]lendor(?) like the female stars of Kuthan.
[The] virgin(?)–Baal coveted her,
he wanted to possess her beauty, Demaron.

The text concludes with what appears to be a marriage feast for Baal and Aštart, unusual in the Ugaritic corpus. There are no other indications that Baal and Aštart were consorts, but the corpus does emphasize the associations between these two deities, present also in Aštart's title "Word-" or "Mouth-of Baal."[121]

Two Ugaritic texts, magical and votive in nature, provide further information on Aštart.[122]

(1) KTU 1.100:

The mother of stallion and mare,
Daughter of Spring, daughter of stone,
Daughter of Heavens and Deep,
Is calling to Shapsh, her mother: (ll. 1–4)

IV: Shapsh, my mother, carry my cry
to Anat (and Athtart) on Inbubu.[123] (ll. 19–20)

VII: Shapsh, my mother, carry my cry
to 'Athtart in Mari. ... (ll. 78ff.)

---

121. Herrmann 1969: 22, no. 43.

122. Translation of KTU 1.100 and UT 5 according to S.B. Parker, in Parker (ed.) 1997: 219–23.

123. The line here reads 'm!/'nt w'[.]ttrt inbbh. Parker gives only the name of Anat instead of both Anat and Astart, the latter of whom I inserted into this translation.

(2) UT 5:[124]

When 'Athtart of Hurri
enters the cistern of the king's house
serve a banquet in the house of the star-gods.

KTU 1.43 refers to Aštart by the epithet *hr*. These texts also provide insights into the range of the goddess' worship: "Carry my cry to 'Attart in Mari" (KTU 1.100) and "when 'Attart of Hurri enters the cistern of the king's house" (KTU 1.43). In summary, Ugaritic literature generally depicts Aštart as martial, a huntress and provider for her family (KTU 1.92). Likewise, in both the *Epic of Keret* and *Aštart the Huntress*, she is portrayed as lovely and desirable.

There are two Egyptian sources pertaining to Aštart's more desirable aspects. The first occurs in the Egyptian text *Aštart and the Tribute of the Sea*,[125] wherein the goddess Aštart, being sent to the Sea to explain that the gods could not send adequate tribute, was demanded herself by the Sea. The text is extremely fragmentary, and the full content of the story is lost.

Another fragment of Egyptian literature that helps to reveal a vaguely sexual nature of Aštart (and in this case of Anat as well) is an invocation against crocodiles from the Harris papyrus. Here, both goddesses are referred to as "the two goddesses who are pregnant but do not bear."[126] There are two potential interpretations for this expression. One is a reference to the sexual relations between these goddesses and Seth, who, being a god of desert and destruction, cannot engender live offspring.[127] Or, one might interpret this as a reference to nubility and a healthy sexuality (a potential for pregnancy) on the part of the goddesses that is never actually used in reproduction.

Two final aspects of Aštart's character in the Egyptian corpus must be mentioned, and these are her associations with horses and with the heavens. The earliest literary evidence for this first association comes from a poem written upon the chariot of a Nineteenth Dynasty pharaoh, where Aštart and Anat are named as the two "hands" of the pharaoh's chariot.[128] Further evidence derives from the artistic representations of Aštart (see below). The latter association is manifest in one of Aštart's Egyptian titles, "Aštart, queen of the heavens and mistress of all the gods."[129]

---

124. Perlman 1978: 134.

125. J.A. Wilson in *ANET*: 17–18.

126. Pritchard 1943: 79. From Magical Papyrus Harris, dated to the Nineteenth or Twentieth Dynasty.

127. Wyatt 1984: 206.

128. Wiggins 1991: 387, esp. note 44. See also Perlman 1978: 192.

129. Perlman 1978: 192.

Qudšu

Qudšu is not a literary character, but a goddess whose name appears in conjunction with a specific style of nude female in the artistic corpus, portrayed nude, *en face*, frequently standing atop a lion, holding lotus blossoms or snakes in her hands. The name Qudšu is Semitic; its radicals have the meaning of "holy" or "sacred" and the name itself means "Holiness." This divine name appeared in the Egyptian repertoire during the Eighteenth Dynasty, when the names of other Semitic deities, such as Rešef, Anat, and Aštart, first appeared in the Egyptian corpus.[130] The concern here is not to define the persona of this goddess, as this is not possible, but to discern which Levantine or Egyptian deity she may represent, or whether she was a goddess in her own right. In recent years she has most frequently been identified with Ugaritic Ašerah or the Egyptian goddess Hathor. Qudšu's associations with the goddess Ašerah began with René Dussaud in 1941 There are several reasons why this identification has been accepted. The first is the presence of the epithet *qdš* in the Ugaritic corpus, usually associated to some degree with Ašerah. A second is the writing of the names "Qudšu-Anat-Aštart" on two of the stelae depicting this goddess. A third argument is the association of both Qudšu and Ašerah with Hathor.

In the Ugaritic corpus, the name/epithet *qdš* often (although not exclusively) appears as a maternal figure.[131] As Ašerah is the primary mother-goddess of the Ugaritic pantheon, it would appear logical that a reference to an otherwise unknown mother-goddess would refer to her. According to Binger, the titles "Ašerah and her sons" or "the sons of Ašerah" occur thirteen times in the Ugaritic corpus; "the sons of *qdš*" occurs seven times. These appellations exist always in parallel with the word *ilm*, "the gods." However, in spite of the Ugaritic fondness for parallelism, the terms *bn aṯrt* and *bn qdš* are never used in parallel to each other, and there is little to no evidence to suggest that the words *aṯrt* and *qdš* are synonymous. One might argue that *qdš* could have served as an epithet of Ašerah, but that it also functioned as an independent noun or adjective.[132] That the title *qdš* could clearly refer to other deities than Ašerah, most notably her servant Qodeš-wa-Amruru, shows that the epithet need not refer exclusively to Ašerah, so the argument for the identification of Ašerah with Qudšu is not entirely persuasive.

The second argument, that Ašerah might be inferred from the inscriptions of Qudšu-Anat-Aštart on the two stelae, is based on the assumption that the Egyptians were referring to the three dominant goddesses of the Levantine

---

130. Leclant 1960: 3.

131. This refers to those instances when the name is solitary, as opposed to the combined name of Qodeš-wa-Amruru.

132. Binger 1997: 59.

pantheon—Ašerah, Anat, and Aštart.[133] However, as Wiggins suggests, there is as yet no explicit evidence that Aštart was a significant member of the Bronze Age Levantine pantheon, certainly not more significant than Šapaš.[134] Furthermore, there is no evidence that three separate goddesses were necessarily intended. According to Winter, it is entirely possible that the word *qdš* as it appears on the two stelae is intended to refer to the goddesses Anat and Aštart.[135] As such, Qudšu could be the combination of these two goddesses, jointly known as "the Sacred."[136] Or, as Wiggins suggests, it is also possible, if not probable, that the name Qudšu refers to a specific and separate Egyptian goddess, who may or may not be identified with the two Levantine goddesses.[137]

A further hypothesis, offered by Maier, is that there is a continuity among the goddesses Hathor, Qudšu, and Ašerah, and that all these goddesses may be cognates of one another, if not the same goddess with different names. The relationship between Hathor and Qudšu derives from the latter's adoption of the former's iconographic motifs. Specifically, Maier argues that Qudšu was adorned with the hair, face, ears, crown, and even snakes of Hathor's iconographic repertoire.[138] Thus, Qudšu = Hathor. The relationship between Hathor and Ašerah derives from the maternal character of both goddesses and, more importantly, their common identification as the *b 'lt gbl*, the "Lady of Byblos."[139] Logically, then, as Hathor and Ašerah are the same, and Hathor and Qudšu are the same, then Qudšu = Ašerah.

This final hypothesis is fraught with methodological difficulties, the most profound of which is the attempt to set limiting, defining characteristics on the Egyptian goddess. Hathor, and the Egyptian deities in general, were far more capable of absorbing new qualities and developing new personae than were, say, the Greek deities, or even necessarily the Levantine. To quote Maier: "Egyptian religion is characterized by, to borrow Gardiner's phrase, a 'chaotic polytheism.' A tendency to create new forms of a god/goddess by instituting his/her worship in new local centers persisted throughout the whole

---

133. Wiggins 1991: 387.

134. *Ibid.*

135. Winter 1983: 112, a hypothesis made difficult by the fact that the word is masculine and singular, while supposedly referring to two female deities. Wiggermann 1998: 52 consistently refers to this goddess as *Qadeš(t)* and *qdš(t)*, apparently for this very reason.

136. Stadelmann 1967: 114-15.

137. Wiggins 1991: 387-88.

138. Maier 1986: 84.

139. Maier 1986: 88ff.

course of Egyptian history."[140] The process of equating two deities, at least one of them Egyptian, based on common attributes is pointless. That Hathor and Ašerah have common attributes may have more to do with the ability of Hathor (or, more correctly, the Egyptian populace) to adopt those attributes of the Levantine goddess which might be "useful" or appealing. I do not, therefore, find it methodologically sound to equate Ašerah with Hathor, or with any other Egyptian goddess for that matter. This precludes an identification of Qudšu with Ašerah through Hathor, and, thus, once again, renders nil the hypothesis that Qudšu must be seen as Ašerah.

The argument that Hathor = Qudšu is even less secure than that identifying the Egyptian goddess as Ašerah. While little can be known about Qudšu from written testimony, her iconography is consistent and distinctive: nude and *en face*. This is in complete contrast to Egyptian and Levantine portrayals of Hathor, which consistently depict her as clothed, paratactic, with cow horns (and often a lunar disk). Furthermore, the association of both goddesses with snakes (which Qudšu frequently carries) is of limited use, as many Egyptian goddesses were, to one extent or another, associated with snakes. Finally, there is the fact that, as mentioned above, Qudšu appeared in the Egyptian corpus only beginning in the Nineteenth Dynasty, in company with several other Levantine deities, and showing a strongly Levantine iconography. The simplest solution is to conclude that the goddess is more Levantine in character than Egyptian, and that her origins at least are to the north. This argues strongly against the hypothesis that she is, in fact, an alternate manifestation of a well-entrenched, long-standing Egyptian goddess. In the end, it appears that Qudšu is simply Qudšu.

On the basis of the literary evidence, there are several goddesses who may have contributed to the persona of Aphrodite. The most probable candidates are the goddesses Ištar and Išhara, who are the most blatantly sexual of all the goddesses. While they both share to a certain degree a military aspect that is only rarely apparent in Greek Aphrodite, it is still possible that remnants of this earlier aspect may be behind the early artistic portrayals of Aphrodite armed. Both Ištar and Išhara also are considered to be beautiful and desirable, and in this aspect of Aphrodite's character they are joined by Ugaritic Aštart as per her roles in the *Epic of Keret* and, more explicitly, in Dijkstra's version of *Aštart the Huntress*. Ašerah as well may play a significant role in the evolution of Aphrodite, for it is from her that the Kyprian may have acquired her association with the sea and, from the Cypriot perspective, her possible relationship to the god of Cyprus.

---

140. Maier 1986: 217.

Levantine Goddess Iconography

The most critical piece of evidence concerning the adoption of Levantine traits into the Cypriot pantheon are the bird-faced figurines that flooded the island at the dawn of the Late Bronze Age. Therefore, for this study we need to identify the meaning of the bird-faced figurines as they existed in the Bronze Age Levant.

Origins of the Nude Goddess

The earliest images of the Nude Goddess are Syrian hand-made figurines.[141] Excavations in Syria, especially those at Ebla and Hama, have shown that the distinctive, nude-female images date well back into the mid-third millennium BCE along the Orontes River, whereas their earliest appearance in Mesopotamia dates only to the very end of the third millennium.[142] Furthermore, the appearance of these images in Mesopotamia is quite brief, with extremely few examples coming from the second millennium. By contrast, not only does the use of these figurines increase during the second millennium in Syria, the iconography seeps into the alternate forms of artistic representations as well. As the Nude Goddess first appears in Syria, and as it is in Syria where her portrayal continues through the Bronze Age and into the Iron Age, logic argues that this use of nudity in iconography is a distinctively Syrian trait.

It is unlikely that just one specific goddess is portrayed in the Nude Goddess motif. I base this observation on the variations in the iconography, not to mention the broad expanses of territory and time in which this motif presented itself.[143]

---

141. Frankfort, Van Buren, and Barrelet believed that these figurines were originally Mesopotamian in origin, possibly deriving from the north of the Diyala region (Barrelet 1968: 77).

142. *Ibid.*, 73. Badre 1980: *passim*. Ingholt 1940: "Niveau J."

143. This conclusion disagrees with that put forth in Winter 1983: 192–99. This recognition of the nude-female motif as Syrian is one of eight conclusions concerning these images determined by Urs Winter. His basic conclusions, based on a complete study of all three types of the motif, are as follows:

    1. The naked woman is a Nude Goddess. This is based not only on her association in the glyptic with other, recognized deities, but also by her wearing of horns in many images.
    2. The Nude Goddess comes from Syria.
    3. The Nude Goddess cannot be associated with any goddesses named in the literature.
    4. The Nude Goddess is not a primary deity in the pantheons of either Syria-Palestine or Mesopotamia.

Syrian Figurines (Ištar and Išḫara)

The earliest known examples, which come from Ebla and date to the EB IVA period (2400–2300 BCE; see fig. 8b), are very schematic in style. Typically, they have pointed heads and hair-styles of applied strips of incised clay. The eyes are pellets of clay pressed flat and pierced in the center, and the noses are molded and prominent. The necks are proportionately long and are decorated with necklaces, either incised, of strips of clay, or both. The chest is

Fig. 8b
Early Bronze Age figurine from Ebla.
TM.83.G.118.

5. The Nude Goddess is the consort of the weather-gods Adad and Amruru in Mesopotamian glyptic.
6. The Nude Goddess is a helpful and intermediary goddess.
7. The Nude Goddess is not just nude, she has sex-appeal.
8. The different manifestations of the Nude Goddess reflect a higher, religious manifestation of "Woman."

My arguments contrary to Winter's analysis are twofold. On the one hand, I do not believe that only one specific goddess is intended by the Nude Goddess motif, basing my contention on the variations in the iconography, not to mention the broad expanses of territory and time in which this motif presented itself. On the other hand, contrary to Winter's hypothesis #3, I argue that not only can a name be offered for this Nude Goddess, but that several may be proposed, once again based on variations in iconography and territory.

Fig. 8c
Middle Bronze Age figurine from Ebla.
TM.92.P.875+TM.94.P.530.

Fig. 8d
Late Bronze Age figurine from Ebla.
TM.88.R.624.

decorated by an incised crisscross, and only occasionally does an example have incised dots that might be recognized as breasts. One remaining base shows a pillar structure flared at the base and, thus, is self-standing. No arms are rendered, but the bodies have an almost *phi* shape, and it is possible that the artist(s) intended that the arms be understood as curving inward with hands under the breasts (as in so many other examples).

Beginning in the Middle Bronze I period (c. 2000 BCE) these images began to take on more detail and a greater degree of sexualization. Four partial Ebla examples show somewhat crude female images, preserved from the waist up.[144] Each has an elaborate headdress, one almost *polos*-like in its high, flat rendering, while the second well-preserved piece shows a strip of clay entirely surrounding the face (minus directly under the chin), incised with small stripes radiating outward from the face. The necks are closer to normal proportions; three have necklaces of incised dots at the base of the neck, while one has a band of clay at the base of the neck, also incised. All four have arms in the *tau* or out-stretched position, and all four have molded breasts on the chest. Two show the incised crisscross between the breasts. One other image from c. 2000–1900 BCE is fully preserved. Much like the other four, it has an elaborate hair-style, incised dot eyes, and a prominent molded nose. While the breasts are not present on this example, the navel is preserved and shows, much like the eyes, a pressed pellet of clay with a single incised dot at the center. At the level of the genitalia are two rows of incised marks, the forerunner of the incised pubic triangle, and the legs are separated by a deep groove.

These images become more prominent later in the Middle Bronze Age (from 1850 BCE), when they begin to show iconography even more reminiscent of the bird-faced figurines (see fig. 8c). Their heads are once again decorated with elaborate coifs, pierced both above the head and to the sides, thus giving the impression of pierced ears as on the Cypriot versions. Eyes and nose are rendered as on their predecessors and, as usual, they wear elaborate necklaces. All have deeply incised navels, prominently incised pubic triangles, and a groove separating the legs. Some of the figurines are *tau*-shaped and show the typical, incised crisscross on the chest. Some have breasts but no crisscrossing, and others have the hands grasping the breasts. Another figurine dating from 1850–1700 BCE shows the basic pattern of arms curving out and holding the breasts, as do two further examples dating to the MB II period (1750–1650 BCE). LBA mold-made versions (see fig. 8d) continue this motif.

Much as at Alalakh, where these images also appear in large quantities over extensive periods of time, the primary female deities at Ebla during the use of the Nude-Goddess figurines were Išḫara and Ištar.[145] Both of these goddesses

---

144. In P. Matthiae's 1995 *Ebla* catalogue (numbers 131–36).

145. That these images only marginally appear in Mari, where Ištar was also a prominent goddess, once again attests to the strong Syrian nature of these images.

are attested in the texts during the period of figurine use in Ebla and Alalakh. However, as the crisscross seems to have martial implications and as the figurines become more prominent in Ebla when Ištar "replaces" Išḫara, it would appear that in Ebla they are more likely to be Ištar. In Alalakh, to the contrary, the evidence of text and spade favor an identification as Išḫara.

Mesopotamian Glyptic (Ašerah and Ištar)

Moving forward in time, and considering the glyptic variations of the Nude Goddess motif, other names and identifications come into play. For example, based on the hypotheses that this Nude Goddess appears in the glyptic as a partner to the deities Adad and Amruru, and that one of her dominant roles appears to be intercession (see note 143), it would appear that this goddess might be the iconographic manifestation in the glyptic art of Ašerah, who in the Mesopotamian literature is the consort of Amruru, is addressed as a merciful goddess, and in the Ugaritic literature is the intercessor between Baal and El. One Sumerian votive possibly refers to her as "voluptuous" (ḫi.li), and according to Wiggins' translation of the Baal Cycle, she even flirts with El. As such, the elements of intercession, consort of Amruru, and sexuality are present. That she is a high-ranking goddess in the Ugaritic pantheon need not contradict the hypotheses of Winter (see note 143), for in the Mesopotamian repertoire she most certainly is not a prominent deity. Thus, one possible identification, especially in Mesopotamia, is Ašerah.[146] However, Barrelet has conducted extensive research on the glyptic motif of armed and winged goddesses in the Mesopotamian repertoire, showing convincingly that both wings and weapons either in the hands or protruding from the shoulders are indicative of the goddess Ištar.[147] These motifs, wings and arms, also appear in the Syrian repertoire, but applied to the Nude Goddess, and Barrelet argues that, based on continuity, these figures continue to represent Ištar, in her Syrian manifestation.[148] The fact that this Nude Goddess often stands atop a

---

146. *Contra* Wiggermann 1998: 51, who sees this deity as the goddess Šala. I believe that both identifications are possible.

147. Barrelet 1955: 222–37. This is based not only on Ištar's persona as a war-like goddess, but, as well, on iconographic parallels to monumental art, where the goddess is named in inscription and is shown with similar attributes as those in the glyptic. It is of interest to note that in certain Mesopotamian seals the armed, winged goddess is shown in the same scene as the Nude Goddess. See Winter's catalogue, nos. 99 and 111. This offers evidence that in Mesopotamia Ištar was seen as distinct from the Nude Goddess.

148. *Ibid.*, 237ff. If one were to follow the theories of Barrelet, then the lion-dominator motif entered the Syrian/Levantine artistic repertoire with the armed- and winged-goddess motif, and, according to her, it originally designated the goddess Ištar. However, the goddess Ištar is not mentioned in the Ugaritic god-lists as a deity of Ugarit,

Fig. 8e
Akkadian period seal impression of Ištar.
Oriental Institute A27903.

lion, as does Ištar in Mesopotamia (see fig. 8e), and that she is often shown next to a star, Ištar's symbol, strengthen this argument. As such, there is a possibility that the nude females portrayed in the Syrian glyptic refer to Ištar.

There is no simple means of categorizing these variations in the motif, to argue that all images with wings or weapons are Ištar and those without are Ašerah, for the variations themselves occur along a continuum. It is perhaps best to see these variations as the multifarious expressions of the symbol sets of the various artists of the ancient Near East, who combined symbols and aspects to arrive at meaningful images that are no longer so clear.

Levantine Plaques and the Egyptian Evidence (Aštart)

It is difficult to interpret the images on the mold-make plaques, since none of the goddesses preserved in the Ugaritic corpus is notable for her erotic qualities—except, possibly, Ašerah—contrary to the goddesses Ištar and Išhara farther inland. As such, the erotic elements of the images must take second place to the other iconographic elements that offer some clue as to the identity and meaning of the Nude Goddess images. In the Levant these nude-female figurines represent the goddess Aštart. We can conclude this is the case based upon the diagnostic elements of (1) the lions, and Aštart's close associations with named goddesses who have lions in their iconography; (2) the horses; and (3) the *potnia theron* motif (see fig. 8f).

---

and there is no suggestion that Ištar and Qudšu (the lion-standers) are the same deity in either Egypt or the southern Levant.

Fig. 8f
Gold Aštart pendant from Ugarit.
Louvre, Inv. AO 14.714.

The nude-goddess-standing-atop-a-lion motif is prominent both in Ugarit, where several of the gold pendants are so rendered, and in Egypt in the iconography of Qudšu. The origin of the goddess-upon-the-lion motif is Mesopotamian glyptic, where the image was indicative of the goddess Ištar. As early as the Old Akkadian period, the goddess is portrayed heavily armed and dominating a lion through the placement of at least one of her feet upon the back of the animal (see fig. 8e). As Ištar is a war-goddess, and as the lion represents the forces of chaos, the image shows a war deity capable of releasing or harnessing the powers of mass destruction.[149]

There is evidence that there was an identification of Aštart with Ištar at Ugarit. KTU 1.118; a bilingual text from Ugarit lists the names of the gods of Ugarit and their Akkadian/Mesopotamian equivalents.[150] Aštart is presented as the western equivalent of Ištar (*ʿttrt* = ᵈIŠTAR.*iš-tar*), although Ugaritic Aštart is in no way as significant in her pantheon as Ištar is in hers, nor does Aštart share Ištar's fully erotic or military character. But this identification,

149. Collon 1987: Chapter Three and 197.

150. See Schaeffer *Ugaritica* V, RS 20.24.; Herdner, *Ugaritica* VII, KTU 1.118; RS 24.264+ 280; and other references in Prechel 1996: 135, no. 341.

nevertheless, allows for speculation as to the sharing of iconographies between the two goddesses.

The second diagnostic element on the Nude Goddess plaques is the horse iconography, once again with the Nude Goddess standing on the animal's back. This horse imagery is found only in Egypt and in the Levantine regions heavily influenced by Egypt, such as Lachish (see fig. 8a) or Tel Qarnayim, in the region of Beth Shan, from which comes a LBA mold depicting the Nude Goddess standing upon a horse. The female, in Egyptian style, holds a bird in each of her hands, which extend out to her sides, and she has the Hathoric hair style. Also Egyptian are the two males (the gods Rešef and Min or Onuris) on either side of her.[151]

The southern Levant was culturally dominated by Egypt in the Late Bronze Age, and in Egypt Aštart was associated with the horse. From the burial chamber of Thutmosis IV came an inscribed chariot calling the pharaoh "Valiant upon the chariot as Aštart."[152] So too, there is an inscription from the Nineteenth Dynasty that reads (in part): "as for the hands of thy chariot they are Anat and Aštart."[153] One further piece of evidence may even come from Ugarit in texts RS 18.039 (=KTU 4.350) and RS 18.041 (=KTU 1.86), wherein the different deities of Ugarit are juxtaposed with the name of an animal. Aštart is mentioned in connection with the horse.[154]

Fig. 8g
Seal impression.
Teissier no. 490.

---

151. Winter 1983: 112; Cornelius 1993: 31; Ben Arieh 1983: *passim*.

152. See Leclant 1960: 22–23. See also Perlman 1978: 191; Stadelmann 1967: 101–3.

153. Translation from Perlman 1978: 192.

154. Leclant 1960: 1.

The inscribed images of Aštart on horseback that come from Egypt are: (1) a stele discovered at the Wâdi 'Abbâd in close proximity to the temple of Seti I, with an inscription that appears to have "Aštart" before a goddess who is armed and wearing an *atef*-crown;[155] (2) an Egyptian(izing) cylinder seal from Beitin depicting a warrior-god and a goddess. This goddess wears the Egyptian white crown flanked by two feathers. In her right hand she holds erect a spear. The hieroglyphs carved before this deity's face read "Aštart";[156] (3) Turin stele 50068, which depicts "an equestrian goddess handling a bow with an inscription containing 'Aštart.'"[157]

It is worth noting that there are several uninscribed images of a young, nude goddess riding a horse from Egypt, whom Leclant and Cornelius accept as portrayals of Aštart.[158] Thus, in Egypt, the nude warrior/chariot-goddess is generally understood to be Aštart. Therefore, in regions heavily influenced by Egypt, we should expect horse imagery to be associated with Aštart, especially if the associated iconography (nude, armed) also suggests this goddess.

Finally, there is the *potnia theron* motif, present both in the glyptic art and on the mold-made plaques (see figs. 8f and 8g). As per the evidence derived from the Ugaritic literary corpus, the most extensive tale currently known about Aštart records that she is a huntress.[159] While Ugaritic Aštart may not possess the explicit erotic qualities that would make the Nude Goddess motif appropriate for such a goddess as Ištar, the mistress of animals motif would easily relate the Nude Goddess image with the Ugaritic hunting goddess. As none of the Ugaritic goddesses can be shown through the literary evidence to be explicitly sexual, the evidence of the alternate iconography rather suggests that in the Levant this image probably refers to the goddess Aštart.

Summary

The Nude Goddess should perhaps be understood as the nude goddess*es*, representing Ištar, Ašerah, Išḫara, Aštart, and Qudšu, if not even more goddesses of whom we, as yet, know little or nothing. For the sake of this study, it is the bird-faced versions of this image that are of particular importance, for

---

155. *Ibid.*, 31.

156. *Ibid.*, 22–23.

157. Cornelius 1993: 24.

158. Leclant 1960: *passim*; Cornelius 1994: 73–75.

159. P. Day, in "Anat: Ugarit's 'Mistress of Animal'" argues that it is the goddess Anat who is intended by the *potnia theron*, based on Anat's roles in three myths where she either desires a hunting weapon (*Myth of Aqhat*), where she encounters Baal while he himself is hunting, or where she goes hunting with Aštart. As Aštart is more clearly portrayed as the Ugaritic huntress, and as alternate forms of this Nude Goddess motif appear to pertain to her, I think it practical to attribute these images to Aštart.

it is they who first appear throughout Cyprus in LC II and demonstrate the arrival of the goddess who would become Aphrodite. In a stroke of simplicity, I would offer that it was the bird-faced figurines from the region of Alalakh that had the greatest impact on Cyprus, due both to their prevalence in that territory and the contacts manifest between Cyprus and Alalakh during the Bronze Age. As it would appear that the bird-faced figurines from Alalakh, as discussed above, represented either Ištar or Išhara or both, and as both of these goddesses are adequately erotic to give rise to such a goddess as Aphrodite, then let me end this section on Bronze Age Levantine goddess iconography by suggesting that it was the goddesses Ištar and Išhara who, through northern Syria, gave rise to the original iconography and persona of the Paphian in Cyprus.

Nevertheless, as was shown above, Cyprus did maintain trade and contacts with several other sites in the Near East, and it would be unreasonable to suppose that the similar iconographies from such areas as Ugarit did not have an effect or impact on the newly emerging cult in Cyprus. Ugaritic Aštart may also have contributed to the Paphian, as well as Egyptian Qudšu. and Ugaritic Ašerah, the "Lady of the Sea." I am loath to ascribe to only one goddess the persona who, in Cyprus, evolved into Aphrodite, but rather I look to a combination of Near Eastern goddesses. Through both iconography and persona I suggest that Išhara and Ištar played dominant roles in this development, but that Aštart, Ašerah, and Qudšu may have also had their parts to play.

But this is only the beginning, for other cultures had their own impact in this process. The goddess who would, and did, become Aphrodite was a mixture of several elements: Levantine, Cypriot, Cretan, Greek, all interacting over the course of several centuries in Cyprus. The Cretan goddess-with-upraised-arms, whoever she might have been intended to represent, had a considerable impact on the Cypriot iconography from the eleventh century onward, and this impact was to continue far beyond the time when Aphrodite had her home on Olympos. The Phoenician colonization of Cyprus, and their movement throughout the Mediterranean at the beginning of the Iron II period, also had a profound influence on the persona and understanding of the Paphian.

IX.
THE PHOENICIAN QUESTION

Aphrodite's cult emerged (and appeared to the Greeks) in Cyprus after extensive contacts with the Levant. But there is a further question in the study of the origins of Aphrodite, and that is what role the Phoenicians played in the emergence of her cult. It is evident that the Greeks believed that Aphrodite (specifically Ourania) was Phoenician in origin, and that the Greek Aphrodite was the Hellenized version of Phoenician Aštart or, according to Herodotos (H. I. 131): "Assyrians call Aphrodite Mylitta; the Arabs call her Alilat, and the Persians Mitran." Following the lead of the Greek historians, modern historians and classicists have suggested that Aphrodite was originally a Phoenician goddess and was introduced into the Greek pantheon by the Phoenicians. This hypothesis is supported not only by the ancient testimony, but also by the evidence of contacts between the Aegean and Phoenicia during the early Iron Age, at precisely that point when the extant evidence suggests that Aphrodite entered into the Greek pantheon (see Chapters Three and Four).

In the analysis of the Phoenicians' role in Aphrodite's origin, the definition of the term "Phoenician" is critical. Contrary to the modern practice, whereby the term "Phoenician" refers to the population inhabiting the area now more-or-less covered by modern-day Lebanon beginning in the early Iron Age (i.e., not the Bronze Age population), the ancient Greeks made no such distinction between Bronze Age and Iron Age "Phoenicians" (or "Sidonians" as was used as a synonym from Homer onward). The Bronze Age "Phoenicians," then, for a modern audience, would have consisted of the Syrian, Amorite, and Canaanite populations. As we have seen, these cultures brought forth an assortment of goddesses who could well parallel, and even be the source of, Greek Aphrodite. However, as the extant data suggest that Aphrodite only appears in Greece in the Iron Age, it is not sound to suggest that the Greeks imported a Levantine, Aphrodite-like goddess directly from the Levant during the Bronze Age.[1] It is likewise not possible to speak of a potential Phoenician origin of the Cypriot goddess discussed in Chapter Six, since the earliest evidence of Aphrodite's sanctuary at Paphos predates the existence of the Iron Age Phoenicians.

---

1. Thus our suggestion that the Bronze Age Levantine influence entered directly into Cyprus during the Late Bronze Age, and only came to influence the Greeks after 1200 BCE.

The Phoenician hypothesis here considered uses the modern sense of the term "Phoenician" as an Iron Age population, and suggests specifically that Aphrodite was introduced into Greece by the Phoenicians as a manifestation of their goddess Aštart at some point in the early Iron Age. The time period considered will be from the end of the Bronze Age to the eighth century, after which time Aphrodite is clearly established in Greece. Contrary to the Cypriot hypothesis, this Phoenician hypothesis holds that Aphrodite was introduced directly from the Levant, without a Cypriot intermediary (although Cyprus will be discussed later in this chapter concerning the later Greek understandings of the goddess Aštart).

In contrast to the extensive materials for contacts between the various populations of the Bronze Age Mediterranean, early-first-millennium contacts between Greece and Phoenicia are rather limited due to the "Dark Age" status of Greece during the Early Iron Age (1200–800 BCE). The majority of data on mainland Greece comes from the Euboian site of Lefkandi and Attica, while on Crete one of our best sites of contact is Kommos (*inter alia*). In the east, most of our extant data comes from the sites of Tyre and Al Mina.

The evidence in both directions shows contacts between Phoenicia and the Aegean as early as the tenth century. The patterns of trade appear to show an export of mainland-Greek (Euboian and Attic) pottery to the East, with a return of Phoenician luxury goods (gold, faience, unguents) to the West, including not only the mainland, but Crete, the Dodecanese, and the Cyclades, as well.[2] This trading pattern occurs within the time period that would allow for the transmission of the cult of Aphrodite: after the evidence from the Linear B tablets, and before the Homeric epics and the Nestor cup.

There are two data, however, that argue strongly against the Phoenician origins of Aphrodite. The first is that, as already established in Chapter Six, there is continuity of the cult of Aphrodite at the sanctuary at Paphos from at least 1200 BCE, if not earlier. Any Phoenician contribution to the origins of this Cypriot goddess must, by definition, come after that date. One possible argument to be made for the Phoenician hypothesis in this instance is that the ancient Greeks who proclaimed the Phoenician origins of Aphrodite may have been referring to the Bronze Age Levant, where excellent cognates for Aphrodite did exist, and which had a considerable impact on the religion of Cyprus, and thus the "Phoenician" origin is actually a Levantine origin through Cyprus. The fact that both Herodotos and Pausanias claim that the cult of Aphrodite was passed from the Phoenicians to the Greeks by way of Cyprus may support this argument.

---

2. Coldstream 1982: 264. For discussion on the contact between the Phoenicians and the Aegean, see Coldstream 1977; Boardman 1980; Coldstream and Bikai 1988; Coldstream 1988; Coldstream 1989; Coldstream 1998.

The second datum is the persona of the Phoenician goddess Aštart, who, according to the Phoenician hypothesis, is Aphrodite's main cognate and progenitress. As will now be discussed, the persona of Aštart is adequately distinct from that of Aphrodite so that it would be difficult, if not impossible, to equate the two.

The Iron Age Persona of Aštart

The literary and iconographic data from the Iron Age complete the picture of Aštart as derived from the Bronze Age evidence considered in the previous chapter, both in terms of continuity and change. One important fact must be borne in mind when considering the evidence for Iron Age Aštart: scholars, both ancient and modern, have tended to see Iron Age Aštart through the lens of Aphrodite. Attributes such as eroticism and even carnality are applied to the Levantine goddess through her identification with the Greek goddess rather than through what few Phoenician inscriptions and *objets d'art* have come down to us. In truth, the few written documents that do remain portray a goddess far more like the Ugaritic Attart than the Hellenic Kythereia, noted for military qualities rather than erotic ones.

In order to avoid this problem, the following survey will only include pre-Hellenic data, so as to present Phoenician Aštart as she existed before being "tainted" by the Greek and Roman authors. In this my methodology differs from that of Bonnet and Delcor, both of whom combine Phoenician and Classical texts to derive a picture of Aštart that shows her to be in many, if not all, respects the *doppelgängerin* of Greek Aphrodite.[3] This lack of discernment is especially ironic in view of Delcor's attestation that the two goddesses must be distinguished from one another, after which he lists the literary references for Aštart as beginning with Lucian (second century CE) and continuing to Macrobius in the fifth century CE.[4] As a result, Delcor comes to the conclusion that Aštart, like Aphrodite and Ištar, was a goddess of love.[5] Likewise, after an extensive examination of the persona of Aštart in Iron Age Phoenicia, Bonnet concluded that Aštart was not merely a goddess of love and fertility, but also a deity associated with war and hunting, the sky and sea, and the protection of the (royal) family.[6] While many of these assertions are based on the epigraphic evidence from Phoenicia, the attributes of "love"" and "fertility" are groundless, and yet are maintained due to a long-standing, inaccurate, tradition.

---

3. Delcor 1986: *passim*; Bonnet 1996: *passim*.

4. Delcor 1986: 1077.

5. *Ibid*.

6. Bonnet 1996: 49.

This study follows the theories of Herrmann, who, after an analysis of the non-Classical evidences for Aštart, came to the conclusion that the goddess was not associated with either love or fertility, but justice, belligerence, and hunting.[7] Such an examination of the Iron Age evidence will allow for an understanding of Aštart in her own right, with her own persona, while simultaneously indicating the extreme differences between Aštart and Aphrodite, thus supporting the argument that Aphrodite is not, in fact, simply the "Greek Aštart."

LITERARY DATA

There is remarkably little to learn about Iron Age Aštart, as the Phoenicians did not record their myths on imperishable materials. We cannot see Aštart interacting with gods or humans as she did in the Ugaritic epics, and, thus, our understanding of the goddess is based solely on royal, funerary, and votive dedications to her. The most prominent difference between Bronze Age and Iron Age Aštart is that, in the later period, Aštart takes on the role of the dominant city goddess, eclipsing both Anat and Ašerah in Sidon and Tyre.

The earliest attestation of the cult of Aštart in Sidon is an inscription on a krater dated to the eighth century BCE:[8]

> Great-Milku, Prie[st]ess of Hurrian Aštart (or possibly "Aštart at the window"). The bones were collected by Ittobaʻal. May she be lamented.

Although this small dedication attests to the presence of a cult of Aštart in Sidon as early as the eighth century, the goddess's actual role in the city cult is only fully expressed in two funerary inscriptions from the end of the sixth and early fifth centuries BCE. Both are of kings of Sidon. The first belongs to King Tabnit:[9]

> I, Tabnit, priest of Aštart, king of the Sidonians, son of Ešmunazor (I), priest of Aštart, king of the Sidonians, repose in this sarcophagus. Whoever you are, whatever man, who will find this sarcophagus, O! do not open it and do not disturb me, for there is no silver by me, there is no gold by me nor any other precious object. I alone rest in this sarcophagus. O! do not open it and do not disturb me, for it a thing abominable to Aštart and if you dare to open upon me and if you dare to trouble me, may you have no descendants among the living under the sun, nor a bed of repose among the Rephaim.

The second inscription is by Tabnit's son Ešmanezer, and is so much longer than that of his father one almost suspects a revolution in inscription tech-

---

7. Herrmann 1969: *passim*.

8. Translation based on Puech in Bonnet 1996: 30–31.

9. KAI 13. Translation based on Lipinski 1995: 128.

nique that allowed for greater verbosity. The beginning of the inscription is quite similar to that of Tabnit, asking that neither the coffin nor the body be disturbed in any way, and calling down curses on whoever would ignore this plea. The second half of the inscription lists those acts of piety that cast light on this study.[10]

> I, a pitiable man, am collected not at my time (read: before my time), son of a few days, the son of a widow am I. I, Esmanezer, King of the Sidonians, son of King Tabnit, King of the Sidonians, grandson of King Ešmanezer, King of the Sidonians, and my mother, Am'Aštart, priestess of Aštart, Our Lady, the Queen, daughter of Ešmanezer, King of the Sidonians. We are they who built the temple for the gods. The temple of Aštart, in Sidon of the Sea-land, and let Aštart dwell there in all her glory. And we are they who built the temple of Ešmun, the Holy Prince, 'NJDLL on the mountain, and let him dwell there in glory. And we are they who built the temple for the gods of the Sidonians in Sidon of the Sea-land, a temple for Baal of Sidon and a temple of Aštart-Name-of-Baal. And to us gave the Lord the King of Dor and Jaffa the fruitful grain lands in the plain of Sharon, for the great things which I did. And we expanded the boundaries of the land belonging to the Sidonians. Whoever you are, king or man, do not open upon me and strip me or remove me from this resting place, and do not remove the coffin of my resting place: The Holy Gods will take him and cut down this king or man, and his offspring forever.

What is first evident from a reading both of this inscription and that of Tabnit is that the priesthood of Aštart was within the royal family. In the case of Tabnit, this is mentioned even before his title "King of Sidon," while for Am'Aštart her title "Priestess of Aštart" likewise comes before her title "Queen of Sidon." It would appear that this religious function is of greater importance (or perhaps prestige) than the actual royal status of the members of the royal family, and it is certainly probable that the relationship of the royal family to the goddess is what justifies their reign (much as Sargon of Akkad attributed his justification to rule to Ištar). That Ešmanezer himself does not use this title might be attributable to his early death: If he was too young upon the death of his father to take up the priesthood, his mother Am'Aštart took it up in his stead.[11]

The inscription also mentions the various temples constructed by this royal family during its reign. The first mentioned is that of Aštart, possibly located on the coastal region of Sidon. This primacy of place combined with the royal priesthood suggest that Aštart was the dominant deity of the city, the city goddess, the Sidonian equivalent of Athena in Athens. That her priesthood runs in the royal family also suggests that her cult is associated with the

---

10. KAI 14. Translation based on Peckham 1987: 83–84.

11. Bonnet 1996: 32–33.

ruling dynasty, making her a dynastic goddess as Ištar in Assyria. Thus, Aštart is a political goddess, possibly the protectress of the city and its royal family, who in turn might justify its power through service to the city's goddess.

Some evidence for the antiquity of Aštart's cult in Tyre comes from an admittedly late source, Josephus Flavius. In his *Against Apion* I, 118, he records that King Hiram I of Tyre:[12]

> cut down the forest of trees from the mountains they call Lebanon, taking them for the roofs of the temples. And having disassembled the ancient temples he constructed a temple of Herakles (read: Melqart) and of Aštart; the first raising of the temple of Herakles was wrought in the month of Peritios.

King Hiram I of Tyre is a contemporary of King Solomon of Israel and, therefore, can be dated to the tenth century BCE. Thus, the cults of both Aštart and Melqart might be dated back at least this far in Tyre. However, as Josephus Flavius refers to older temples in the city, it is possible that these cults go back even further. Unfortunately, no data either written or archaeological offer insight into this issue as yet.

A second piece of evidence casting light on the role of Aštart in Tyre is a treaty concluded between King Esarhaddon of Assyria and King Baal of Tyre in 670 BCE. At the end of this treaty, in typical Near Eastern fashion, the gods of the two regions are invoked to protect the treaty and to punish any who would transgress it. The Phoenician deities invoked are as follows:[13]

> May Ba'al Šamaim, Ba'al Malagee, and Ba'al Saphon raise an evil wind against your ships to undo their moorings and tear out their mooring pole, may a strong wave sink them in the sea and a violent tide [rise] against you.

> May Melquarth and Ešmun deliver your land to destruction and your people to deportation; may they [uproot] you from your land and take away the food from your mouth, the clothes from your body, and the oil for your anointing.

> May Aštart break your bow in the thick of battle and have you crouch at the feet of your enemy, may a foreign enemy divide your belongings.

It is evident from this invocation that Aštart, like her Ugaritic equivalent, is still associated to some degree with warfare and the military. It is actually rather ironic that while modern scholars have so avidly recognized Aštart as a fertility goddess, it is the three Baals who threaten with the powers of nature, while Aštart maintains her power through battle and force of arms. Although it is certainly possible that Tyrian Aštart's military connotations arise from the Akkadian context, where she would be closely aligned with Assyrian Ištar and, thus, partake of some of this latter goddess's attributes, especially militarism, Aštart's role as dynastic/city goddess, as well as her earlier associa-

---

12. See Appendix B 9.1.

13. Translation from Parpola and Watanabe 1988: 27.

tions with battle, make it just as conceivable that her military aspects are applicable to her in Tyre as well as in Assyria.

Two other small inscriptions remain from the early Iron Age. One is a small ivory box from Ur inscribed in Phoenician dating to the seventh century:[14]

> This coffer here 'MTB'L, daughter of PT'S, servant of our lord, has offered as a gift to her lady Aštart; may she bless her. In his days, [the days] of our lord....', son of YSD'R.

The second inscription is upon a small plaque from Sarepta, dated also to the seventh century:

> "This statue SHLM, son of M'P'L, son of 'ZY, made to Tanit-Aštart."[15]

These are the very few written testimonies concerning the cult of Aštart in Phoenicia. Only a little more evidence is presented in the Hebrew Bible (notably in Kings 1 and 2, Judges, and 1 Samuel), although much of it is merely condemnatory in nature.[16] That Aštart is the city goddess of Sidon is mentioned twice, in 1 Kgs 11:5 and 2 Kgs 23:13, although it is probable that both Sidon and Tyre are intended in these passages where the term "Sidonian," much as with Homer, meant either "Sidonian and Tyrian" or more simply "Phoenician." There is slight evidence that Aštart was worshipped also in the Philistine cities in 1 Sam 31:10, where it is recorded that: "They (the Philistines) put Saul's armor in the temple of Aštaroth, and they fastened his body to the wall of Beth Shan."[17]

Such are the literary and epigraphic testimonia that have come down to us concerning the cult of Aštart in the early Iron Age in the Levant. Her cult extended from northern Phoenicia possibly as far south as the Philistine pentopolis, depending on how one wishes to interpret 1 Sam 31:10. Little is known of the nature of the goddess—not as we know the crafty side of Athena or the hunting prowess of Artemis. Aštart is clearly a goddess concerned with the city, whether Sidon or Tyre, and, according to the inscriptions from Sidon, is closely allied with the royal family, who provides her priest(ess)hood. That she has military connotations is suggested both in the Tyrian treaty with Assyria and, once again, in the passage from 1 Samuel. In at least some instances, she is paired with a male deity, Baal in Sidon, where she also has a temple as

---

14. Amadasi Guzzo 1990: 59.

15. *Ibid.*, 62.

16. Perlman 1978: 100ff. for full references. All biblical citations are from the Oxford Annotated Bible with the Apocrypha, Revised Standard Version.

17. Another use of the word *štrwt* (Aštoret) appears in Deut 7:13 and 28: 4, 18, and 51, where the word refers to the fertility of the flocks. It is not entirely clear how this usage of the word might relate to the name of the goddess, if at all, but it may be slight evidence for fertility aspects of Aštart in the Hebrew Bible.

Aštart Name-of-Baal, or Melqart/Herakles in Tyre. She just as frequently appears alone.

As was the case with the Ugaritic tablets, there is nothing in the written data that hints at any erotic attributes of the goddess. Less than at Ugarit, really, for we do not even have tales where she is invoked as a standard of beauty, as in the *Epic of Kirta*, or desired by another god, as in the tales of Yamm and Baal. Once again, then, it becomes necessary to examine the iconographic evidence closely to determine if, as in the Bronze Age, the fairly erotic, nude-goddess motif may be applied to Aštart.

Fig. 9a
Statuette of Aštart from Seville.
Museo Arqueológico, R.E.P. 11.136.

ICONOGRAPHY

There is, fortunately, one relatively unambiguous example of Aštart iconography in the Iron Age, although, both in time and space, it is somewhat
removed from the main focus of this study. This piece (see fig. 9a) is a votive
figure from El Carambolo, Seville, Spain and dates to the seventh century BCE.
This bronze figure, standing 16.5 cm high, shows a seated nude female. Her
hair, textured, is short in front and lies just above her eyes, while the remainder is past shoulder-length and falls in front of her shoulders to lie just above
her breasts. The facial features are rendered in molding and show Egyptian
influence. The breasts are molded in the round and stand out prominently
from the chest. Her right arm, broken off between the elbow and wrist, is bent
at the elbow and rises forward in the traditional gesture of benediction. The
left arm is missing entirely. The stomach is somewhat rounded and the navel
is distinct. No genitalia are indicated. The thighs bend out from the torso at
a right angle, and the knees again bend at a right angle from the thighs. The
feet are well preserved with the toes rendered by incision, and they rest atop
a cubical foot rest.

The dedication reads: "This throne was made by B'lytn, son of D'mmlk,
and by 'bdb'l, son of D'mmlk, son of Ys'l, for Aštart-*hr*, our Lady, because she
heard the voice of their words [prayers]."[18] The *'strt hr*, meaning either "Hurrian Aštart" or "Aštart at the window," was also applied to Ugaritic Aštart.
Thus, the one extant, identified image of Aštart in the Iron Age Phoenician
world shows a female portrayed in the nude in a gesture of benediction.[19]

The remaining evidence for Iron Age Aštart iconography comes predominantly from continuity of iconography from the Bronze Age, a tricky matter,
as the Bronze Age iconography is ambiguous in nature. The continuity in the
archaeological record, combined once again with elements of Aštart's distinctive imagery (lions and horses), and the use of these images on cultic items
all point to the sacred nature of these images in general, and their interpretation as specifically Aštart in the Phoenician world in particular.

The greatest evidence for continuity occurs in Syria at the site of Hama.
The lower remains of an Aštart plaque came to light from Level H, dated to

---

18. Bonnet 1996: 161.

19. Although there is a possibility that this image was originally clothed, this is unlikely.
    The statue is seated and attached to the throne/chair, so that any clothing adorning the
    statue would, of necessity, have to cover the chair. As the throne was an important
    aspect of Aštart's royal statue, it is unlikely that the artist would have chosen to cover
    it. That the statue may have been covered by some manner of precious metal in the
    form of clothing is also unlikely, as there remains no evidence that another material
    was either originally attached to the figure or subsequently removed. Likewise, once
    again, the connection between the statue and her throne would have made the appli-
    cation of an additional, covering material difficult.

1550–1450 BCE.[20] A second example, this one more fully preserved, comes from Level F, dated to the Iron I period, or 1200–900 BCE (see fig. 9b).[21] Three final examples comes from Level E in the eighth century.[22] All these, except the unclear example from Level H, show a nude female *en face* holding her breasts in her hands. This tendency for an individual site to maintain the use of these images during and through the so-called Dark Ages is repeated in Palestine, where more extensive excavation has yielded greater results. Megiddo, studied above in Chapter Seven, had yielded Aštart plaques from Levels VII (1350–1150 BCE) through III (780–650 BCE).[23] Gezer has produced such images from the fourteenth century through the ninth,[24] and Ashdod, excavated by Dothan, has examples from the mid-fifteenth century continuously through to the early sixth century BCE.[25] Finally, there is the southern site of

Fig. 9b
Late Bronze Age Aštart plaque from Hama.
Ingholt, Pl. XXIV, no. 5.

20. Ingholt 1940: Pl. XX.

21. *Ibid.*, Pl. XXIV.

22. *Ibid.*, Pl. XXXII.

23. Böhm 1990: 83 with noted bibliography.

24. *Ibid.* Note also Holland's appendix C in Dever 1975.

25. Ashdod publications in *'Atiqot* 7 (1967), 9 (1971), 10 (1973), and 15 (1982).

Gerar, where Petrie discovered "goddess plaques" from strata ranging from 1700–600 BCE.[26] Some sites show the presence of the images in question during the transition from Bronze to Iron Age, as at Tel Zeror[27] and Beth Shemesh.[28] Excavations at other sites have revealed the presence of these plaques as late as the Neo-Babylonian period, such as the Syrian sites of Khan Sheikoun,[29] Neirab,[30] and Tel Halaf.[31] Beyond plaques, images of this nude female clasping her breasts are also present in the round from Phoenicia. One, from Akhziv, eighth to sixth centuries, is a terra-cotta, mold-made, hand-worked and painted image, unworked only in the back.[32] Her breasts are prominently rendered and, except for the lack of emphasis on the genitalia, is in all respects similar to the Bronze and Iron Age images. A similar bronze female standing atop a tripod base dates to the eighth to seventh centuries, although no more definite place of origin is known than simply "Phoenicia."[33]

The continual production and use of these images from the Bronze Age into the Iron Age, corroborated by the possibility of a nude-female representing the goddess Aštart during the Bronze Age as per the Levantine materials, provides a strong argument that the identification of these plaques is continuous from the Bronze Age and, thus, are intended to be understood as Aštart in the Levant. The only difficulty in identifying these images as the goddess of Phoenicia is their relative paucity in Phoenicia itself, especially from such sites as Sidon and Tyre. However, one must remain cognizant of the small extent of excavations in these areas, due to the presence of modern cities directly atop the ancient. However, it is significant that in all excavated areas north, south, east and west of Phoenicia proper, such as Hama, and within Phoenicia proper, such as Akhziv, these plaques have come to light. This suggests that their paucity in Phoenicia is due more to lack of excavation than a true absence.

That these images are intended to represent Aštart is further maintained by the iconography, where, as in the Bronze Age, the nude female represented is often shown in conjunction with either lions or horses. The association with horses is most blatant in the use of these images as decoration on horse paraphernalia, both in ivory and, less commonly, bronze. An example of the

---

26. Petrie 1928: Tables 35 and 36.

27. Stern 1993: 1524–26.

28. Böhm 1990: 83.

29. Comte du Mesnil du Buisson 1928: 178–84.

30. Carriere et Barrois 1927: 201–5.

31. Oppenheim 1962: 12–13.

32. Moscati 1988: Figure 37.

33. *Ibid.*, Figure 112.

latter, a horse's head-piece, comes from Tell Tainat in southeastern Turkey and dates to the late eighth or early seventh century BCE.[34] This object is divided into two registers, an upper and a lower. The theme of the upper register is of a male hero on one bent knee contending with four lions, two on either side of him. The lower register shows two nude-female figures holding their breasts and standing atop lions' heads. Their hairstyles are "Hathoric" in nature, and both wear elaborate necklaces, bracelets and anklets. The breasts are rendered in the round, and their genitalia are accentuated by incised dots. In all respects they are strongly reminiscent of the Bronze Age versions of goddesses. This is not only evident in the emphasis on sexual characteristics, but as well on the association with lions.[35]

North Syrian-style bronze horse adornments such as this were also discovered in the east Greek regions of Samos and Miletos. One well-preserved example from Samos shows not only the nude-female motif but also the strong association with lions—both lion heads and lions *couchant*.[36]

The motif of the Nude Goddess associated with horses through her appearance on objects of horse paraphernalia, and as well associated with lions through the use of their combined iconography on said objects, is well represented among the hoards of ivories brought to light at Nimrud and dating to the eighth century BCE. Although these items were recovered by excavation within the limits of Assyria proper, the style of these ivories is predominantly North Syrian and Phoenician, having been "exported" to the Assyrian heart land through conquest, booty, and the (forced) importation of Levantine crafts people.[37] In his catalogue of ivory equestrian bridle-harness ornaments from Nimrud, Orchard lists ten "Naked Maidens with Lotus Flowers and Lions."[38] One example of such an image is represented on Plate XXVIII (see fig. 9c) of the catalogue, which shows an ivory, triangular object with a nude female in the center of the triangle. While her face and breasts are worn away, it is easy to make out that the female stood *en face* with her arms out to either side of her body, grasping flowers in either hand. The genital triangle is rendered by carving, and no navel is visible. Like the nude females from the Tainat bronze, she wears both bracelets and anklets (the neck is impossible to make out). She stands atop the head of a crouching lion, whose face is effaced but whose paws are carefully rendered with claws and a mane detailed with incision. All around this scene is a continuous guilloche pattern.

---

34. Kantor 1962: 93–95.

35. *Ibid.*, 101.

36. *Ibid.*, 108–9.

37. Barnet 1982: Chapter Seven.

38. Orchard 1967: 27–29 and Plates XXVIII–XXXI.

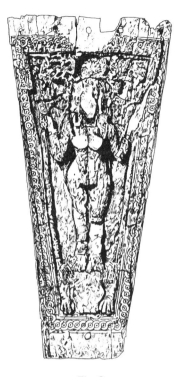

Fig. 9c
Ivory horse blinker from Nimrud.
Orchard, #135, Plate XXVIII.

A second example is shown on Plate XXIX of Orchard. Here, once again, is a triangular piece in ivory, with the nude female image in the center of the triangle. She stands *en face* with her arms to either side, this time grasping a small lion by the rear paw in each hand. Her hair is similar to that of the votive from Seville, with blunt-cut bangs and tresses hanging over the shoulders to lie just above the breasts. Her ears stand out 90 degrees from her face, and her eyes are rendered by incision. She wears an elaborate necklace and anklets, and while the navel is rendered by an incised dot, neither the breasts nor the genitalia are emphasized or decorated. Above the head of the female is a winged solar disk. Below her feet, as is visible from the side, is a lotus, upon which the female stands. A similar image, in an even better state of preservation, is shown on Plate XXX of Orchard's catalogue (see fig. 9d).

Beyond the "nude maiden with lions" motif, the nude female appears in four more examples of equestrian decoration, either standing on lotus flowers without lions or shown holding ibex or birds. It is clear that these motifs—the nude female, either with or without her lion—were of importance in the

Fig. 9d
Ivory horse blinker from Nimrud.
Orchard, #137, Plate XXX.

iconographic repertoire. That Aštart in the Bronze Age was associated with
both of these animals—horse and lion—in literature and iconography suggests
that a similar, if not the same, image is meant to be conjured here. If Aštart
were a patroness of horses, then perhaps her image upon that animal would
have protective value.

Another item that shows the close association between the nude female,
lions and religion is a cult stand from Ta'anach dating back into the tenth century BCE.[39] The bottom register of this rectangular, cubical, terra-cotta stand
depicts a nude female standing between two (relatively) large lions. The
female is rather crudely wrought, being hand-made. Her hair is a small strip
of clay laid atop her head; her face consists of two pressed-in pellet eyes, a
molded nose, and a mouth rendered by a light, straight incision below the
nose. Her breasts, set awkwardly low on her torso so that they are beneath arm

---

39. Hestrin 1987: 61.

level, are molded and protruding. The legs are straight molded lines of clay, with both feet turned out to either side and with toes rendered by incision. Between the legs is a deeply incised hole, apparently representing the vagina. Her arms extend to either side of the body, curving upward at the (purely theoretical) elbows, and the hands, like the feet, are detailed by incision. In each hand the female grasps an ear of both of the lions, who, like the female, are portrayed completely *en face*. Only the fronts of the lions are visible, with their faces in high relief against the backing of the stand, detailed by incision with manes, eyes, ears, nostrils, whiskers, teeth, and claws. Like those of the female, their legs are simply applied strips of clay. The profiles of the rest of the lions' bodies are rendered on the lateral sides of the stand, not visible from the front.[40] It is clear that what is here portrayed is the Nude Goddess dominating two lions, similar in many respects to the nude females on the ivory horse ornaments holding lions on either side of the body. Hestrin suggests that this Nude Goddess tentatively might be identified as Ašerah, based on the association between this goddess and lions.[41] However, the association between Ašerah and lions depends upon the identification of Egyptian Qudšu as Ašerah, as it is only Qudšu who is named on her imagery standing upon a lion. As Wiggins has noted, the identification of Ašerah as Qudšu is not definite, and it is not methodologically sound to associate Ašerah and lions.[42]

The association of these nude-female images with cultic items and, thus, the divine sphere, is also suggested by their presence on model shrines from Tel Qasile and Akhziv, with similar models coming as well from Cyprus. The so-called "*naos*" ("temple") from Tel Qasile dates to the tenth century BCE (Stratum X) and was discovered lying on the floor of Temple 131 in front of a raised platform.[43] The terra-cotta object is rendered with a full Egyptian architectural façade, with rims both above and below the central images extending out from the face of the image. There are pivot holes within these extensions indicating where wooden doors were attached, covering the *naos* interior. Within the *naos* are two broken images that, from their remains, appear to be two nude females who were holding their breasts. To date, only the legs of these images remain.[44] The overall structure of the *naos* suggests that, when in use, the doors would have been closed, thus veiling the female/

---

40. *Ibid.*, 66, Figure 4.

41. *Ibid.*, 70ff.

42. Wiggins 1991: 384–89.

43. Mazar 1980: 82.

44. The positioning of the upper body is based on the outline of the break lines on the back "wall" of the *naos*. Although the high relief of the bodies is missing, this outline shows a silhouette similar in form to the nude-goddess plaques with arms extending out from the shoulders and reaching in toward the chest. See Mazar 1980, *passim*.

goddess figure(s) from public view. Then, the doors, on specific occasions, could be opened to reveal the figure(s). Two other sections of this object are broken off: some manner of handle on the bottom extension of the façade, and what appears to have been a crouching lion on the top of the *naos*. If this latter identification is correct, than the Tel Qasile *naos* gives one more indication of the association between the Aštart images and lions. In any case, the shrine-like imagery of the object, its location within a sanctuary, and the ability to "hide" the goddesses within the shrine point to a divine nature both for the object itself and for the identification of the female images.

A similar shrine from Phoenicia, and now in the Museum of the American University, Beirut, shows a central niche edged with neatly recessed panels and flanked on either side by nude female images, this time outside of the so-called *naos* instead of within.[45] Once again, the hairstyle of the Seville votive is to be seen, and the nude goddesses wear elaborate necklaces and bracelets. The breasts are molded in the round, and the hands lie under the breasts, either supporting them, as in other examples in this study, or lying on the stomach below the breasts. Both the tresses of the females and the interior of the niche were painted with black paint.[46] Shrines such as these, although without the nude-goddess elements, come not only from Jordan, but also from Cyprus. The majority of the shrines from this latter context come from Amathus, which was subject to considerable Phoenician influence from the end of the Iron I period. Although these small model shrines from Amathus lack the Nude Goddess, they nevertheless often enclose within the *naos* an anthropomorphic figure, either female or male. In some instances, the image within the model is more aniconic than anthropomorphic, appearing as a clay cylinder decorated with pressed-on clay dots. Culican argues that these dots are intended to represent either roses or perhaps stars, and, thus, these images are aniconic images of the "Rose Goddess" or "Queen of Heaven," to wit, Aphrodite-Kypris-Aštart.[47] As other references to aniconic images of Aphrodite and Aštart, such as the stone from Palaipaphos, are later in date by several centuries,[48] it is perhaps better to refrain from any specific identification of the deity implied with these model shrines and trends toward aniconism. However, the close associations between Amathus, the Cypriot model shrines, and Aphrodite argue in favor of an Aphrodite-Aštart identification in the Cypriot context, while the nude-goddess imagery present in the Levant would argue for associations with Aštart.

---

45. Culican 1976: 53.

46. *Ibid.*

47. *Ibid., passim.*

48. Soyez 1972: *passim.*

Ultimately, what do these data mean in relation to the iconography and persona of Aštart in the Iron Age? The use of the Nude-Goddess plaques in the Levant from the Bronze Age through the Iron Age makes a strong claim for continuity of iconography, a claim that is strengthened by the continued use of horse and lion imagery present in the north Syrian- and Phoenician-made horse adornments from north Syria and Nimrud, as well as the cult stand from Tel Ta'anach. Furthermore, the votive dedication from Seville, specifically naming the goddess, portrays this goddess as a nude female. Is it possible, then, to recognize the Iron Age goddess plaques as representations of Aštart? I would argue "yes" in spite of the fact that the sexualized nature of the iconography finds no parallels in the written sources concerning this goddess, much as was the case in the Bronze Age.

The identification of these images as Aštart receives further support from their presence in the southern regions of Israel and Judah, where the literature records the names of very few female deities, to wit Aštart (Aštoreth/ Aštaroth) and Ašerah. The Queen of Heaven, as recorded in Jeremiah quoted above, might be either of these goddesses, although Aštart's associations with Ištar, the Mesopotamian Queen of Heaven, may strengthen the argument in her favor. That these images of nude females portrayed *en face* with emphasis on the sexual characteristics and shown either grasping the breasts, or flora or fauna to either side of the body do not represent the goddess Ašerah is suggested both by the lion iconography and the frequent association with horse paraphernalia, and, possibly, by the proliferation of a different style of goddess image in Palestine during the Iron II period. These are the "pillar figurines," female figurines that have a molded head, arms grasping the breasts in long-standing Near Eastern fashion, but with the lower body cylindrical in the general shape of a pillar or column. The work of Kletter suggests that these images might represent Ašerah due to their adherence to the description of images of that goddess in the Bible.[49] If there is a possibility to distinguish between the iconographies of the two named goddesses revered in Iron Age Palestine, perhaps the non-columnar images refer to Aštart.

It is important to remain aware that this identification only applies to the Levant, including Syria, Phoenicia proper, and possibly the southern regions of Israel and Judah. Heading west, toward Cyprus and the Greek world, the matter of identification becomes increasingly more complicated. As the works of H. Kantor and S. Böhm have shown, these Aštart plaques and images become common in the Cypriot and Greek repertoires in the Late Geometric-Early Archaic Ages. However, as discussed above in Chapter Three, in the Iron Age these images are not necessarily associated with any specific god or goddess. This is especially so in the Greek world, where nude-goddess figurines appear in sanctuaries ranging from Aphrodite to Athena to Eileithyia to Zeus in Crete.

---

49. Kletter 1996: *passim.*

Although the presence of such images usually suggests the presence of a goddess cult (notably in Crete, where the only god with whom they are found is "baby" Zeus), no specific goddess can be identified in their iconography.

One other iconographic motif remains that, like the plaques, may portray the goddess Aštart, although once again the lack of written material makes this identification tentative. This image is the so-called "Smiting Goddess," a female image shown brandishing a weapon in either hand while striding forward in typical Egyptian pose. According to Negbi, only six such images have come to light from the Bronze Age, none with a clear provenance or chronology, although a tentative date of the mid-second millennium is possible.[50] Four of these figures are clothed, while the remaining two are nude, one of which, from Hauran, is also portrayed standing upon two lions. This combination of nudity and lions suggests an identification as Aštart, although this is the only example of a goddess upon a lion shown in the smiting pose, and this figurine is strongly influenced by Anatolian styles.[51]

Similar bronze images derive from Phoenician Iron Age contexts, although the exact date of some of these remain debated.[52] One such example is published by Falsone, an example datable solely by style as, once again, the provenance is unclear.[53] This figure, like the majority of the Bronze Age examples, is clothed in a long dress, visible only where it connects the striding legs at the bottom of the image. The image wears a large, Hathor-disk upon the head, and has blunt bangs and short hair. From the head protrude four (probably originally five) horns, two on either side of the head bending forward and one above the forehead curving upward. The facial features are well-wrought, and the eyes were originally inlaid. The figure holds up her right arm from the shoulder, bent 90 degrees at the elbow, and the left arm extends down along the body and bends forward from the elbow. Both fists are clenched and probably originally held weapons.[54] The waist is small, and the figure steps forward with her left leg, thus offering a counterbalance to the raised right arm. Stylistically, Falsone dates this statuette to the eighth century BCE.[55]

On the basis of style, it is possible that this image represents Baalat Gubal, the city goddess of Byblos, who is strongly identified with both Hathor and Isis in the Egyptian pantheon.[56] That one of the possible Iron Age statuettes comes from Byblos would certainly support this argument and, thus, in this

---

50. Negbi 1976: 84–86.

51. *Ibid.*, 84.

52. Falsone 1986: 68.

53. *Ibid.*, 53.

54. *Ibid.*, 55.

55. *Ibid.*, 75.

56. Bonnet 1996: 20–22.

context, it might be prudent to identify the image here as Baalat Gubal.[57] However, two other examples attributable to the Iron Age come from both Palestine (Tel Dan) and Phoenicia proper (Qal'at Faqra) and, thus, offer evidence that a deity beyond just the city goddess of Byblos is represented, at least in other contexts.[58] The prominence of Aštart in Phoenicia during the eighth century and her identification as a war-goddess as per the written testimonia in both the Bronze and Iron Ages suggest that the smiting goddess might in some instances represent the goddess Aštart.

In conclusion, Iron Age Aštart is in most ways identical to her Bronze Age counterpart. From the inscriptional evidence she is a goddess concerned with justice and the preservation of the royal family; she protects the dead; and, like Išhara, guards the oaths of kings, using her influence in battle to punish the wrong-doer. In many respects she is like Ištar. As with her Bronze Age counterpart, only the iconography of Iron Age Aštart hints at sexual nature, being portrayed as a nude female both on terra-cotta plaques and on one inscribed bronze votive statue. The discontinuity between the literary portrayal of the goddess and her iconographic portrayal is, probably, due primarily to continuity between Ištar/Išhara and Aštart iconography in the LBA, and continuity between Bronze Age and Iron Age portrayals of this goddess. Thus, Aštart, as the western equivalent of Ištar, took part in Syrian Ištar's iconography. This rather awkward iconography then remained in continual use.

It is important to note how strong the differences are between Phoenician Aštart and Greek Aphrodite. As discussed in Chapter Two, Aphrodite is primarily a goddess of love and sex; Aštart is a goddess associated with justice and royalty; her erotic iconography is quite difficult to explain in light of her literary portrayals. To suggest that the Greeks adopted the Phoenician goddess and turned her into Aphrodite is not methodologically sound, as, apart from gender, these two goddesses had little to do with one another. Thus, for reasons of chronology and spread of cult as mentioned above, and the fact that Phoenician Aštart is simply not a good cognate for Greek Aphrodite, one must accept the fact that the Phoenician hypothesis is not viable.

This does, however, leave the question of how the two goddesses came to be associated with each other in the first place. Other than in iconography, Aštart is far closer in persona to either Athena or Hera.[59] Why was she seen as the eastern Aphrodite? The answer to this question lies in the relationship both goddesses had with the island of Cyprus.

---

57. Falsone 1986: 68.

58. *Ibid.*, 67.

59. At the Etruscan site of Pyrgi, Aštart is, in fact, equated with Uni/Juno. See Colonna 1984–85: *passim* for information about the sanctuaries and the discovery of the gold-leaf inscriptions. For a translation of and commentary on the Phoenician inscription (KAI 277), see Bonnet 1996: 120–25, 161; Peckham 1987: 87.

Aštart Arrives in Cyprus: Kition[60]

It was in the tenth century when Cyprus, and the Aegean as well, came once again under explicit Levantine influence. [61] In Cyprus, Phoenicians settled Kition in approximately 850 BCE, rebuilding the city deserted for over a century and dedicating the newly reconstructed Temple 1 to their main deity: Aštart.[62] That they were, in fact, inhabitants of Tyre, or possibly from both Tyre and Sidon, is evident in an eight-line inscription dating to the Archaic Age discovered in Sardinia and known as the Nora inscription:[63]

> Temple of the cape of Nogar, which is in Sardinia. May it be prosperous! May Tyre, the mother of Kition, be prosperous! Construction that constructed Nogar in the honor of Pumay!

Both literary and archaeological evidence offer various dates for the foundation of the Phoenician settlement at Kition. The literary evidence dates the settlement to the very beginnings of the Iron Age, when the Greek foundation myths of Cyprus claim that Kition was founded by King Belos, king of the Sidonians, who, likewise, assisted the Achaean king Teukros to take possession of Salamis.[64] As such, Kition would have been inhabited by Sidonians (or perhaps a combination of Sidonians and Tyrians) after the fall of Troy.

A somewhat later date is offered by Menander, who says that Hiram I, king of Tyre, at the beginning of his reign, "undertook a campaign against the Itykaians, who had not paid their tribute, and when he had again made them subject to him, returned home" (*Ant.* VIII, 146).[65] If this is the case, then Kition (the understood identification of "Itykaians") must have been under the authority of Hiram's father Abibaal during the tenth century BCE.[66]

The archaeological evidence lowers the date of the Phoenician settlement a bit further. The earliest style of pottery found in quantities suggesting a new

60. The following sections are in no way intended to examine, *in toto*, the cults of either Aštart or Aphrodite in Cyprus, but, rather, simply offer an explanation as to how these two goddesses may have come to be associated. Anja Ulbrich of the University of Heidelberg is currently undertaking a full examination of the cults of Aštart and Anat in Iron Age Cyprus.

61. According to both Bikai and Karageorghis, Phoenician settlement of Cyprus began as early as the eleventh century BCE, as per the wide-scale presence of Phoenician pottery at the cemetery of Palaipaphos-*Skales*. Karageorghis 1983: *passim*; Bikai 1994: 31. By both literary and archaeological evidence, the first actual Phoenician colony in Cyprus was Kition.

62. Karageorghis 1976: Chapter Five.

63. Translation based on Dupont-Sommer 1974: 83.

64. Karageorghis 1976: 95.

65. Katzenstein 1973: 84.

66. Karageorghis 1988: 152.

population at Kition is red-slip I ware, a style diagnostic of the mid-ninth century.[67] Much of this pottery was discovered within the reconstructed temple overlying the remains of the Bronze Age Temple 1 in Kition's Area 2.

Approximately one hundred fifty years separate the final years of the Cypriot sanctuaries in Kition from their Phoenician reconstructions, a period that is represented in the archaeological record by a thick layer of alluvial deposit at the site.[68] The new Phoenician temple was constructed entirely on top of the previous Temple 1, making use of the ashlar foundations, while the constructors piously removed the older votives and placed them in *bothroi* outside of the new temple.

The chronology, the founders, and the deity of this new temple are supported by an inscription discovered in the temple on a shard of red-slip ware. The orthography of the inscription is Phoenician and dates, according to Dupont-Sommer, to sometime between 850 and 800 BCE.[69] The shard was found in a context preceding the burning and rebuilding of the temple in 800 BCE, thus confirming this hypothesis. The inscription reads:[70]

> [In me]morium. Moula shaved this hair (from his head), and he invok[ed the Lady Aš]tart, and Aš[tart heard his voice. And he offered (as a sacrifice): for Moula, a sheep and a l[amb with] this hair; for the household of Moula, a sheep. [This] recipient [here], Moula completed with [this] hair seven times, because of the vo[w] of Tamassos.

Apparently Moula is taking part in a ritual whereby the hair of the dedicant is offered to the goddess, either in fulfillment of a vow, as it would appear above, or during a liminal point in life, such as preceding marriage. This was an established practice in the Phoenician cult of Aštart, for it is described in two other documents of the Classical Age.

The first of these is an inscription dating to 400–350 BCE on alabaster written in black ink discovered on the Bamboula hill. On the top of side A is written "TKLT," interpreted by Masson-Sznycer and Delcor as "total (of expenses)," thus referring to the personnel on the payroll of the temple of Aštart in Kition—the goddess who is mentioned throughout the various listings.[71] Line 12 on side A of the list records the "GLBM," the barbers of the temple.[72] Both Delcor and Dupont-Sommer identify these as those barbers who cut the token locks of hair to be dedicated to the goddess.[73]

---

67. Karageorghis 1976: 95.

68. Karageorghis 1973a: 20.

69. Dupont-Sommer 1974: 90–94; Guzzo Amadasi and Karageorghis 1977: 149: D 21.

70. Translation based on Dupont-Sommer 1974: 91; Peckham 1987: 85.

71. Delcor 1979: 148.

72. *Ibid.*, 156.

73. *Ibid*; Dupont-Sommer 1974: 92

A further bit of evidence comes from Lucian of Samosata of the second century CE, who in his work *De Dea Syria*, section VI, notes a ritual whereby:[74]

> They (the inhabitants of Byblos) shave their heads as do the Egyptians at the
> death of Apis. The women who refuse to cut their hair are punished in the
> following manner: They set their beauty out for an entire day, at a market
> only open to foreigners, and the money for these women is brought as an
> offering to Aphrodite.

This evidence is more remote concerning the cult of Aštart in Kition, both in
time and place. It does, however, link the dedication of hair to a sacred practice involving the goddess Aštart (referred to as Aphrodite by the Classical
authors).[75]

The historical events occurring in Phoenicia at the time of the foundation
of the settlement at Kition also suggest that the principle temple of Kition was
dedicated to Aštart. Between the years 887 and 856 BCE, the temporarily unit-
ed cities of Tyre and Sidon were under the authority of King Ethbaal, who
established the supremacy of the cult of Aštart during his reign, having himself
been her high priest before his kingship.[76] This practice, whereby secular
kings were also the (high) priests of Aštart, continues into the Classical Era,
as is evident in the inscription recorded on the fifth-century sarcophagus of
King Tabnit I of Sidon, mentioned above.

Both the inscription of Moula and the shard upon which it was written
show that Kition and its chief temple were erected no later than the middle
of the ninth century BCE. It is logical that the city deity of a new Phoenician
outpost would be the chief deity of the mother city, Ethbaal's Aštart, as is
recorded in Moula's dedicatory inscription.

While the Phoenicians had their original stronghold on the island of
Cyprus at Kition, over the centuries they spread out to have considerable
influence over the entire island. As early as the ninth and eighth centuries BCE
they had reached the mining districts of Meniko in the center of the island.[77]
Between 950 and 750 BCE the *Skales* tomb complex brought forth gold
répoussée plaques decorated with Aštart- and Hathor-style figures.[78] Likewise, a stele of mid-seventh-century Phoenician manufacture was discovered
at Pyla, northeast of Kition.[79] Eventually, Phoenician products and elements
of Phoenician culture and religion covered the entire island.[80]

---

74. *Ibid*; Lipinski 1995: 96. See Appendix B 9.2.

75. Herrmann 1969: *passim*.

76. Karageorghis in Moscati 1988: 155.

77. Karageorghis 1988: 161–62.

78. Maier and Karageorghis 1984: 149.

79. Karageorghis 1988: 161.

80. *Ibid.*, 153.

Aštart Meets the Paphian: Amathus

One of the more important sites of Phoenician settlement and influence for this study is the ancient city of Amathus, which in Roman times was considered to be, along with Paphos, one of the most important Aphrodite sanctuaries in the Roman world.[81] Amathus is especially interesting for the study of the origins of Aphrodite as it is here that the Phoenicians came into contact with an Eteo-Cypriot population still in control of the area, and one might imagine that it was here that a Cypriot cult occurred side-by-side with the Phoenician. It is unfortunate that the archaeological data are limited by the presence of a Roman sanctuary and a Christian basilica over the remains of the Archaic sanctuary.[82]

According to the mythical tradition handed down through Theopompos, Amathus was founded by King Kinyras of Paphos when he was driven from Paphos by the arrival of the Achaeans lead by Agapenor of Tegea returning from Troy. He and his followers, moving eastward, established the kingdom of Amathus and re-instituted the cult of the Paphian goddess there. The first half of this tale is partly supported by the archaeological evidence, which shows no Bronze Age settlement at the site.[83] Only one red polished I vase from the Early Bronze Age was discovered in a grave of the Cypro-Geometric period. Furthermore, the site is not mentioned in the list of city names of Cyprus in the Medinet Habu inscription of c. 1186 BCE, which mentions no cities between Kourion and Kition.[84]

Human occupation at the site is evident only from the eleventh century BCE.[85] At this date a small ceramic deposit was buried in a pit near the ancient palace, and it is also the possible date of a grave on the city acropolis that later tradition attributes to Ariadne.[86] The style of this tomb, a shaft dug into rock and covered with slabs, is typical of earlier periods in Cypriot funerary architecture. Both this tomb and the area of the sanctuary of Aphrodite produced stone gaming *cupulae* prevalent in Cyprus during the Bronze Age. This, com-

---

81. Hermary 1993: 180.

82. *Ibid.*, 181.

83. Aupert 1985: 230. "En ce qui concerne la chronologie du site, nos recherches ont rélévé une première occupation à l'époque néolithique, suivie d'une apparement longue période d'abandon: quelques objets de l'Age du Bronze, dont deux seulement ont été trouvés en fouille dans des tombes de date ultérieure, ne suffisent pas à attester l'existence d'un établissement à cette époque." See also Hermary 1993: 171.

84. Aupert 1997: 19.

85. Hermary 1987: 376.

86. Aupert 1997: 19. Contrary to the evidence of this tradition, there does not appear to have been any pronounced Minoan presence at Amathus as discernible in the ceramic repertoire.

bined with the lack of Mycenaean wares at Amathus, argues that the population was, as per the mythical tradition, Eteo-Cypriot.[87] This possibility is further strengthened by the fact that, up until the fourth century BCE, the city
used two official languages, Greek and an undeciphered language known as
Eteocypriot.[88] Although Aegean-style spits and knives were found among the
funerary remains of the city as early as 1050, the Aegean element at Amathus
never grew in prominence as it did at Paphos and Salamis, and the city
remained essentially "native" at least until the eighth century.[89]

It is difficult to determine through archaeology whether a cult of Paphia
was established at this early period, for the site of the later temple, located on
the city acropolis, shows no remains older than the eighth century.[90] If the
Cypriots under King Kinyras did establish a cult to the Paphian at Amathus,
either they did so with no archaeologically visible sanctuary, or the location
of their cult site is, as yet, undetermined. Aupert suggests that the Amathu-
sians continued the cults of Bronze Age Cyprus, worshipping a male horned
god and the female deity adored at Paphos, which would accord well with the
foundation myth. Evidence for the Horned God lies in scraps of later evidence:
small sculptures of priests wearing bull masks and the tale related by Ovid of
the Cerast legend, wherein Aphrodite turned horned monsters into bulls.[91]
Evidence for the goddess lies in the presence of several goddess-with-
upraised-arms found in the ancient tombs of the city, as well as the above-men-
tioned tale.[92]

In the eighth century, Amathus becomes a grand city, and this is when the
earliest traces of a sanctuary appear on the city acropolis.[93] The question
remains whether or not either or both of these events are due to the Phoenicians. According to Aupert, during this century the Phoenicians were also
present and active establishing a city alongside the Eteo-Cypriots. The very
ancient Phoenician inscriptions from Moutti Sinoas, a hill summit 10 km north
of the settlement, attests to a Semitic cult here.[94] The Phoenician influence on

87. Hermary 1987: 376–77; Aupert 1997: 20–21.

88. Aupert 1997: 21–22.

89. *Ibid.*, 23. As per the discussions of East–West trade in the early Iron Age mentioned
     above, Amathus is understood as a main port-of-call between the Aegean and Phoe-
     nicia, visible in the high number of Euboian, then Attic, ceramics at the site. In spite
     of this, it appears to have retained its indigenous culture longer than the rest of the
     island.

90. Hermary 1987: 376–77.

91. Aupert 1997: 23.

92. *Ibid.*

93. Hermary 1987: 378–79.

94. Aupert 1997: 24.

the city is supported also by the ceramic assemblage of the eighth and seventh centuries, when the graves at Amathus show a high proportion of Phoenician pottery among their goods. Furthermore, the ceramics from the votive remains of the eighth-century sanctuary show either an origin or a strong inspiration from the Near East.[95] Notable among the latter of these are terra-cotta goddess images, similar in iconography to the goddess plaques of the Levant. Two of these, now in Limassol, are votive figurines showing the upper half (the remains are broken) of a female whose hands curve into the body to support the breasts.[96] One is mold-made, the other hand-rendered. Neither of them show the hair-styles typical of the Phoenician images of this period, and, as such one might suggest that they are of Cypriot manufacture. However, beyond the positioning of the arms, they show no affinities to either the bird-faced or normal-faced images of the Cypriot Bronze Age, and, thus, considering their chronology, they may be seen as purely Phoenician in inspiration.

If we are to understand that the cult of Amathus arrived with the earliest, Eteo-Cypriot settlers, then we must recognize that a pre-Phoenician, arguably Paphian, goddess was worshipped in the city as early as the eleventh century BCE. With the arrival of the Phoenicians in the eighth century, the city expanded. Expansion was the result of either Phoenician influence or, perhaps, the revenues that the Phoenicians brought with them, which led to the construction of the earliest known sanctuary to the goddess, eventually Aphrodite, at Amathus. It appears at least probable that the cult of this goddess was originally practiced by both populations of Amathus, Eteo-Cypriot and Phoenician, to judge from the prevalence of both goddess-with-upraised-arms and Aštart-plaque votives at the sanctuary. One "Goddess of Cyprus" was simultaneously identified as the Paphian, Aštart, and eventually by the Greek settlers as Aphrodite. It is this syncretism, the commonality of the cult of Cyprus, and not a common erotic persona, to which one might attribute the original identification of Aphrodite with Aštart: Aphrodite = Paphia = Goddess of Cyprus =Aštart.

Aštart "Becomes" Aphrodite

PHOENICIAN INFLUENCE IN IRON AGE CYPRIOT ICONOGRAPHY

Even though the Phoenicians never did exert extensive political control over Cyprus, their presence from the ninth century did have a profound influence on the arts of the island, most critically in the Cypriot goddess iconography, as, once again, the Near Eastern iconography made itself manifest in the religion of Cyprus.

---

95. Hermary 1987: 380.

96. *Ibid.*, Figures 2 and 3.

From this renewed Levantine influence beginning in 850–750 (Cypro-Geometric III), a new goddess iconography appears in Cyprus, replacing the purely occidentalized style of the previous two centuries. This new iconography is manifest both in terra-cotta figurines (such as those just mentioned at Amathus) and in gold/gold-foil images of the Cypriot goddess. As J. Karageorghis noted, these images are not exclusively Levantine in their iconography, but rather a mixture of Levantine, Cypriot, and Aegean styles.[97] They mix the nudity typical of the Levantine iconography with the upraised arms of the Cretan style and the jewelry and facial characteristics prevalent in Cyprus since the Chalcolithic Age.

One such example of this new style is a terra-cotta plaque from Famagousta, currently in the Louvre (see fig. 9e).[98] Here, on a plaque with strong parallels to Levantine versions,[99] is a nude-female figure in high relief. The

Fig. 9e
Famagousta fixture.
Hajiprodromou Collection.

---

97. Karageorghis 1977: Chapter Seven.

98. Caubet and Yon 1974: *passim*.

99. *Ibid.*, 120ff.

top of her head is rendered flat, as though she is wearing a *polos*. The face is painted, with the brows coming together and leading into the prominent nose, while the eyes are only slightly visible. Around her neck is a painted line indicating a simple necklace. The breasts are slight and molded, and the arms extend up from the shoulders to the head, where the hands touch the *polos*. Painted lines on either shoulder probably indicate further jewelry. The navel is indicated by a painted rosette pattern, and the pubic triangle is also painted. There is one painted swastika on either thigh, the knees are decorated with painted circles, and the ankles are also adorned with painted lines.

The full frontal, nude characteristics of the image are strongly Syrian in character, especially the careful delineation of the genitalia and the navel. The position of the arms recalls the upraised posture of the Minoan-style figurines both in Crete and Cyprus. The painted decoration on the neck and arms shows the same emphasis on jewelry, especially the necklace, of traditional Cypriot female figurines.

A similar image appears in gold foil from a tomb at Lapithos (see fig. 9f). Here, once again, is a female figure *en face* and completely nude. The top of her head is surmounted by a *polos*, while her arms, bent at the elbows, are held up vertically on either side of her head as with the traditional goddess-with-upraised-arms of the previous periods. Her breasts are molded, and the pubic triangle is rendered in faintly incised lines. A deep groove separates the legs, and the feet are pointed sideways.

Fig. 9f
Gold foil image from Lapithos.
Cyprus Museum, Inv. 403/40.

Fig. 9g
Incense box.
Metropolitan Museum of Art. 74.51.5163

A final, and especially interesting example, from Cypro-Geometric III, is a limestone box decorated at either end with low-relief images of a nude goddess-with-upraised-arms from Kythrea (see fig. 9g).[100] These female images show, yet again, the amalgamous iconography of the Cypro-Geometric III style. The hair is stylized (although not really flat enough to be identified as a *polos*), and the facial features are beautifully rendered with closed eyes and small mouth. The arms, extending out from the shoulders and bending at right angles at the elbows, rise vertically on either side of the head. Two incised lines around the neck indicate one or two necklaces. The breasts are molded dots; the navel is incised, as is the pubic triangle. The legs, fully molded, are separated, and the feet are well-formed, and even have incised toes.

This style of box continues through the Cypro-Archaic period, and is especially noteworthy for its associations with the cult of Aphrodite. According to Myres, some broken fragments from boxes with similar dimensions and overall style were discovered bearing inscriptions in Syllabo-Cypriot. As the pieces were uniformly burnt, Myres surmised that they may have functioned as incense-burners.[101] On two of these the inscriptions are still legible, while the remainder are reconstructed:

---

100. Karageorghis 1977: 153.

101. Myres 1914: 304.

#1831: "I am (the gift) of Prototimos, the priest of the Paphian; and he offered me to Paphian Aphrodite."

#1832: "I belong to the Paphian, and Onasithemis dedicated me."

#1834–42: "I belong to the Paphian."[102]

The boxes come primarily from Kythrea and Tamassos, both of which were famous in antiquity for their sanctuaries of Paphian Aphrodite.[103] The close association of these boxes with cult places of Aphrodite, her name as receiver of the dedication on the boxes, and the possible use of these boxes in sacred practice (i.e., incense burners) all suggest that the boxes were closely linked to the cult of that goddess at least in the Archaic Age, although the general continuity of cult on Cyprus argues that even the earliest Cypro-Geometric III boxes were associated with her. It would appear that these nude female images are closely linked with the Paphian goddess, shown to be Aphrodite in the previous chapter, and are possibly even intended to be images of that goddess.

From 850, and continuing into the Cypriot Archaic Age, the goddess iconography of Cyprus once again shows strongly orientalizing features due to the influx of a Levantine population. The explicit sexuality that was the dominant characteristic in the Late Cypriot Bronze Age and the Phoenician Iron Age emerges once again at precisely the time when it would appear that the Paphian goddess is brought fully into the Greek consciousness and imagination. This offers an explanation as to why the later Greeks, such as Herodotos, believed this goddess to be Phoenician in origin, either as a manifestation of Aštart or even Ištar/Mylitta from Babylon. Seeing a similar iconography for the Paphian among the Phoenicians, who appeared to worship this goddess as the "goddess of Cyprus," lead understandably to a Greek (mis-)conception that the Phoenician goddess of Cyprus and the Greek goddess of Cyprus were one and the same, that they were identical deities, and that the one derived from the other.

---

102. *Ibid.*

103. Karageorghis 1977: 153.

X.
APHRODITE BECOMES GREEK

The ancient Greeks clearly thought of Aphrodite as eastern, and the farther east their contacts reached, the more oriental Aphrodite became. In the days of Homer and Hesiod she was thought to be Cypriot.[1] For Herodotos, she was more Phoenician in origin, her cult traveling from Ashkalon to Cyprus before heading farther west.[2] Later, for Pausanias, Aphrodite Ourania was considered to have been originally worshipped by the Assyrians, who taught her cult to the Phoenicians, who, in turn, transmitted it to the Cypriots, before it was passed on to the Greeks.[3] But Aphrodite was not an oriental goddess. She emerged slowly from Cypriot, Levantine, and Aegean influences, all left to simmer together in Cyprus for centuries during the Dark Ages before finally emerging and establishing her cult in the Greek world. Aphrodite was Cypriot.[4]

Overview of the Developmental Process

In the Middle and Late Bronze Ages, merchants actively traded along the coasts of the Eastern Mediterranean, exchanging goods and ideas among Cyprus, the Levant, and the neighboring regions. Evidence for such trade between Cyprus and the Levant is especially strong in Ugarit, Alalakh, and in the south at Tel el-'Ajjul and Megiddo, but it cannot be denied that the entire Levantine culture had a profound influence on Cypriot culture at this time.

---

1. *Theogony*, ll. 187-202, *Odyssey*, Bk. VIII, ll. 386-89.

2. *Histories* I.105, 2-3.

3. Pausanias I, 14, 7. If Alexander the Great had reached China who knows what might have happened! Actually, Alexander did reach as far as India, yet no attestations of Aphrodite's Indian origins have come to light in spite of the combined erotic/violent characteristics of such goddesses as Durga and Kali. The movement eastward of Aphrodite's alleged origins only go so far as the cult of Ištar. As such, although the ancient Greeks did continue to push the earliest manifestation of their goddess farther and farther to the east, this was within limits, and must most logically be explained by the perceived identification of Aphrodite with Ištar (through Aštart, no doubt) as the Greeks themselves came to find this goddess farther and farther afield.

4. An interesting note to bear in mind is the fact that the Phoenicians themselves did not automatically establish the cult of this goddess in their colonies. Consider the Phoenician settlement at Thasos, where the Phoenician cult of Melqart became the Greek cult of Herakles. The presence of Phoenicians did not necessitate the arrival of Aphrodite, or even Aštart.

From the Levant the Cypriots came into contact with different Near Eastern deities, such as Baal, El, Ašerah, Aštart, Anat, Rešef, Šapaš, Qudšu, Išḫara, and Ištar, and from the Late Cypriot Bronze Age it becomes apparent that at least some of these deities were adopted into the Cypriot pantheon. One piece of evidence for this is the Ugaritic letter mentioning "Baal, Aštart, Anat, Šapaš, and all the other gods of Alašiya." Far more profound and far-reaching, however, is the architecture and iconography that appear in Cyprus during the LC I and LC II periods. The sanctuary and temple architecture that appears at such locations as Enkomi, Kition, and Paphos is notably Near Eastern in character. What seems to be a new god appears in the Cypriot iconographic repertoire, a god wearing a kilt and a horned helmet, and who may even carry a spear and be associated with metallurgy, ingots, and animals. Likewise, a new type of goddess figurine appears simultaneously all over the island. This new iconography shows a female completely nude with strikingly prominent breasts and hips, bedecked with necklaces, earrings, and bracelets. Sometimes she carries a child; more often she does not, and by the LC III period she is no longer viewed as a *kourotrophos* at all. The figurines and feminine votives discovered at Kition and Paphos during the Late Bronze Age, and the continuity of cult observable at Paphos during the following periods, indicate that a goddess cult was prevalent at different, prominent, far-flung reaches of Cyprus by no later than LC II.

Of all the Levantine deities exposed to Cyprus, Išḫara was the most likely progenitress of Aphrodite. Išḫara was revered in Alalakh, a close trading neighbor of Cyprus. It is apparent that the bird-faced figurines that were used for a millennium at Alalakh were associated with this goddess (and, as well, her close cognate Ištar). And finally, Išḫara's character is most like that of Greek Aphrodite. Išḫara is specifically a sexual goddess, possibly even the bridal aspect of Ištar, and she is also a goddess concerned with affairs of justice and the punishment of wrong-doers.

Possibly through Alalakh, the Cypriots were exposed also to the cult of Ištar, who is, probably, the second-most likely progenitress of Aphrodite. The close associations of this goddess with sex, love, the heavens, birds/doves, and even warfare make her an excellent parallel to Aphrodite. Furthermore, the presence of this goddess, and Išḫara as well, at Alalakh gives a reasonable hypothesis as to why Greek Aphrodite did, in fact, share so many qualities with these Mesopotamian goddesses.

Furthermore, Cyprus maintained trade and contacts with several other sites in the Near East, and it would be unreasonable to suppose that iconographies from such areas as Ugarit did not have any effect or impact on the newly emerging cult in Cyprus. Ugaritic Aštart may have contributed to the Paphian, as well as Egyptian Qudšu, the "Mistresses of the Heavens." Likewise, the literature suggests certain relationships between Aphrodite and such goddesses as Ugaritic Ašerah, the "Lady of the Sea." Through iconography and persona, I suggest that Išḫara and Ištar played dominant roles in the development of the Paphian, with only minor influences from the goddesses Aštart, Ašerah, and Qudšu.

When the end of the Bronze Age fell on the Eastern Mediterranean, Mycenaeans and Minoans migrated to Cyprus and established new homes for themselves. One of the first places to be inhabited by the Mycenaeans was Paphos, one of the more prominent cult centers of a Cypriot goddess, and the continuity of architecture and votive offerings attest that the newcomers adopted the cult of the local goddess. From the Minoans the Cypriots adopted a new type of iconography, the goddess-with-upraised-arms, and it is possible that elements of the Minoan and Cypriots goddesses fused at this time, creating a goddess who was still essentially Cypriot, but familiar and recognizable to the Minoans. In the eleventh century there was considerable cultural interchange between Cyprus and Crete, and in the tenth century and beyond, relations were open between Cyprus and the entire Aegean, especially Crete. At this time, several elements of Cypriot art and style made their way into the Cretan repertoire. It is entirely probable that knowledge of this Cypriot goddess reached Crete, where she merged with the goddess of Kato Symi, thus, paving her way for acceptance into this Aegean community.

By as early as the late tenth century, and certainly by the mid-ninth century, the Phoenicians set off westward from the Levantine coast to trade and to inhabit many parts of the Mediterranean. From 850 BCE they colonized Cyprus and introduced the cult of Aštart on the island. The re-introduction of Near Eastern art and iconography eventuated the "re-sexualization" of the Cypriot goddess iconography, and the deity later known through the Syllabo-Cypriot inscriptions as "Wanassa" or "Paphia," once again appeared nude and heavily bejeweled.

As trade and relations warmed in the eastern Mediterranean, a new iconography was introduced into the sanctuary located at Kato Symi in Crete, evidenced by the dedication of one, possibly two, nude-female figurines during the Protogeometric and Geometric Ages. Sanctuaries of the Geometric/ Early Archaic period were found at Olous and Axos; inscriptions and iconography establish that these sanctuaries were dedicated in part to Aphrodite. From the early Archaic period onward, the cult of this new goddess Aphrodite spread throughout the Greek world, touching upon Kythera, Corinth, Samos, Lesbos, and Naukratis among other sites. But it was always recognized that this new goddess was essentially eastern in orientation, with her primary sanctuary at Paphos and her epithets of *Kypris* and *Paphia*.

The goddess who would, and did, become Aphrodite was a mixture of several elements: Levantine, Cypriot, Cretan, Greek, all interacting over the course of several centuries, predominantly in Cyprus. The Phoenician colonization of Cyprus, as well as the Phoenician spread throughout the Mediterranean at the beginning of the Iron II period, also had a profound influence on the persona and understanding of the Paphian. In the Iron Age and later, seeing the iconography and domain of the Phoenician Aštart, the Greeks came to associate their Cypriot goddess with the Phoenician Cypriot goddess. Aštart became the "parallel" of Aphrodite, and the Phoenicians were credited with the introduction of her cult into Greece.

The Greek Adaptation of Aphrodite's Persona

Questions remain concerning the passage of this goddess into the Greek pantheon. What qualities did the Paphian lose in her transmission from east to west? How did the Greeks Hellenize this goddess to conform to their own worldviews? What qualities endured from the earliest manifestation of the goddesses into the Classical persona? These issues can be addressed based on the known qualities of the Near Eastern goddesses who contributed to Aphrodite's final form and on the persona of Aphrodite herself. It is unfortunate that more cannot be said about the Cypriot goddess, Paphia/Wanassa, who first emerged in Cyprus at the end of the Bronze Age—we must await further advances in our understanding of Eteocypriot.

LESSENING OF MARTIAL PROWESS

The most obvious difference between Greek Aphrodite and her Levantine progenitresses (and possibly Minoan as well, considering the iconography of the "armed goddess" in Minoan glyptic) is her relation to warfare and her belligerent nature. If Aphrodite is, in fact, the western descendant of the Near Eastern goddesses of love and war, how did the Greeks, who proclaimed her to be the same goddess as Aštart, do away with the more militaristic aspects of her character?

The Greek Aphrodite did maintain some militaristic attributes: her early arms-bearing *xoana* on Kythera, Sparta, and Corinth, later repeated by Hellenistic and Roman artisans. But these images appear to have confused even the ancients: Roman school boys were asked why the statue of Aphrodite in Lakedaimonia was armed.[5] Furthermore, the later rendering of these images, most notably the one from Corinth, portrayed the goddess not bearing arms in a threatening pose, but in the nude, admiring her reflection in the inner mirror of the shield.[6] By Roman times, the nude Venus surrounded by winged Erotes "playing" with the weapons of Ares was a common artistic motif.[7] Although Aphrodite is shown armed in the Lydos dinos, the *gigantomakhy* theme militarized all the deities, and, therefore, Aphrodite is armed not due to her own persona, but due to the overall motif.

---

5. Quintilien, *Inst. Orat.*, II, 4, 26. Pirenne-Delforge 1994: 193. Flemberg 1991: *passim*.
6. Williams 1986: 15.

Turning from the iconography to a literary and anthropological perspective, Aphrodite's role in military affairs is as the creator of conflicts. Examining Greek mythology through a structuralist approach,[8] it becomes apparent that the Greek deities possess power in opposite/opposing forms. Demeter, the goddess of grain, can withhold her gift and, thus, be a goddess of famine, as in the *Homeric Hymn to Demeter*. Apollo, the god of healing, can also send plague, as in the opening lines of the *Iliad*. Dionysos, who causes drunkenness and madness, can also restore sanity—it was he who taught humans to dilute wine with water so as to avoid drunkenness. Persephone, the queen of the dead, is also the herald of springtime and new life. Artemis the Virgin is the protectress of children and women in labor, but a woman who dies a quick and painless death is said to have been struck down by the arrows of Artemis.

Aphrodite, the goddess of sex, is never portrayed as a goddess of chastity. However, as the goddess of love, she can use her powers either to inflict love or to withhold it, and thereby cause the worst wars recounted in the tales of the heroic world. For Homer in the Archaic Age, she instigated the Trojan War by causing Helen to fall in love with Paris. For Aiskhylos in the Classical era, she brought about the death of the Lemnian men by causing the Lemnian women to be repugnant to their husbands. A century later, for Euripides, she caused the death of Hippolytos by filling Phaidra with love for the hero. In Roman times, Aphrodite was (at least in terms of the literature) considered responsible for the Punic Wars through her instigation of the Trojan War, by causing Dido to fall in love with Aineas, and by giving rise to the Roman royalty through her affair with Ankhises.

Aphrodite certainly should not be labelled as a war-goddess, especially when contrasted to Athena and Hera. She did, however, play a significant role in the war ideology of ancient Greece through her ability to begin and, less frequently, end wars. Aphrodite's nature is quite dissimilar to that of the highly belligerent Ištar or of the huntress Aštart. Nevertheless, remnants of an earlier, mortal character are preserved in the literature, both concerning her early iconography and her role in the instigation of wars.

THE MORTAL-LOVER MOTIF

Whereas Aphrodite appears to have lost a martial emphasis upon her introduction into the Greek pantheon, she did acquire traits that rendered

---

7. For a general discussion of this motif, see D. Michaelides in *Engendering Aphrodite*, forthcoming.

8. Strauss 1963: *passim*.

her persona more Hellenic in character. Two of these are the motif of the goddess with a mortal lover and the motif of the goddess who conceals.

In the Greek pantheon certain goddesses typically had sexual relations with mortal men. Thus Aphrodite and Adonis, Phaëthon, and Ankhises; Eos and Tithonos; Thetis and Peleus; Kirke and Odysseus; Kalypso and Odysseus; and Demeter and Iasion all are part of a common mythological archetype.

Boedeker notes that this motif is common to the Indo-European tradition.[9] The Vedic goddesses Surya and Ushas take mortal lovers/husbands, and the Phrygian Kybele takes as her paramour the mortal Attis.[10] To the west, this motif is paralleled by Irish Macha, who marries a mortal farmer, and Welsh Rhiannon, who marries the mortal prince Pwyll. However, the goddess with mortal paramour appears also in non-Indo-European literature. Perhaps the best-known example, as noted by Boedeker, is Mesopotamian Ištar, who propositions Gilgameš, whereupon she is rebuked by Gilgameš for turning all her former mortal lovers into animals (Tablet VI, col. i).[11] In Norse mythology Freyja pines for her lost mortal husband Oðr.

Since Aphrodite stands between the Greek and Near Eastern traditions, it is fruitless to try to identify a specific tradition that spawned this trait. The Adonis myth clearly stems from Near Eastern tradition, whereas Aphrodite's tryst with Phaëthon, the son of Eos, places the affair more firmly in the realms of Indo-European lore.

THE GODDESS WHO CONCEALS

In her work *The Power of Thetis*, L. Slatkin takes the goddess with mortal lover aspect one step further, contending that the mortality of the lover (or resultant son) leads to a secondary, Indo-European motif: the goddess who conceals—a goddess who hides for his protection a mortal hero, either a lover or the mortal son of a mortal lover.[12] Thus, Aphrodite conceals both Paris and Aineas in the *Iliad*, Eos conceals Tithonos in the *Homeric Hymn to Aphrodite*, and Kalypso and Kirke conceal the hero Odysseus in the *Odyssey*.

Slatkin's assertion that this motif is Indo-European derives from her belief that it is intimately connected to the goddess-with-mortal-lover motif, which she accepts as Indo-European. I disagree with Slatkin's argument on two grounds. First, the theme of the goddess who conceals is not necessarily related to that of the goddess with mortal lover. Second, the theme is not Indo-European in origin, but Greek.

---

9. Boedeker 1974: 68ff.

10. *Ibid*.

11. *Ibid*: 64–65.

12. Slatkin 1991: 40ff.

Filling out the examples listed by Slatkin, the goddesses who conceal (mortal) heroes are: Athena, who conceals both Erikhthonios as an infant (Ion: 20–24, 260–74) and Odysseus in Skheria (*Odyssey*, VII: 17–23); Kalypso, who conceals Odysseus on Orgygia (*Odyssey*, V); Kirke, who also hides Odysseus on Aiaia (*Odyssey*, XII); Aphrodite, who conceals Paris from Menelaos (*Iliad*, III: 373–75), and Aineas (*Iliad*, V: 311–18); Persephone, who conceals Adonis in Hades (*Panyassis*, F. 25[13]); Eos, who conceals Tithonos in her palace upon his arrival at old age (*Homeric Hymn to Aphrodite* V: 218–38); and possibly even Rhea, who conceals the infant Zeus in Crete from his paidophontes father Kronos (*Theogony* 468–84). Two points to notice are that (1) the concealment may take place not only for the sake of protecting the hero, but for the sake of "kidnapping" him; and (2) the hero concealed is not necessarily the lover or child of the concealing goddess. This latter aspect is most apparent with Athena and Odysseus and Aphrodite and Paris.[14] As such, it is not practical to link this motif with that of the goddess with mortal lover.

The motif cannot be of Indo-European origin, as it does not occur in any mythology except the Greek, where it occurs with some frequency.[15] Although it would appear to present yet one more parallel between Eos and Aphrodite, it must be noted that one of the goddesses who most often is associated with this characteristic is non-Indo-European Athena. Furthermore, it is reasonable to posit that this motif began in Greece with Athena, became a *Leitmotif* of the wanderings of Odysseus, and, thus, lead to further concealments of that hero by the more clearly Indo-European goddesses in the *Odyssey*. It is meaningful in determining the origin as non-Indo-European that both Persephone and Aphrodite share in this characteristic, and that it is specifically Adonis whom Persephone hides almost draws the motif back into the realm of the Near East. The goddess-who-conceals motif, therefore, should not be considered Indo-European, but Greek, where it is applied to several goddesses regardless of origin, including Aphrodite.

---

13. Detienne 1994: 2.

14. One could make the rather tortuous argument that, as Friedrich argues, Helen, as well as Aphrodite, derives from the Indo-European dawn-goddess. Thus, Aphrodite saves Paris, who is the lover of Aphrodite's alternate manifestation as dawn-goddess in the Greek pantheon. This puts considerable stress on Ockham's razor, especially in light of the arguments against Aphrodite's derivation from the Indo-European dawn-goddess already presented throughout this work.

15. Three apparently similar motifs appear in the Arthurian legends: (1) Vivian's concealing Lancelot; (2) Elain's concealing Galahad; and (3) Morgana's hiding Mordred. However, as these legends are all quite late, even for the Arthurian cycle, they cannot be used as evidence for the goddess-who-conceals motif in the Celtic repertoire.

NON-FERTILITY-ORIENTED SEX

More difficult questions are: When did the concept of non-fertility-oriented sex come into being, and how did Aphrodite come to be the patroness of that form of sexuality? Was this a distinctively Greek trait or did the perceived distinction between maternity and sexuality occur even before the Hellenization of the goddess?

In contrast to the proper wife (Hera) and the proper mothers (Demeter, Thetis), Aphrodite was not involved in the "work" aspect of sexuality, i.e., producing legitimate children in a proper familial setting.[16] Rather, Aphrodite presided over the "inappropriate" aspects of sexuality: uncontrolled and misplaced desire (Phaidra), adultery (Helen), and deception (Hera and Zeus in the *Iliad*). As such, she not only controlled the power to unravel society through destruction of the legitimate family, but she focused attention on the essentially feminine nature of this power. By seeking sex outside marriage, the Greek woman had the potential to disgrace her family, to upset the political maneuverings of the *pater familias*, and to cause the paternal estate to pass on to the wrong clan through a lover and/or an illegitimate child (cf. "The Murder of Eratosthenes"). To the Greeks, Aphrodite was the ultimate embodiment of feminine destructive power through uncontrolled feminine sexuality.[17]

This may explain the starkly different roles played by Aphrodite and her earlier sisters. Although Mesopotamian literature does portray the dangerous and less savory aspects of Inanna/Ištar, she also embodies aspects of positive power, the ability to overcome the destructive forces of chaos, as in her defeat of the KUR-monster[18] her support of the "just" kings of Mesopotamia, on whom she showered peace and prosperity, and the sudden disappearance of earthly fertility upon Ištar's captivity in the netherworld. Aštart played a similar role both in the Bronze and Iron Ages. As a military goddess, she upheld the just, punished the wrong-doer, and protected the dead.

All these positive aspects were denied to Aphrodite; her powers in Greek literature were mostly limited to the mischievous, the painful, and the humbling.[19] Sappho's first poem expresses the pain wrought by her unrequited love and asks Aphrodite to inflict a similar pain on the objects of the poet's affections. In *Homeric Hymn V*, Aphrodite laughs at the gods whom she caused to "mingle in love" with mortal women; she is forced to stop only

16. Carson 1990: 149–53.

17. Carson 1990: *passim*; Demand 1994: *passim*.

18. See Bruschweiler 1985: *passim*.

19. This is not to suggest that Aphrodite herself was portrayed as necessarily evil or humbled. Her two great humiliations in the literature are *Homeric Hymn V* and the *Song of Demodokos*. Otherwise, especially in the songs of Sappho, she appears as a

when Zeus uses her own powers against her, causing her to put a mortal child under her belt. For Homer, it is Aphrodite who must aid the queen of the gods in seducing Zeus in order place a sleeping spell upon him. The list of wars and victims claimed by the power of Aphrodite have already been noted. To maintain order in the cosmos, Aphrodite had to be portrayed as subordinate, either to Hera in the *Iliad*, to Zeus in *Homeric Hymn* V, or to her husband (almost) in the *Song of Demodokos*.

The dichotomy of maternity and sexuality may also be seen in the Near Eastern goddesses.[20] Inanna is highly sexual,[21] and yet she is not portrayed as a mother-goddess. Išhara is specifically portrayed as a goddess of sex, and yet she is never described as having children. It is entirely possible that this eroticism *sans enfants* is not necessarily a specifically Greek characteristic (although the negativity associated with it appears to be), but perhaps a trait that appeared in the Paphian from Late Bronze Age times through contact with the Levant, and was preserved through Aphrodite's induction into the Greek pantheon.[22]

Conclusion

Aphrodite was "Hellenized"; she became for the Greeks a divinity who existed in accordance (for the most part) with their worldview. The goddess lost much of her martial character in her transition from Levant to Cyprus to Crete and, finally, to Greece. However, certain aspects of her earlier persona lingered long enough to confuse even the Romans. The motif of the goddess with a mortal lover is found in the Near East and Greece. Regardless of whether the goddess acquired this aspect of her character from the one or the other, it does set her on common ground with many other goddess of the Greek pantheon. Likewise, Aphrodite, as did Athena, Kalypso, Persephone, and Rhea (among others), assumed the characteristic of the goddess who conceals, a distinctively Greek characteristic. The disassociation of maternity and sexuality visible in Aphrodite certainly is well in accord with

---

glorious, beautiful, divine being, trailing beauty in her wake. The aspects of pain and humiliation are inflicted by her, not aspects of her own persona.

20. Bahrani 1996: 7–13; Budin in "Creating a Goddess of Sex." In the "Engendering Aphrodite" publication, forthcoming.

21. Note Inanna/Ištar's association with prostitution and, in particular, Ištar's amazing sexual stamina in *Ištar Will Not Tire* (B. Foster, *Before the Muses*, Vol. II, p. 584).

22. Friedrich suggests that the separation of the erotic from the maternal is not specific to any culture, but is an ingrained development of the human psyche, an acquired mechanism against incest and an inevitable reaction against the Oedipal conflict, whereby the individual cannot associate a mother (or father) figure with sexual accessibility. Friedrich 1978: 190ff.

the perceived understanding of these concepts as presented in ancient Greek literature and cult practice, and, thus, might be understood as a further Hellenization of the goddess. However, this same dichotomy also occurs in the Near East, and, thus, it just as likely that this aspect of Aphrodite was with the goddess from the beginning, translating from Near Eastern through Cypriot to Greek.

We certainly cannot say that the goddess was entirely feared or not welcomed in ancient Greece. Certainly Mimnermos remembered her more pleasant attributes, and Sappho welcomed the goddess from Crete amid great rejoicing. There is ambiguity in the Greek portrayal of Aphrodite, just as, for the Greeks, there was perceived ambiguity concerning the origins of this goddess and her arrival into Greece. Some believed her to be Cypriot, others Phoenician. In the end, to a certain extent, all were correct. She was a goddess originally from Syria and the Levant, brought to Cyprus, where she absorbed not only the "local flavor," but elements of Minoan and, eventually, Iron Age Phoenician iconography as well. So created, she came to the Aegean by way of Crete, where she Hellenized into the Greek goddess of love and sex.

APPENDIX A

DEITIES IN THE LINEAR B TEXTS

Name:	*Region where named:*[1]	*Tablet Number(s):*
Ares	Knossos, Pylos	Fp 14.2[2]
Artemis	Pylos	Es 650, PY Un11[3]
Athena	Knossos	V 52.1[4]
Demeter	Pylos (?)	En 02 (?)[5]
Dione	Pylos	Kn 02 [Tn316][6]
Dionysos	Pylos, Khania	Xa 06,[7] Gq5[8]
Drimios	Pylos	Kn 02 [Tn316][9]
Eileithyia	Knossos	Gg 705.1, Od 714-15[10]
Enyalios	Knossos	V 52.2[11]
Erinys	Knossos	Fh 390, Fp 1.8, V 52[12]
Hephaistos	Knossos	KN L 588[13]
Hera	Pylos, Thebes	Kn 02 [Tn316][14]
Hermes	Pylos, Thebes, Knossos	KN D311; PY Nn1357, Tn316, Un219; THOf31[15]
Iphemedeia	Pylos	Kn 02 [Tn316][16]
Manasa	Pylos	Kn 02 [Tn316][17]
Marineus	Knossos, Thebes	X 508, Gg 713[18]
Pade	Knossos	Fp 1.4, 48.2, Fs 8.B, Ga 456.1, 953.2[19]
Paiwon	Knossos	V 52.2, C 394[20]

1. Hägg 1997: 165.
2. Hiller 1997: 211.
3. Ventris and Chadwick 1958: 127.
4. Hiller 1997: 211.
5. Ventris and Chadwick 1958: 127.
6. *Ibid.*, 286-87.
7. *Ibid.*, 127.
8. Hallager and Vlasaki 1997: 171.
9. Ventris and Chadwick 1958: 286-87.
10. Hiller 1997: 211.
11. *Ibid.*
12. Hiller 1997: 211.
13. Ventris and Chadwick 1958: 127.
14. *Ibid.*, 286-87.
15. Nosch 2000: 211.
16. Ventris and Chadwick 1958: 286-89.
17. *Ibid.*
18. Palmer 1979: *passim.*
19. Hiller 1997: 211.
20. *Ibid.*

Peleia	Pylos	Kn 02 [Tn316][21]
Pipituna	Knossos	Fp 13.1[22]
Posidaeia	Pylos	Kn 02 [Tn316][23]
Poseidon	Knossos, Pylos	V52.2, X5560,[24] Kn 02 [Tn316][25]
Potnia Asiwa	Pylos	PY 1206[26]
P. Dapuritojo	Knossos	Gg 702.2, Oa 745.2[27]
Potnia Iqcja	Pylos	AN 1281[28]
P. Newopeo	Pylos	Cc 665[29]
Potnia Sito	Mycenae	MY Oi 701.3[30]
Qerasija	Knossos	Fh 5475, Fp1.6; 5.1; 6.2; 13.2; 14.2; 16.2; 48.2[31]
Trisheros	Pylos	PY Fr 1204, Tn 316.5[32]
Zeus	Knossos, Pylos, Khania	Fp 1.2, Fs 51.2, E 842.1, Fp 5,[33] Kn 02 [Tn316],[34] KH Gq 5[35]

21. Ventris and Chadwick 1958: 286-87.
22. Hiller 1997: 211
23. Ventris and Chadwick 1958: 286-87.
24. Hiller 1997: 211
25. Ventris and Chadwick 1958: 286-87.
26. Chadwick 1957: 125ff.
27. Hiller 1997: 211
28. Palaima 1988: 75.
29. *Ibid.*, 83.
30. Melena and Olivier 1991: 88.
31. Hiller 1997: 211
32. Olivier et al. 1973: 230.
33. Hiller 1997: 211
34. Ventris and Chadwick 1958: 286-87.
35. Hallager and Vlasaki 1997: 171.

"HISTORY" OF THE GREEK GODS

Name:	Linear B?[1]	BA Iconography?[2]	Archaic Icon?	Classical Icon?	BASc?
Apollo	? (*Paiwon*)	No	Bow & Arrows	Archery, youth	X
Aphrodite	No	? (Nude Goddess)[3]	No	Swans, Nudity, Flora	X
Artemis	Yes	Yes (*Potnia Theron*)	*Potnia Theron* (Wings?)	Archery	X
Athena	Yes	Yes (Goddess w/ Spear)[4]	Spear, crest, *Aegis*, arms, owl		X
Ares	Yes	Yes (Shield God)	Warrior	Warrior	
Demeter	? (*Potnia Sito*)	Yes (Grain Goddess)	Holding Grain	Torch	X
Dione	Yes	No	No	No	
Dionysos	Yes	?(*Posei Theron*)[5]	Wine & Animals	Wine & wild things	X
Eileithyia	Yes	No	No	No	X
Erinys	Yes	No	No	No	
Hades	No	No	No	No	
Hephaistos	Yes	No	?	Lame, smith	X
Hera	Yes	? (Enthroned Goddess)	No	No	
Hermes	Yes	No	Herald	Herald, Caduceus, winged sandals and cap	X
Hestia	No	No	No	No	?
Iris	No	No	Herald	Wings	
Persephone	No	? (Flower Goddess)	Grain or Torch	Torch	X
Poseidon	Yes	No	Trident?	Trident	
Zeus	Yes	? (Smiting God)	Thunderbolt	Thunderbolt	X

In this table, the identification of the BA iconography is based upon similarities with the earliest Iron Age iconography of the deities in question. Where it would appear that a deity-type is present in the BA iconography (such as Hera), but that deity has no specific Early Archaic Age iconography, a "?" is used.

Deities with an "X" in the Bronze Age Sanctuary column have sanctuaries (which in later years are attributed to them), which have archaeological evidence dating back to the Bronze Age. However, it is possible in many of these instances that assimilation took place between an indigenous deity and a later Greek deity (notably with Zeus on Crete, Aphrodite and Hermes at Kato Symi, and perhaps Apollo Maleatas).

1. Ventris and Chadwick 1956: 125–29.
2. Bronze Age iconography: Is there iconography from the Bronze Age which would suggest this deity? The same question for both Archaic and Classical iconography. BASc indicates "Bronze Age Sanctuary."
3. There is also the possibility that the goddess-with-spear may represent an early Aphrodite-type, based on the early IA portrayals of this goddess with Ares or armed herself, and based on the literary accounts of her earliest statues being armed (Kythera, Sparta, Corinth).
4. Some would also argue that the snake-goddess should represent Athena as well. As she is not portrayed with snakes in her earliest Archaic iconography, this is not here being considered.
5. The Posei Theron of BA iconography is shown with birds. Dionysos is portrayed in Archaic art with tigers and other wild beasts. Thus the ambiguity.

EARLY GREEK SANCTUARIES AND TEMPLES (PRE-500 BCE)

Aphaia:	Aigina:	c. 600 BCE[1]
Aphrodite:	Kato Symi:	MMII ff.[2]
	Olous:	Proto- or Geometric[3]
	Corinth:	Protogeometric–7th century BCE[4]
	Argos:	end of the 7th century BCE
	Troizen:	c. 550 BCE[5]; 7th century BCE[6]
	Miletos:	7th century BCE[7]
	Taras:	7th century BCE[8]
	Axos:	Late Archaic Age[9]
	Berezan:	6th century BCE
	Istros:	6th century BCE
	Dichova (Lakonia):	6th–5th century BCE[10]
	Samos (inscription):	no later than 6th century BCE[11]
	Naukratis:	late 7th –early 6th centuries BCE[12]
	Santa Venera:	6th century BCE[13]
Apollo:	Epidauros (Maleatas):	Mycenaean[14]
	Amyklai:	10th century BCE[15]
	Thermon:	10th–8th century BCE[16]
	Eretria:	8th century BCE[17]
	Dreros:	8th century BCE[18]
	Asine (Pythaios):	pre-710 BCE[19]
	Ptoion:	7th century BCE[20]
	Phanai (Chios):	Geometric[21]
	Didyma:	Geometric[22]
	Thebes:	Geometric[23]
	Asine:	Geometric[24]

1. Bergquist 1967:55
2. Lebessi 1972: *passim*.
3. Renard 1967: 576–77.
4. Williams 1986: *passim*.
5. Bergquist 1967:55
6. Pirenne-Delforge 1994: 182 no. 70.
7. Graeve 1995: 195–203.
8. Schindler 1998: 147–48.
9. Levi 1930-31: *passim*.
10. Delivorrias 1968: 153.
11. Michel 1900: #832.
12. Coulson and Leonard 1982: 372.
13. Schindler 1998: 184ff.; Ammermann 1991: 201.

14. Desborough 1972, 283.
15. Desborough 1972: 280.
16. Coldstream 1977: 324.
17. Coldstream 1977: 321.
18. Desborough 1972: 285; Coldstream 1977: 321.
19. Coldstream 1977: 327.
20. Coldstream 1977: 328.
21. *Ibid.*
22. *Ibid.*
23. *Ibid.*
24. *Ibid.*

	Naxos:	Geometric[25]
	Naxos (Sicily):	Geometric[26]
	Volos:	Geometric[27]
	Delos:	c. 700 BCE[28]
	Delphi:	c. 600 BCE[29]
	Kalydon:	c. 600 BCE[30]
	Paros:	c. 550 BCE[31]
	Argos:	c. 500 BCE[32]
Artemis:	Sparta:	c. 700 BCE[33]; 10th century BCE[34]
	Dreros:	8th century BCE[35]
	Lousoi (Arkadia):	Geometric[36]
	Mavriki (Arkadia):	Geometric[37]
	Ephesos:	Geometric[38]
	Aulis:	Geometric[39]
	Pherai:	Geometric[40]
	Brauron:	Geometric[41]
	Delos:	c. 700 BCE[42]
	Kalydon:	c. 600 BCE[43]
	Paros:	c. 550 BCE[44]
Athena:	Athens:	Mycenaean-9th century BCE[45]
	Kameiros:	10th century BCE[46]
	Sparta:	10th century BCE[47]; 9th century BCE[48]
	Delphi:	c. 600 BCE[49]; 9th century BCE[50]
	Tegea:	Geometric[51]
	Ialysos:	Geometric[52]
	Lindos:	Geometric[53]
	Emporio:	Geometric[54]

25. *Ibid.*
26. *Ibid.*
27. *Ibid.* The cult statue that has recently come to light is the oldest so far known in Greece. This may indicate an even earlier date for the sanctuary than originally believed.
28. Bergquist 1967:55
29. *Ibid.*
30. *Ibid.*
31. *Ibid.*
32. *Ibid.*
33. Bergquist 1967:55
34. Desborough 1972: 278.
35. Desborough 1972: 285; Coldstream 1977: 321.
36. Coldstream 1977: 328.
37. *Ibid.*
38. *Ibid.*
39. *Ibid.*
40. *Ibid.*
41. *Ibid.*
42. Bergquist 1967:55
43. Bergquist 1967:55
44. Bergquist 1967:55
45. Coldstream 1977: 328
46. Desborough 1972: 278.
47. Desborough 1972: 278.
48. Coldstream 1977: 328.
49. Bergquist 1967:55
50. Desborough 1972: 279.
51. Coldstream 1977: 327-328.
52. *Ibid.*
53. *Ibid.*
54. *Ibid.*

	Miletos:	Geometric[55]
	Phokaia:	Geometric[56]
	Syracuse:	Geometric[57]
	Kieron (Philia):	Geometric[58]
	Larisa:	c. 600 BCE[59]
Demeter:	Eleusis:	Mycenaean? ff.[60]
Dionysos:	Ayia Irini:	10th century BCE[61]
Eileithyia:	Amnisos:	Minoan?- 8th century ff. BCE[62]
(Hephaistos):	Lemnos[63]	
Hera:	Argos:	c. 800 BCE[64]
	Samos:	c. 650 BCE[65]; Protogeometric[66]; 8th century BCE[67]
	Perachora (Akraia):	c. 8th century BCE[68]
	Delos:	8th century BCE[69]
	Tiryns:	750–650 BCE[70]
	Olympia:	c. 650 BCE[71]
	Solygeia[72]	
Herakles:	Thasos:	c. 500 BCE[73]
Hyakinthos:	Amyklai:	Mycenaean?[74]
Kabeiroi:	Thebes:	8th century BCE[75]
Nemesis:	Rhamnous:	c. 500 BCE[76]
Nike:	Athens:	Mycenaean?[77]
Pan:	Aspripetra Cave (Kos):	8th century BCE[78]
Poseidon:	Isthmia:	10th century BCE[79]
	Kalaureia:	c. 500 BCE[80]

55. *Ibid.*
56. *Ibid.*
57. *Ibid.*
58. *Ibid.*
59. Bergquist 1967:55
60. *Ibid.*, 328.
61. Desborough 1972: 281.
62. Coldstream 1977: 317.
63. *Ibid.*, 328.
64. Bergquist 1967:55
65. *Ibid.*
66. Desborough 1972: 280.
67. Coldstream 1977: 317.
68. *Ibid.*, 321.

69. *Ibid.*
70. *Ibid.*, 326.
71. Bergquist 1967:55
72. *Ibid.*, 328.
73. *Ibid.*, 55
74. Coldstream 1977: 328.
75. *Ibid.*
76. Bergquist 1967:55.
77. *Ibid.*
78. Coldstream 1977: 328.
79. Gebhard 1993: *passim*; Coldstream 1977: 328.
80. Bergquist 1967:55.

Zeus:	Dikte:	Minoan? ff.[81]
	Ida:	Minoan? ff.[82]
	Mt. Hymettos:	Protogeometric[83]; 9th century BCE[84]
	Dodona:	Geometric[85]
	Pherai:	Geometric[86]
	Ithome:	Geometric[87]
	Olympia:	c. 650 BCE[88]
Hero	at Sparta:	9th century BCE[89]
Unknown:	Aetos (Ithika):	10th–9th centuries BCE[90]
	Antissa:	9th century BCE[91]

81. Boardman 1961: *passim*.
82. Coldstream 1977: 328.
83. Desborough 1972: 278.
84. Coldstream 1977: 328.
85. Coldstream 1977: 328.
86. *Ibid.*

87. *Ibid.*
88. Bergquist 1967:55.
89. *Ibid.*
90. *Ibid.*
91. *Ibid.*

Appendix B
TEXT TRANSCRIPTIONS

CHAPTER I.

1.1 Homer, *Odyssey*, VIII, 360–64

τὼ δ'ἐπεὶ ἐκ δεσμοῖο λύθεν κρατεροῦ περ ἐόντος,
αὐτίκ' ἀναΐξαντε ὁ μὲν Θρήκηνδε βεβήκει,
ἡ δ'ἄρα Κύπρον ἵκανε φιλομμειδὴς 'Αφροδίτη
ἐς Πάφον, ἔνθα τέ οἱ τέμενος βωμός τε θυήεις.

1.2 Herodotos, *Histories* I.105, 3

ἔστι δὲ τοῦτο τὸ ἱρόν, ὡς ἐγὼ πυνθανόμενος εὑρίσκω, πάντων ἀρχαιότατον ἱρῶν,
ὅσα ταύτης τῆς θεοῦ· καὶ γὰρ τὸ ἐν Κύπρῳ ἱρὸν ἐνθεῦτεν ἐγένετο, ὡς αὐτοὶ
Κύπριοι λέγουσι, καὶ τὸ ἐν Κυθήροισι Φοίνικές εἰσι οἱ ἱδρυσάμενοι ἐκ ταύτης τῆς
Συρίης ἐόντες.

1.3 Pausanias 1, XIV, 7

πλησίον δὲ ἱερόν ἐστιν 'Αφροδίτης Οὐρανίας. πρώτοις δὲ ἀνθρώπων 'Ασσυρίοις
κατέστη σέβεσθαι τὴν Οὐρανίαν, μετὰ δὲ 'Ασσυρίους Κυπρίων Παφίοις καὶ
Φοινίκων τοῖς 'Ασκάλωνα ἔχουσιν ἐν τῇ Παλαστίνῃ, παρὰ δὲ Φοινίκων Κυθήριοι
μαθόντες σέβουσιν·

CHAPTER II.

2.1 Hesiod, *Theogony*, ll. 203–6

Ταύτῃ δ'ἐξ ἀρχῆς τιμὴν ἔχει ἠδὲ λέλογχε
μοῖραν ἐν ἀνθρώποισι καὶ ἀθανάτοισι θεοῖσι,
παρθενίους τ'ὀάρους μειδήματά τ'ἐξαπάτας τε
τέρψιν τε γλυκερὴν φιλότητά τε μειλιχίην τε.

2.2 Homeric Hymn V, 68–74

Ἴδην δ' ἵκανεν πολυπίδακα, μητέρα θηρῶν
Βῆ δ' ἰθὺς σταθμοῖο δι' οὔρεος· οἳ δὲ μετ' αὐτὴν
σαίνοντες πολιοί τε λύκοι χαροποί τε λέοντες,
ἄρκτοι παρδάλιές τε θοαὶ προκάδων ἀκόρητοι
ᾖσαν· Δ δ' ὁρόωσα μετὰ φρεσὶ τέρπετο θυμὸν
καὶ τοῖς ἐν στήθεσσι βάλ' ἵμερον· οἳ δ'ἅμα πάντες
σύνδυο κοιμήσαντο κατὰ σκιόεντας ἐναύλους.

2.3 Homeric Hymn V, 1-6

Μοῦσά μοι ἐννέπε ἔργα πολυχρύσου ᾿Αφροδίτης
Κύπριδος, ἥτε θεοῖσιν ἐπὶ γλυκὺν ἵμερον ὦρσε
καί τ᾿ ἐδαμάσσατο φῦλα καταθνητῶν ἀνθρώπων
οἰωνούς τε διπετέας καὶ θηρία πάντα,
ἠμὲν ὅσ᾿ ἤπειρος πολλὰ τρέφει ἠδ᾿ ὅσα πόντος·
πᾶσιν δ᾿ἔργα μέμηλεν ἐυστεφάνου Κυθερείης.

2.4 Mimnermos, frag. 1, ll. 1-3

Τίς δὲ βίος, τί δὲ τερπνὸν ἄτερ χρυσέης ᾿Αφροδίτης;
    τεθναίην, ὅτε μοι μηκέτι ταῦτα μέλοι,
κρυπταδίη φιλότης καὶ μείλιχα δῶρα καὶ εὐνή·

2.5 Sappho I

σὺ δ᾿, ὦ μάκαιρα,
μειδιαίσαισ᾿ ἀθανάτῳ προσώπῳ
ἤρε᾿ ὄττι δηὖτε πέπονθα κὤττι
δηὖτε κάλημμι,

κὤττι μοι μάλιστα θέλω γένεσθαι
μαινόλα θύμῳ· τίνα δηὖτε πείθω
ἄψ σ᾿ ἄγην ἐς Ϝὰν φιλότατα; τίς σ᾿ ὦ
Ψάπφ᾿, ἀδικήει;

καὶ γὰρ αἰ φεύγει, ταχέως διώζει·
αἰ δὲ δῶρα μὴ δέκετ᾿, ἀλλὰ δώσει·
αἰ δὲ μὴ φίλει, ταχέως φιλήσει
κωὐκ ἐθέλοισα.

ἔλθε μοι καὶ νῦν, χαλέπαν δὲ λῦσον
ἐκ μερίμναν, ὄσσα δέ μοι τέλεσσαι
θῦμος ἰμέρρει, τέλεσον· σὺ δ᾿αὔτα
σύμμαχος ἔσσο.

2.6 Aeschylus, *Eumenides* ll. 215-18

Κύπρις δ᾿ ἄτιμος τῷδ᾿ ἀπέρριπται λόγῳ,
ὅθεν βροτοῖσι γίγνεται τὰ φίλτατα.
εὐνὴ γὰρ ἀνδρὶ καὶ γυναικὶ μόρσιμος
ὅρκου 'στὶ μείζων τῇ δίκῃ φρουρουμένη.

2.7 Homeric Hymn V, 34-40

τῶν δ᾿ἄλλων οὐ πέρ τι πεφυγμένον ἔστ᾿ ᾿Αφροδίτην
οὔτε θεῶν μακάρων οὔτε θνητῶν ἀνθρώπων.
καί τε παρὲκ Ζηνὸς νόον ἤγαγε τερπικεραύνου,
ὅστε μέγιστός τ᾿ἐστὶ μεγίστης τ᾿ἔμμορε τιμῆς.

καί τε τοῦ, εὖτ'ἐθέλοι, πυκινὰς φρένας ἐξαπαφοῦσα
ρηιδίως συνέμιξε καταθνητῇσι γυναιξίν,
Ἥρης ἐκλελαθοῦσα, κασιγνήτης ἀλόχου τε,

2.8 Sophokles, frag. 941

ὦ παῖδες, ἤ τοι Κύπρις οὐ Κύπρις μόνον,
ἀλλ' ἐστὶ πολλῶν ὀνομάτων ἐπώνυμος.
ἔστιν μὲν Ἅιδης, ἔστι δ'ἄφθιτος βίος,
ἔστιν δὲ λύσσα μανιάς, ἔστι δ' ἵμερος
ἄκρατος, ἔστ' οἰμωγμός. ἐν κείνῃ τὸ πᾶν
σπουδαῖον, ἡσυχαῖον, ἐς βίαν ἄγον.
ἐντήκεται γάρ πλευμόνων ὅσοις ἔνι
ψυχή· τίς οὐχὶ τῆσδε τῆς θεοῦ βορός;
εἰσέρχεται μὲν ἰχθύων πλωτῷ γένει,
χέρσου δ'ἔνεστιν ἐν τετρασκελεῖ γονῇ,
νωμᾷ δ' ἐν οἰωνοῖσι τοὐκείνης πτερόν...
ἐν θηρσίν, ἐν βροτοῖσιν, ἐν θεοῖς ἄνω.
τίν' οὐ παλαίουσ' ἐς τρὶς ἐκβάλλει θεῶν;
εἰ μοι θέμις–θέμις δὲ–τἀληθῆ λέγειν,
Διὸς τυραννεῖ πλευμόνων ἄνευ δορός,
ἄνευ σιδήρου· πάντα τοι συντέμνεται
Κύπρις τὰ θνητῶν καὶ θεῶν βουλεύματα.

2.9 Maximus of Tyre, *Orations*, frag. 159

λέγει που καὶ Σαπφοῖ ἡ Ἀφροδίτη ἐν ᾄσματι·
...σύ τε κἄμος θεράπων Ἔρος.

2.10 Homeric Hymn to Aphrodite 247–57

Αὐτὰρ ἐμοὶ μέγ' ὄνειδος ἐν ἀθανάτοισι θεοῖσιν
ἔσσεται ἤματα πάντα διαμπερὲς εἵνεκα σεῖο,
οἳ πρὶν ἐμοὺς ὀάρους καὶ μήτιας, αἷς ποτε πάντας
ἀθανάτους συνέμιξα καταθνητῇσι γυναιξί,
τάρβεσκον· πάντας γὰρ ἐμὸν δάμνασκε νόημα.
νῦν δὲ δὴ οὐκέτι μοι στόμα χείσεται ἐξονομῆναι
τοῦτο μετ' ἀθανάτοισιν, ἐπεὶ μάλα πολλὸν ἀάσθην,
σχέτλιον, οὐκ ὀνοταστόν, ἀπεπλάγχθην δὲ νόοιο,
παῖδα δ' ὑπὸ ζώνῃ ἐθέμην βροτῷ εὐνηεῖσα.
τὸν μέν, ἐπὴν δὴ πρῶτον ἴδῃ φάος ἠελίοιο,
Νύμφαι μιν θρέψουσιν ὀρεσκῷοι βαθύκολποι.

2.11 Athenaios, *Deipnosophistai*, XIII, 600, b

ἐρᾷ μὲν ἁγνὸς οὐρανὸς τρῶσαι χθόνα,
ἔρως δὲ γαῖαν λαμβάνει γάμου τυχεῖν·

ὄμβρος δ'ἀπ'εὐνάοντος οὐρανοῦ πεσὼν
ἔκυσε γαῖαν· ἡ δὲ τίκτεται βροτοῖς
μήλων τε βοσκὰς καὶ βίον Δημήτριον·
δενδρῶτις ὥρα δ' ἐκ νοτίζοντος γάμου
τέλειος ἐστί. τῶν δ' ἐγὼ παραίτιος.

2.12 Athenaios, *Deipnosophistai*, XIII, 600, a

ἐρᾷ μὲν ὄμβρου γαῖ', ὅταν ξηρὸν πέδον
ἄκαρπον αὐχμῷ νοτίδος ἐνδεῶς ἔχῃ.
ἐρᾷ δ' ὁ σεμνὸς οὐρανὸς πληρούμενος
ὄμβρου πεσεῖν εἰς γαῖαν Ἀφροδίτης ὕπο.
ὅταν δὲ συμμιχθῆτον ἐς ταὐτὸν δύο,
φύουσιν ἡμῖν πάντα καὶ τρέφουσ' ἅμα,
δι' ὧν βρότειον ζῇ τε καὶ θάλλει γένος.

2.13 Euripides, *Hippolytos*, ll. 447–50

φοιτᾷ δ' ἀν' αἰθέρ', ἔστι δ' ἐν θαλασσίῳ
κλύδωνι Κύπρις, πάντα δ' ἐκ ταύτης ἔφυ·
ἥδ' ἐστὶν ἡ σπείρουσα καὶ διδοῦσ' ἔρον,
οὗ πάντες ἐσμὲν οἱ κατὰ χθόν' ἔκγονοι.

2.14 Hesiod, *Theogony*, ll. 188–95

Μήδεα δ'ὡς τὸ πρῶτον ἀποτμήξας ἀδάμαντι
κάββαλ'ἀπ' ἠπείροιο πολυκλύστῳ ἐνὶ πόντῳ,
ὡς φέρετ' ἂμ πέλαγος πουλὺν χρόνον· ἀμφὶ δὲ λευκὸς
ἀφρὸς ἀπ'ἀθανάτου χροὸς ὤρνυτο, τῷ δ'ἔνι κούρη
ἐθρέφθη· πρῶτον δὲ Κυθήροισιν ζαθέοισιν
ἔπλητ', ἔνθεν ἔπειτα περίρρυτον ἵκετο Κύπρον·
ἐκ δ' ἔβη αἰδοίη καλὴ θεός, ἀμφὶ δὲ ποίη
ποσσὶν ὑπὸ ῥαδινοῖσιν ἀέξετο.

2.15 Pausanias, 3, XXIII, 1

Κύθηρα δὲ ἡ πόλις ἀναβάντι ἀπὸ Σκανδείας στάδια ὡς δέκα. τὸ δὲ ἱερὸν τῆς
οὐρανίας ἁγιώτατον καὶ ἱερῶν ὁπόσα Ἀφροδίτης παρ' Ἕλλησίν ἐστιν
ἀρχαιότατον· αὐτὴ δὲ ἡ θεὸς ξόανον ὡπλισμένον.

2.16 Pausanias, 3, XV, 10

προελθοῦσι δὲ οὐ πολὺ λόφος ἐστὶν οὐ μέγας, ἐπὶ δὲ αὐτῷ ναὸς ἀρχαῖος καὶ
Ἀφροδίτης ξόανον ὡπλισμένης.

2.17 Pausanias 2, V, 1

'Ανελθοῦσι δὲ ἐς τὸν 'Ακροκόρινθον ναός ἐστιν 'Αφροδίτης· ἀγάλματα δὲ αὐτή τε ὡπλισμένη καὶ ῞Ηλιος καὶ ῞Ερως ἔχων τόξον.

2.18 Inscription from Athens

'Επὶ ἱερείας 'Ηγησιπύλης.
ἐπ' Εὐθίου ἄρχοντος, ἐπὶ τῆς
Αἰαντίδος δωδεκάτης πρυ-
τανείας ᾗ Ναυσιμένης
Ναυσικύδου Χολαπγεὺς
ἐγραμμάτευεν· Σκιποφοριῶ-
νος ἔνηι καὶ νέαι· Καλλίας Λ[υ-]
σιμάχου ῞Ερμειος εἶπεν- ὅπ[ι-]
ζαν οἱ ἀστυνόμοι οἱ ἀεὶ λανχ[ά-]
νοντες ἐπιμέλειαν ποιῶντα[ι]
τοῦ ἱεροῦ τῆς 'Αφροδίτης τῆς
Πανδήμου κατὰ τὰ πάτρια. τύ-
χηι ἀγαθέι, δεδόχθαι τῆι βου-
λῆι· τοὺς προέδρους οἳ ἂν λάχω-
σιν προεδρεύειν εἰς τὴν ἐπιοῦ-
σαν ἐκκλησίαν προσαγαγεῖν τὸν
[ο]ἰκεῖον τῆς ἱερείας καὶ χρηματίσαι
[π]ερὶ τούτων, γνώμην δὲ ξυνβάλλε-
[σ]θαι τῆς βουλῆς εἰς τὸν δῆμον ὅ-
[τ]ι δοκεῖ τῆι βουλῆι· τοὺς ἀστυνό-
μους τοὺς ἀεὶ λαχόντας, ὅταν ἦι
ἡ πομπὴ τῆι 'Αφροδίτηι τέι Πανδή-
μωι, παρασκευάζειν εἰς κάθαπσι[ν]
τοῦ ἱεροῦ περιστεράν καὶ περιαλε[ῖ-]
[ψαι] τοὺς βωμοὺς καὶ πιττῶσαι τὰ[ς]
[θύρας] καὶ λοῦσαι τὰ ἴδη· παρασκευ-
[άσαι δὲ κα]ὶ πορφύραν ὁλκὴν
——— τὰ ἐπὶ τ ———

CHAPTER III.

3.1 Hymn 1.113

Idám sréshtham jyótishäm jyótir ágäe citráh praketó ajanishta víbhvä
Yáthä prásütä savitúh saváya evá rátry usháse yónim äraik
Rúsadvatsä rúsatï svetyágäd áraig u krishná sádanäny asyäh
Samänábandhü amríte anücí dyávä várnam carata äminäné

3.2 Hymn 1.123. 8-9

Sadrísïr adyá sadrísïr íd u svó dïrghám sacante várunasya dháma
Anavadyás trinsátam yójanäny ékaikä krátum pári yanti sadyáh
Jänaty áhnah prathamásya náma sukrá krishnád ajanishta svitïcí
Ritásya yóshä ná mináti dhámáhar-ahar nishkritám äcárantï

3.3 Hymn 1.92.10

Púnah-punar jáyamänä puräní samänám várnam abhí súmbhamänä
Svaghníva kritnúr víja äminänä mártasya deví jaráyanty áyuh

3.4 Hymn 1.49.2

Supésasam sukhám rátham yám adhyásthä ushas tvám
Ténä susrávasam jánam právädyá duhitar divah

3.5 Hymn 5.79.6-8

Aíshu dhä vïrávad yása úsho maghoni süríshu
Yé no rádhansy áhrayá maghäväno árasata sújäte ásvasünrite
Tébhyo dyumnám brihád yása úsho maghony á vaha
Yé no rádhänsy ásvyä gavyá bhájanta süráyah sújäte ásvasünrite
Utá no gómatïr ísha á vahä duhitar divah
Säkám súryasya rasmíbhih sukraih sócadbhir arcíbhih sújäte ásvasünrite

3.6 Hymn 1.123.10

Kanyèva tanvà sásadänän éshi devi devám íyakshamänam
Samsmáyamänä yuvatíh purástäd ävír vákshänsi krinushe vibhätí

3.7 Hymn 1.124.7-8

Abhrätéva punsá eti praticí gartärúg iva sanáye dhánänäm
Jäyéya pátya usatí suvá ushá hasréva ní rinïte ápsah
Svásä svásre jyáyasyai yónim äraig apaity asyáh praticákshyeva
Vyuchánti rasmíbhih süryaayänjy ànkte samanagá iva vráh

3.8 Poetic Edda

Þegi þú, Freyja! þik kann ek full-görva;

esa þér vamma vant:
Ása ok Alfa, es her inni ero,
    hverr hefir þinn hór vesið.
Þegi þú, Freyja! þu-ert fordaeða,
    ok meini blandin miök:
Sitztu at broeðr þínom siðo' blíð regin,
    ok myndir þú pá, Freyja, frata.

3.9 Poetic Edda

Rannt at Óði ey þreyandi,
skutosk þer fleiri und fyrir-skyrto.
Hleypr þú, Óðs vina, úti á nóttom,
sem með höfrom Heiðrún fari.

3.10 Nestor cup

Νέστορος: ε[2-3]ι̣: εὔποτ[ον]: ποτέριο[ν:]
hὸς δ'ἂ<ν> τὸδε π[ίε]σι: ποτερί[ο]: αὐτίκα̣ κênον
hίμερ[ος: haιρ]έσει: καλλιστε[φά]ν̣ο: 'Αφροδίτες.

3.11 Linear B tablet

[?]-*de-u-ki-jo-jo* / *me-no*
di-ka-ta-jo / *di- we*   OIL 1
da-da-re-jo-de   OIL 2
pa-de   OIL 1
pa-si-te-o-i   OIL 1
qe-ra-si-ja   OIL [1?]
a-mi-ni-so / *pa-si-te-o-i*   <OIL> [2?]
e-ri-nu   OIL 3
*47-da-de   OIL 1
a-ne-mo / *i-je-re-ja*   OIL 4
to-so   OIL 3 2 2

CHAPTER IV.

4.1 Herodotos, Bk. I, 105

καὶ ἐπείτε ἐγένοντο ἐν τῇ Παλαιστίνη Συρίη, Ψαμμήτιχός σφεας Αἰγύπτου
βασιλεὺς ἀντιάσας δώροισί τε καὶ λιτῇσι ἀποτρέπει τὸ προσωτέρω μὴ πορεύεσθαι.
οἱ δὲ ἐπείτε ἀναχωρέοντες ὀπίσω ἐγίνοντο τῆς Συρίης ἐν 'Ασκάλωνι πόλι, τῶν
πλεόνων Σκυθέων παρεξελθόντων ἀσινέων ὀλίγοι τινὲς αὐτῶν ὑπολειφθέντες
ἐσύλησαν τῆς οὐρανίης 'Αφροδίτης τὸ ἱρόν. ἔστι δὲ τοῦτο τὸ ἱρόν, ὡς ἐγὼ
πυνθανόμενος εὑρίσκω, πάντων ἀρχαιότατον ἱρῶν, ὅσα ταύτης τῆς θεοῦ· καὶ γὰρ

τὸ ἐν Κύπρῳ ἱρὸν ἐνθεῦτεν ἐγένετο, ὡς αὐτοὶ Κύπριοι λέγουσι, καὶ τὸ ἐν Κυθήροισι
Φοίνικές εἰσι οἱ ἱδρυσάμενοι ἐκ ταύτης τῆς Συρίης ἐόντες.

4.2 Babylonian Inscription

a-n[a] ᵈMi-[š]ar²
[D]ur²-R[i]²-[m]uš²ki
ᵐᵈNa-ra-am-ᵈEN.ZU
mar ᵐI-pí-iq-ᵈAda[d...]
a-n[a] ba-la-ṭì-š[u...]

4.3 Pausanias 2, XIX, 6

τὰ δὲ ξόανα Ἀφροδίτης καὶ Ἑρμοῦ, τὸ μὲν Ἐπειοῦ λέγουσιν ἔργον εἶναι, τὸ δὲ
Ὑπερμήστρας ἀνάθημα. ταύτην γὰρ τῶν θυγατέρων μόνην τὸ πρόσταγμα
ὑπεριδοῦσαν ὑπήγαγεν ὁ Δαναὸς ἐς δικαστήριον, τοῦ τε Λυγκέως οὐκ ἀκίνδυνον
αὐτῷ τὴν σωτηρίαν ἡγούμενος καὶ ὅτι τοῦ τολμήματος οὐ μετασχοῦσα ταῖς
ἀδελφαῖς καὶ τῷ βουλεύσαντι τὸ ὄνειδος ηὔξησε. κριθεῖσα δὲ ἐν τοῖς Ἀργείοις
ἀποφεύγει τε καὶ Ἀφροδίτην ἐπὶ τῷδε ἀνέθηκε Νικεφόρον.

4.4 Pausanias 2, XX, 8

Ὑπὲρ δὲ τὸ θέατρον Ἀφροδίτης ἐστὶν ἱερόν, ἔμπροσθεν δὲ τοῦ ἕδους Τελέσιλλα ἡ
ποιήσασα τὰ ᾄσματα ἐπείργασται στήλῃ. καὶ βιβλία μὲν ἐκεῖνα ἔρριπταί οἱ πρὸς
τοῖς ποσίν, αὐτὴ δὲ ἐς κράνος ὁρᾷ κατέχουσα τῇ χειρὶ καὶ ἐπιτίθεσθαι τῇ κεφαλῇ
μέλλουσα.

4.5 Pausanias 2, XXV, 1

Ἡ δ' ἐς Μαντίνειαν ἄγουσα ἐξ Ἄργους ἐστὶν οὐχ ἥπερ καὶ ἐπὶ Τεγέαν, ἀλλὰ ἀπὸ
τῶν πυλῶν τῶν πρὸς τῇ Δειράδι. ἐπὶ δὲ τῆς ὁδοῦ ταύτης ἱερὸν διπλοῦν πεποίηται,
καὶ πρὸς ἡλίου δύνοντος ἔσοδον καὶ κατὰ ἀνατολὰς ἑτέραν ἔχον. κατὰ μὲν δὴ
τοῦτο Ἀφροδίτης κεῖται ξόανον, πρὸς δὲ ἡλίου δυσμὰς Ἄρεως· εἶναι δὲ τὰ
ἀγάλματα Πολυνείκους λέγουσιν ἀναθήματα καὶ Ἀργείων, ὅσοι τιμωρήσοντες
αὐτῷ συνεστρατεύοντο.

4.6 Pausanias 3, XIII, 8-9

Ἥρας δὲ ἱερὸν Ὑπερχειρίας κατὰ μαντείαν ἐποιήθη, τοῦ Εὐρώτα πολὺ τῆς γῆς
σφισιν ἐπικλύζοντος. ξόανον δὲ ἀρχαῖον καλοῦσιν Ἀφροδίτης Ἥρας· ἐπὶ δὲ
θυγατρὶ γαμουμένῃ νενομίκασι τὰς μητέρας τῇ θεῷ θύειν.

4.7 Pausanias, 3, XV, 10-11

προελθοῦσι δὲ οὐ πολὺ λόφος ἐστὶν οὐ μέγας, ἐπὶ δὲ αὐτῷ ναὸς ἀρχαῖος καὶ
Ἀφροδίτης ξόανον ὡπλισμένης. ναῶν δὲ ὧν οἶδα μόνῳ τούτῳ καὶ ὑπερῷον ἄλλο
ἐπῳκοδόμηται Μορφοῦς ἱερόν. ἐπίκλησις μὲν δὴ τῆς Ἀφροδίτης ἐστὶν ἡ Μορφώ,
κάθηται δὲ καλύπτραν τε ἔχουσα καὶ πέδας περὶ τοῖς ποσί· περιθεῖναι δέ οἱ

Τυνδάρεων τὰς πέδας φασὶν ἀφομοιοῦντα τοῖς δεσμοῖς τὸ ἐς τοὺς συνοικοῦντας τῶν γυναικῶν βέβαιον. τὸν γὰρ δὴ ἕτερον λόγον, ὡς τὴν θεὸν πέδαις ἐτιμωρεῖτο ὁ Τυνδάρεως, γενέσθαι ταῖς θυγατράσιν ἐξ Ἀφροδίτης ἡγούμενος τὰ ὀνείδη, τοῦτον οὐδὲ ἀρχὴν προσίεμαι· ἦν γὰρ δὴ παντάπασιν εὔηθες κέρδου ποιησάμενον ζῴδιον καὶ ὄνομα Ἀφροδίτην θέμενον ἐλπίζειν ἀμύνεσθαι τὴν θεόν.

4.8 Pausanias 3, XVII, 5

Ἐν ἀριστερᾷ δὲ τῆς Χαλκιοίκου Μουσῶν ἱδρύσαντο ἱερόν, ὅτι οἱ Λακεδαιμόνιοι τὰς ἐξόδους ἐπὶ τὰς μάχας οὐ μετὰ σαλπίγγων ἐποιοῦντο ἀλλὰ πρός τε αὐλῶν μέλη καὶ ὑπὸ λύρας καὶ κιθάρας κρούσμασιν. ὄπισθεν δὲ τῆς Χαλκιοίκου ναός ἐστιν Ἀφροδίτης Ἀρείας· τὰ δὲ ξόανα ἀρχαῖα εἴπερ τι ἄλλο ἐν Ἕλλησιν.

4.9 Pausanias 2, X, 4-5

Οὗτος μὲν δὴ παρείχετο ὁ περίβολος τοσάδε ἐς μνήμην, πέραν δὲ αὐτοῦ ἄλλος ἐστὶν Ἀφροδίτης ἱερός· ἐν δὲ αὐτῷ πρῶτον ἄγαλμά ἐστιν Ἀντιόπης· εἶναι γὰρ οἱ τούς παῖδας Σικυωνίους καὶ δι' ἐκείνους ἐθέλουσι καὶ αὐτὴν Ἀντιόπην προσήκειν σφίσι. μετὰ τοῦτο ἤδη τὸ τῆς Ἀφροδίτης ἐστὶν ἱερόν. ἐσίασι μὲν δὴ ἐς αὐτὸ γυνή τε νεωκόρος, ᾗ μηκέτι θέμις παρ' ἄνδρα φοιτῆσαι, καὶ παρθένος ἱερωσύνην ἐπέτειον ἔχουσα· λουτροφόρον τὴν παρθένον ὀνομάζουσι· τοῖς δὲ ἄλλοις καθέστηκεν ὁρᾶν ἀπὸ τῆς ἐσόδου τὴν θεὸν καὶ αὐτόθεν προσεύχεσθαι. τὸ μὲν δὴ ἄγαλμα καθήμενον Κάναχος Σικυώνιος ἐποίησεν, ὅς καὶ τὸν ἐν Διδύμοις τοῖς Μιλησίων καὶ θηαίοις τὸν Ἰσμήνιον εἰργάσατο Ἀπόλλωνα· πεποίηται δὲ ἔκ τε χρυσοῦ καὶ ἐλέφαντος, φέρουσα ἐπὶ τῇ κεφαλῇ πόλον, τῶν χειρῶν δὲ ἔχει τῇ μὲν μήκωνα τῇ δὲ ἑτέρᾳ μῆλον.

4.10 Pausanias 1, XXII, 3

Ἀφροδίτην δὲ τὴν Πάνδημον, ἐπεί τε Ἀθηναίους Θησεὺς ἐς μίαν ἤγαγεν ἀπὸ τῶν δήμων πόλιν, αὐτήν τε σέβεσθαι καὶ Πειθὼ κατέστησε· τὰ μὲν δὴ παλαιὰ ἀγάλματα οὐκ ἦν ἐπ'ἐμοῦ, τὰ δὲ ἐπ'ἐμοῦ τεχνιτῶν ἦν οὐ τῶν ἀφανεστάτων.

4.11 Pausanias 1, XIX, 2

ἐς δὲ τὸ χωρίον, ὃ Κήπους ὀνομάζουσι, καὶ τῆς Ἀφροδίτης τὸν ναὸν οὐδεὶς λεγόμενός σφισίν ἐστι λόγος· οὐ μὴν οὐδὲ ἐς τὴν Ἀφροδίτην, ἣ τοῦ ναοῦ πλησίον ἕστηκε. ταύτης γὰρ σχῆμα μὲν τετράγωνον κατὰ ταὐτὰ καὶ τοῖς Ἑρμαῖς, τὸ δὲ ἐπίγραμμα σημαίνει τὴν Οὐρανίαν Ἀφροδίτην τῶν καλουμένων Μοιρῶν εἶναι πρεσβυτάτην. τὸ δὲ ἄγαλμα τῆς Ἀφροδίτης τῆς ἐν Κήποις ἔργον ἐστὶν Ἀλκαμένους καὶ τῶν Ἀθήνησιν ἐν ὀλίγοις θέας ἄξιον.

4.12 Athenaios XIII, 569, d

Καὶ Φιλήμων δὲ ἐν Ἀδελφοῖς προσιστορῶν ὅτι πρῶτος Σόλων διὰ τὴν τῶν νέων ἀκμὴν ἔστησεν ἐπὶ οἰκημάτων γύναια πριάμενος, καθὰ καὶ Νίκανδρος ὁ Κολοφώνιος ἱστορεῖ ἐν τρίτῳ Κολοφωνιακῶν φάσκων αὐτὸν καὶ πανδήμου

'Αφροδίτης ἱερὸν πρῶτον ἱδρύσασθαι ἀφ'ὧν ἠργυρίσαντο αἱ προστᾶσαι τῶν οἰκημάτων.

4.13 Hesiod, *Theogony* 933-37

... Αὐτὰρ Ἄρηι
ῥινοτόρῳ Κυθέρεια Φόβον καὶ Δεῖμον ἔτικτε
δεινούς, οἵ τ' ἀνδρῶν πυκινὰς κλονέουσι φάλαγγας
ἐν πολέμῳ κρυόεντι σὺν Ἄρηι πτολιπόρθῳ,
'Αρμονίην θ', ἣν Κάδμος ὑπέρθυμος θέτ' ἄκοιτιν.

4.14 Pausanias 9, XVI, 3-4

'Αφροδίτης δὲ Θηβαίοις ξόανά ἐστιν οὕτω δὴ ἀρχαῖα ὥστε καὶ ἀναθήματα
'Αρμονίας εἶναί φασιν, ἐργασθῆναι δὲ αὐτὰ ἀπὸ τῶν ἀκροστολίων, ἃ ταῖς Κάδμου
ναυσὶν ἦν ξύλου πεποιημένα. καλοῦσι δὲ Οὐρανίαν, τὴν δὲ αὐτῶν Πάνδημον καὶ
'Αποστροφίαν τὴν τρίτην· ἔθετο δὲ τῇ 'Αφροδίτῃ τὰς ἐπωνυμίας ἡ 'Αρμονία, τὴν μὲν
Οὐρανίαν ἐπὶ ἔρωτι καθαρῷ καὶ ἀπηλλαγμένῳ πόθου σωμάτων, Πάνδημον δὲ ἐπὶ
ταῖς μίξεσι, τρίτα δὲ 'Αποστροφίαν, ἵνα ἐπιθυμίας τε ἀνόμου καὶ ἔργων ἀνοσίων
ἀποστρέφῃ τὸ γένος τῶν ἀνθρώπων· πολλὰ γὰρ τὰ μὲν ἐν βαρβάροις ἠπίστατο ἡ
'Αρμονία, τὰ δὲ καὶ παρ' Ἕλλησιν ἤδη τετολμημένα, ὁποῖα καὶ ὕστερον ἐπὶ τῇ
'Αδώνιδος μητρὶ καὶ ἐς Φαίδραν τε τὴν Μίνω καὶ ἐς τὸν Θρᾷκα Τηρέα ᾄδεται.

4.15 Sappho, Poem II

δεῦρύ μ' ἐκ Κρήτας ἐπ[ὶ τόνδ]ε ναῦον
ἄγνον, ὅππ[ᾳ τοι] χάριεν μὲν ἄλσος
μαλί[αν], βῶμοι δὲ τεθυμιάμε-
νοι [λι]βανώτῳ·
ἐν δ' ὕδωρ ψῦχρον κελάδει δι' ὕσδων
μαλίνων, βρόδοισι δὲ παῖς ὁ χῶρος
ἐσκίαστ', αἰθυσσομένων δὲ φύλλων
κῶμα κατέρρει·
ἐν δὲ λείμων ἱππόβοτος τέθαλεν
ἠρίνοισιν ἄνθεσιν, αἱ δ' ἄηται
μέλλιχα πνέοισιν [
[   ]
ἔνθα δὴ σὺ ... ἔλοισα Κύπρι
χρυσίαισιν ἐν κυλίκεσσιν ἄβρως
ὀμμεμείχμενον θαλίαισι νέκταρ
οἰνοχόαισον

4.16 Athenaios, *Deipnosophistai*, XV, 675f-76c

κατὰ δὲ τὴν τρίτην πρὸς ταῖς εἴκοσιν 'Ολυμπιάδα ὁ 'Ηρόστρατος, πολίτης ἡμέτερος
ἐμπορίᾳ χρώμενος καὶ χώραν πολλὴν περιπλέων, προσχών ποτε καὶ Πάφῳ τῆς
Κύπρου ἀγαλμάτιον 'Αφροδίτης σπιθαμιαῖον, ἀρχαῖον τῇ τέχνῃ, ὠνησάμενος ἥει

φέρων εἰς τὴν Ναύκρατιν. καὶ αὐτῷ πλησίον φερομένῳ τῆς Αἰγύπτου ἐπεὶ χειμὼν αἰφνίδιον ἐπέπεσεν καὶ συνιδεῖν οὐκ ἦν ὅπου γῆς ἦσαν, κατέφυγον ἅπαντες ἐπὶ τὸ τῆς Ἀφροδίτης ἄγαλμα σώζειν αὐτοὺς αὐτὴν δεόμενοι. ἡ δὲ θεὸς (προσφιλὴς γὰρ τοῖς Ναυκρατίταις ἦν) αἰφνίδιον ἐποίησε πάντα τὰ παρακείμενα αὐτῇ μυρρίνης χλωρᾶς πλήρη ὀδμῆς τε ἡδίστης ἐπλήρωσεν τὴν ναῦν ἤδη ἀπειρηκόσι τοῖς ἐμπλέουσιν τὴν σωτηρίαν διὰ τὴν πολλὴν ναυτίαν γενομένου τε ἐμέτου πολλοῦ· καὶ ἡλίου ἐκλάμψαντος κατιδόντες τοὺς ὅρμους ἧκον εἰς τὴν Ναύκρατιν. καὶ ὁ Ἡρόστρατος ἐξορμήσας τῆς νεὼς μετὰ τοῦ ἀγάλματος, ἔχων καὶ τὰς αἰφνίδιον αὐτῷ ἀναφανείσας χλωρὰς μυρρίνας, ἀνέθηκεν ἐν τῷ τῆς Ἀφροδίτης ἱερῷ· θύσας δὲ τῇ θεῷ καὶ ἀναθεὶς τῇ Ἀφροδίτῃ τἄγαλμα, καλέσας δὲ καὶ ἐφ' ἑστίασιν ἐν αὐτῷ τῷ ἱερῷ τοὺς προσήκοντας καὶ τοὺς οἰκειοτάτους ἔδωκεν ἑκάστῳ καὶ στέφανον ἐκ τῆς μυρρίνης, ὃν καὶ τότε ἐκάλεσε Ναυκρατίτην.

4.17 Thucydides, VI, 46

ἔς τε τὸ ἐν Ἔρυκι ἱερὸν τῆς Ἀφροδίτης ἀγαγόντες αὐτοὺς ἐπέδειξαν τὰ ἀναθήματα, φιάλας τε καὶ οἰνοχόας καὶ θυμιατήρια καὶ ἄλλην κατασκευὴν οὐκ ὀλίγην, ἃ ὄντα ἀργυρᾶ πολλῷ πλείω τὴν ὄψιν ἀπ' ὀλίγης δυνάμεως χρημάτων παρείχετο·

4.18 Strabo, VI, ii, 6

Οἰκεῖται δὲ καὶ ὁ Ἔρυξ λόφος ὑψηλός, ἱερὸν ἔχων Ἀφροδίτης τιμώμενον διαφερόντως, ἱεροδούλων γυναικῶν πλῆρες τὸ παλαιόν, ἃς ἀνέθεσαν κατ' εὐχὴν οἵ τ' ἐκ τῆς Σικελίας καὶ ἔξωθεν πολλοί· νυνὶ δ' ὥσπερ αὐτὴ ἡ κατοικία λειπανδρεῖ τὸ ἱερόν, καὶ τῶν ἱερῶν σωμάτων ἐκλέλοιπε τὸ πλῆθος.

CHAPTER VI.

6.1 Homeric Hymn V, ll. 58–59

ἐς Κύπρον δ'ἐλθοῦσα θυώδεα νηὸν ἔδυνεν,
ἐς Πάφον· ἔνθα δέ οἱ τέμενος βωμός τε θυώδης.

6.2 Homer, *Odyssey*, VIII, ll. 362–66

ἡ δ'ἄρα Κύπρον ἵκανε φιλομμειδὴς Ἀφροδίτη
ἐς Πάφον, ἔνθα τέ οἱ τέμενος βωμός τε θυήεις.
ἔνθα δέ μιν Χάριτες λοῦσαν καὶ χρῖσαν ἐλαίῳ
ἀμβρότῳ, οἷα θεοὺς ἐπενήνοθεν αἰὲν ἐόντας,
ἀμφὶ δὲ εἵματα ἕσσαν ἐπήρατα, θαῦμα ἰδέσθαι.

6.3 Pausanias, 8,V, 2

Ἀγαπήνωρ δὲ ὁ Ἀγκαίου τοῦ Λυκούργου μετὰ Ἔχεμον βασιλεύσας ἐς Τροίαν ἡγήσατο Ἀρκάσιν. Ἰλίου δὲ ἁλούσης ὁ τοῖς Ἕλλησι κατὰ τὸν πλοῦν τὸν οἴκαδε ἐπιγενόμενος χειμὼν Ἀγαπήνορα καὶ τὸ Ἀρκάδων ναυτικὸν κατήνεγκεν ἐς Κύπρον, καὶ Πάφου τε Ἀγαπήνωρ ἐγένετο οἰκιστὴς καὶ τῆς Ἀφροδίτης κατεσκευάσατο ἐν Παλαιπάφῳ τὸ ἱερόν· τέως δὲ ἡ θεὸς παρὰ Κυπρίων τιμὰς εἶχεν ἐν Γολγοῖς καλουμένῳ χωρίῳ.

6.4 Tacitus, *Historiae* II, 3

Conditorem templi regem Aeriam vetus memoria, quidam ipsius deae nomen id perhibent. Fama recentior tradit a Cinyra sacratum templum deamque ipsam conceptam mari huc adpulsam; sed scientiam artemque haruspicum accitam et Cilicem Tamiram intulisse, atque ita pactum ut familiae utriusque posteri caerimoniis praesiderent. Mox, ne honore nullo regium genus peregrinam stirpem antecelleret, ipsa quam intulerant scientia hospites cessere: tantum Cinyrades sacerdos consulitur. ... Sanguinem arae obfundere vetitum: precibus et igne puro altaria adolentur, nec ullis imbribus quamquam in aperto madescunt. Simulacrum deae non effigie humana, continuus orbis latiore initio tenuem in ambitum metae modo exsurgens, set ratio in obscuro.

CHAPTER VII.

7.1 Homer, *Odyssey*, Bk. IV: 82-85

.....ὀγδοάτῳ ἔτει ἦλθον·
Κύπρον Φοινίκην τε καὶ Αἰγυπτίους ἐπαληθείς,
Αἰθίοπάς θ' ἱκόμην καὶ Σιδονίους καὶ Ἐρεμβοὺς
καὶ Λιβύην.

CHAPTER VIII.

8.1 Hymn to Ištar

5.	*ša-at me-li-ṣi-im ru-à-ma-am la-ab-ša-at*
6.	*za-'-na-at in-bi mi-ki-a-am ù ku-uz-ba-am*
7.	*ᵈIŠTAR me-li-ṣi-im ru-à-ma-am la-ab-ša-at*
8.	*za-'-na-at in-bi mi-ki-a-am ù ku-uz-ba-am*
9.	*[ša]-ap-ti-in du-uš-šu-pa-at ba-la-ṭú-um pí-i-ša*
10.	*si-im-ti-iš-ša i-ha-an-ni-i-ma ṣi-ha-tum*
11.	*šar-ha-at i-ri-mu ra-mu-ú re-šu-us-sa*
12.	*ba-ni-à-a ši-im-ta-à-ša bi-it-ra-a-ma i-na-ša ši-it-a-ra*

8.2 The Myth of Ashtarte, the Huntress (KTU 1.92)

⁽²⁾ᶜ*ṯtrt ṣwdt [tṣdn šdm]*
⁽³⁾*tlk bmdbr [ktn]*
[wkbkbm]⁽⁴⁾*thdtn*
whl[l(?)   ]
⁽⁵⁾*wtglt thmt.ᶜl*[yt mdbr]*
⁽⁶⁾*yṣi.ǵlh thmd*[nh ᶜṯtrt]*
⁽⁷⁾*mrhh ladrt l*[tṣb]*

[bkm] $^{(8)}$ *ṭṭb* ^{c}*ṭṭrt bǧl*
[lymnh] $^{(9)}$*qrẓ tšt.*
lšmal*[h tšt] $^{(10)}$*arbh.*
^{c}*nh tšu w[tphn]*
$^{(11)}$*aylt tǧpy ṭr.*
^{c}*n*[ṭr xxx]* $^{(12)}$*bq*r.*
mrḥh.ti[hd bydh]
šbrh bm ymn.
tr*[my]l*ṯr[?]
$^{(14)}$*ts*p*l b^{c}l.^{c}bb.*
[ṭṭ]b*.lbt*[h]
$^{(15)}$*ṭr abh il.ṭṭrm*
[wt]š*lḥ*[m]
$^{(16)}$*tšlḥm yrh.ggn.*
[wtšlḥm] $^{(17)}$*k[ṭ]r ḥrš.*
hssm [ ]
$^{(18)}$*x[xxxxx]b*m ^{c}ttr[t]*
$^{(19)}$*[ ]t*r*[abh il]*
$^{(20)}$*[ ]*
$^{(21)}$*[ ]*
$^{(22)}$*[ ]*

$^{(23)}$*[wy^{c}n ^{c}ṭṭ]r*t bnǧr krm*
$^{(24)}$*[n^{c}mt bnt].abh.krm ar*
$^{(25)}$*[tks bšr]h*.mḥtrt.pṭtm*
$^{(26)}$*[t^{c}l ^{c}]l*h.ušpǧt tišr*
$^{(27)}$*[wnf^c*mh.nšat ẓl kkbkbm*
$^{(28)}$*[k]b*d* km kbkbt kṭn*
$^{(29)}$*[b]ṭ*lt b^{c}l yhmdnh.*
yrṭy $^{(30)}$*[nf^{c}mh*.dmrn.*
lpnh yrd $^{(31)}$*[?]aliy*n* b^{c}l.*
šm[h] rgbt.
yu $^{(32)}$*[h]b* mn[th(?)].*
wyrmy q*rnh $^{(33)}$*[l]n*ǧr**
[wy^c]nyh pdr.ttǧr $^{(34)}$*[b^{c}l]*
[xxx b]šrk.al ttn.ln $^{(35)}$*[^{c}l]*
[xxxxxa] l* t*tn lrbd
$^{(36)}$*[p npš npš] b^{c}l thwyn*
$^{(37)}$*[hm brlt rk]b ^{c}rpt*
$^{(38)}$*[hn xxxx y]n.wmnu dg*
$^{(39)}$*[xxxxx]l*aliyn b^{c}l*
$^{(40)}$*[wyšm]h *.rkb ^{c}rpt*

CHAPTER IX.

9.1 Josephus, *Against Apion* I, 118

ἐπί τε ὕλην ξύλων ἀπελθὼν ἔκοψεν ἀπὸ τοῦ λεγομένου ὄρους Λιβάνου, κέδρινα ξύλα εἰς τὰς τῶν ἱερῶν στέγας, καθελών τε τὰ ἀρχαῖα ἱερὰ καινοὺς ναοὺς ᾠκοδόμησεν τόν τε τοῦ Ἡρακλέους καὶ τῆς Ἀστάρτης, πρῶτόν τε τοῦ Ἡρακλέους ἔγερσιν ἐποιήσατο ἐν τῷ Περιτίῳ μηνί.

9.2 Lucian, *De Dea Syria*, section VI

καὶ τὰς κεφαλὰς ξύρονται ὅκως Αἰγύπτοι ἀποθανόντος Ἄπιος. γυναικῶν δὲ ὁκόσαι οὐκ ἐθέλουσι ξύρεσθαι, τοιήνδε ζημίην ἐκτελέουσιν· ἐν μιῇ ἡμέρῃ ἐπὶ πρήσει τῆς ὥρης ἵστανται· ἡ δὲ ἀγορὴ μούνοισι ξείνοισι παρακέαται, καὶ ὁ μισθὸς ἐς τὴν Ἀφροδίτην θυσίη γίγνεται.

BIBLIOGRAPHY

A Campo, A.L. *Anthropomorphic Representations in Prehistoric Cyprus: A Formal and Symbolic Analysis of Figurines, c. 3500-1800 B.C.* Paul Åströms Förlag. Jonsered. 1994.

Ahlström, G.W. "An Archaeological Picture of Iron Age Religions in Ancient Palestine." *Stud Or* 55:3 (1984), 115-146.

Akurgal, E. *Ancient Civilizations and Ruins of Turkey: From Prehistoric Times until the End of the Roman Empire.* Haset Kitabevi. Istambul. 1978.

Albright, W.F. "Astarte Plaques and Figurines from Tell Beit Mirsim." In *Mélanges Syriens offerts à Monsieur René Dussaud.* Librairie Orientaliste Paul Geuthner. Paris. 1939.

Alexiou, S. "Η μινοικη θεα μεθ'υψωμενων χειρων." *Kret Chron* 12 (1958), 179-299.

Alkim, U.B. *Anatolia I (From the Beginnings to the End of the 2nd Millennium B.C.* Nagel Publishers. Geneva. 1970.

Alkire, L.G. (Jr.) *Periodical Title Abbreviations: by Abbreviation.* Vol. 1. 11th edition. Gale Research Inc. London. 1998.

Alpözen, T.O., A.H. Özdas and B. Berkaya. *Commercial Amphoras of the Bodrum Museum of Underwater Archaeology.* Bodrum museum of Underwater Archaeology Publication No, 2. Bodrum. 1995.

Al-Radi, S.M.S. *Phlamoudhi Vounari: A Sanctuary Site in Cyprus.* Paul Åströms Förlag. Göteborg. 1983.

Ammerman, R.M. "The Naked Goddess: A Group of Archaic Terracotta Figurines from Paestum." *AJA* 95 (1991), 203-230.

Archi, A. "La religione e il culto nel Periodo Protosiriano." In P. Mattthiae et al. 1995.

————. "Divinités Sémitiques et Divinités de Substrat: le cas d'Ishhara et d'Ishtar à Ebla." *M.A.R.I.* 7 Paris. 1993, 71-78.

Arnaud, D. *Recherches au pays d'Ashtata: Emar [Mission archéologique de Meskené-Emar]* VI/3. Editions Recherches sur les civilizations 1985-87. Paris. 1986.

Assante, J. "The KAR.KID/ḫarimtu, Prostitute or Single Woman? A Reconsideration of the Evidence." *UF* 30 (1998), 5-96.

Astour, M.C. "Some New Divine Names from Ugarit." *JAOS* 86 (1966), 277-284.

Åström, P. "A Cypriote Cult Scene." *Journal of Prehistoric Religion* 2 (1988), 5-11.

————. "Relations between Cyprus and the Dodecanese in the Bronze Age." In Dietz and Papachristodoulou (eds.). 1988, 76-79.

305

————. "Comments on the Corpus of Mycenaean Pottery in Cyprus." In *MEM*.

Åström, P. et al. *Excavations at Kalopsidha and Ayios Iakovos in Cyprus.* SIMA, vol. 2. Lund. 1966.

————. *The Middle Cypriot Bronze Age.* Håkan Ohlssons Boktrycker. Lund. 1957.

Aufrecht, T. *Die Hymnen des Rigveda.* Adolph Marcus. Bonn. 1877.

Aupert, P. "Amathus During the First Iron Age." *BASOR* 308 (1997), 19-26.

————. "Argos aux VIIIe-VIIe siècles: Bourgade ou Métropole?" *ASAA* LX (1982), 21-32.

Aupert, P. et al. *Guide d'Amathonte.* De Boccard Edition-Diffusion. Paris. 1996.

Avigad, N. "Two Ammonite Seals Depicting the Dea Nutrix." *BASOR* 225 (1977), 63-66

Badre, L. "Late Bronze and Iron Age Imported Pottery from the Archaeological Excavations of Urban Beirut." In Karageorghis and Stampolidis (eds.). 1998, 73-83.

————. *Les figurines anthropomorphes en terre cuite à l'âge du bronze en Syrie.* Institute Français d'Archéologie du Proche Orient. Librairie Orientaliste Paul Geuther. Paris. 1980.

Bahrani, Z. "The Hellenization of Ishtar: Nudity, Fetishism, and the Production of Cultural Differentiation in Ancient Art." *The Oxford Art Journal* 19:2 (1996), 3-16.

Barlow, J.A., D.L. Bolger and B. Kling (eds.) *Cypriot Cermaics: Reading the Prehistoric Record.* A.G. Leventis Foundation and the University Museum of Archaeology and Anthropology, University of Pennsylvania. Philadelphia. 1991.

Barnstone, W. *Sappho and the Greek Lyric Poets.* Schocken Books. New York. 1988.

Barnett, R.D. *Ancient Ivories in the Middle East.* The Hebrew University of Jerusalem. Jerusalem. 1982.

Barrelet, M-Th. *Figurines et reliefs en terre cuite de la Mesopotamie antique I. Potiers, termes de metier, procedes de fabrication et production.* Bibliothèque archéologique et historique. LXXXV. Librairie Orientaliste Paul Geuthner. Paris. 1968.

————. "Deux déesses Syro-Phéniciennes sur un bronze du Louvre." *Syria* XXXV (1958), 27-44.

————. "Les Déesses Armées et Ailées." *Syria* XXXII (1955), 222-260.

Bass, G.F. "Beneath the Wine Dark Sea: Nautical Archaeology and the Phoenicians of the Odyssey." In Coleman and Walz (eds.). 1997, 71-101.

————. "A Bronze Age Shipwreck at Ulu Burun (Kas): 1984 Campaign." *AJA* 90 (1986), 269-296.

————. "Cape Gelidonya and Bronze Age Maritime Trade." In Hoffner (ed.). 1973, 29-38.

————. "The Earliest Seafarers in the Mediterranean and the Near East." In G.F. Bass (ed.) *A History of Seafaring Based on Underwater Archaeology*. Thames & Hudson. New York. 1972.

————. *Cape Gelidonya: A Bronze Age Shipwreck*. Transactions of the American Philosophical Society. New Series – Volume 57, Part 8. Philadelphia. 1967.

Baurain, C. *Chypre et la Mediterranée orientale au Bronze récent: Synthese historique*. École Française d'Athènes. Paris. 1984.

Baurain, C. and C. Bonnet. *Les Phéniciens: Marins des trois continents*. Armand Colin. Paris. 1992.

Bayhan, S. *Priene, Miletus, Didyma*. Keskin Color. Ankara. 1997.

Begg, P. *Late Cypriot Terracotta Figurines: a study in context*. Paul Åströms Förlag. Jonsered. 1991.

Belgiorno, M.R. "Transmission di elementi iconografici ciprioti ed egei dell'Età del Bronzo nell'Età del Ferro." In Musti et al. (eds.). 1991, 465–478.

Ben-Arieh, S. "A Mould for a Goddess Plaque." *IEJ* 33 (1983), 72–77 & Pl. 8.

Ben-Arieh, S. and G. Edelstein. "The Tombs and Their Contents," in "Akko Tombs near the Persian Garden." *'Atiqot* 12 (1977), 1–88.

Benton, S. "The Ionian Islands." *BSA* 32 (1931–32).

Bergoffen, C.J. *A Comparative Study of the Regional Distribution of Cypriote Pottery in Canaan and Egypt in the Late Bronze Age*. Doctoral Dissertation. New York University. 1990.

Bergquist, B. *The Archaic Greek Temenos. A Study of Structure and Function*. Dissertation. University of Uppsala. 1967.

Berranger, D. *Recherches sur l'histoire et la prosopographie de Paros à l'époque Archaïque*. Faculté des Lettres et Sciences humaines de l'Université Blaise-Pascal. Nouvelle serie, 36. 1992.

Betancourt, P.P. "Middle Minoan Objects in the Near East." In Cline and Harris-Cline (eds.). 1998, 5–12.

Bevan, E. "Ancient Deities and Tortoise-Representation in Sanctuaries." *BSA* 83 (1988), 1–6.

Bikai, P. "The Phoenicians in Cyprus." In Karageorghis (ed.). 1994, 31–38.

Binger, T. *Asherah: Goddess in Ugarit, Israel and the Old Testament*. Journal for the Study of the Old Testament Supplement Series 232. Sheffield Academic Press. Sheffield. 1997.

Boardman, J. *Athenian Black Figure Vases*. Thames & Hudson. London. 1991.

————. *The Greeks Overseas: Their Early Colonies and Trade*. New and enlarged edition. Thames & Hudson. New York. 1980.

————. *The Cretan Collection in Oxford: The Dictean Cave and Iron Age Crete*. Oxford at the Clarendon Press. Oxford. 1961.

Boedeker, D.D. *Aphrodite's Entry into Greek Epic*. Lugduni Batavorum. E.J. Brill. Leiden. 1974.

Böhm, S. *Die <<Nackte Göttin>>: zur Ikonographie und Deutung unbeklei- deter weiblicher Figuren in der frühgriechischen Kunst.* Verlag Philipp von Zabern. Mainz am Rhein. 1990.

Bolger, D. "Figurines, Fertility, and the Emergence of Complex Society in Pre- historic Cyprus." *Current Anthropology* 37 #2 (1996), 365-373.

————. "Engendering Cypriot Archaeology: Female Roles and Statuses Before the Bronze Age." *Opuscula Atheniensia* XX: 1, 1994, 9-16.

————. "The Feminine Mystique: Gender and Society in Prehistoric Cypriot Studies." *RDAC* 1993, 29-41.

————. "The Archaeology of Fertility and Birth: A Ritual Deposit from Chalcolithic Cyprus." *JAR* 48 (1992), 145-164.

————. *Erimi-Pamboula: A Chalcolithic Settlement in Cyprus.* BAR Interna- tional Series 443. Oxford. 1988.

Bonnet, C. *Astarté: dossier documentaire et perspectives historiques.* Consiglio Nazionale delle Ricerche. Rome. 1996.

Bonnet, C., E. Lipinski and P. Marchetti (eds.). *Religio Phoenicia: Acta Colloquii Namurensis habiti 14 et 15 mensis Decembris anni 1984.* Studia Phoenicia IV. Société des Études Classiques. Namur. 1986.

Bordreuil, P. "Ventes." *Syria* LXII (1985), 171-186.

————. "Ashtart de Mari et les Dieux d'Ougarit." In *M.A.R.I.* 4. (1985) 545- 548.

————. "Une Inscription Phenicienne Champlevée des Environs de Byblos." *Semitica* XXVII (1977), 23-28.

Bousquet, J. "Le Temple d'Aphrodite et d'Ares à Sta Lenika." *BCH* 62 (1938), 386-408.

Brumfield, A. "Aporreta: Verbal and Ritual Obscenity in the Cults of Ancient Women." In Hägg (ed.). 1996.

Broneer, O. "Eros and Aphrodite on the North Slope of the Acropolis in Athens." *Hesperia* 1 (1932), 31-55.

Brüschweiler, F. *Inanna: La déesse triomphante et vaincue dans la cosmologie sumérienne: recherche lexicographique.* Editions Peeters. Leuven. 1987.

Buchanan, B. *Catalogue of Ancient Near Eastern Seals in the Ashmolean Mu- seum Vol. I: Cylinder Seals.* Oxford University at the Clarendon Press. Oxford. 1966.

Buchner, G. and D. Ridgway. *Pithekoussai I: La Necropoli: Tombe 1-723 Scavate dal 1952 al 1961.* Accademia Nazionale dei Lincei. Giorgio Bretschneider. Milan. 1993.

Buchner, G. and C.F. Russo. "La coppa di Nestore e un'inscrizione metrica da Pithecusa dell'VIII secolo av. Cr." *Rend Linc* 10 (1955), 215-234.

Buck, C.D. *Introduction to the Study of the Greek Dialects; Grammar, Selected Inscriptions, Glossary.* Ginn and Co. Boston. 1928.

Buitron-Oliver, D. and E. Herscher. "The City-Kingdoms of Early Iron Age Cyprus in Their Eastern Mediterranean Context." *BASOR* 308 (1997), 5–8.

Bunnens, G. *L'expansion phénicienne en Méditerranée: essai d'interprétation fondé sur une analyse des traditions littéraires.* Institute historique belge de Rome. Brussels. 1979.

Burdajewicz, M. *The Aegean Sea Peoples and Religious Architecture in the Eastern Mediterranean at the Close of the Late Bronze Age.* BAR International Series 558. Oxford. 1990.

Burkert, W. "Greek Temple-builders: Who, Where and Why?" in Hägg (ed.). 1996.

————. *The Orientalizing Revolution: Near Eastern Influence on Greek Culture in the Early Archaic Age.* Harvard University Press. Cambridge. 1992.

————. "Oriental and Greek Mythology: The Meeting of Parallels." in *Interpretations of Greek Mythology.* Jan Bremmer and Fritz Graf (eds.). Barnes & Noble. Totowa. 1986.

————. *Greek Religion.* Harvard University Press. Cambridge. 1985.

Burt, E.C. *Erotic Art: an annotated bibliography with essays.* G.K. Hall & Co. Boston. 1989.

Bury, J.B. and R. Meiggs. *A History of Greece.* MacMillan Press. London. 1987.

Buschor, E. "Aphrodite und Hermes." *Ath Mitt* 52 (1957), 77–86.

Cadoux, C.J. *Ancient Smyrna: A History of the City from the Earliest Times to 324 A.D.* Basil Blackwell. Oxford. 1938.

Camp, J.McK. *The Athenian Agora: Excavations in the Heart of Classical Athens.* Thames & Hudson. New York. 1986.

Campbell, D.A. *Greek Lyric I.* Harvard University Press. London. 1982.

Caquot, A. and M. Sznycer. *Ugaritic Religion.* E.J. Brill. Leiden. 1980.

Carpenter, J.R. "Excavations at Phaneromeni." In *Studies in Cypriot Archaeology.* (ed.). Biers and Soren. UCLA. Los Angeles. 1981, 59–66.

Carpenter, T.H. *Art and Myth in Ancient Greece: A Handbook.* Thames & Hudson. London. 1991.

Carrière, B. and A. Barrois. "Fouilles de l'École Archéologique Française de Jerusalem Effectuées à Neirab du 24 Septembre au 5 Novembre 1926." *Syria* 8 (1927), 126–142, 201ff.

Carson, A. "Putting Her in Her Place: Women, Dirt and Desire." In Halperin, Winkler and Zeitlin (eds.). 1990, 135–169.

Cartledge, P. *Sparta and Lakonia: A Regional History 1300–362 B.C.* Routledge & Kegan Paul. London. 1979.

Catling, H. "Reflections upon the Interpretation of the Archaeological Evidence for the History of Cyprus." In *Studies Presented in Memory of P. Dikaios.* Nicosia. 1979: 194–205.

————. "The Achaean Settlement of Cyprus." In *MEM*, 33–39.

————. "A Cypriot Bronze Statuette in the Bomford Collection." In *Alasia I*: 1971, 15-32.

————. *Cypriot Bronzework in the Mycenaean World*. Oxford University at the Clarendon Press. Oxford. 1964.

Caubet, A. and M. Yon. "Deux Appliqués Murales." *RDAC* 1974, 112-131.

Chadwick, J. "Potnia." *Minos* VI (1957), 117-129.

————. *The Mycenaean World*. Cambridge University Press. Cambridge. 1980.

Chavalas, M.W. *Emar: The History, Religion, and Culture of a Syrian Town in the Late Bronze Age*. CDL Press. Bethesda. 1996.

Clamer, C. "A Gold Plaque from Tel Lachish." *Tel Aviv* 7 (1980), 152-162.

Clifford, R.J. "Phoenician Religion." *BASOR* 279 (1990), 55-64.

Cline, E. *Sailing the Wine-Dark Sea: International trade and the Late Bronze Age Aegean*. BAR International Series 591. London. 1994.

————. "Amenhotep III and the Aegean: A Reassessment of Egypto-Aegean Relations in the 14th Century." *Orientalia* 56 (1987), 1-36.

Cline, E.H. and D. Harris-Cline (eds.). *The Aegean and the Orient in the Second Millennium: Proceedings of the 50th Anniversary Symposium, Cincinnati, 18-20 April 1997*. Aegaeun 18. Université de Liège and University of Texas at Austin. Austin. 1998.

Cohen, B. "The Anatomy of Kassandra's Rape: Female Nudity Comes of Age in Greek Art." *The Source* 12-13 (1992-1993), 37-46.

Coldstream, J.N. and G.L. Huxley. *Kythera; Excavations and Studies Conducted by the University of Pennsylvanian Museum and the British School at Athens*. Noyes Press. Park Ridge. 1973.

Coldstream, J.N. and P.M. Bikai. "Early Greek Pottery in Tyre and Cyprus: Some Preliminary Comparisons." *RDAC* 1988², 35-44.

Coldstream, J.N. "The First Exchanges between Euboeans and Phoenicians: Who Took the Initiative?" In S. Gitin, A. Mazar and T. Dothan (eds.). 1998a. 353-360.

————. "Crete and the Dodecanese: Alternative Eastern Approaches to the Greek World during the Geometric Period." In Karageorghis and Stampolidis (eds.). 1998b, 255-262.

————. "Early Greek Visitors to Cyprus and the Eastern Mediterranean." In Tatton-Brown (ed.). 1989, 90-96.

————. "Greeks and Phoenicians in the Aegean." In Niemeyer (ed.). 1982, 261-275.

————. "Kythera: The Change from Early Helladic to Early Minoan." in R.A. Crossland and A. Birchall (eds.). *Bronze Age Migrations in the Aegean: Archaeological and Linguistic Problems in Greek Prehistory*. Duckworth Ltd. London. 1973. 33-36.

————. "Cypro-Aegean Exchanges in the 9th and 8th Centuries B.C." In *Praktika* 1972, 15-22.

————. "Some Cypriot Traits in Cretan Pottery, c. 950-700 B.C." In *RBCC*. 257-263.

————. *Geometric Greece*. Methuen & Co., Ltd. London. 1977.

————. "Kition and Amathus: Some Reflections on Their Westward Links during the Early Iron Age." In *CBOO*, 321-329.

Coleman, J.E. "Ancient Greek Eurocentrism." In Coleman and Walz (eds.). 1997, 175-220.

Coleman, J. E. et al. *Alambra: A Middle Bronze Age Settlement in Cyprus: Archaeological Investigations by Cornell University 1974-1985*. Paul Åströms Förlag. Jonsered. 1996.

Coleman, J.E. and C. A. Walz (eds.). *Greeks and Barbarians: Essays on the Interactions between Greeks and Non-Greeks in Antiquity and the Consequences for Eurocentrism*. CDL Press. Bethesda. 1997.

Collon, D. *The Seal Impressions from Tell Atchana/Alalakh*. Ph.D. Dissertation, Columbia University. 1975.

Colonna, G. "Novita Sui Culti Di Pyrgi." *Rend Pont*. LVII (1984-85), 57-88.

Conzelmann, H. "Corinth und die Mädchen der Aphrodite." *Göttingen Nachrichten*. 1967, 246-261.

Cook, R.M. *Greek Painted Pottery*. Third Edition. Routledge Press. London. 1997.

Cook, S.A. *The Religion of Ancient Palestine in the Light of Archaeology*. British Academy. London. 1925.

Cornelius, I. "Anat and Qudshu as the <<Mistress of Animals>> Aspects of the Iconography of the Canaanite Goddess." *SEL* 10 (1993). 21-45.

Corpus Inscriptionum Graecarum. A. Boeckhius (ed.). Berolini.

Corpus Vasorum Antiquorum. Italia, Museo Nazionale di Villa Giulia in Roma, a Cura de G.Q. Giglioli. Casa Editria d'Arte Bestetti E. Tumminelli. Rome.

Coulson, W.D.E. and Al. Leonard, Jr. "Investigations at Naukratis and Environs, 1980 and 1981." *AJA* 86 (1982), 361-380.

————. *Cities of the Delta, Part 1: Naukratis. Preliminary Report on the 1977-78 and 1980 Seasons*. Undena Publications. Malibu. 1981

Courtois, J.C. "Vestiges Minoens a Enkomi." In *RBCC*, 158-172.

————. "Le sanctuaire du dieu au lingot d'Enkomi-Alasia." In Schaeffer (ed.). 1971.

Courtois, J.C., J. Largarce et E. Lagarce. *Enkomi et le bronze récent à Chypre*. Imprimerie Zavallis. Nicosia. 1986.

Courtois, J.C. and J. Webb. *Les cylindres-sceaux d'Enkomi: Fouilles françaises 1957-1970*. Mission archéologique française d'Alasia. Nicosia. 1987.

Crielaard, J.P. "Surfing on the Mediterranean Web: Cypriot Long-distance Communications during the Eleventh and Tenth Centuries B.C." In Karageorghis and Stampolidis (eds.). 1998, 187-204.

Cross, F.M. *Canaanite Myth and Hebrew Epic: Essays in the History of the Religion of Israel*. Harvard University Press. Cambridge. 1973.

Crowley, J.L. *The Aegean and the East: An Investigation into the Transference of Artistic Motifs between the Aegean, Egypt, and the Near East in the Bronze Age.* Paul Åströms Förlag. Jonsered. 1989.

Culican, W. "A Terracotta Shrine from Achzib." *ZDPV* 92 (1976), 47-53.

Cureton, W. *Spicilegium Syriacum.* Leiden. 1855.

Curtis, A. *Ugarit (Ras Shamra).* William B. Ecrdmans Publishing Co. Grand Rapids. 1985.

Dalley, S. "Near Eastern Patron Deities of Mining and Smelting in the Late Bronze and Early Iron Ages." *RDAC* 1987, 61-66.

Daux, G. "Chronique des Fouilles 1968." *BCH* 93 (1969), 419-430, 946-954.

——————. "Chronique des Fouilles 1967." *BCH* 92 (1968), 241-256, 625-632.

Davidson, G.R. *Corinth, Volume XII: The Minor Objects.* ASCSA. Princeton. 1952.

Davidson, H. *Gods and Myths of Northern Europe.* Penguin Books. Baltimore. 1964.

Dawson, W.R and T.E. Peet. "The So-Called Poem on the King's Chariot." *JEA* 19 (1933), 167-174.

Day, P.L. 'Anat: Ugarit's "Mistress of Animals." *JNES* 51 (1992), 181-190.

de Cree, F. "The Black-on-Red or Cyprus Phoenician Ware." In Lipinski (ed.). 1991.

de Franciscis, A. "Ancient Locri." *Archaeology* 11/3 (1958), 206-212.

Delcor, M. "Le Personnel du Temple d'Astarté à Kition d'après une Tablette Phénicienne (CIS 86 A et B)." *UF* 11. 1979.

——————. "Astarte." *LIMC*, vol. III (supplement). 1986, 1077-1085.

Delivorrias, A.S. "Χρονικα" *AD* 23 (1968).

Delivorrias, A., G. Berger-Doer and A. Kossatz-Deissmann. "Aphrodite." *LIMC*, vol. II. 1984, 2-151.

Demand, N. *Birth, Death, and Motherhood in Classical Greece.* Johns Hopkins University Press. Baltimore. 1994.

Demargne, P. *La Crète dédalique: études sur les origines d'une renaissance.* Bibliothèque des Écoles Françaises d'Athèns et de Rome, 164. E. de Boccard. Paris. 1947.

Demetriou, A. *Cypro-Aegean Relations in the Early Iron Age.* SIMA LXXXIII. Paul Åströms Förlag. Göteborg. 1989.

De Moor, J.C. *An Anthology of Religious Texts from Ugarit.* E.J. Brill. Leiden. 1987.

——————. "'Athtartu the Huntress (KTU 1.92)." *UF* 17 (1986), 225-230.

Desborough, V.R. "Mycenaeans in Cyprus in the 11th Century B.C." In *MEM*, 79-87.

——————. *The Greek Dark Ages.* St. Martin's Press. New York. 1972.

Des Gagniers, J. and V. Karageorghis. *Vases et figurines de l'Âge du bronze à Chypre: céramique rouge et noire polie.* Presses de l'Université Laval. Québec. 1976.

Detienne, M. *The Gardens of Adonis: Spices in Greek Mythology.* Princeton University Press. Princeton. 1994.

Dever, W.G. "Excavations at Gezer." *BA* XXX #2 (1967), 47-62.

Dietrich, B.C. "Minoan Religion in the Context of the Aegean." In Krzyszkowska, O. and L. Nixon (eds.). 1983, 55-60.

Dietrich, M., O. Lorentz and J. Sanmartin (eds.). *Keilalphabetischen Texte aus Ugarit.* Ugarit-Verlag. Münster. 1995.

Dietz, S. and I. Papachristodoulou. *Archaeology in the Dodecanese.* National Museum of Denmark. Copenhagen. 1988.

Dijkstra, M. "The Myth of Astarte, the Huntress (KTU 1.92): New fragments." *UF* 26 (1994), 113-126.

Dikaios, P. *Enkomi: Excavations 1948-1958.* Vol. 1-3. Verlag Philipp von Zabern. Mainz am Rhein. 1969-1971.

————. "The Excavations at Erimi, 1933-1935." *RDAC* 1936, 1-81.

————. "Les Cultes Préhistoriques dans l'Île de Chypre." *Syria* 13 (1932), 345-354.

Dodds, E.R. *The Greeks and the Irrational.* University of California Press. Berkeley. 1963.

Donner, H. and W. Rölling. *Kanaanäische und Aramäische Inschriften.* Otto Harrassowitz. Wiesbaden. 1962-.

Donohue, A.A. *Xoana and the Origins of Greek Sculpture.* American Classical Studies 15. Scholar's Press. Atlanta. 1988.

Dossin, G. "Les Inscriptions des Statues de Mari (1952)." *CRAI* 1953.

————. *Mission archéologique de Mari IV.* Librairie Orientaliste Paul Geuthner. Paris. 1968.

————. "Le Pantheon de Mari." In *Studia Mariana* (ed.). A. Parrot. E.J. Brill. Leiden. 1950.

Dothan, T. "Minoan Elements and Influence at Athienou, Cyprus." In *RBCC*, 173-177.

Dothan, T. and A. Ben-Tor. *Excavations at Athienou.* Qedem 16. The Hebrew University of Jerusalem. Jerusalem. 1983.

Douglas Van Buren, E. *Clay Figurines of Babylonia and Assyria.* Yale Oriental Series XVI. Yale University Press. New Haven. 1930.

Drerup, H. "Zur Entstehung der griechischen Tempelringhalle." In *Festschrift für Friedrich Matz.* Verlag Philipp von Zabern. Mainz. 1962, 32-38.

————. "Prostashaus und Pastashaus: zur Typologie des griechischen Hauses." *Marb W Pr* 1967, 6-17.

————. *Griechesche Baukunst in Geometrischer Zeit.* Vondenhoech & Ruprecht. Göttingen. 1969.

Driessen, J. and A. Farnux (eds.). *La Crète Mycenienne: Actes de la Table Ronde Internationale organisée par l'École française d'Athènes.* BCH Supplément 30. Athens. 1997.

Drioton, E. et J. Vandier. *L'Egypte: des origines à la conquete d'Alexandre*. Presses Universitaires de France. Paris. 6th ed. 1984.

Dugand, J-E. "Aphrodite-Astarte (de l'etymologie du nom d'Aphrodite)." In *Hommage à Pierre Fargues (philologie, littératures et histoire anciennes)*. Annales de la Faculté des Lettres et Sciences Humaines de Nice. No. 21. Paris. 1974.

Du Mesnil du Buisson, Comte. "Une Campaigne de Fouilles à Khan Sheikoun." *Syria* 13 (1932), 171-184.

Dunand, M. *Fouilles de Byblos*. Tome V. Librairie d'Amerique et d'Orient, Adrien Maisonneuve. Paris. 1973.

Dunayevsky, I. and A. Kempinski. "The Megiddo Temples." *ZDPV* 89 (1973), 161-187.

Dupont-Sommer, A. "Les Phéniciens à Chypre." *RDAC* 1974, 75-94.

Dussaud, R. *Les Anciennes Religions Orientales: Les Religions des Hittites et des Hourrites, des Phéniciens et des Syriens*. Presses Universitaires de France. Paris. 1945.

————. *Les Découvertes de Ras Shamra (Ugarit) et l'Ancien Testament*. Librairie Paul Geuthner. Paris. 1941.

————. "Culte funeraire et culte chthonien à Chypre à l'âge du bronze." *Syria* 13 (1932).

Edwards, I.E.S. "A Relief of Qudshu-Astarte-Anath in the Winchester College Collection." *JNES* XIV (Jan-Oct, 1955), 49-51.

Edwards, R. "The Story of Theseus." In Ward et al. (eds.). 1970.

Edzard, D.O. "Pantheon und Kult in Mari." *Rencontre Assyriologique Internationale* XV. Paris. 1967. 51-71.

Engelmann, H. and R. Merkelbach. *Die Inschriften von Erythrai und Klazomenai*. Teil II. Rudolf Habelt Verlag. Bonn. 1973.

Engelmann, H., D. Knibbe, R. Merkelbach. *Die Inschriften von Ephesos*. Teil IV. Rudolf Habelt Verlag. Bonn. 1980.

Enmann, A. "Cyprus und der Ursprung des Aphroditekultes." *Memoires de l'Academie des Sciences de Saint-Petersbourg*. VII serie, Tome XXXIV. (1886), 1-85.

Epstein, C. "An Interpretation of the Megiddo Sacred Area During Middle Bronze II." *IEJ* 15 (1965), 204-221.

Eriksson, K.O. *Red Lustrous Wheel-Made Ware*. Paul Åströms Förlag. Jonsered. 1993.

Evans, A.J. *The Palace of Minos at Knossos*. Vol. I. Macmillan & Co., Ltd. London. 1921.

Falsone, G. "Anath or Astarte? A Phoenician Bronze Statuette of the <<Smiting Goddess>>." In Bonnet et al. 1986, 53-76.

Farnell, L.R. *The Cults of The Greek States*. Aegaean Press. Chicago. 1971.

Finkelberg, M. "Minoan Inscriptions on Libation Vessels." *Minos* 1990, 43-85.

Fischer, P.M. *Prehistoric Cypriot Skulls: A Medico-Anthropological, Archaeological and Micro-Analytical Investigation.* Paul Åströms Förlag. Göteborg. 1986.

Flemberg, J. *Venus Armata: Studien zur bewaffneten Aphrodite in der griechisch-römischen Kunst.* Skrifter Utgivna av Svenska Institutet i Athen, 8, X. Stockholm. 1991.

Fleming, D.E. "The Emar Festivals: City Unity and Syrian Identity under Hittite Hegemony." In Chavalas (ed.). 1996.

————. *The Installation of Baal's High Priestess at Emar: A Window on Ancient Syrian Religion.* Harvard Semitic Series 42. Scholars Press. Atlanta. 1992.

Flourentzos, P. "Selected Antiquities of Red Polished Ware from Cypriot Private Collections." *Op Ath* XIV:3, 1982, 21–26.

————. "Notes of the Red Polished III Plank-Shaped Idols from Cyprus." *RDAC* 1975, 29–35.

Foley, H. (ed.). *The Homeric Hymn to Demeter: Translation, Commentary, and Interperative Essays.* Princeton University Press. Princeton. 1994.

Fontenrose, J. Review of Boedeker's Aphrodite's Entry into Greek Epic. *CW* LXX (1977), pp. 460–461.

Foster, B.R. *Before the Muses: An Anthology of Akkadian Literature.* CDL Press. Bethesda. 1993.

Frankel, D. "On Cypriot Figurines and the Origins of Patriarchy." *CA* 38 (1997), 84.

Frankel, D. and A. Tamvaki. "Cypriot Shrine Models and Decorated Tombs." *AJBA* 2 (1973), 39–44.

Frankel, D. and J. Webb. *Marki Alonia: An Early and Middle Bronze Age Town in Cyprus: Excavations 1990–1994.* Paul Åströms Förlag. Jonsered. 1996.

Frankfort, H. *Art and Architecture of the Ancient Orient.* The Pelican History of Art. Penguin Books. 1989.

Frantz-Szabó. "Ishara." In *RlA*, Fünfter Band. 1980, 177–178.

Frayne, D. *The Royal Inscriptions of Mesopotamia, Early Periods, Vol. 4: Old Babylonian Period (2003–1595).* University of Toronto Press. Toronto. 1990.

French, E. "Development of Mycenaean Terracotta Figurines." *BSA* 66 (1971) 102–187.

Friedrich, P. *The Meaning of Aphrodite.* University of Chicago Press. Chicago. 1978.

Frost, H. "On a Sacred Cypriot Anchor." In Starcky and Hours (eds.). 1982, 161–166.

Fuhrmann, H. "Locri." *Arch Anz* 1941, 648ff.

Gawlikowska, Kr. "Eshtar et Ishtar à Mari au IIIè millenaire." *Rocznik Orientalistyczny.* XLI/2 (1980), 25–28.

Gardner, E.A. *Naukratis II.* Trübner & Co. London. 1888.

————. "The Early Ionic Alphabet." *JHS* 7 (1886), 220-239.

Gardner, P. "Statuette of Pallas from Cyprus." *JHS* 2 (1881), 326-331.

Gaster, T.H. "The Egyptian 'Story of Astarte' and the Ugaritic Poem of Baal." *Bibliotheca Orientalis*. Jaargang IX (1952), 82-85.

Gebhard, E.R "The Evolution of a pan-Hellenic Sanctuary: From Archaeology toward History at Isthmia." In *Greek Sanctuaries: New Approaches*. Ed by N. Marinatos and R. Hägg. Routledge Press. 1993, 154-177.

Gelb, I.J. "The Inscription of Jibbit-Lim, King of Ebla." *Stud Or* 55 (1984), 213-229.

Gesell, G.C. *Town, Palace, and House Cult in Minoan Crete*. Paul Åströms Förlag. Göteborg. 1985.

————. "The Place of the Goddess in Minoan Society." In Krzyszkowska and Nixon (eds.). 1983, 93-99.

Getz-Preziosi, P. *Early Cycladic Sculpture: An Introduction* (Revised Edition). J. Paul Getty Museum. Malibu. 1994.

Gilmour, G. "Aegean Influence in Late Bronze Age Funerary Practices in the Southern Levant." In S. Campbell and A. Green (eds.). *The Archaeology of Death in the Ancient Near East*. Oxbow Monographs 51. Oxford. 1995.

————. "Aegean Sanctuaries and the Levant in the Late Bronze Age." *BSA* 88 (1993), 125-134.

Gitin, S., A. Mazar and E. Stern (eds.). *Mediterranean Peoples in Transition: Thirteenth to Early Tenth Centuries BCE*. Israel Exploration Society. Jerusalem. 1998.

Gittlen, B.M. "The Cultural and Chronological Implications of the Cypro-Palestinian Trade During the Late Bronze Age." *BASOR* 241 (1981), 49-59.

Gjerstad, E. "The Colonization of Cyprus in Greek Legend." *OA*. Vol. III. Institutum Romanum Regni Sueciae. 1944, 107-123.

Gordon, C.H. *Ugaritic Literature, a Comprehensive Translation of the Poetric and Prose Texts*. Pontificium Institutum Biblicum. Rome. 1949.

Goring, E. "Pottery Figurines: The Development of a Coroplastic Art in Chalcolithic Cyprus." *BASOR* 282-283 (1991), 153-161.

Gow, A.S.F. *Theocritus, edited with a Translation and Commentary*. 2nd ed. Cambridge University Press. Cambridge. 1952.

Graeve, V.v. "Milet 1992-1993." *ArchAnz* 1995, 195-203.

Graham, A.J. "The Odyssey, History, and Women." In B. Cohen (ed.) *The Distaff Side: Representing the Female in Homer's Odyssey*. Oxford University Press. Oxford. 1995, 3-16.

Gray, G.B. "The Excavations at Gezer and Religion in Ancient Palestine." *The Expositor* 7 (1909), 423-442.

Greco, E. *Il Pittore di Afrodite*. Museo del Sannio. Benevento. 1970.

Griffin, A. *Sikyon*. Clarendon Press. Oxford. 1982.

Grigson, G. *The Goddess of Love*. Stein & Day Publishers. 1977.

Groneberg, B. "Ein Ritual an Ishtar." In *M.A.R.I.* 8. Paris. 1997.

————. "Die sumerisch-akkadische Inanna/Ishtar: Hermaphroditos?" *WO* XVII (1986), 25–46.

Guarducci, M. "Due Pezzi Insigni del Museo Nationale Romano: Il "Trono-Ludovisi" e l'"Acrolito Ludovisi." *Bollettino d'Arte* 33–34 (1985); Settembre-Dicembre, 1–20.

Guarducci, M. (ed.) *Inscriptiones Creticae*. La Libreria dello Stato. Rome. 1935.

Gubel, E. and P. Bordreuil. "Statuette Fragmentaire Portant le nom de la Baalat Gubal." *Semitica* XXXV (1985), 5–11.

Gubel, E., E. Lipinski and B. Servais-Soyez (eds.). *Redt Tyrus/Sauvons Tyr*. Studia Phoenicia I–II. Uitgeverij Peeters. Leuven. 1983.

Gubel, E. "Art in Tyre during the First and Second Iron Age: A Preliminary Survey." In Gubel et al., 1983, 23–46.

Gulick, C.B. (ed.). *The Deipnosophists*. Harvard University Press. Cambridge. 1967.

Guzzo Amadasi, M.G. "Two Phoenician Inscriptions Carved in Ivory: Again the Ur Box and the Sarepta Plaque." *Orientalia* 59: 1-2 (1990), 58–66.

Guzzo Amadasi, M.G and V. Karagoerghis. *Fouilles de Kition III. Inscriptions Phéniciennes*. Department of Antiquities, Cyprus. Nicosia. 1977.

Haas, V. *Geschichte der Hethitischen Religion*. E.J. Brill. Leiden. 1994.

Hadley, J.M. *Yahwey's Asherah in the Light of Recent Discovery*. Ph.D. Dissertation. St. John's College, Cambridge University. 1989.

Hadjioannou, K. "On the Identification of the Horned God of Engomi-Alasia." In Schaeffer (ed.). 1971.

————. "On Some Disputed Matters of the Ancient Religion of Cyprus." *RDAC* 1978, 103–110.

Hägg, R. (ed.) *The Role of Religion in the Early Greek Polis: Proceedings of the Third International Seminar on Ancient Greek Cult, Organized by the Swedish Institute at Athens, 16–18 October 1992*. Svenska Institutet i Athen. Stockholm. 1996.

Hägg, R. "Religious Syncretism at Knossos?" In Driessen and Farnous (eds.). 1997, 163–168.

————. "Geomentric Sanctuaries in the Argolid." In Piépart (ed.). 1992. 9–35.

Hallager, E. and M. Vlasaki. "New Linear B Tablets from Khania." In Driessen and Farnous (eds.). 1997, 169–174.

Halperin, D. J. Winkler, and Fr. Zeitlin (eds.). *Before Sexuality: The Construction of Erotic Experience in the Ancient Greek World*. Princeton University Press. Princeton. 1990

Hampe, R. and E. Simon. *The Birth of Greek Art, from the Mycenaean to the Archaic Period*. Oxford University Press. New York. 1981.

Handy, L.K. *Among the Host of Heaven: the Syro-Palestinian Pantheon as Bureaucracy*. Eisenbrauns. Winona Lake. 1994.

Head, B.V. *Catalogue of the Greek Coins of Ionia*. British Museum. London. 1892.

Heimpel, W. "A Catalogue of Near Eastern Venus Deities." *Syro-Mesopotamian Studies*, vol. 4, issue 3. December 1982.

Heinz, M. and R. Senff. "Die Grabung auf dem Zeytintepe." *ArchAnz* 1995, 220–223.

Herbillon, J. *Les cultes de Patras, avec une prosopograhie Patréenne*. Johns Hopkins Press. Baltimore. 1929.

Hermary, A. "Votive Offerings in the Sanctuaries of Cyprus, Rhodes and Crete during the Late Geometric and Archaic Periods." In Karageorghis and Stampolidis (eds.). 1998, 265–275.

——————. "Les fouilles françaises d'Amathonte." In Yon (ed.). 1993, 167–193.

——————. "Amathonte de Chypre et les Phéniciennes." In Lipinski (ed.). 1987, 375–388.

Herrmann, W. "Ashtart." *MIO* XV (1969), 6–55.

Herscher, E. "Southern Cyprus, the Disappearing Early Bronze Age, and the Evidence from Phaneromeni." In *Studies in Cypriot Archaeology*. (ed.). by J.C. Biers and D. Soren. UCLA Press. 1981. 79–82.

Herter, H. "Die Ursprünge des Aphroditekultes." from *Kleine Schriften*. E. Vogt (ed.) Wilhelm Fink Verlag. Munich. 1975, 28–42.

Hess, R.S. "Divine Names in the Amarna Texts." *UF* 18 (1986), 149–168.

Hestrin, R. "The Cult Stand from Ta'anach and Its Religious Background." In Lipinski (ed.). 1987. 61–77.

Higgins, R. *Minoan and Mycenaean Art*. Thames & Hudson. New York. 1989.

Hill, G. *A History of Cyprus*. Cambridge University Press. Cambridge. 1940.

Hiller, S. "Cretan Sanctuaries and Mycenaean Palatial Administration at Knossos." In Driessen and Farnoux (eds.). 1997.

Hiller von Gaertringen, F. "Die Älteste Inschrift von Paros." *Jahreshefte des Österreichischen Archäologischen Institutes in Wien*. V (1902).

——————. *Inschriften von Priene*. Druk und Verlag von Georg Reimer. Berlin. 1906.

Honeyman, A.M. "The Phoenician Inscriptions of the Cyprus Museum." *Iraq* V–VI (1939), 104–108.

Hood, S. "Mycenaean Settlement in Cyprus and the Coming of the Greeks." In *MEM*, 40–50.

Hooker, J.T. "Minoan and Mycenaean Settlement in Cyprus: A Note." In *Praktika* 1985.

Hoffmann, H. "Foreign Influence and Native Invention in Archaic Greek Altars." *AJA* 57, no. 3 (July, 1953), 189–195.

Hoffner, H.A. (ed.) *Orient and Occident: Essays presented to Cyrus H. Gordon on the Occasion of His Sixty-fifth Birthday*. Verlag Butzon & Bercker Kevelaer. Neukirchener Verlag. Neukirchen-Vluyn. 1973.

Hogarth, D.G., H.L. Lorimer and C.C. Edgar. "Naukratis, 1903." *JHS* 25 (1905), 105ff.

Holland, T.A. *A Typological and Archaeological Study of Human and Animal Representations in the Plastic Art of Palestine During the Iron Age.* Unpublished Dissertation. Oxford. 1975.

————. "Figurine Plaque from Gezer." in Dever et al., *Gezer II: Report of the 1967-70 Seasons in Fields I and II.* Vol. II. Hebrew Union College. Jerusalem. 1975.

Hollander, L.M. *The Poetic Edda.* 2nd ed., revised. University of Texas Press. Austin. Second Edition. 1962.

Hollinshead, M.B. "'Adyton,' 'Opisthodomos,' and the Inner Room." *Hesperia* 68 (1999), pp-pp.

Huffnor, H.B. *Amorite Personal Names in the Mari Texts: A Structural and Lexical Study.* Johns Hopkins Press. Baltimore. 1965.

Hulin, L. "Marsa Matruh 1987, Preliminary Ceramic Report." *JARCE* XXVI (1989), 115-126.

Hurwit, J.M. *The Art and Culture of Early Greece, 1100-480 B.C.* Cornell University Press. Ithaca. 1985.

Huxley, G.L. *Acheans & Hittites.* The Queen's University. Belfast. 1960.

Ingholt, H. *Rapport préliminaire sur sept campaignes de fouilles à Hama en Syrie (1932-1938).* Ejnar Munksgaard. Copenhagen. 1940.

Inscriptiones Graecae. Consilio et Auctoritate Academiae Litterarum Regiae Boriassicae editae. Berolini. Apud Georgium Reimerum. 1873-1914.

Ioannides, G.C. (ed.), *Studies in Honour of Vassos Karageorghis.* Association of Cypriot Studies. Nicosia. 1992.

Isler, H.P. *Studia Ietina II.* Universität Zürich, Archäologisches Institut. Eugen Rentsch Verlag. Zürich. 1984.

Jackson, H. "A Black-Figure Neck-Amphora in Melbourne: The Nudity of Kassandra." *Mediterranean Archaeology* 9/10 (1996/97), 53-75.

Jacobsen, T. "The Graven Image." In Miller et al. (eds.). 1987.

————. *The Treasures of Darkness: A History of Mesopotamian Religion.* Yale University Press. New Haven. 1976.

Jamot, P. "Travaux de l'École Française d'Athèns." *CRAI* 1938.

Jenkins, R.J.H. *Dedalica: A Study of Dorian Plastic Art in the Seventh Century B.C.* Cambridge University Press. Cambridge. 1936.

Johansen, K.F. *Les vases sicyoniens; étude archéologique.* E. Champion. Paris. 1923.

Johnston, A.W. and A.K. Andriomenou. "A Geometric Graffito from Eretria." *BSA* 84 (1989), 217-220.

Jost, M. *Sanctuaires et Cultes d'Arcadie.* École Française d'Athènes. Paris. 1985.

Kadletz, E. "Pausanias 1.27.3 and the Route of the Arrhephoroi." *AJA* 86 (1982), 445-446.

Kanta, A. "Cult, Continuity and the Evidence of Pottery at the Sanctuary of Syme Viannou, Crete." In Musti et al. (eds.). 1991.

Kanta, A. and A Karetsou. "From Arkadhes to Rytion. Interactions of an Isolated Area of Crete with the Aegean and the East Mediterranean." In Karageorghis and Stampolidis (eds.). 1998, 159–173.

————. "Cypriot Connections in the Area of Arkadhes, Crete." In *CAA*, 159–170.

Kantor, H.J. "A Bronze Plaque with Relief Decoration from Tell Tainat." *JNES* XXI (1962), 93–117.

Karageorghis, J. "On Some Aspects of Chalcolithic Religion in Cyprus." *RDAC* 1992, 17–27.

————. *La grande déesse de Chypre et son Culte à travers l'iconographie de l'époque néolithique au VIème s. a.C.* Maison de l'Orient Mediterranéen Ancien. Lyons. 1977.

Karageorghis, V. *The Coroplastic Art of Ancient Cyprus*. Volumes 1–6. A.G Leventis Foundation. Nicosia. 1991–1998c.

————. "'Astarte' in Naxos?" In Karageorghis and Stampolidis (eds.). 1998a, 121–126.

————. *Greek Gods and Heroes in Ancient Cyprus*. Commercial Bank of Greece. Athens. 1998b.

————. "L'archéologie française et le Bronze Récent à Chypre." In Yon (ed.). 1993.

————. *Tombs at Palaipaphos 1. Teratsoudhia 2. Eliomylia.* Leventis Foundation. Nicosia. 1990.

————. "Cyprus." In S. Moscati (ed.). *The Phoenicians*. Bompiani. Milan. 1988.

————. "New Light on Late Bronze Age Cyprus." In *Praktika* 1985b.

————. *Palaepaphos-Skales: An Iron Age Cemetery in Cyprus.* Ausgrabungen in Alt-Paphos auf Cypern 3. Universitätsverlag Konstanz. Konstanz. 1983.

————. *Cyprus: From the Stone Age to the Romans.* Thames & Hudson. London. 1982.

————. *Ancient Cyprus: 7,000 years of Art and Archaeology.* Louisiana University Press. Baton Rouge. 1981.

————. "Some Reflections on the Relations Between Cyprus and Crete." In *RBCC*, 199–203.

————. "The Goddess with Uplifted Arms in Cyprus." In *Scripta Minora 1977–78: in honorem Einari Gjerstad*. Lund. 1977.

————. *A View from the Bronze Age: Mycenaean and Phoenician Discoveries at Kition.* Dutton. New York. 1976.

————. "Kypriaka II." In *RDAC* 1975, 58–68.

————. "Kition: Mycenaean and Phoenician." *PBA* LIX (1973)a, 1–27.

————. "Chronique des Fouilles à Chypre en 1972." *BCH* 97 (1973)b, 635–8.

————. "Two Religious Documents of the Early Cypriot Bronze Age." *RDAC* 1970, 10–13.

————. "Αι Σχεσεις Μεταξυ Κυπρου και Κρητης κατα τον 11ον ΑΙ. π.Χ." In Πεπραγμενα του Β' Διεθνους Κρητολογικου Συνεδριου. Τομος Α'. Athens. 1968, 180–185.

Karageorghis, V. (ed.) *Cyprus in the 11th Century B.C.* University of Cyprus. Nicosia. 1994.

————. (ed.) *Archaeology in Cyprus 1960–1985.* A.G. Leventis Foundation. Nicosia. 1985a.

Karageorghis, V. and D. Michaelides (eds.) *Cyprus and the Sea.* University of Cyprus. Nicosia. 1995.

Karageorghis, V., D. Michaelides, et al. *Tombs at Palaepaphos.* A.G. Leventis Foundation. Nicosia. 1990.

Karageorghis, V. and M. Demas. *Excavations at Kition: V. The Pre-Phoenician Levels.* Department of Antiquities, Cyprus. Nicosia. 1985.

Karageorghis, V. and N.C. Stampolidis (eds.). *Eastern Mediterranean: Cyprus–Dodecanese–Crete 16th–6th cent. B.C.: Proceedings of the International Symposium held at Rethymon–Crete in May 1997.* A.G. Leventis Foundation. Athens. 1998.

Katzenstein, H.J. "Phoenician Deities Worshipped in Israel and Judah during the Time of the First Temple." In Lipinski (ed.). 1991, 187–191.

————. *The History of Tyre: From the Beginning of the Second Millennium B.C.E. until the Fall of the Neo-Babylonian Empire in 538 B.C.E.* The Schocken Institute for Jewish Research. Jerusalem. 1973.

Keel, O. and C. Uehlinger. *Göttinnen, Götter und Gottessymbole: Neue Erkenntnisse zur Religionsgeschichte Kanaans und Israels aufgrund bisland unerschlossener ikonographischer Quellen.* Herder. Freiburg. 1992.

Keil, J. "Aphrodite Daitis." *Jahreshefte des Österreichischen Archäologischen Institutes in Wien.* Band XVII (1914).

Kempinski, A. *Megiddo: A City-State and Royal Centre in North Israel.* Verlag C.H. Beck. Munich. 1989.

Kenna, V.E.G. *Corpus of Cypriote Antiquities 3. Catalogue of the Cypriote Seals of the Bronze Age in the British Museum.* SIMA XX: 3. Göteborg. 1971.

Kirchhoff, A. *Studien zur Geschichte des Griechischen Alphabets.* C. Bertelsmann. Gütersloh. 1887.

Kirk, G.S. *The Nature of Greek Myths.* Penguin Books. Hamondsworth. 1974.

Kletter, R. *The Judean Pillar-Figurines and the Archaeology of Ashera.* BAR International Series 636. Oxford. 1996.

Knapp, A.B. *Copper Production and Divine Protection: Archaeology, Ideology and Social Complexity on Bronze Age Cyprus.* Paul Åströms Förlag. Göteborg. 1986.

————. "Alashiya, Caphtor/Keftiu and Eastern Mediterranean Trade: Recent Studies in Cypriot Archaeology and History." *JFA* 12/2 (1985), 231-250.

————. "An Alashiyan Merchant at Ugarit." *Tel Aviv* 10/1 (1983), 38-45.

Knapp, A.B. (ed.) *Sources for the History of Cyprus, Volume II: Near Eastern and Aegean Texts from the Third to the First Millennia BC.* Greece and Cyprus Research Center. 1996.

Knapp, A.B. and L. Meskell. "Bodies of Evidence on Prehistoric Cyprus." *CAJ* 7:2 (1997), 183-204.

Knapp, A.B. et al. "The Prehistory of Cyprus: Problems and Prospects." *Journal of World Prehistory* 8 #4 (1994), 377-453.

Koch-Harnack, G. *Erotische Symbole: Lotosblüte und gemeinsamer Mantel auf antiken Vasen.* Gebr. Mann Verlag. Berlin. 1989.

Kochavi, M. "Tell Zeror." in *The New Encyclopaedia of Archaeological Excavations in the Holy Land.* E. Stern (ed.). Israel Exploration Society. Jerusalem. 1993.

Kourou, N. "Αιγαίο και Κύπροσ κατά την Πρώιμη Εποχή των Σιδήρου: Νεώτερες εχελίχεις." In CAA, 217-230.

Kovacs, D. (ed.). *Children of Heracles; Hippolytus; Andromache; Hecuba/ Euripides.* Harvard University Press. Cambridge. 1995.

Kramer, S.N. (ed.). *Mythologies of the Ancient World.* Anchor Books, Doubleday Press. New York. 1961.

Krebernik, M. *Die Personennamen der Ebla-Texte: Eine Zwischenbilanz.* Dietrich Reimer Verlag. Berlin. 1988.

Krzyszkowska, O. and L. Nixon (eds.). *Minoan Society: Proceedings of the Cambridge Colloquium 1981.* Bristol Classical Press. Bristol. 1983.

Kuhrt, A. *The Ancient Near East: c. 3000-330 BC.* Routledge Press. New York. 1995.

Kurke, L. "Pindar and the Prostitutes, or Reading Ancient 'Pornography'." *Arion* vol. 4, no. 2. (Fall 1996), 49-75.

Kyrieles, H. *Führer durch das Heraion von Samos.* Krene Verlag. Deutsches Archäologisches Institut. Athens. 1981.

Laffineur, R. and J. Crowley (eds.). ΕΙΚΩΝ. *Aegean Bronze Age Iconography: Shaping a Methodology.* Aegaeum 8. University of Liège. Liège. 1992.

Lagarce, J. "Enkomi. Fouilles françaises." In Yon (ed.). 1993, 91-106.

Lambert, W.G. "Metal-working and Its Patron Deities in the Early Levant." *Levant* 23 (1991), 183-186.

————. "The Pantheon of Mari." In *M.A.R.I.* 4. (1985), 525-540.

————. "Išhara." *RlA*, Fünfter Band, 1980, 176-177.

Lambrou-Phillipson, C. *Hellenorientalia: The Near Eastern Presence in the Bronze Age Aegean, ca. 3000–1100 B.C.: Interconnections Based on the Material Record and the Written Evidence: Plus Orientalia: A Catalogue of Egyptian, Mesopotamia, Mitannian, Syro-Palestinian, Cypriot and Asian Minor Objects from the Bronze Age Aegean.* Paul Åströms Förlag. Göteborg. 1990.

Lance, H.D. "Gezer in the Land and in History." *BA* XXX #2 (1967), 34–47.

Langlotz, E. "Aphrodite in den Gärten." *SHA*. Band XXXVIII (1953/54).

Laroche, E. *Textes mythologiques hittites en transcription.* Éditions Klincksieck. Paris. 1965.

Lazzarini, M.L. *Le formule delle dediche votive nella Grecia arcaica.* Classe di Scienze Morali – Memorie, Vol. XIX, Ser. 8. Rome. 1976.

Lebessi, A. "Ιερον Ερμου και Αφροδιτης εισ Συμην Βιαννου". *PAAH* 1974, 222–227.

————. "Ιερον Ερμου και Αφροδιτης παρα την Κατω Συμην Βιαννου". *AAA* 6 (1973a), 104–113.

————. "Ιερον Ερμου και Αφροδιτης εισ Συμην Βιαννου." *PAAH* 1973b, 188–199.

————. "Ιερον Ερμου και Αφροδιτης εισ Συμην Κρητης." *PAAH* 1972, 93–203.

Leclant, J. "Astarté à Cheval d'apres les Representations Égyptiennes." *Syria* XXXVII (1960), 1–67.

Leekley, D. and R. Noyes. *Archaeological Excavations in the Greek Islands.* Noyes Press. Park Ridge. 1975.

Leick, G. *Sex and Eroticism in Mesopotamian Literature.* Routledge Press. London. 1994.

Lemerle, P. "Chronique des Fouilles." *BCH* 61 (1937), 441ff.

Levi, D. "I bronzi di Axos." *ARSIA*. 13–14 (1930–1931), 50–57.

Lévi-Strauss, C. *Structural Anthropology.* Basic Books. New York. 1963.

Lipinski, E. *Dieux et Déesses de l'Universe Phénicien et Punique.* Studia Phoenicia XIV. Uitgeverij Peeters & Department Oosterse Studies. Leuven. 1995.

Lipinski, E. (ed.) *Studia Phoenicia IV: Phoenicia and the Bible.* Uitgeverij Peeters. Leuven. 1991.

————. (ed.) *Studia Phoenicia V: Phoenicia and the East Mediterranean in the First Millennium B.C.* Uitgeverij Peeters. Leuven. 1987.

Lippold. "Sikyon" in *PW*. 1923.

Litke, R.L. *A Reconstruction of the Assyro-Babylonian God-Lists AN: ^{d}A-nu-um and AN: Anu šá Amēli.* Yale Babylonian Collection. New Haven. 1988.

Lloyd-Jones, H. (ed.). *Sophocles Volume 3—Fragments.* Harvard University Press. Cambridge. 1996.

Lolos, Y.G. "Late Cypro-Mycenaean Seafaring: New Evidence from Sites in the Saronic and the Argolic Gulfs." In Karageorghis and Michaelides (eds.). 1995, 65–88.

Lubsen-Admiraal, St. and Joost Crouwel. *Cyprus & Aphrodite*. SDU uitgeverij, 's-Gravenhage. 1989.

Lucie-Smith, E. *Sexuality in Western Art*. Thames and Hudson. London. 1991.

MacDonell, A.A. "The Usas Hymns of the Rgveda." *JRAS* 1932, 345-371.

MacQueen, J.G. *The Hittites and Their Contemporaries in Asia Minor*. Rev. (cd.). Thames & Hudson. New York. 1986.

Maier, F.G. "Evidence for Mycenaean Settlement at Old Paphos." In *MEM*, 68-78.

————. "The Paphian Shrine of Aphrodite and Crete." In *RBCC*, 228-234.

————. "Kinyras and Agapenor." In *CBOO*, 311-320.

————. "The Temple of Aphrodite at Old Paphos." *RDAC* 1975, 69-80.

Maier, F.G. and V Karageorghis. *Paphos: History and Archaeology*. A.G. Leventis Foundation. 1984.

Mallory, J.P. *In Search of the Indo-Europeans: Language, Archaeology, and Myth*. Thames & Hudson. New York. 1989.

Mallowan, M.E.L. "The Excavations at Tall Chagar Bazar, and an Archaeological Survey of the Habur Region, 1934-5." *Iraq* 3.1 (1936), 1-86.

Marchetti, P. "Mythes et Topographie d'Argos I. Hermès et Aphrodite." *BCH* 117 (1993), 211-223.

Margueron, J.-Cl. "Palais de Mari: figurines et religion populaire." *M.A.R.I.* 8 (1997).

————. "Quatre Campagnes de Fouilles à Emar (1972-1974): un bilan provisoire." *Syria* LII (1975), 53-85.

Markoe, G. "The Phoenicians on Crete: Transit Trade and the Search for Ores." In Karageorghis and Stampolidis (eds.). 1998, 233-240.

Masson, E. *Cyprominoica*. Paul Åströms Förlag. Göteborg. 1974.

Masson, O. "Remarques sur les Cultes Chypriotes à l'Époque du Bronze Recent." In *MEM*, 110-121.

————. *Les Inscriptions Chypriotes Syllabiques: Recueil Critique et Commenté*. Éditions E. de Boccard. Paris. 1961.

Masson, O. et T.B. Mitford. *Les Inscriptions Syllabiques de Kouklia-Paphos*. Ausgrabungen in Alt-Paphos auf Cypern, Band 4. Universitätsverlag Konstanz GMBH. 1986.

Mastrokostas, E.I. "Παρατηρησεις επι Επιγραφων." *AAA* 31 (1970), 427-8.

Matthäus, H. "Cyprus and Crete in the Early First Millennium B.C.: A Synopsis with Special Reference to New Finds from the Idean Cave of Zeus." In Karageorghis and Stampolidis (eds.). 1998, 127-156.

Matthiae, P., Fr. Pinnock and G.S. Matthiae (eds.). *Ebla: Alle origini della civilita urbana*. Electa. Milan. 1995.

May, H.G. *Material Remains of the Megiddo Cult*. University of Chicago Press. Chicago. 1935.

Mazar, A. "The Excavations at Tel Beth Shean." In Silberman and Small (eds.). 1997.

————. *Archaeology of the Land of the Bible: 10,000–586 B.C.E.* Doubleday Books. New York 1992.

————. "The Excavations at Tel Beth-Shean in 1989-1990." In *Biblical Archaeology Today, 1990.* Israel Exploration Society. Jerusalem. 1990.

————. *Excavations at Tell Qasile, Part 1: The Philistine Sanctuary: Architecture and Cult Objects.* Qedem 12. Hebrew University of Jerusalem. 1980.

McGovern, P. "Beth-Shan." *ABD*, 693–696. 1992.

Megaw, A.H.S. "Archaeology in Cyprus, 1949-1950." *JHS* 71 (1951), 258–260.

Meiggs, R. and D. Lewis. *A Selection of Greek Historical Inscriptions to the End of the 5th Century B.C.* Clarendon Press. Oxford. 1988.

Melas, E.M. *The Islands of Karpathos, Saros and Kasos in the Neolithic and Bronze Age.* SIMA 68. Paul Åströms Förlag. Göteborg. 1985.

Melena, J.L and J.-P. Olivier. *Tithemy: The Tablets and Nodules in Linear B from Tiryns, Thebes and Mycenae.* Minos Supplement #12. 1991.

Mercer, S.A.B. *The Tell-El-Amarna Tablets.* Macmillian Co. Toronto. 1939.

Merrillees, R.S. "Mother and Child: A Late Cypriot Variation on an Eternal Theme." *Mediterranean Archaeology* I (1988), pp. 42–56.

————. "A 16th Century B.C. Tomb Group from Central Cyprus with Links both East and West." In *CBOO*, 69–90.

————. "Representation of the Human Form in Prehistoric Cyprus." *Op Ath* XIII (1980), 171–184.

Mertens, M. "Corinto e l'Occidente nelle Immagini la Nascita di Pegaso e la Nascita di Afrodite." In *Corinto e l'Occidente.* Instituto per la Storia e l'Archeologia della Magna Grecia-Taranto. Taranto. 1994.

Meyer, M.A. *History of the City of Gaza: From the Earliest Times to the Present Day.* The Columbia University Press. New York. 1907.

Michel, Ch. *Recueil d'Inscriptions Grecques.* H. Lamertin. Bruxelles. 1900.

Miller, P.D. Jr. "Aspects of the Religion of Ugarit." in Miller et al. (eds.). 1987.

Miller, P.D. Jr., P.D. Hanson and S.D. McBride (eds.). *Ancient Israelite Religion: Essays in Honor of Frank Moore Cross.* Fortress Press. Philadelphia. 1987.

Mogelonsky, M.K. *Early and Middle Cypriot Terracotta Figurines.* Ph.D. Dissertation. Cornell University. New York. 1988.

Monti, P. *Ischia: Archeologia e Storia.* Universita degli Studi di Salerno. 1979.

Morgan, G. "Aphrodite Cytherea." *TAPA* 108 (1978), 115–120.

Morpurgo, A. *Mycenaeae Graecitatis Lexicon.* Romae in Aedibus Athenaei. Rome. 1963.

Morris, D. *The Art of Ancient Cyprus.* Phaidon Press. Oxford. 1985.

Moscati, S. (ed.). *The Phoenicians.* Bompiani. Milan. 1988.

————. *An Introduction to the Comparative Grammar of the Semitic Languages.* Otto Harrassowitz. Wiesbaden. 1969.

Motz, L. *The Beauty and the Hag: Female Figures of Germanic Faith and Myth.* Fassbaender. Wien. 1993.

Muhly, J.D. "Phoenicia and the Phoenicians." In *Biblical Archaeology Today: Proceedings of the International Congress on Biblical Archaeology.* ASOR. Jerusalem. 1985. 177-191.

————. "Homer and the Phoenicians: The Relations between Greece and the Near East in the Late Bronze and Early Iron Ages." In *Berytus* 19 (1970), 19-64.

————. "The Land of Alashiya: References to Alashiya in the Texts of the Second Millennium B.C. and the History of Cyprus in the Late Bronze Age." In *Praktika* 1972, 201-219.

Müller, H-P. "Religionsgeschichtliche Beobachtungen zu den Texten von Ebla." *ZDPV* 96 (1980), 1-19.

Musti, D. et al. *La Transizione dal Miceneo all'Alto Arcaismo: Dal palazzo alla città.* Consiglio Nazionale delle Ricerce. Rome. 1991.

Myres, J.L. *Handbook of the Cesnola Collection of Antiquities from Cyprus.* The Metropolitan Museum of Art. New York. 1914.

Na'aman, N. "The Ishtar Temple at Alalakh." *JNES* 39 (1980), 209-14.

Nagy, Gr. *Greek Mythology and Poetics.* Cornell University Press. New York. 1990.

Näsström, Br.-M. *Freyja – the Great Goddess of the North.* Lund Studies in histories of Religions, Volume 5. Lund. 1995.

Negbi, O. "Levantine Elements in the Sacred Architecture of the Aegean at the Close of the Bronze Age." *BSA* 83 (1988), 339-357.

————. *Canaanite Gods in Metal: An Archaeological Study of Ancient Syro-Palestinian Figurines.* Tel Aviv University. Tel Aviv. 1976.

————. *The Hoards of Goldwork from Tell el-'Ajjul.* SIMA XXV. Göteborg. 1970.

Neils, J. *The Youthful Deeds of Theseus.* Giorgio Bretschneider Editore. Rome. 1987.

Nicolaou, K. "The First Mycanaeans in Cyprus." In *MEM*, 51-61.

————. *Ancient Monuments of Cyprus.* Department of Antiquities, Republic of Cyprus. Nicosia. 1968.

Niemeyer, H.G. *Phonizier im Westen.* Verlag Philipp von Zabern. Mainz am Rhein. 1982.

Nilsson, M.P. *A History of Greek Religion.* Clarendon Press. Oxford. 1925.

Nosch, M.-L. B. "Schafherden unter dem Namenspatronat von Potnia und Hermes in Knossos." In F. Blakolmer (ed,) *Österreichische Forschungen zur Ägäischen Bronzezeit 1998.* Phoibos Verlag. Wien. 2000, 211-215.

Oden Jr. R.A. *Studies in Lucean's 'De Syria Dea'.* Harvard Semitic Monograph 15. Scholars Press. Missoula. 1977.

O'Flaherty, W.D. *The Rig Veda.* Penguin Classics. London. 1981.

Ohly, D., E. Buschor and K. Verneisel. "Heraion 1959." *Ath Mitt* 74 (1959), 1-74.

Olivier, J.-P., L. Godart, C. Seydel and C. Sourvinou. *Index généraux du Linéaire B*. Incunabula Graeca, vol. LII. Rome. 1973.

Olympios, Th. "Συλλογη Ανεκδοτων Παριωον Επιγραφων." Αθηναιον. 5 (1877), 1-48.

Orchard, J.J. *Equestrian Bridle-Harness Ornaments: Catalogue and Plates*. British School of Archaeology in Iraq. 1967.

Orphanides, A.G. "The Interpretation of the Bronze Age Terracotta Anthropomorphic Figurines from Cyprus." In Vandenabeele and Laffineur (eds.). 1991, 39-45.

————. "A Classification of the Bronze Age Terracotta Anthropomorphic Figurines from Cyprus." *RDAC* 1988, pt. 1, 187-199.

————. *Bronze Age Anthropomorphic Figurines in the Cesnola Collection at the Metropolitan Museum of Art*. Paul Åströms Förlag. Göteborg. 1983.

Owens, G. "All Religions Are One: Astarte/Ishtar/Ishassaras/Asasarame: The Great Mother Goddess of Minoan Crete and the Eastern Mediterranean." *Cretan Studies* 5 (1996).

Palaima, T.G. *The Scribes of Pylos*. Incunabula Graeca, vol. LXXXVII. Rome. 1988.

Palmer, L.R. "Some New Mycenaean Functional Gods?" *NESTOR* 6:2 (1979), 1338-1339.

Papadopoulos, T.J. "Cyprus and the Aegean World: Links in Religion." In *CAA*, 171-184.

Pardee, D. *Les Textes Para-Mythologiques de la 24e Campagne (1961)*. Éditions Recherche sur les Civilizations. Paris. 1988.

Parke, H.W. *Festivals of the Athenians*. Cornell University Press. Ithaca. 1977.

Parker, S.B. (ed.) *Ugaritic Narrative Poetry*. SBL Wrtings from the Ancient World Series Volume 9. Scholars Press. 1997.

Parpola, S. and K. Watanabe. *Neo-Assyrian Treaties and Loyalty Oaths*. Helsinki University Press. Helsinki. 1988.

Parrot, A. *Mission Archéologique de Mari I: Le Temple d'Ishtar*. Librairie Orientaliste Paul Geuthner. Paris. 1967.

————. *Mission Archeologique de Mari III: Les Temples d'Ishtarat et de Ninni-Zaza*. Librairie Orientaliste Paul Geuthner. Paris. 1958.

Payne, H. *Perachora 1: The Sanctuaries of Hera Akraia and Limesnia*. Clarendon Press. Oxford. 1940.

Peckham, B. "Phoenicia and the Religion of Israel: The Epigraphic Evidence." in Miller et al. (eds.). 1987.

Pelagatti, P. "Naxos 2: Ricerche topografiche e scavi 1965-1970. Relazione preliminare." *BdA* 57 (1972), 211-220.

Peltenburg, E.J. "Constructing Authority: The Vounous Enclosure Model." *Op Ath* XX: 10 (1994), 157-162.

————. "Birth Pendants in Life and Death: Evidence from Kissonerga Grave 263." In Ioannides (ed.). 1992, 27-36.

————. "The Beginnings of Religion in Cyrpus." In Peltenburg (ed.). 1989.

————. "The Evolution of the Cypriot Cruciform Figurine." *RDAC* 1982, 12-14.

————. "Some Implications of Recent Lemba Project Radiocarbon Dates for the Later Prehistory of Cyprus." In J. Reade (ed.). 1981.

————. "Lemba Archaeological Project, Cyprus, 1976-77: Preliminary Report." *Levant* 11 (1979), 9-45.

Peltenburg, E.J. (ed.). *Early Society in Cyprus.* Edinburgh University Press. 1989.

Peltenburg, E.J. et al. *Lemba Archaeological Project Volume II.1A: Excavations at Kissonerga-Mosphilia 1979-1992.* Paul Åströms Förlag. Jonsered. 1998.

————. *Lemba Archaeological Project Volume II.2: A Ceremonial Area at Kissonerga.* Paul Åströms Förlag. Göteborg. 1991.

Peltenburg, E.J. and E. Goring. "Terracotta Figurines and Ritual at Kissonerga-Mosphilia." In Vandenabeele and Laffineur (eds.). 1991.

Peltenburg, E.J., D.L. Bolger, E. Goring and C. Elliott. "Kissonerga-Mosphilia 1987: Ritual deposit, Unit 1015." *RDAC,* 1988 (1), 43-52.

Penglase, Ch. *Greek Myths and Mesopotamia: Parallels and Influence in the Homeric Hymns and Hesiod.* Routledge Press. London. 1994.

Perlman, A.L. *Asherah and Astarte in the Old Testament and Ugaritic Literatures.* Unpublished Ph.D. Dissertation. Graduate Theological Union. 1978.

Petrie, F. *Ancient Gaza: Volumes I-IV.* British School of Archaeology in Egypt. London. 1933.

————. *Gerar.* British School of Archaeology in Egypt. London. 1928.

Picard, Ch. *Manuel d'Archéologie Grecque. La Sculpture: Period Archaïque.* A. Picard. Paris. 1935.

Piérart, M. (ed.) *Polydipsion Argos: Argos de la fin des palais mycéniens à la constitution de l'État classique.* BCH Supplément XXII. Paris. 1992.

Pinnock, F. "Erotic Art in the Ancient Near East." In *CANE IV.*

Pomponio, F. "I Nomi Divini nei Testi di Ebla." *UF* 15 (1983), 141-156.

Popham, M. "Connections Between Crete and Cyprus Between 1300-1100 B.C." In *RBCC,* 178-191.

Popham, M.R., L.H. Sackett and P.G. Themelis (eds.). *Lefkandi I: The Iron Age.* Thames and Hudson. London. 1980.

Porada, E. "The Cylinder Seals of the Late Cypriot Bronze Age." *AJA* 52 (1948), 178-198.

Poursat, J.-C. *Catalogue des ivoires mycéniens dy musée national d'Athènes.* École Française d'Athènes. Athènes. 1977.

Prechel, D. *Die Göttin Ishara: Ein Beitrag zur altorientalischen Religionsgeschichte.* Ugarit-Verlag. Münster. 1996.

Preziosi, D. and L.A. Hitchcock. *Aegean Art and Architecture.* Oxford University Press. Oxford. 1999.

Pritchard, J. (ed.) *Ancient Near Eastern Texts Relating to the Old Testament* (ANET). Princeton University Press. Princeton. 1965.

Prückner, H. *Die Lokrischen Tonreliefs: Beitrag zur Kultgeschichte von Lokroi Epizephyrioi*. Philipp von Zabern. Mainz. 1968.

Puech, E. "The Canaanite Inscriptions of Lachish and Their Religious Background." *Tel Aviv* 13-14 (1986-1987), 13-25.

Raubitschek, A.E. *Dedications from the Athenian Akropolis: A Catalogue of the Inscriptions of the Sixth and Fifth Centuries B.C.* Archaeological Institute of America. Cambridge. 1949.

Reade, J (ed.) *Chalcolithic Cyprus and Western Asia*. British Museum Occasional Paper No. 26. 1981.

Rebuffat, R. Review of Boedeker's Aphrodite's Entry into Greek Epic, in *RA* 1977, 324-325.

Redford, D.B. *Egypt, Canaan, and Israel in Ancient Times*. Princeton University Press. Princeton. 1993.

——————. "New Light on the Asiatic Campaigning of Horemheb." *BASOR* 211 (1973), 36-49.

Rehak, P. "New Observations on the Mycenaean 'Warrior Goddess.'" *ArchAnz* 99 (1984), 535-545.

Rehm, A. *Didyma: Zweiter Teil: Die Inschriften*. Verlag Gebr. Mann. Berlin. 1958.

Reiner, Er. "A Sumer-Akkadian Hymn of Nana." *JNES* 33 (1974), 221-236.

Renard, L. "Notes d'Architecture Proto-Géometrique et Géometrique en Crète." *Ant Cl* 36 (1967), 566-595.

Renfrew, C. *Archaeology and Language: The Puzzle of Indo-European Origins*. Cambridge University Press. New York. 1987.

——————. "The Typology and Chronology of Cycladic Sculpture." In Thimme (ed.). 1977, 59-70.

——————. *The Emergence of Civilization: The Cyclades and the Aegean in the Third Millennium B.C.* Methuen & Co. Ltd. London. 1972.

——————. "The Development and Chronology of the Early Cycladic Figurines." AJA 73 (1969), 1-32.

Richter, T. "Die Lesung des Göttesnamens AN.AN.MAR.TU." *Studies on the Civilization and Culture of Nuzi and the Hurrians* 9 (1998), 135-137.

Ridgway, Br. and R.T. Scott. "The Lokrian Pinakes: A Review Article." *Archaeology* 26/1 (1973), 43-47.

Ridgway, D. *The First Western Greeks*. Cambridge University Press. Cambridge. 1992.

Riis, P.J. "The Syrian Astarte Plaques and Their Western Connections." *Berytus* IX, 2 (1949), 69-90.

Roberts, J.J.M. *The Earliest Semitic Pantheon: A Study of the Semitic Deities Attested in Mesopotamia Before Ur III*. Johns Hopkins University Press. Baltimore. 1972.

Robertson, N. "The Riddle of the Arrhephoria at Athens." *HSPh* 87 (1983), 241–288.

————. "The Goddess on the Ingot in Greco-Roman Times." *RDAC* 1978, 202–205.

Roebuck, C. "The Grain Trade between Greece and Egypt." *CPh* 45 (1950), 236–247.

Roehl, H. *Imagines Inscriptionum Graecarum Antiquissimarum*. Berolini. 1908.

Romano, Ir. *Early Greek Cult Images*. Ph.D. Dissertation, University of Pennsylvania. 1980.

Ronen, A. "Core, Periphery and Ideology in Aceramic Cyprus." *Quartär*, Band 45/46. 1995, 177–206.

Ronen, A. and Y. Winter. "Eyal 23–a Lower Palaeolithic Site in the Eastern Sharon, Israel." *Quartär*, Band 47/48. 1997, 177–188.

Rose, H.J. *A Handbook of Greek Mythology*. Methuen & Co. Ltd. 1964.

Ross, J.F. "Gezer in the Tell el-Amarna Letters." *BA* XXX #2 (1967), 62–70.

Roussel, P. "Rapport sur les travaux de l'École Française d'Athèns durant l'année 1938-1939." *CRAI* 1939, 269–286.

Rowe, A. *The Four Canaanite Temple of Beth-Shan: Part I: The Temples and Cult Objects*. University of Pennsylvania. Philadelphia. 1940.

————. *The Topography and History of Beth-Shan*. University of Pennsylvania. Philadelphia. 1930.

Roy, J. "Pausanias, VIII, 5, 2–3 and VIII, 53, 7: Laodice Descendant of Agapenor; Tegea and Cyprus." *Ant Cl* 56 (1987), 192–200.

Rutkowski, B. "Religious Architecture in Cyprus and in Crete in the Late Bronze Age." In *RBCC*, 223–227.

————. *The Cult Places of the Aegean*. Yale University Press. New Haven. 1986.

Samuelson, A.-Gr. *Bronze Age White Painted I Ware in Cyprus: A Reinvestigation*. Paul Åströms Förlag. Jonsered. 1993.

Sandars, N.K. *The Sea Peoples: Warriors of the Ancient Mediterranean*. Thames & Hudson. New York. 1987.

Schachter, A. *Cults of Boiotia*. University of London Institute of Classical Studies. Bulletin Supplement Number 38.1. 1981.

Schaeffer, Cl. F.-A. "An ingot god from Cyprus." *Antiquity* XXXIX (1965), 56–57.

Schaeffer, Cl.F.-A. (ed.) *Palais Royal d'Ugarit*. Imprimerie Nationale. Paris. 1955ff.

Schaeffer, Cl.F.-A et al. *Alasia: Première Série*. Mission Archéologique d' Alasia. Paris. 1971.

Schaeffer-Forrer, Cl. F.-A. et al. *Corpus des Cylindres-sceaux de Ras Shamra-Ugarit et d'Enkomi-Alasia*. Editions Recherche sur les Civilizations. Paris. 1983.

Schefold, K. *Myth and Legend in Early Greek Art.* H.N. Abrams, Inc., Publishers. New York. 1966.

Schindler, R. *The Archaeology of Aphrodite in the West.* Ph.D. Dissertation. University of Michigan. 1998.

Schmidt, G. *Kyprische Bildwerke aus dem Heraion von Samos.* Deutsches Archäologisches Institut. Rudolf Habelt Verlag. Bonn. 1968.

Schweitzer, B. *Greek Geometric Art.* Phaidon Press. Cologne. 1969.

Senff, R., und M. Heinz. "Arbeiter am Zeytintepe im Jahre 1994." *ArchAnz* 1997, 114–118.

Shaw, J. "Kommos in Southern Crete: an Aegean Barometer for East-West Interconnections." In Karageorghis and Stampolides (eds.). 1998, 13–24.

————. "Phoenicians in Southern Crete." *AJA* 93 (1989), 165–183.

Shields, E.L. *The Cults of Lesbos.* Dissertation. Johns Hopkins University. Baltimore. 1917.

Siebert, G. "Hermes." *LIMC*, vol. V. 1990, 285–290.

Silberman, N.A. and D.B. Small (eds.). *The Archaeology of Israel: Constructing the Past, Interpreting the Present.* Sheffield Academic Press. Sheffield. 1997.

Simms, Robert. Database of sacrificial inscriptions from the Greek world. http://willard.emma.troy.ny.us/~rsimms/.

Simms, R.R. *Foreign Religious Cults in Athens in the Fifth and Fourth Centuries B.C.* Unpublished Ph.D. Dissertation. University of Virginia. 1985.

Simon, C.G. *The Archaic Votive Offerings and Cults of Ionia.* Ph.D. Dissertation. University of California, Berkeley. 1986.

Simon, E. *Die Götter der Griechen.* Hirmer Verlag. Munich. 1985.

————. *Festivals of Attica: An Archaeological Commentary.* University of Wisconsin Press. Madison. 1983.

Sissa, G. "Maidenhood without Maidenhead: The Female Body in Ancient Greece." In Halperin, Winkler, and Zeitlin. 1990, 339–364.

Sjöqvist, E. *Problems of the Late Cypriot Bronze Age.* The Swedish Cyprus Expedition. Stockholm. 1940.

————. "Ajios Jakovos" in *SCE I.* 1927–1931.

Skiadas, A. Αρκακος Λυρισμος I. Ελλενικη Ανθρωπιστικη Εταιρεια. Athens. 1979.

Slatkin, L.M. *The Power of Thetis: Allusion and Interpretation in the Iliad.* University of California Press. Berkeley. 1991.

Smith, M. *The Ugaritic Baal Cycle.* Volume 1. E.J. Brill. Leiden. 1994.

Smith, W. *A Dictionary of Greek and Roman Biography and Mythology.* Vol. I. London. 1880.

Soyez, Br. "Le Betyle dans le Culte de l'Astarté Phenicienne." *MUSJ* XLVII (1972), 149–169.

Stadelmann, R. *Syrisch-Palästinensische Gottheiten in Ägypten.* E.J. Brill. Leiden. 1967.

Stampolidis, N. "Imports and Amalgamata: The Eleutherna Experience." In Karageorghis and Stampolidis (eds.). 1998, 175-184.

Starky, J. and F. Hours (eds.). *Archéologie au Levant: Recueil à la mémoire de Roger Saidah*. Maison de l'Orient. Lyon. 1982.

Stern, E. *Excavations at Tel Mevorakh: Part Two: The Bronze Age*. Qedem 18. Hebrew University of Jerusalem. 1984.

————. (ed.) *The New Encyclopaedia of Archaeological Excavations in the Holy Land*. Israel Exploration Society. Jerusalem. 1993.

Stewart, A. *Art, Desire, and the Body in Ancient Greece*. Cambridge University Press. Cambridge. 1997.

Stewart, E. and J. Stewart. *Vounous 1937-38*. C.W.K. Gleerup. Lund. 1950.

Stewart, J. *Tell el-'Ajjul: The Middle Bronze Age Remains*. SIMA XXXVIII. Göteborg. 1974.

————. "When Did Base-Ring Ware First Occur in Palestine?" *BASOR* 138 (1955), 47-49.

Stieglitz, R.R. "Ebla and the Gods of Canaan." In *Eblaitica: Essays on the Ebla Archives and the Eblaite Language*. Vol. 2. C.H. Gordon (ed.). Eisenbrauns. Indiana. 1990.

Supplementum Epigraphicum Graecum. Alphen aa den Rija. Sijtheff and Noordhoff.

Swiny, S. *The Kent State University Expedition to Episkopi Phaneromeni, 2*. SIMA 74, 2. Nicosia. 1986a.

————. "The Philia Culture and Its Foreign Relations." In *CBOO*. 1986b. 12-28.

————. "Sotira-Kaminoudhia and the Chalcolithic Early Bronze Age Transition in Cyprus." In *Archaeology in Cyprus 1960-1985*. Nicosia. 1985a. 115-124.

————. "The Cyprus American Archaeological Research Institute Excavation at Sotira-Kaminoudhia and the Origins of the Philia Culture." In *Proceedings of the Second International Congress of Cypriot Studies. Vol. A: Ancient Section*. Nicosia. 1985b.

————. "An Anthropomorphic Figurine from the Sotira Area." *RDAC* 1983, 56-59.

————. "Bronze Age Settlement Patterns in Southwest Cyprus." *Levant* 13 (1981), 51-87.

Symeonoglou, S. *The Topography of Thebes from the Bronze Age to Modern Times*. Princeton University Press. 1985.

Tatton-Brown, V. (ed.). *Cyprus and the East Mediterranean in the Iron Age*. British Museum Publications. London. 1989.

Taylor, J. *Myrtou-Pigadhes: A Late Bronze Age Sanctuary in Cyprus*. Ashmolean Museum. Oxford. 1957.

Teissier, B. *Ancient Near Eastern Cylinder Seals from the Marcopoli Collection*. University of California Press. Berkeley. 1984.

Thimme, J. (ed.) *Art and Culture of the Cyclades in the Third Millennium B.C.* University of Chicago Press. Chicago. 1977.

Thompson, H. *Mekal, the God of Beth Shean.* Brill. Leiden. 1970.

Thureau-Dangin, F. "Un Hymne à Ishtar de la Haute Époque Babylonienne." *RAA* XXII (1925), 169-177.

————. "Inscriptions Votives sur des Statuettes de Ma'eri." *RAA* XXXI (1934), 137-144.

Torelli, M. "Per la definizione del commercio greco-orientale: il caso di Gravisca." *PP* 37 (1982), 304-325.

————. "I culti di Locri." *AttiTaranto* 16 (1976), 147-156.

Tuempel, K. "Ares und Aphrodite: Eine Untersuchung über Ursprung und Bedeutung ihrer Verbindung." *Jahrbuch für klassische Philologie*, Supplement Eleven. 1880.

————. "Aphrodite" in *PW*, I, 2.

Tufnell, O. et al. *Lachish II (Tel ed-Duweir): The Fosse Temple.* Oxford University Press. London. 1940.

————. *Lachish IV (Tel ed-Duweir): The Bronze Age.* Oxford University Press. London. 1958.

Tzedakis, Y. "Cypriot 'Influences' on the Geometric Pottery of Western Crete." In *RBCC*, 192-198.

Uehlinger, C. "Nackte Göttin. B" *RlA* 9 1./2. 1998, 53-64.

Ussishkin, D. "Lachish." In *ABD*, 114ff. 1992.

————. "Excavations at Tel Lachish–1973-1977, Preliminary Report." *Tel Aviv* 5 (1978), 1-97.

Vagnetti, L. "Stone Sculpture in Chalcolithic Cyprus." *BASOR* 282-283 (1991), 139-151.

————. "Some Unpublished Chalcolithic Figurines." *RDAC* 1975, 1-4.

————. "Preliminary Remarks on Cypriot Chalcolithic Figurines." *RDAC* 1974, 24-34.

Vandenabeele, F. "Kourotrophoi in the Cypriot Terracotta Production from the Early Bronze Age to the Late Archaic Period." *RDAC* 1988 (2), 25-34.

Vandenabeele, F. and R. Laffineur (eds.). *Cypriote Terracottas. Proceedings of the First International Conference of Cypriote Studies, Brussels-Liège-Amsterdam, 29 May-1 June, 1989.* Brussels-Liège. 1991.

van der Toorn, K., B. Becking and P.W. van der Horst (eds.). *Dictionary of Deities and Demons in the Bible.* E.J. Brill. Leiden. 1995.

van Leuven, J.C. "Mycenaean Goddesses Called Potnia." *Kadmos* 18 (1979), 112-129.

Venit, M.S. *Greek Painted Pottery from Naukratis in Egyptian Museums.* American Research Center in Egypt Catalogues, Volume 7. Eisenbrauns. Winona Lake. 1988.

————. *Painted Pottery from the Greek Mainland Found in Egypt, 650–450 B.C.* Unpublished Doctoral Dissertation, New York University. New York. 1982.

Ventris, M and J. Chadwick. *Documents in Mycenaean Greek: 300 Selected Tablets from Knossos, Pylos & Mycenae.* Cambridge University Press. Cambridge. 1959.

Vermeule, E. *Toumba Tou Skourou: The Mound of Darkness.* The Harvard University Cyprus Archaeological Expedition and the Museum of Fine Arts, Boston. 1974.

Vermeule, E. and F. Wolsky. *Toumba Tou Skourou: A Bronze Age Potters Quarter on Morphou Bay In Cyprus.* The Harvard University Cyprus Archaeological Expedition and the Museum of Fine Arts, Boston. 1990.

Vianu, M.A. "Aphrodite orientales dans le bassin du Pont-Euxin." *BCH* 121/1 (1997).

Vichos, Y. and Y. Lolos. "The Cypro-Mycenaean Wreck at Point Iria in the Argolic Gulf: First Thoughts on the Origin and the Nature of the Vessel." In *In Poseidons Reich: Archäologie unter Wasser.* Zaberns Bildbände zur Archäologie, 23. Mainz von Zabern. 1995.

Virolleaud, C. *Le palais royal d'Ugarit V: Textes en cuneiformes alphabetiques des archives sud, sud-ouest et du petit Palais.* "Mission de Ras Shamra" Tome XI. Imprimerie National. Paris. 1965.

Von Bissing, F.W. "Naukratis." *BSRAA.* 39 (1951).

Von Oppenheim. *Tell Halaf IV: Die Kleinfunde aus historischer Zeit.* Walter de Gruyter & Co. Berlin. 1962.

Voyatzis, M.E. "Arcadia and Cyprus: Aspects of Their Interrelationship Between the Twelfth and Eighth Centuries B.C." *RDAC* 1985, 135–163.

Walls, N.H. *The Goddess Anat in Ugaritic Myth.* SBL Dissertation Series 135. Baltimore. 1992.

Walter, H. "Korinthische Keramik." *Ath Mitt* 74 (1959), 57–68.

Walz, C.A. "Black Athena and the Role of Cyprus on Near Eastern/Mycenaean Contact." In Coleman and Walz (eds.). 1997, 1–27.

Ward, A.J., W.R. Connor and R.B. Edwards (eds.). *The Quest for Theseus.* Pall Mall Press. London. 1970.

Ward, W.A. "La Déesse nourriciere d'Ugarit." *Syria* XLVI (1969), 225–239.

Waterhouse, H. and R. Hope Simpson. "Prehistoric Laconia: Part II." *BSA* 56 (1961) 114–175.

Watkins, T. "The Chalcolithic period in Cyprus: the background to current research." In J. Reade (ed.). 1981, 9–20.

Watson, W.G.E. "The Goddesses of Ugarit: A Survey." *SEL* 10 (1993), 47–59.

Webb, J.M. "Cypriote Bronze Age Glyptic: Style, Function and Social Context." In Laffineur and Crowley (eds.). 1992a, 113–121.

————. "Funerary Ideology in Bronze Age Cyprus. Towards the Recognition and Analysis of Cypriot Ritual Data." In *Studies in Honour of Vassos Karageorghis.* A.G. Leventis Foundation. Nicosia. 1992b, 87–99.

————. "A Cypriote Caprid Goddess?" *RDAC* 1988 (1), 275-279.

————. "Late Cypriot Altars and Offering Structures." *RDAC* 1977, 113-132.

Webb, J.M. and D. Frankel. "Characterizing the Philia Facies: Material Culture, Chronology, and the Origin of the Bronze Age in Cyprus." *AJA* 103 (1999), 3-43.

Weidner, E.F. "The Inscription from Kythera." *JHS* 59 (1939), 137-138.

Weiss, H. (ed.). *Ebla to Damascus: Art and Archaeology of Ancient Syria.* University of Washington Press. Seattle. 1985.

West, M.L. *The East Face of Helicon: West Asiatic Elements in Greek Poetry and Myth.* Clarendon Press. Oxford. 1997.

————. (ed.) *Theogony.* Oxford University Press. 1966.

Westenholz, J.G. "Love Lyrics from the Ancient Near East." In *CANE* IV.

White, D. "1987 Excavations on Bate's Island, Marsa Matruh: Second Preliminary Report." *JARCE* XXVI (1989), 87-114.

————. "Excavations on Bate's Island." *JARCE* XXIII (1986), 51-84.

Wiegand, T. *Sechster Vorläufiger Bericht über die von den Königlichen Museen in Milet und Didyma Unternommenen Ausgrabungen.* Verlag der Koenigl. Akademie der Wissenschaften. Berlin. 1908.

Wiggermann, F.A.M. "Nackte Göttin (Naked Goddess). A" *RlA* 9 1./2. 1998, 46-53.

Wiggins, S.A. *A Reassessment of 'Asherah': A study According to the Textual Sources of the First Two Millennia B.C.E.* Verlag Butzon & Bercker Kevelaer. Darmstadt. 1993.

————. "The Myth of Asherah: Lion Lady and Serpent Goddess." *UF* 23 (1991), 383-394.

Will, E. *Corinthiaka: Recherches sur l'Histoire et la Civilization de Corinthe des Origines aux Guerres Médiques.* E.de Boccard. Paris. 1955.

Williams II, C.K. "Archaic and Classical Corinth." In *Corinto e l'Occidente.* Instituto per la Storia e l'Archeologia della Magna Grecia-Taranto. Taranto. 1994.

————. "Corinth and the Cult of Aphrodite." In *Corinthiaca: Studies in Honor of Darrell A. Amyx.* (ed.). M.A. Del Chiaro. University of Missouri Press. Columbia. 1986, 12-24.

Williams, D. "Sophilos in the British Museum." In *Greek Vases in the J. Paul Getty Museum.* J. Paul Getty Museum. Malibu. Volume 1 (1983), 9-34.

Winter, U. *Frau und Göttin: Exegetische und ikonographische Studies zum weiblichen Gottesbild im Alten Israel und in dessen Umwelt.* Universitätsverlag Freiburg Schweiz. Vandenhoeck & Ruprecht. Göttingen. 1983.

Wiseman, D.J. *The Alalakh Tablets.* British Institute of Archaeology at Ankara. London. 1953.

Woodard, R.D. "Linguistic Connections between Greeks and Non-Greeks." In Coleman and Walz (eds.). 1997, 29-60.

Woodward, A.M. "Sparta. Votive Inscriptions from the Acropolis." *BSA* 30 (1928-1930).

Woolley, Sir L. *Alalakh: An Account of the Excavations at Tell Atchana in the Hatay, 1937-1949.* Oxford University Press. London. 1955.

Wright, G.E. "Iron: The Date of Its Introduction into Common Use in Palestine." *AJA* 43 (1939), 458-463.

Wright, G.R.H *Ancient Buildings in Cyprus*, Vols. I and II. E.J. Brill. Leiden. 1992.

————. "Pre-Israelite Temples in the Land of Canaan." *PEQ* 103 (1971), 17-32.

Wu Yü-hung. *A Political History of Eshnunna, Mari and Assyria during the Early Old Babylonian Period (from the end of Ur III to the Death of Samsi-Adad).* Institute of the History of Ancient Civilizations, North East University. Changchun. 1994.

Wyatt, N. "The 'Anat Stela from Ugarit and Its Ramifications." *UF* 16. 1984, 327-337.

Wyatt, W.F. Review of Boedeker's Aphrodite's Entry into Greek Epic. In "Book Reviews," *CPh* LXXIII (1978), 169-171.

Xella, P. "Aspekta religiöser Vorstellungen in Syrien nach den Ebla- und Ugarit-Texten." *UF* 15 (1983), 279-290.

Xenophontos, C. "Picrolite, Its Nature, Provenance, and Possible Distribution Patterns in the Chalcolithic Period of Cyprus." *BASOR* 282-283 (1991), 127-138

Yamauchi, E.M. "Cultic Prostitution: A Case Study in Cultural Diffusion." In Hoffner (ed.). 1973, 213-222.

Yavis, C. *Greek Altars: Origins and Typology.* St. Louis University Press. 1949.

Yon, M. "Kition in the Tenth to Fourth Centuries B.C." *BASOR* 308 (1997), 9-18.

————. "Le Royaume de Kition: Epoque archaïque." In Lipinski (ed.). 1987, 357-374.

————. "Chypre et la Crète au XIè S." In *RBCC*, 241-248.

Yon, M. (ed.) *Kinyras: l'Archéologie française à Chypre.* Travaux de la Maison de l'Orient. Lyon. 1993.

Zadok, R. "West Semitic Material from Emar." *AION* 51 (1991), 120-135.

Selected Index

Due Date	Date Returned
T MARCH 15, 10	MAR 2 5 2010
T MARCH 08, 11	MAR 1 7 2010
NOV 2 5 2011	NOV 2 4 2011
T NOV 29 11	DEC 1 3 2011
APR 1 8 2012	APR 0 5 2012
JUN 2 8 2012	
APR 1 4 2015	APR 1 4 2015
	DEC 0 6 2016

www.library.humber.ca